I0918838

The Lost Tradition:
Mothers and Daughters
in Literature

THE LOST TRADITION
Mothers and Daughters in Literature

EDITED BY
CATHY N. DAVIDSON
AND E. M. BRONER

Frederick Ungar Publishing Co.
New York

Library of Congress Cataloging in Publication Data
Main entry under title:

The Lost tradition.

  Bibliography: p.
  Includes index.
   1. Mothers and daughters in literature—Addresses,
essays, lectures. I. Davidson, Cathy N., 1949-
II. Broner, E. M.
PN56.5.M67L6   809'.933'54   79-4832
ISBN 0-8044-2083-1
ISBN 0-8044-6112-0 pbk.

Dedication

There are a number of mothers and daughters whose inspiration I wish to acknowledge: my grandmother, Mae Notari, a wise lady; Ann Luvisi; Amalia Deyo, Mary Deyo Krasney, and Kelly Krasney; Sharon Notari; Mary Lou Shioji Notari; Marlene Fineman Notari; Inez, Karen, and Jo Jo Davidson; and Leeann Collura, who communicated a love of literature to her daughter.

C.N.D.

To daughters who mothered me or my work:
Hindi Brooks, scriptwriter, Santa Monica, California
Phyllis Chesler, Ph.D., psychologist-writer, New York City
Milka Cizik, artist, Bezalel Academy, Jerusalem
Cynthia Fuchs Epstein, Ph.D., sociologist, New York City
Jody Hoy, Ph.D., academic administrator, California
Eleanor Johnson, director, Emmatroupe, New York City
Bea Kreloff, artist, New York City
Lucy Lippard, writer, New York City
Grace Paley, writer, New York City
Lily Rivlin, writer, New York City
Kathryn Kish Sklar, Ph.D., historian, UCLA
Marjean Kettunen Zegart, educator, Mill Valley, California
In memory of Ellen Moers, a literary woman and connector of women, and
    Nancy Lynn Schwartz, age 26, scriptwriter, Los Angeles, the daughter half
    of a mother-daughter writing team.

E.M.B.

Together we thank the many contributors who worked to make this book a history and not just an assemblage of two dozen essays. We thank the bibliographers who spent hours in libraries documenting a literature of matrilineage nearly forgotten. Finally, and most of all, we thank each other.

Contents:

vii

III   Columbia's Daughters

IV   A Trinity of Mothers

V   Mother as Medusa

VI   The New Matrilineage

VII *Bibliography*

Foreword

CATHY N. DAVIDSON AND E. M. BRONER

We have already heard the story of fathers and sons, of mothers and sons, even of fathers and daughters. But who has sung the song of mothers and daughters? And yet, as the twenty-four essays in this volume and the bibliography attest, we have forty centuries of a literature of mothers and daughters. *The Lost Tradition: Mothers and Daughters in Literature* is a looking back in order to look forward, a looking inward in order to look out. We are at the beginning of new discovery and renewal of ancient relationships.

Our collaboration on this project began in November of 1975 at a Midwest Modern Language Association meeting when members of the Women's Caucus voted to hold a special workshop on mothers and daughters in literature at their next convention. Esther had just published a novel, *Her Mothers*, that fall and had been working on the mother-daughter relationship historically and personally. She had also been rewriting Jewish ceremonies to reincorporate women into ancient ritual. Her *Women's Haggadah* was published in *Ms.* that following spring. Cathy was teaching women's studies courses which increasingly emphasized how mothers and daughters were portrayed in literature. The next summer Cathy was a visiting professor of Sacred Science at the Franciscan Institute of St. Bonaventure University. With the Women Religious studying there, she discussed matriarchy, medieval patriarchy, and the masculinization of theology by the Church Fathers.

With this mixed background in poetry and pedagogy, mysticism and activism, we coordinated the 1976 workshop on mothers and daughters in literature. We asked that this session be nonhierarchical, a sharing rather than a criticizing, a bridging of generations. The main paper was copresented by a scholar-mother and her daughter. We celebrated that night with film, poetry, and readings from the literature of mothers and daughters.

Later in 1976, we began to collect essays and art for a special issue of *Women's Studies*. We discovered a photographer, Harriette Hartigan, who had gone with midwives around Michigan, photographing home births. We published two of her photographs, "Daughters Born." We found a poet-printmaker, Catherine Claytor–Becker, who made art of the distance and closeness between mothers and daughters. And we heard from literally hundreds of women who wished to contribute to the project. Their response is what engendered our present collection, this wealth of material dealing with a neglected subject.

As our backgrounds differ, so do those of our contributors. They come from the East—New York, Pennsylvania, New Jersey, Massachusetts, Connecticut; the South—Florida, Georgia, Virginia, Louisiana; the Midwest—Michigan, Wisconsin; and the West—Oregon, California, New Mexico. They come from Canada and Israel. Their ages differ—from one young graduate student to a distinguished scholar who published her first work in 1935. Some teach in community colleges; some in universities; some are independent scholars. They range from department chairpersons to visiting lecturers. We have anthropologists, social scientists, and literary critics. Their approaches are as varied as their training: Jungian archetypal criticism, Freudian, psycho-linguistic, historical, formalistic, autobiographical, socio-political, and mythological. They have worked with the polytheistic cultures of the ancient Near East and with the contemporary culture of the Native American Indian. Their approaches are both professional and personal. In three essays, mothers and daughters even write together. All contribute to the body of feminist criticism.

Among the early papers we heard delivered in St. Louis at the 1976 MMLA meetings was one on the controversial and sometimes violent relationship between mid-Victorian mothers and daughters. Another was a mourning for the mother-daughter relationship in contemporary fiction. We found mothers and daughters to be embattled.

But over the past year there has been a new trend, with many scholars finding other paths to our mothers. By searching in unusual literature—in the private or hidden literatures of diary, tale, myth, song, and autobiography—women have been restoring the blurred image of our mothers. There has been an embracing of the maternal past.

This history, this text, begins over four thousand years ago and points to the future. But perhaps further studies will deal in more detail with still other topics: mother-daughter relationships in eighteenth-century English literature; or in continental literature of other centuries; or in the literatures of the Far East; or of Third World peoples; or with such fine French Canadian authors as Gabrielle Roy, Marie-Claire Blais, and Anne Hébert. The literature of mothers and daughters is rich and more topics are yet to be discovered. But much has already been revealed. Adrienne Rich has reminded many of the paper writers that we are *Of Woman Born*. Phyllis Chesler, Nancy Chodorow, Ellen Moers, and Carroll Smith-Rosenberg are among the other mother-critics invoked in these essays. We are trying to fill the silences that Tillie Olsen made us hear.

Perhaps because of the nature of this collection, the letters we have received from our contributors display a rare warmth. And our own coediting has carried out the natural process of mothering: exchange of experience, comforting, tenderness, and respect on both of our parts for one another.

Together, as daughter-scholars, we all search for the stranger who has been our mother. We find her in our body memories, in our gestures towards the world. Collectively, we hail her. She approaches, and we recognize ourselves.

Michigan
February, 1979

The Lost Tradition:
Mothers and Daughters
in Literature

Part One
THE LOST MOTHER

Introduction

When we seek the literature of mothers and daughters, we are looking for a lineage not traced in any genealogy. We are tracking our roots back to ancient mothers whose origins are the earth itself but whose traces are as dust. They have no names throughout history, these mothers and daughters. Changelings, they are listed at birth and on tombstones without their conceiver's name, born and buried as daughter/wife/mother.

We who make history, who retrace history, must erect new stones and inscribe them with the lost names.

We begin by recalling the Demeter and Persephone of myth, and remember the wrath a mother can vent upon an earth which has permitted her beloved daughter to be defiled and abducted. But it is no easy task to find Demeter's footprints in the sands of time. Too often we see Persephone leaving her mother to return to the nether kingdom. As the essays in this section illustrate, patriarchal tradition separates mother and daughter—and all for the taste of a few pomegranate seeds.

The five essays which begin this history show both how and why the mothers and daughters of literature and myth gradually became isolated from one another. Professor Judith Ochshorn's opening essay documents our initial loss, our fall from deity to devalued woman. It describes a time, long ago, in the ancient Near East, when there was "relative unimportance attached to sexual identity . . . for the female as goddess or cultic celebrant was as powerful and indispensable as the male, and therefore daughters were valued as much as sons." It was a golden time when the literature about mothers and daughters "describes their straightforward, unreserved, unambivalent love for each other."

In Sumeria, a woman priest wrote hymns of praise to her mother-goddess. The priestess Enheduanna's poetry is taken out of the realm of the most specialized scholarship for the first time and is made available here to a wider audience.

But the goddesses were buried and the one God of the Old Testament reigned. Yet, Ochshorn shows, even the misogyny of Biblical times did not prevent the relationship of Ruth and Naomi. In the book of *Ruth*, important actions are "initiated by women . . . and the witnesses and commentators are 'the women of the neighborhood.'" Ruth and Naomi bring pleasure and comfort to one another (as is implied by Naomi's Hebrew name, "Nechama," which means "consolation").

In the next essay, a mother-daughter scholarly team shows how, earlier and concurrently, the Greeks repressed their "awe for the mother-goddess" and attempted to force the once powerful goddesses "into molds." Professors Ida H. Washington and Carol E. W. Tobol suggest that the myth of rape and seduction of goddesses (such as Persephone, Leda, or Europa) was one of the "principal ways the Greek invaders dealt with their predecessors' goddesses, thereby bringing about their 'death' as protecting, powerful dieties."

A figure who breaks out of the mold is Clytemnestra. She rejects the "patriarchal claim to wifely fidelity" when her husband Agamemnon sacrifices their daughter Iphigenia for favorable winds that will take his armies to Troy. Clytemnestra becomes the avenging fury denied her daughter. She is, or would be, the grain goddess Demeter who would lay barren the whole earth as her life is made bárren. But our furies are defeated, and the lesson is clear. Clytemnestra is executed by her son. For thousands of years the mouths of the furies are stopped, the howls silenced.

Professor Nikki Stiller, a medievalist, searches another "dark age" and the literature of "half a dozen languages" for the sound of other lost voices. Since the written record of medieval times is by men—and usually aristocratic men, says Stiller—there are "silences." We do not know "what went on beside the childbed, or while the ladies were dressing, or between two gossips."

In unexpected places, Stiller discovers how women learned to be women, from their mothers and surrogate mothers. By looking at what the misogynistic literature condemned, she discovers a kind of female bonding, "the older woman advising the younger woman." The hag/witch/mother-in-law/adviser, although a stock figure, represents "the male fear of the bond between woman and woman, mother and daughter." She movingly concludes, "Even though Mother Eve was . . . deprived of her daughters, women . . . [were] able to form those bonds among themselves which can only be called familial."

Professor Stiller deals with the hidden record of medieval times. With the Renaissance, there is a public record. Demeter can once again nurse and cradle her Persephone. The new humanism and liberalism allowed women to give public counsel to each other, to advise from the nursery. This is the bulk of the written literature by women in the Renaissance.

The women's writing of the time is different from the male literature—"eloquent, fervent, and touching," says Professor Betty S. Travitsky. The mothers write personally, directly, and warmly. Their writings, in fact, may have marked the beginning of a difference between the male and female approach to letters: the woman as journalist and diarist; the man objective about his material and abstracted from it.

With Shakespeare, however, Demeter is again separated from Persephone. Professor Myra Glazer Schotz, using a Jungian, archetypal approach, discusses the significance of the motherless daughters who abound in Shakespeare's world: "Where is the mother of Jessica? Desdemona? Ophelia? What woman carried in her womb Regan, Goneril, *and* Cordelia?" In Shakespeare, Demeter's role is diminished. Pluto-Zeus becomes important. In *Pericles*, it is the father-figure who searches out the daughter and brings about the reunion with the mother. In *The Tempest*, mother and daughter are forever isolated. Mother Nature becomes Father Prospero. Prospero is the "wifeless father, sole educator of his daughter, magician whose books teach him control over the natural world."

By the time Western civilization has "progressed" into the high Renaissance, with our greater writer, we mothers and daughters are lost to one another.

E.M.B.
C.N.D.

Mothers and Daughters in Ancient Near Eastern Literature

Accounts of unusually close mother-daughter relationships appear in some of the earliest literature of the ancient Near East. At times, the divine mother-child relationship predominates, and where the child is female, the nature of the bond between mother and daughter is pictured as incomparably intense.

Before we can look at this literature of mothers and daughters, it must be emphasized that much of ancient literature expresses the outlook of a milieu quite alien to our own, a milieu in which both official religions and popular cults seem to have served as the matrix of the culture. The goddesses and gods of the ancient Near East were immanent and interventionist, simply "present" in the lives of the people. Above all, divinity was conceived of in anthropomorphic terms. It was widely held that gods and goddesses loved, hated, bore offspring either in or out of marriage, ate, drank, prospered, sickened, died, suffered jealousy, anguish, bereavement, experienced happiness, victories—in short, enjoyed and endured all of the vicissitudes of humans, only writ large.

Both the male and female deities encountered in this literature are sexually active, with multiple relationships often based on blood ties as well as marriage. Sexual liaisons occur either in or out of wedlock and are engaged in by a variety of partners, i.e., divine parents, divine parents and children, divine brothers and sisters, or divinities and mortals who are sometimes later deified. Most often, these relationships are not monogamous. Indeed, the notions of incest or illegitimacy in divine "families" fall outside the pale of the ancient mind just as divine maternity is not viewed as limiting the active powers and sexuality of the goddesses.

Given the shifting affections and loyalties between spouses implicit in a nonmonogamous family structure, the intensity of female bonding as compared to most divine mother-son affiliations may be partly due to the absence of a sexual component, typical of the frequently incestuous relationships between divine mothers and their sons. Also, the closeness shown between mothers and daughters might have been reenforced by the relative unimportance attached to sexual identity as the ground of divine power, for the female as goddess or cultic celebrant was as powerful and indispensable as the male, and therefore daughters were valued as much as sons.

More important, while an aura of devotion surrounds some mother-son, father-daughter interrelations—Isis and Horus or Athena and Zeus—the ambivalence which so strongly marks other of these filial relationships is conspicuously absent from the mother-daughter literature. For example, in Greek literature there are few counterparts in the attitudes of mothers and daughters toward each other (with the exception of Electra) which bear comparison with Hesiod's account of how Gaia arranges for the castration of her son/husband Ouranos.[1]

Likewise, in Mesopotamian literature divine daughters do not countermand their mothers the way they do their fathers. The goddess Ishtar threatens to raise the dead so they will outnumber the living if her father Anu refuses her demand for vengeance against the hero Gilgamesh.[2] Nor do divine mothers consign their daughters to death for half the year as the goddesses Inanna and Ishtar annually commit their deified sons/husbands, Dumuzi and Tammuz, to the awful Netherworld for their failure to pay them proper homage.[3]

Similarly, there are no counterparts in Canaanite myth or epic of threats by goddesses against their divine mothers to rival the terrifying violence with which the goddess Anath, in her martial aspect, threatens her father El if he refuses to grant her brother/consort Baal a palace of his own.[4] And in Egyptian tales of mothers and daughters, there are no parallels to the myth which recounts how Isis almost fatally poisons her "father" Rā to force him to reveal to her his secret name of power.[5]

In addition, there are no conflicts between divine mothers and daughters which even approximate the struggle for the kingship of the gods which runs like a leitmotif through ancient Near Eastern texts, and involves only males. In seeming conformity to changing priorities in communities of worshippers, the younger male gods replace the older (or their fathers) as the active executors of divine authority, even while the more ancient male deities become the increasingly remote heads of divine pantheons. Myths relate the movement to center stage of the younger Sumerian god Enlil for the older An, the Akkadian Marduk for Anu, the Canaanite Baal for El, the Egyptian Osiris for Rā, and the Greek Zeus for Kronus.

By way of contrast, younger female divinities do not usurp the powers of their goddess-mothers in quite the same fashion. Some goddesses like Isis over time emerged as powerful, syncretistic deities. In her own evolution, by the end of the first millenium, she came to embody the characteristics of all the major female fertility deities of the Mediterranean world. But her ascendance did not altogether eclipse the worship of these other goddesses, nor were they her "mothers." On the contrary, the literary treatment of mothers and daughters in this early time most often describes their straightforward, unreserved, unambivalent love for each other. The ties uniting them are sometimes shown as so close that in one reading of the Demeter-Korè myth, for example, Korè is viewed as a personification of the great goddess Demeter as Maiden, or as a younger form of the Corn or Grain-Mother even at the same time that she functions as her divine daughter.[6]

One of the earliest and most passionate statements of female filial devotion is found in *The Exaltation of Inanna* by Enheduanna (c. 2300 B.C.E.). Poet, high priestess, and princess, Enheduanna was the daughter of Sargon the Great and the first in a line of royal high priestesses (many of whose names are now known), who served the temples of Akkad continuously for the next five hundred years. As theologian, poet, and hymnographer, Enheduanna seems to have had a great impact on later writers. Her poetry was widely popular during the Old Babylonian period, and her stature in the eyes of her people may be gauged by her virtual apotheosis in later theological literature.

The Exaltation of Inanna is one of the earliest extant Akkadian hymns, part of a great cycle written for the temples of Sumer and Akkad, and regarded as "a major piece of Mesopotamian theology."[7] It extols the power of the Sumerian fertility goddess Inanna; narrates Inanna's role among civilized people; establishes Enheduanna's identification with her surrogate mother, Inanna; and concludes with a splendid celebration of Inanna's cultic primacy in the city-states of Ur and Uruk, the ancient centers of Sumerian religion. Furthermore, it is noteworthy that in *The Exaltation of Inanna* Enheduanna at times employs imagery suggestive of the human rather than the divine, as when she refers to the goddess as "righteous woman" and "my lady." Even more startling is her humanization of the goddess. Enheduanna fuses Inanna's identity with her own when she refers to her not by name but as one "suitable for the high priesthood."

In the passages that follow, Enheduanna elaborates on the character and power of this many-faceted fertility goddess, her divine "mother." Contrasting sharply with the celebration of divine female sexuality in Mesopotamian myth and poetry commemorating the Sacred Marriage rites, in which the goddess Inanna and later her prototype Ishtar "took" royal human lovers, here her "daughter" Enheduanna minimizes her sexual aspect and pictures Inanna as autonomous and awesome in her power. Rather than providing for the stability of the throne and the fertility of the land by having intercourse with the king, probably through her avatars or high priestesses, Inanna emerges in this hymn as the awful goddess of war, the personification and deification of the raging, destructive forces in nature which neither deities nor people can withstand, and the judge and punisher of people, dispensing to them "their just deserts." And while Enheduanna distances herself from other divinities by referring to them only by name—for example, An, Enlil, the "great Anunna"—she refers to her divine mother both by name, symbolic of her power, and as "my lady":

9. Like a dragon you have deposited venom on the land
10. When you roar at the earth like Thunder, no vegetation can stand up to you.
11. A flood descending from its mountain,
12. Oh foremost one, you are the In-   of heaven and earth![8]
anna
18. Beloved of Enlil,[9]   you fly about in the nation.
20. Oh my lady, at the sound of you   the lands bow down.
21. When mankind   comes before you
22. In fear and trembling   at (your) tempestuous radiance,
23. They receive from you   their just deserts.[10]
34. Oh my lady, The Anunna,   the great gods,
35. Fluttering like bats   fly off from before you to the clefts,
36. They dare not walk   in your terrible glance.
37. Who dare not proceed   before your terrible countenance.[11]

When humanity withholds its worship of Inanna as a vegetation and fertility goddess, she is shown as terrible in her vengeance:

43. In the mountain where homage is withheld from you
     vegetation is accursed.
44. Its grand entrance   you have reduced to ashes
45. Blood rises in its rivers for you, its people have nought to drink.
46. It leads its army captive before you of its own accord.
55. Its woman no longer speaks
     of love   with her husband.[12]

Later in "The Invocation of Inanna," Enheduanna again identifies herself with Inanna, the "brilliantly righteous *woman*," or her mother, whose praise she recites in reverence and love.

The intensity of the mother-daughter bond, articulated from the point of view of the daughter in *The Exaltation of Inanna*, is represented by the behavior of the mother in the Demeter-Korè myth, enacted and reenacted in one of the most enduring and widespread rituals in the ancient world, the Eleusinian Mysteries.[13] As the goddess of agriculture and the civilized arts and social order based on it, and as the sister of Zeus, Demeter could lay as ancient a claim to divine provenance as her brother. In fairly typical, nonmonogamous fashion, Demeter mothers three children, Korè, Iacchus, and Plutus, but only the first was to play a central role along with her mother in literature and ritual. Performed in the sacred dramas of the Greater and Lesser Mysteries every fall and spring, the story line of the myth which recapitulated the ritual was quite simple.

With the consent of Zeus, Demeter's daughter is abducted and raped by their brother Hades, and carried off by him to the underworld to become his august queen, Persephone. Inconsolable, Demeter wanders in search of her daughter, and on the tenth day arrives at Eleusis where, in disguise, she is welcomed and becomes a nursemaid to the infant prince. Replicating the experience of Isis when she journeys to Phoenicia in search of Osiris' body, Demeter is discovered by the queen in the act of burning away the mortal parts of the baby, and the goddess then reveals her true identity in all of her splendor and might. She orders a temple built in her honor where she gives way to her awful bereavement, and she refuses to do her job.

The earth becomes barren and humanity is threatened with starvation until the return of Persephone to her mother is arranged. It is curious that Zeus braved Demeter's anger in the first place, unless Hades required the presence of the goddess' daughter as his consort in order to legitimize his rule. At any rate, there is no suggestion that Hades or Zeus possess countervailing power against Demeter's wrath and refusal to function in her customary way, and Hades is able to retain his queen for one third of the year only through trickery, by feeding Persephone addictive pomegranate seeds before her reunion with her mother. Moreover, it is only after Persephone's restoration to Demeter as Korè that the Grain-Mother consents to disseminate the knowledge of agriculture throughout the world.

Unquestionably, the primary affiliation here is between mother and daughter, the strength of which may be measured by the power of Demeter's opponents and by her willingness to bring the earth to the brink of extinction if Korè is denied to her. In this contest, Demeter's connections with her consorts (Zeus, Poseidon, or Dionysus) as well as her sons are shown as negligible. Unlike some of the mother-son, father-daughter relationships discussed above, there is nothing ambivalent in her love for her daughter. Just as Demeter's mourning sets in motion the passage of the seasons, so it is her love for Korè which brings her back from the dead each year and signals their turn. And it is Demeter's rescue of her daughter which came to symbolize for her worshippers the possibility of immortality for themselves.

The Bible shares the cultural belief of the ancient Near East in the interpenetration of the divine and secular in everyday life. But while polytheistic literature provides evidence of the inclusion of women as well as men in just about every aspect of temple life and popular cult as initiates, celebrants, and priests, parts of the Bible represent men in a special and closer relation to God than women. Men are usually dominant in cult, war, governance, family life, and social structure, and as transmitters of divine commandments or embodiments of divine purpose. But beyond all that, many Biblical passages express profound ambivalence toward women, and fear of their normal bodily functions and sexuality.

The God of monotheism is shown as different from polytheistic deities in His overriding concern for justice, compassion, and righteousness. However, within the parameters of the moral and spiritual universe of monotheism, while women are shown as recipients of divine judgment and grace, they also are often described, in comparison to men, as less capable of moral judgment and more tied to the material than the moral or spiritual aspects of existence. At times, female sexuality symbolizes the community's idolatry or is shown as endangering the pursuit of righteousness by men. At other times, women are portrayed as receiving less of God's compassion, justice, and righteousness than men, seemingly only on account of their sex.

This ambivalence toward women is carried over into views of their importance as mothers. Though women are valued for "building up" their husband's houses and barrenness is considered their greatest shame, there are conflicting, nonmaternal motifs in portions of the Bible. For example, the virtue of women as wives is defined in terms of their roles as economic producers rather than mothers (*Proverbs*, 31:10–31), and in two of the three books titled by women's names in the Old Testament and Apocrypha, Esther and Judith save their people by their beauty and sexuality, and neither are mothers. Even when a woman physically gives birth to Jesus, and thereby enables his redemptive mission, she is shown as of relatively slight account in that mission and in early cult. (It was only centuries later that the central role of the Virgin Birth was attested in the rise of Mariology in both the Western and Eastern churches.)

When mothers and daughters are mentioned, it is usually in order to illustrate the enormity of Israel's abominations. As one instance, Ezekiel writes of sinning Israel, and has God say:

"Have you not committed lewdness in addition to all your abominations? Behold, every one who uses proverbs will use this proverb about you, 'Like mother, like daughter.' You are the daughter of your mother, who loathed her husband and her children; and you are the sister of your sisters, who loathed their husbands and their children. Your mother was a Hittite and your father an Amorite, and your eldest sister is Samar'ia, who lived with her daughters to the north of you; and your younger sister, who lived to the south of you, is Sodom with her daughters. Yet you were not content to walk in their ways, or do according to their abominations; within a very little time you were more corrupt than they in all your ways. As I live, says the Lord God, your sister Sodom and her daughters have not done as you and your daughters have done" (*Ezekiel*, 16:43–9).

Against this backdrop of deep ambivalence toward women, the book of *Ruth* stands virtually alone. It seems no wonder that it took approximately five hundred years for it to be included in the final redaction, for it is different in tone and emphasis from the rest of the canon. The primary affectional relationships are between women, and the whole narrative hinges on female affiliation and mother-daughter love.

Ruth chooses to leave her own people and country because of her love for her mother-surrogate, Naomi, and the expression of that love is among the most tender of personal passages about the *feelings* of people for each other in the Old Testament. As her mother-in-law is about to leave Moab for her own land, Ruth says:

> "Entreat me not to leave you or to return from following you; for where
> you go I will go, and where you lodge I will lodge; your people shall
> be my people, and your God my God; where you die I will die, and
> there will I be buried. May the Lord do so to me and more also if even
> death parts me from you" (*Ruth*, 1:16–7).

Compared with this daughter-mother devotion, there is no special
affection ascribed to Ruth's marriage to her first husband, Naomi's
deceased son, or for her future husband Boaz. In fact, Boaz initially
treats Ruth kindly because he values her filial affection for his kins-
woman, Naomi. Throughout, Ruth does what Naomi tells her to do.
She works to support her, marries her kinsman Boaz to continue the
name of Naomi's son, and presents Naomi with security and a grandson
to nurse in her old age after she suffers the loss of her own husband
and two sons:

> Then the women said to Na'omi, "Blessed be the Lord, who has not
> left you this day without next of kin: and may his name be renowned
> in Israel! He shall be to you a restorer of life and a nourisher of your
> old age; for your daughter-in-law who loves you, who is more to you
> than seven sons, has borne him." Then Na'omi took the child and laid
> him in her bosom, and became his nurse. And the women of the
> neighborhood gave him a name, saying, "A son has been born to
> Na'omi" (*Ruth*, 4:14–7).

Ruth provides for Naomi in her old age. Naomi, in turn, provides
a husband for her daughter-in-law through the custom of her people,
levirate marriage. And Ruth is rewarded for her love for Naomi with
status explicitly comparable to that held by Leah and Rachel, "who
together built up the house of Israel" (*Ruth*, 4:11), for though she bears
but one son, he is the grandfather of David (*Ruth*, 4:17). Interestingly,
the action in this book is initiated by women; the central result—the
birth of David's ancestor—issues from the love of "mother" and "daughter" for each other; and the witnesses and commentators are "the women
of the neighborhood."

It should be recalled that Ruth the Moabite came from a polytheistic
society where women might well have held higher status in cult than
they did in the later days of ancient Israel, and therefore she may share
in the autonomy exhibited by other alien women—for example, the
Queen of Sheba, Jezebel, Delilah. Also, while surviving daughters are
told by God that they must marry within their father's tribe to preserve

his inheritance (*Numbers*, 36:6–9), Naomi's easy acceptance of Ruth as the perpetuator of her son's name is in line with Old Testament permissiveness toward intermarriage between Hebrew men and foreign women.

Much more significant, the book of *Ruth* originated in an early period, prior to the almost total masculinization of Israel's rituals and the hardening of attitudes toward women in the exilic and postexilic periods. It was a time which still tolerated the cultic leadership of a few great women like the judge Deborah, the soldier Jael, and the prophetess Chuldah, variously shown as judges and saviors of Israel, active agents of God's intentions or authenticators of part of the Pentateuch. Though Deborah, Jael, and Chuldah are all initially identified as wives of their husbands while important men are rarely identified as the husbands of anyone, they nevertheless are shown as strong and responsible individuals in their own right, acting in close concert with God's purposes.

It is only in this earlier time, when women were valued more and seen as capable of autonomous, brave actions indispensable to the survival of their people, that women like Naomi and Ruth could be valued as mothers and daughters. They emerge as whole and feeling persons, acting in their own behalf, providing for each other, and, through their mutual love, for the ancestry of the first great king of Israel. In this sense, the story of their moving, unconditional love for each other is part of the long tradition of close mother-daughter bonding so conspicuous in the polytheistic literature of the ancient Near East.

Notes
[1] Hesiod, *Theogony*, translated by Richard Lattimore, 1st printing, 1959 (Ann Arbor: University of Michigan Press, 1970), lines 155–82, 459–506.
[2] *The Epic of Gilgamesh*, translated by N. K. Sandars (Middlesex, England: Penguin Books, Ltd., 1960), p. 85.
[3] See, for example, Samuel Noah Kramer, *The Sacred Marriage Rite* (Bloomington: Indiana University Press, 1969), pp. 119–22.
[4] Cyrus H. Gordon, "Canaanite Mythology," in Samuel Noah Kramer (ed.), *Mythologies of the Ancient World* (New York: Anchor Books, 1969), p. 204.
[5] John A. Wilson, "Egyptian Myths, Tales, and Mortuary Texts," in James B. Pritchard (ed.), *Ancient Near Eastern Texts Relating to the Old Testament*, 3rd edition (Princeton: Princeton University Press, 1969), "The God and His Unknown Name of Power," pp. 12–14.
[6] Jane Ellen Harrison, *Mythology* (New York: Harbinger Books, 1924), p. 59.
[7] Enheduanna, *The Exaltation of Inanna*, translated by William W. Hallo and J. J. A. Van Dijk (New Haven: Yale University Press, 1968), p. 3.
[8] Enheduanna, p. 15.

[9] Enlil is the son of An and Ki and, by the third millenium, the active head of the Sumerian pantheon.

[10] Enheduanna, p. 17.

[11] Enheduanna, p. 19.

[12] Enheduanna, p. 21.

[13] See, for example, Sterling Dow and Robert F. Healey, S. J., *A Sacred Calendar of Eleusis*, Harvard Theological Studies, XXI (Cambridge: Harvard University Press, 1965); and C. Kerenyi, *Eleusis: Archetypal Image of Mother and Daughter*, translated by Ralph Manheim (New York: Bollingen Press, 1967).

Kriembild and Clytemnestra — Sisters in Crime or Independent Women?

We think of the woman seeking independence as a twentieth-century phenomenon; our research into the traditions of Greece and Germany,[1] however, suggests that she may be as old as the very roots of our culture. As we began our investigation, we expected to find forerunners of the present rebellion of daughters against their mothers' homebound existence in such figures as Kriemhild and Clytemnestra, but the results of our research have led us to believe that these early epic characters were involved in a far more elemental struggle.

The Burgundian princess Kriemhild is the leading female figure of the great Germanic folk epic *Das Nibelungenlied*. She moves from inconspicuous domesticity, to a place of command, and finally dies by the sword she has been wielding. Kriemhild's relationship to her family, particularly to her widowed mother, Uta, is a close one. The first "action" of the epic shows Kriemhild confiding a disturbing dream to her mother, which Uta then interprets as a symbolic foreshadowing of subsequent tragic events. Of her father we learn only that he has bequeathed to his heirs with his kindgom a name honored for deeds of glory and courage.

Uta is only a peripheral character in the *Nibelungenlied*, but every mention of her shows a strong mother figure, protecting, guiding, and rewarding those around her. The male-oriented transmission of this epic preserved a version which would lead us to believe that authority was completely in the hands of the men, but it is evident that women often held ruling power.[2] Uta's children treat her with respect and consult her when plans are made and decisions taken. A visit to Queen Uta is a necessary part of every arrival and departure at the castle, and messengers who report to Uta are often rewarded with rich gifts. When her children engage in tournaments or set out on journeys to distant lands, it is to Uta that they turn both for counsel and for the proper dress to indicate their wealth and rank, and it is she who gives directions to the serving women for the preparation of their garments. Her position as matriarch of the clan is firmly established, as is made clear by the formulaic labels given to her children: Kriemhild is called "Uta's daughter," and her brothers frequently receive the appellation "Uta's sons."

The close bond of warm affection and understanding between Kriemhild and her mother, which persists through the entire epic, does not prevent Kriemhild from rejecting her mother's advice and choosing her own course of action independently. Kriemhild's first rejection of her mother's value system comes in the argument which follows Uta's interpretation of Kriemhild's dream. Uta, according to the tradition which reaches us, maintains that the only way for a woman to attain happiness is through a man's affection, while Kriemhild insists that she will never marry, for she does not want to suffer the pain that is the price of love ("wie líebé mit leide zu jungest lônen kan," *Nibelungenlied*, 17).[3]

The Swiss scholar Nelly Dürrenmatt observes that the depiction of male and female character is very different in early Germanic literature: men grow and develop new traits in the course of an epic, while women only reveal qualities already inherent in their personalities.[4] The traits hidden within the fair Kriemhild, and gradually disclosed, are vigorous ones: assertiveness, independence of action, devotion not to her children but to a cause, all combined with the tragic flaw of pride.

Kriemhild becomes the wife of Sigfrid, despite her resolve to remain single, but her new surroundings are more patriarchal than those to which she was accustomed. She reacts by behaving in an even more overtly independent manner and by striving to attain more of the visible emblems of power than her mother enjoyed. Uta is, in the extant version, above all a parent, but the role of mother never assumes a primary place in Kriemhild's life. Rejecting the maternal place to which she was expected to confine herself, she leaves the child of her first marriage behind when she returns to her homeland, and even after Sigfrid's murder by her own people, she refuses to go back with her father-in-law to the care of her son. She shows even less interest in the child of her second marriage, using him as a bargaining lever in persuading Attila to do her will and spending no time in grief or horror when he is decapitated before her eyes at a banquet.[5]

Kriemhild's rebellious speech and action are also the immediate cause of the series of events that lead to Sigfrid's death. First she boasts immoderately to Brunhild and taunts her with having submitted to Sigfrid on her wedding night, thus revealing secrets entrusted by Sigfrid and provoking his statement that wives who exhibit unseemly behavior ("ungefüge," 862) should be chastised into a state of disciplined obedience.

Then, when Kriemhild realizes that her words have put her husband's life in danger, she tries to undo the damage and protect him by embroidering a cross on his cloak immediately over his one vulnerable spot,[6] and by enlisting Hagen to watch over him. Kriemhild is as skillful with her needle and thimble as her mother, but it should be noted that she employs these skills on her own initiative rather than at the behest of others. But Sigfrid's eventual death makes Kriemhild economically independent, for she acquires the Nibelung hoard which belonged to him. With it she starts out to hire and equip the army which is yet another manifestation of her search for power, until Hagen, sensing her intention to destroy him, steals the treasure and sinks it in the Rhine.

Revenge for Sigfrid's murder and for her loss of independence becomes the cause to which Kriemhild devotes all her energies from this time on. Again she finds herself at uneven odds with the world. Her second marriage to Attila, the most powerful man in the world, is recommended by her mother to put an end to her grief and loneliness, but for Kriemhild it is only a means to achieve the revenge she craves. She bides her time until the birth of a son enables her to ask what she will from Attila, and she is able to lure her brothers and Hagen to their destruction at the court of the Huns.

It is ironical that, after the forces of both sides have been almost completely wiped out, the only surviving Burgundian warriors are Gunther and Hagen, just those whom Kriemhild wanted most to kill. The final blood bath, in which Gunther, Hagen, and Kriemhild all perish, can be interpreted as concluding the fulfillment of dire prophecies made at the beginning of the epic, but there is another aspect of the situation which also deserves attention.

After Gunther is killed, and Hagen still will not reveal where the Nibelung hoard is concealed, Kriemhild seizes Sigfrid's sword and cuts off Hagen's head. The anger which impels Kriemhild's last desperate and token attempt to regain lost independence cannot be the result of economic need, for she is married to the wealthiest and most powerful man in the world. The execution of Gunther and the slaying of Hagen over the possesssion of the hoard can only derive from the same traits of pride and desire for personal power which initiated the conflict between Kriemhild and Brunhild and precipitated the chain of events leading to the final disaster.[7] To satisfy this desire, Kriemhild must not only avenge her first husband's murder by killing Hagen, but she must also regain possession of the wealth which was rightfully hers as Sigfrid's widow, so that she will have power separate from her present husband Attila. The frustration of this recovery of independent identity leads to her impulsive murder of Hagen and to her subsequent execution by Hildebrand in the name of justice.

The Greek epic tradition also contains a major female figure, Clytemnestra, whose life represents a woman's attempt to gain overt power in a patriarchal system. The mother here, Leda, is a shadowy figure, who is best known as one of Zeus' many conquests. Yet this indicates that she may have been a pre-Greek goddess, since rape by a god was one of the principal ways the Greek invaders dealt with their predecessors' goddesses, thereby bringing about their "death" as protecting, powerful deities. The Greeks fought constantly to repress the awe for the mother-goddess, who, like the strong-minded German heroine, reappeared in one form or another throughout Greek mythology. This is clearly seen in the rape/death of Persephone in the Eleusinian tradition. However, the Leda whom we know from extant literature shows only the nurturing-mother side of feminine power, and is subject to the whims of the patriarchal god Zeus and of her mortal husband Tyndareus. In the mold into which the Greeks forced her, she was the mother of four famous children: the Dioscuri Castor and Pollux, fair Helen of Troy, and her sister Clytemnestra.

The story of Clytemnestra was probably included in a series of short oral narratives referred to as the "Nostoi," or "Homecomings," of famous men. Traces of these are found in the *Odyssey*, but the works themselves have been lost to us, since they were obscured by the far greater Homeric works. The tales related in these "Homecomings" were preserved in the oral tradition and were picked up repeatedly by the early Greek poets as themes.

By these bards we are shown a Clytemnestra who seems to have started out to follow the traditional route of the daughter of a famous family, restricted to the wife-mother role. After Clytemnestra was tricked into sacrificing Iphigenia, however, she turned her back on the maternal role. Her desire to avenge her daughter's betrayal by Agamemnon was so great that she became the antithesis of the nurturing mother figure and, like Kriemhild, sought more obvious power. The nurse of her son Orestes smuggled the baby boy away to family friends in another part of Greece to prevent Clytemnestra from killing him, the only male heir to the throne, and Electra's life with her is generally portrayed as miserable. But in the constricting society into which she had married she could not seek power alone. She sought out her husband's worst enemy, Aegisthus,[8] and taking him as her lover, forced him to act as her figurehead, thus rejecting the patriarchal claim to wifely fidelity. She then proceeded to rule the country in her husband's absence. This regency revealed yet another facet of Clytemnestra's nature: she enjoyed the personal power she had as ruler, and her unwillingness to relinquish it undoubtedly reinforced the decade-old desire for revenge. She, with some help from Aegisthus, prepared a violent reception for Agamemnon on his return from the Trojan War.

Except for a few scattered references in Homer (for example, *Odyssey* xi, 421–434), all of the early Greek literature about this series of events has been lost.[9] However, from a Cretan disc seal of about 700 B.C.[10] to a series of red-figured vases at the beginning of the fifth century (including Berlin F 2301 and Vienna 1103), most of the pre-Aeschylean illustrations show Clytemnestra holding the murder weapon, either a sword or a double axe.

Aeschylus' is the earliest extant narration which focuses on Clytemnestra's action against Agamemnon. Her masculine strength of character ("ανδρόβουλον . . . κέαρ," line 11) is strongly contrasted with the weakness of her lover, who does not even make his entrance until line 1577 (less than one hundred lines from the end of the drama) and is depicted as a weak braggart whom Clytemnestra flatters into obedience. He claims that he, too, took a part in the plot against Agamemnon, but no one in the audience could have had many doubts about who directed the affair. Sophocles and Euripides also acknowledged Clytemnestra's strength of character, although they handled the story in less traditional fashion than Aeschylus.

The story goes on from Agamemnon's death to the slaying of Clytemnestra by her son Orestes, an act of revenge which includes a telling blow against independent women. That her death is an execution rather than a murder is clearly indicated by the tradition that Apollo inspired the deed. Also, even though Clytemnestra's Furies rise up and pursue Orestes, Athena exonerates him when he comes to her as suppliant, backed by Apollo's lines, "The mother is no parent of that which is called her child, but only nurse of the new-planted seed that grows"

(*Eumenides* 658–659, translated by R. Lattimore). This was a widely held biological theory of the time, and Aeschylus picked it up to strengthen his case against Clytemnestra, and with her any woman who attempted to overstep the patriarchally defined bounds of decency.

Between the stories of Clytemnestra and Kriemhild there are striking similiarities. Both women tried to take the traditionally masculine path toward power when faced with crises in their lives. Clytemnestra's vengeance for the sacrifice of Iphigenia parallels Kriemhild's revenge for the death of Sigfrid. Both turn from the role of mother, in which they had been confined. Each commits her last deed of revenge from mixed motives: Kriemhild murders when she cannot retrieve the wealth that would give her independence, and Clytemnestra is reluctant to relinquish ruling power to her returned spouse. Finally, both women fail to recover their independence and die in the struggle.

Though this study started by assuming that the daughters were the independent women, our results would point in the other direction, to the consequences of denying rights to women who have known them. Daughters seeking personal power evidently have ancient roots in Kriemhild and Clytemnestra, who both first tried the passive resistance patterns of their mothers in a restrictive environment. Neither, however, could find her own final answer in these models: the "ἀνδρόβουλονκεαρ" (masculine nature) of Clytemnestra and the "ungefüge" (unseemly behavior) of Kriemhild showed them by nature unwilling to be confined to the paths that became traditional. The means to which they turned were primitive and violent, criminal by both ancient and modern standards, and brought about their own destruction. Their actions make them sisters in crime, but the very violence of their deeds shows the intensity of their need for independent identity. Both tales reveal traces of an earlier matriarchal society in which the mother is not only a nurturing figure, but also protects, guides, and rewards her offspring, lovers, and associates. The stories show both Kriemhild and Clytemnestra against the backdrop of a society where woman is limited to her nurturing role and forbidden the influence which other roles give her. Both women in their frustration turn their backs on the one beneficent role remaining to them and become instead avenging furies. Their violence carries a warning of the disaster which threatens those who frustrate the need for total fulfillment found only in the full range of the positive female potential.

Notes

1 As a mother-daughter team with separate specializations in German and Greek literature, respectively, we have worked together on a number of research projects. Cf., e. g., "Werther's Selective Reading of Homer," *Modern Language Notes*, Vol. 92, No. 3 (April 1977).

2 Cf., among others, Parzival's mother Herzeloyde and his first wife Belacane.

3 All references to the *Nibelungenlied* will be by the traditional strophe numbers, and to Greek literature by line numbers, within the text.

4 Nelly Dürrenmatt, *Das Nibelungenlied im Kreis der höfischen Dichtung* (Lungern: Burch, 1945), p. 184.

5 An alternate version of the Nibelung story relates that Kriemhild deliberately sacrificed her young son by inciting him to strike Hagen, who then killed him.

6 According to legend, Sigfrid had bathed in dragon's blood and had so become invulnerable except for one spot on his back, where a linden leaf had fallen unnoticed.

7 Cf. Nelly Dürrenmatt, *op. cit.*, 192 ff., for an interesting discussion of the place of pride in Kriemhild's story.

8 Agamemnon and Aegisthus had a grandfather in common, Pelops, who was cursed by the gods for breaking a promise. He had two sons, Atreus and Thyestes. Thyestes seduced Atreus' wife, and in revenge Atreus served Thyestes his own children for dinner. Atreus was Agamemnon's father; Thyestes was Aegisthus' parent.

9 Stesichorus' *Oresteia* is known to us from later lists of the poet's works. Simonides is also said to be the author of an *Oresteia*.

10 Published by Carlo Anti in *Archaeologike Ephemeris* I (1953–54), pp. 180–188.

Eve's Orphans: Mothers and Daughters in Medieval English Literature

In *The Heroine of the Middle English Romances*, Adelaide Evans Harris remarks that mothers are, in medieval literature, conspicuous by their absence.[1] But, surely, one responds in protest, a literature spanning roughly four hundred years and half a dozen languages—I refer only to Western Europe—must depict *some* mothers and provide some clues as to how they behaved toward their children, particularly toward the children who were like them in mind and body: toward their daughters. And, since official history is meagre in this regard, one looks to the poetry and unofficial prose of the period in the hope of finding there some indication of how women learned, in those distant and shadowy centuries, to *be* women, since their roles could have been learned only in part from men.

Seeking representations of medieval mothers and daughters brings some problems common to all scholarship in that period. Only the clergy and the gentlefolk were literate, by and large; the literature is, then, from the outset, that of an elite group. Information about the majority of people is scarce and difficult to obtain. Except for an occasional reference to a sturdy yeoman or peasant, the aristocratic poets depicted those around them, those they knew.[2] Thus, whatever we glean about mothers and daughters will be not only from the pens of men, for the most part, but from the pens of aristocratic men or from those of the clergy. What we find in the literature about mothering will be, primarily, about mothering in the upper reaches of society. Perhaps mothers were more important to peasants and guildspeople—when the women could survive childbirth. But the courtly ladies customarily surrendered their offspring to wet nurses; children were sent at tender ages to neighboring courts for aristocratic training; and children, particularly girls, were married off when very young.[3] Contact between aristocratic mother and highborn child of either sex was distinctly limited. What the majority of women did we simply do not know.

The next difficulty in finding mothers and daughters in medieval literature arises from the fact that most writers were men in a society which was sexually segregated.[4] Many important parts of women's lives were hidden from the eyes of men.[5] Given even the largest heart and most humane mind, given the powers of observation of a Chaucer, for example, what went on beside the childbed, or while the ladies were dressing, or between two gossips, as in "The Wife of Bath's Tale," was unknown and uncharted. A medieval man would have had relatively little access to women in their own world, even if he had wanted to gain knowledge of what took place there. Exceptions exist; the authors of the *Ancrene Wisse* and *Hali Meidenhad*, tracts written for women, seem to have known and liked women, seem to have been acquainted with their private ways. In general, however, the world of womb and loom lay outside men's province and, naturally or unnaturally, male authors were not terribly concerned with distinctly feminine functions such as childbirth and mothering. Even when women begin to take active roles in the literature—after, for example, the chivalric period and its apotheosis in *The Song of Roland* where only one woman has a bit part—these roles are romantic, not maternal. Even in the courtly literature, written in good part for women and controlled by them to some extent, the relation of the woman to the man is important, and not that of a woman to her children. The occasional major role played by a mother—as in the *Percival* of Chretien de Troyes—is that of mother to a male child, to son. This holds true for much Marian imagery as well.

Finally, the strength of the patriarchy was such that it managed to subsume the emotional functions of mothering and fathering together. We find more than a few father-daughter relationships depicted in medieval literature: in elegiac poems such as *Pearl*, in romances such as *Floris and Blancheflor*, and in the lives of female saints. Medieval theories of procreation, such as that of Aquinas, emphasize the course of the sperm; husbands more or less owned their wives and children; and a daughter's entire life and livelihood depended upon whether or not her father would provide a dowry, approve a husband, or make arrangements with a nunnery. These economic, philosophical, and social bonds underpinned the greatest father-daughter relationship, that of a woman to the patriarchal godhead.[6] Thus we find an emotional reliance on the father which in more recent times has been associated with motherhood. We see this particularly in the religious literature: in the *Ancrene Wisse*, where three sisters turn to a kindly priest for rules of conduct to govern their exclusively feminine lives; in *Iuliene*, the heroine of which both identifies with and rebels against her earthly father; in *Seinte Marharete*, the heroine therein gaining strength from "the heavenly Lord . . . fosterer and father of helpless children"[7] [my translation].

To recapitulate: depiction of mother-daughter relationships is rare in medieval literature for three reasons. First, it is the literature of an aristocratic culture in which children were at a remove from their mothers. Secondly, the extant writings are by and large the production of men who would not have had access to the woman's world. Lastly, the father was of such socioeconomic importance that when parent-child relationships are depicted they tend to be father-son or father-daughter relationships. Nonetheless, our humanity being what it is, if we look deep enough and hard enough, through all the barriers of class, male authorship, and paternal domination, we begin to glimpse our mothers at last: in an occasional reference, a fleeting portrait, and in a whole series of substitutes and surrogates, a hidden gallery of the women who made women what they were and are.

Natural Mothers

Natural mothers are represented by and large as being on their daughters' side. One recalls the prologue to "The Wife of Bath's Tale." The Wife informs the pilgrims that the ruse she employed to catch her young husband was taught her by her "dame" (*Chaucer*, p.81, 1.576). We glimpse an intimacy here, some counsel by the kitchen fire, in regard to an important survival technique: snaring a man. But mothers, while sympathetic and even conspiratorial, were not always presented as being so successful in their advice. In the *fabliau*, or comic tale, of *Dame Sirith*, for example, the good woman of the title bemoans the fate of her daughter, and we feel, in the midst of the comedy, the tie of empathy and mutual helplessness. Dame Sirith relates that she had a beautiful daughter, none fairer, who had a very fine husband, also "the best":

> My daughter loved him all too well,
> And this I deeply regret,
> For one day he went on a journey,
> And this is what ruined my daughter.

> When her husband was out of town,
> A wily cleric came around,
> Seeking my daughter's favors.
> But she would have none of that.
> He was not to have his way
> In anything he wished to do with her.
> Then this cleric began to bewitch
> And turned my daughter into a bitch.
> This is my daughter of whom I speak:
> For sorrow of her my heart must break.[8]
>
> [my translation]

Both the Wife of Bath and Dame Sirith appear in comic works, and it has been suggested that a kind of counterculture literature existed in the medieval period, a literature in which women figured vividly.[9] Perhaps whatever women do has always seemed funny to men, or perhaps this comic literature, unofficial, out of the mainstream, included dimensions of life thought indecorous at the time. Evocation of domesticity was not a medieval forte.

The Book of the Knight of Tour-Laundry, while having serious overtones and being indeed a kind of "treatise on social ethics,"[10] is, again, not of Leavis' Great Tradition. It is notably domestic. Geoffrey de la Tour Laundry, a widower who wrote for his three daughters, portrays their mother playing the part of adviser and protector; with commendable honesty, he portrays her endeavoring to protect them from his own well-meaning but ill-founded advice, and from the carelessness of all men:

> "Ye say, and so do all other men, that a lady or damsel is the better worth when she loveth paramours, and that she shall be the more gay and of fair manner and countenance, and how she shall do great alms to make a good knight . . .
>
> "But these words cost to them but little to say for to get the better and sooner the grace and good will of their paramours. For of such words, and others much marvellous, many a one useth full oft. But, howbeit that they say that 'For them and for their love they do it,' in good faith, they do it only for to enhance themself and for to draw unto them the grace and vainglory of the world.
>
> "Therefore, I charge you, my fair daughters, that in this matter ye believe not your father . . ."[11]

She goes on to say that men are deceivers. Again, we see a protective mother, concerned for her daughters' well-being, and not entirely sanguine about the nature of men. There is no hint of rivalry or distrust, and no *blame* accrues to the daughters for involvement in courtly love.

Some natural mothers are presented as so distrustful of men, so concerned with protecting their daughters from them, that they are seen encouraging their daughters to withdraw from the world entirely. In *The Lives of Women Saints of Our Countrie of England*,[12] a veritable troop of women seem eager to shield their young ones from the life of married woe depicted in *Hali Meidenhad*.[13] St. Keyna's mother envisages the girl's beatitude while the child is in her belly (*Saints*, p.39); a nameless woman brings her daughter to St. Brigide to save the girl from a marriage (*Saints*, p.42); and St. Mildred's mother sends her to a cloister in France (*Saints*, p.63). We are told in two cases of the saint's mother having been violated: the mother of St. Brigide (*Saints*, p.40) and the mother of St. Edith (*Saints*, p.102). I believe these details are included not out of sensationalism but to show causality: the convent might not have been the earthly paradise but it was closer to it, these details imply, than the ordinary life of woman. In several legends, daughter and mother enter a religious house together, as in the account of St. Werburge (*Saints*, p.59), and in one legend, a mother, daughter, and *granddaughter* are shown living in a nunnery (*Saints*, p.59). A serious problem for feminists to consider: in encouraging their daughters to remain virginal and thus childless, these mothers are in some way denying the worth of motherhood, invalidating their own experience, even if this was possibly the only way in which they could protect their daughters and their daughters' autonomy, to some extent, in the medieval period.

Mother Surrogates: the Old Hag

The figure of the female go-between which emerges in the Renaissance—the sympathetic busybody of *Romeo and Juliet*, for example—comes from the medieval figure of the old woman who has great knowledge in love. The old woman is frequently presented as a hag, almost a witch, and the reason for this seems fairly clear. A literature composed by men is filtered through their fears, as it were. The Old Hag who furthers the cause of the beautiful young maiden is a version of the mother-in-law: the fearsome powers of all women and mothers is attributed to an older female figure.[14] Also revealed is the male fear of the bond between woman and woman, mother and daughter, as if a magical power lay in female generation: there is tacit acknowledgement by these male authors of the strength and persistence of the mothering instinct in relation to creatures of its own kind.

I turn once more to the Wife of Bath—but this time to her fantasies in the classic wish fulfillment sequence which constitutes her tale. The culpable knight meets up with the wise but hideous hag who at the appropriate moment rewards him by turning into a fair young woman; the Wife of Bath is here both mother and daughter at once. The Old Hag, that is, with her accumulated wisdom helps the young woman inside her accomplish the young woman's ends. We recall that the Wife of Bath's mother, in the prologue, is reported to have taught her how to enchant a man; in the fantasy, the Old Hag takes over the mother's role—but with much more power and control.

The literary ancestor of the Wife of Bath appears in one of the most popular works of the period, *Le roman de la rose* (*The Romance of the Rose*).[15] The Old Hag here is not so much an enchantress as a lascivious meddler, one who is privy to the young woman's desires and who works hard to bring the lover and the rose, the maiden, together, seeming to take vicarious pleasure in the match:

> "I'll tell you in advance, 'tis not my wish
> To set your thoughts on love; but, if your will
> Is strong to intermeddle in such things,
> I'll gladly show you all the roads and paths
> That once I trod before my beauty fled."
> (*Rose*, p.269)

The narrator, echoing the misogynistic point of view of Jean de Meun,[16] comments:

> Then, like the false and servile crone she was,
> She recommenced her prating, with the thought
> That by her doctrines she might cozen me
> To fool myself with honey licked from thorns.
> (*Rose*, p.269)

The Duenna, as she is called in this translation, although "The Old One" would be a more correct term, deals in illusion and the manipulation of human nature: a woman must disguise her ailments and her lacks, employ her tears to gain men's sympathy, see to it that her table manners express a delicacy she really doesn't have, etc. Especially,

> "With care should women always imitate
> The wolf when she desires to steal a sheep.
> That she may fail not, and be sure of one,

27

> A thousand she assails; she never knows,
> Before she has him caught, which one she'll get.
> A woman everywhere should spread her nets
> To capture all the men . . ."
>
> (*Rose*, p.283)

Of course, Jean de Meun was a satirist, and here the Old Hag is confessing, "telling all," to a masculine figure. But beyond the satiric conventions of misogyny lies that peculiar fear of women which permeates medieval thought. Images of entrapment, as in the passage above, abound. As in the Wife of Bath's narrative, the Old Hag has the knowledge which the young women lack, and can advise the young on setting snares for men. This kind of representation reflects, I believe, the way men thought women must have counseled their daughters.

In *Sir Gawain and the Green Knight*, the threatening nature of the Old Hag-Young Woman alliance becomes clearer. There are two women at table in Bercilak's castle, a beautiful young woman, she of the green girdle who will attempt to seduce Sir Gawain, and an old crone with "black brows" and "sour" lips.[17] The poet describes both women in the same stanza: they seem to be opposites. As it turns out, however, the young woman is simply an extension, a projection, of the old one, her flesh in its youthful guise; in other words, a kind of daughter. The old woman, it also turns out, is none other than that puissant and dangerous sorceress of the Arthurian legends, Morgan. Gawain's manhood has been tested in this work, and although all he receives is a nick in the neck, Morgan has been responsible for this and indeed for the whole plot against Arthur's court. There is no one so high and mighty, Bercilak explains, that Morgan cannot "tame" him.[18] The beautiful young woman is only an agent of the old, but her power of seduction is threatening to Gawain, too. Together, the two generations of women are especially dangerous: they present a double threat to Gawain's manhood, and to his very life. This explains Gawain's otherwise inexplicable tirade against women and, indeed, makes a woman the prime mover of the plot. The Old Hag, then, seems to represent women's power, and to symbolize the help women could not get from their real mothers, as in "The Wife of Bath's Tale," or the fears of men as to the strength young women might indeed have gotten from the old.

Mother Surrogates: Foster Mothers

The second kind of mother surrogate, the foster mother, is a creature of the shadows. Like the real mother, she is sympathetic and powerless.

Even the abbesses of the period, we must remember, were always accountable to male authority; even the Virgin Mother, when she is permitted to address her daughters at all, counsels meekness and obedience. But what is most significant in regard to foster mothers and their daughters, I believe, is the desire of one to protect the other, although they are not related by blood.

Although we find foster mothers in romances and lays as well, I will focus here on the saints' lives where the adoptive impulse seems to have prospered. *Seinte Marharete* is paradigmatic in this regard, and we encounter in it an actual "fostremodre."[19] Margaret's real mother has died. While she is tending her foster mother's sheep, she is spotted and desired by one Olibrius who, as in many of these legends, tries to win her by wooing and threatening, then by torture, and who, finally, in frustration and fury, has her put to death. Important for this discussion, however, is the way the foster mother behaves when Olibrius puts Margaret in prison. Margaret's father has thrown her out, abandoned her, as it were, but her foster mother comes to visit her in prison, and brings her bread for food and the drink of a knight.[20] Thus, she recognizes Margaret's valor, sympathizes with her suffering, and performs the most basic of motherly functions: nurture. She can do nothing about her foster daughter's plight, of course, and, submerged in a crowd of onlookers, she must wait as passively as they do while Margaret struggles with a devil-dragon in her cell.

Of St. Ethelburge, "virgin and Abbesse," we are told that having "found her father a moste cruell persecutor and enemie of her faithful mynde and endeauors," she flees his house, whereupon her brother provides her with "a spritual teacher named Hildelitha, a woman as well excellentlie learned in the liberall sciences, as verie expert, in skill of religious discipline and life" (*Saints*, pp.52–53). St. Ethelburge, in turn, surpasses the other nuns in "vertue and holynes, and at last was chosen mother or Abbesse of them all" (*Saints*, p.53). St. Elflede lived "vnder the holie gouernment of the vertuous Ladie and Abbesse Merwenne: who loued her as her owne daughter, and taught her, as her owne bowells" (*Saints*, p.101). The abbesses, then, are not seen as severe authority figures but as protectors and educators. In a rule such as that of the *Sustris Menouresses Enclosid*, the woman in charge seems to be in that position in order to "gif licence," to loosen the rules, as it were, and not to impose them unfeelingly from above.[21]

The Virgin Mother Mary does not intercede on behalf of her daughters as much as one might have thought; as she was made to mother a son, this is often where her concern is directed. She does occasionally address her daughters, however, comforting and teaching them. In one instance, she goes so far as to save a pregnant nun from the wrath of her superiors.[22] In *The Revelations of Saint Birgitta*, a late medieval work of the fifteenth century, the "moder of God spekyth" directly to Birgitta on several occasions, most intimately and notably in the passage on the "mantelle of mekenes":[23]

> I am called by all the mother of mercy. In truth, daughter, the mercy of my son made me merciful, and his suffering made me have compassion . . . Therefore, you, my daughter, come and hide under my mantle, which is outwardly despicable but inwardly is beneficial for three things. First, it shelters from tempestuous winds. Secondly, it keeps from biting cold. Thirdly, it defends from rain. This mantle is my meekness.[24]
>
> [my translation]

In other words, she advises Birgitta to gain strength through self-abasement, to seek a shelter in gentleness, a place to hide from the cruelty and strife of the world. What other counsel could a medieval mother or mother surrogate give? All even the Queen of Heaven could offer her daughters was a certain compassion for their plight. And the example of meekness, a genuine and general Christian virtue, of course provided women with a mode of survival yet might well have made it more difficult for them, in succeeding generations, to have changed their lot.

Women mothered other women. The bonds between them, described infrequently in a male-oriented literature, seem strong. The protecting and sheltering impulse—the desire to keep another, younger woman from hurt—predominates in the representation of mothers and surrogates in medieval English literature. We can see this even in "The Clerk's Tale," where Griselda's mothering instincts appear so negligible. Walter, Griselda's husband, we recall with a shudder, has taken away Griselda's children, and has told her that he has had them slain; she declares that, even so, she has been and "evere schal" be a "humble servant" to the man she thinks the murderer of her little boy and girl.[25] Although the tale is clearly an allegory, Patient Griselda representing the soul and Walter standing for God, the implications for the strength of medieval motherhood seem grim. However, we find Griselda—outcast, childless, humiliated, and in the degrading position of having to prepare for and approve of her husband's new wife—speaking these words to Walter in reference to his young bride:

> "One thing I beg of you, and warn, too,
> That you do not prick with torments
> This tender maiden, as you have done to me.
> For she has been brought up more
> Delicately, and, I would venture to suppose,
> She could not endure adversity
> As could a creature brought up in poverty."[26]
>
> [my translation]

Griselda does not yet know, as she speaks these lines, that the lovely girl is really her natural daughter whom Walter has not in fact had slain. But her impulse—overcoming even the famous humility—is to shield the young woman from the harshness of the man and his demands.

If one of the ambitions of the patriarchy was to sever the bonds between mothers and their female children, to make of women a nation of orphans, then I think we can say that, despite the strictures of misogyny in the medieval world, the patriarchs did not succeed. Even though Mother Eve was in many ways deprived of her daughters, women then and now have been able to form those bonds among themselves which can only be called familial, and have desired to love, nurture, and protect each other; to be, in short, mothers to others and finally, one hopes, to themselves.

Notes

[1] (Cleveland: Western Reserve University Press, 1928), p.38.

[2] An exception to this is Langland's *Piers Plowman*. And I will not be dealing here with the more egalitarian culture of Anglo-Saxon times.

[3] Harris, p.38; see also Ann S. Haskell, "The Paston Women on Marriage in Fifteenth Century England," *Viator*, Vol. 4 (1973), 459–471.

[4] This problem in regard to classical Greek literature is admirably handled by Sarah Pomeroy, *Goddesses, Whores, Wives and Slaves: Women in Antiquity* (New York: Schocken, 1973).

[5] Doctors sometimes refused to treat women; see Vern Bullough, "Medieval Medical Views of Women," *Viator*, Vol. 4 (1973), 487–501.

[6] See Mary Daly, *Beyond God the Father* (Boston: Beacon Press, 1973).

[7] E. J. Dobson, ed., *The English Text of the Ancrene Riwle* (London: Oxford University Press, 1972); S.T.R.O. d'Ardenne, ed., *Se Liflade ant te Passiun of St. Iuliene* (Oxford: Early English Text Society, 1961); Frances M. Mack, ed., *Seinte Marharete* (Oxford: Early English Text Society, 1958), p.19.

[8] J. A. W. Bennett and G. V. Smithers, eds., *Early Middle English Verse and Prose* (Oxford: Clarendon Press, 1966), p.77. This is a thirteenth-century tale.

[9] See Phillippe Verdier, "Woman in the Marginalia of Gothic Manuscripts and Related Works," in *The Role of Woman in the Middle Ages*, ed. Rosemarie Thee Morewedge (Albany: State University of New York Press, 1975), p. 121 ff.

[10] *Later Medieval English Prose*, ed. William Matthews (New York: Appleton-Century-Crofts, 1963), p. 262.

[11] *Later Medieval English Prose*, pp. 279–280.

[12] C. Horstmann, ed. (London: Early English Text Society, 1886). These *Lives*, compiled at the end of the sixteenth century, draw upon medieval and Anglo-Saxon sources. Page numbers follow references and are given parenthetically within the text.

[13] F. J. Furnivall, ed. (New York: Greenwood Press, 1969).

[14] Such disparate thinkers as Sigmund Freud in *Wit and Its Relation to the Unconscious* and Robert Briffault in *The Mothers* have confirmed that fear and ridicule of the mother-in-law stems from the incest taboo.

[15] Guillaume de Lorris and Jean de Meun, *The Romance of the Rose*, translated by Harry W. Robbins (New York: Dutton, 1962). Page numbers are given parenthetically within the text and refer to this edition. I include this French work since it was popular and influential in England; Chaucer himself translated a part of it.

[16] Guillaume de Lorris, author of Part I, is sympathetic to *fin amors*, courtly love, and thus to female figures in general.

[17] J. R. R. Tolkien and E. V. Smithers, eds. (Oxford: Clarendon Press, 1968), p. 27.

[18] *Sir Gawain and the Green Knight*, p. 67.

[19] See particularly Marie de France's "Lai le Freine" ("The Lay of the Ash Tree"); see note 7, *Marharete*, p. 19.

[20] *Marharete*, p. 20.

[21] See the edition of Walter W. Seton (Oxford: Early English Text Society, 1962).

[22] Cf. Johannes Herolt, *Miracles of the Blessed Virgin Mary*, translated by C. C. Swinton Bland (London: Routledge, 1928); also, Beverly Boyd, ed., *The Middle English Miracles of the Virgin* (San Marino, Ca.: The Huntington Library, 1964).

[23] William Patterson Cumming, ed. (London: Early English Text Society, 1929).

[24] *The Revelations of Saint Birgitta*, pp. 100–101.

[25] From *The Canterbury Tales* in *The Works of Geoffrey Chaucer*, ed. F. N. Robinson (Boston: Houghton-Mifflin, 1957), p. 110, II. 824–25.

[26] *The Canterbury Tales*, p. 112, II. 1037–43.

The New Mother of the English Renaissance: Her Writings on Motherhood

After serving for centuries as the target of a Christian misogynism, Renaissance women benefited from the development of an expanded conception of woman as a human being. In England, due to the relatively late onset of humanism and the advent of religious reform, the new Renaissance theories resulted in the development of a "new mother" who was learned and pious, responsible for raising her children and developing her own potential. From a historical perspective, the evolution of the role of the woman in English Renaissance society became centered in the woman as mother. At the same time, there was no interest in changing the subordinate legal status of women, or in allowing them to engage in public life. Consequently, the development of the role of the "new mother" was central to the expectations and experiences of the Renaissance woman who, in the context of Renaissance reality, would one day hope to find in her experience as a mother the outlet for her creative, spiritual, and intellectual needs.

There was significant interest in women generally, as well as in the mother specifically, on the part of two related but distinct groups of English Renaissance thinkers. The first group was composed of such early humanist scholars as Sir Thomas More, Desiderius Erasmus, Juan Luis Vives, Richard Hyrde, and Sir Thomas Elyot. The second group of conscious innovators was composed of religious reformers (who tended to become predominantly Puritan over the period). The orientations of both groups of thinkers—English humanists and religious reformers—were in many ways similar. Both were profoundly serious, and both subordinated human and materialistic goals to heavenly ones.

The theories of the humanists found their main expression in the writings of Juan Luis Vives, who was brought to England by Catherine of Aragon, the first queen of Henry VIII, to educate Princess Mary. In his *Instruction of a Christen Woman*, dedicated to Queen Catherine, Vives, attempting to fit this newly learned woman into a private life style, stated that a woman, should "study . . . if nat for her own sake, at the least wyse for her chyldren, that she maye teache them and make them good . . . For that age childhood can do nothynge it selfe but counter-fayte and folowe others, and . . . taketh its fyrst conditions and infor-mation of mynde [from the] mother . . . . Therfore it lyeth more in the mother than men wene, to make the conditions of the chyldren."[1] It was through her own prior learning that the mother would be enabled to fulfill this responsibility; for, as Vives states with typical humanistic fervor, "the study of lerning . . . occupieth ones mind holly, . . . and lifteth it up from the remembraunce of such thinges as be foul." (I, 17–18) These same ideas are expressed both in Vives' other writings, and in the writings of the other humanists.[2]

Bartholomaeus Batty may be taken as typical of the religious reform-ers. In his *Christian mans closet*, Batty states, "mothers by the commande-ment of God, ought to have no lesse care and charge belonging unto them, then the Fathers and masters, touching the good government of their sonnes, daughters and servants."[3]

The recognition, in the Renaissance, of the importance of the mother's influence, which today seems obvious and even restrictive, must be appreciated as an advance against medieval thinking, which charged the father with the responsibility for the education of children.[4] There are few medieval tracts on women's education in English, and most of those which were written were intended for women entering the religious life.[5] However, one tract, entitled *The Northern Mothers Blessing* (1420), confirms and illustrates that the training and aspirations of medieval lay women were limited to such narrow and unlettered goals as humility, silence, obedience, and chastity.[6]

Conversely, the historical existence of "Tudor paragons," or nu-merous illustrious sixteenth- and seventeenth-century Englishwomen, is a fact which can be explained in the light of the development of the new theories of the humanists and reformers concerning women.[7] Among extant writings by these prodigies are some illuminating writ-ings on motherhood by Renaissance mothers. These writings are per-sonal, even intimate, and are addressed by individual women to indi-vidual children, under individual circumstances. However, despite their variations, the tracts, considered as a group, do yield a consistent accumulation of evidence on the thinking of Renaissance English mothers. The examination of these writings which follows groups the tracts in accordance with their foci, and attempts to analyze them in the context of the developing Renaissance theories on the role of the mother, in order to answer such questions as the following: Did these mothers acquiesce in the new thinking on their role and responsibility? Alternately, did they wish—or dare—to venture for themselves beyond the social and professional limitations of their time? If not, did they aspire for greater opportunity for their daughters than they had realized themselves? Or did they accept the newly enhanced, but private, status for both themselves and for their daughters, and therefore address themselves differently to their sons than to their daughters?

The survey of writings on motherhood by English Renaissance mothers begins with two tracts addressed to married daughters. The first is the diary of Lady Grace (Sherrington) Mildmay (1552–1620). At fifteen, following a rigorous Puritan upbringing, Grace was married to Anthony Mildmay, son of a Puritan official.[8] Her diary is actually a journal of reminiscences and reflections written late in her life, and was not intended for publication. However, it was addressed to Lady Mildmay's daughter, Mary, whose children's upbringing concerned their grandmother deeply. The long preface to the journal is entitled "Experience I conned to my child"; it contains Lady Mildmay's most intimate thoughts on the education of the young, and it constitutes evidence of the interest in and concern about the education of children which was developing among mothers of the Renaissance.

The following excerpt serves to illustrate Lady Mildmay's thoughts: "All that are . . . born into this world shall either be . . . electe children of God, or be . . . cast out from God into Hell to be the children of the devill . . . . Wherefore it is a matter of great importance to bring up children unto God, . . . and in the exercise of that teaching we teach and instruct ourselves unto the same end, which is life everlasting" (p. 228). In other words, children must be taught properly so that they escape damnation; their education, therefore, is a matter of great importance. Here is the distillation of the substance of the reformers' tracts by a woman who had obviously absorbed and accepted their contents.

Lady Mildmay specifies certain subjects for the curriculum of her grandchildren. Among these are "Scriptures, to read them with all diligence and humility every day," history, "whereby we may be instructed to . . . follow the example of true and faithful subjects . . . [and] whereby we may avoyd all treasons and treacherous attempts . . . " and philosophic works, "worthie works, sometimes to be read for recreation" (p. 227). Lady Mildmay is addressing the needs of two generations—the mother (her daughter) who wishes to teach her children, and the children themselves, but her interest, essentially, is in educating the young child. However, the fact that she has a dual purpose in writing to a mother about young children deflects her from such specifics as a schedule for every hour of the child's day to general principles of childrearing.

The same rather oblique focus on the needs of the young child is embodied in another tract dedicated to a younger woman who is herself a mother; this is a short work entitled the *Countesse of Lincolnes Nurserie*[9] by Elizabeth Knevet Clinton, Countess of Lincoln (1574–1630?). The treatise, which is addressed by the Countess to her daughter-in-law, Briget, consists, essentially, of a series of religious justifications for breast feeding.[10] Obviously a discussion of breast feeding must be addressed to the mother, to define her duties, although it is the infant who is the ultimate object of concern in such a treatise.

In addressing her daughter-in-law, the Countess cites the biblical examples of Eve, Sarah, Hannah, and Mary as precedents for the nursing of one's children. She interprets the precept "to marry and bear children" to mean to nourish and hold the children as well as to carry them during pregnancy. She asserts that those who fail to nurse their children show "unmotherly affection, idlenesse, desire to have liberty to gadd from home, . . . and the like evils" (p. 13). Finally, she alleges that hired nurses are often neglectful and that if harm befalls the child, the mother is equally responsible with the nurse. She states, "the child at your breast . . . is the Lord's own instruction . . . instructing you to show that you are his new born babe by your earnest desire after his word" (p. 20).

A comment should be added about the attitude of the Countess. At midpoint in her work she states, "I might say more, but I leave the larger and learneder discourse here-of unto men of art, and learning: only I speake of so much as I reade, and know in my owne experience, which if any of my sexe, and condition do receave good by, I am glad" (pp. 11–12). This statement demonstrates the humility and submissiveness of the Countess, who did not consider herself the equal of men, and who did not consider it her perogative to write books of advice. It also demonstrates her hesitancy to publish even materials of sober, unobjectionable character. It is from her conception of herself as a new mother that the publication of the Countess' *Nurserie* sprang. Therefore, the Countess' tract, and those of the other women who are discussed here, can not be considered merely the female counterparts to the seventeenth-century advice books by men,[11] for statements like the Countess' are to be found in each of the published tracts on motherhood by the new mothers of the English Renaissance.

One other tract in the period is addressed by a mother to a daughter,[12] although this daughter was apparently a younger child, because the writer's instructions were addressed directly to her. This curious tract, called the *Mothers counsell . . .* [13] is by an unknown mother, M. R., and shows not only a knowledge of religious doctrine, but a familiarity with the poetry of Edmund Spenser, since several verses are quoted, without acknowledgement, from the *Faerie Queene*.[14]

This change in the conception of the dignity and intellectuality of women from 1420 to 1630 is shown clearly by a comparison of this tract with the earlier *Northern Mothers Blessing* (which I mentioned earlier). Both works emphasize such traditional virtues as chastity, humility, and temperance, but the approaches of the two authors are radically different. In the medieval tract, for example, the daughter is cautioned:

> My doughter gif thou be a wife, wisely thou werke,
> Looke ever thou love God and the holy Kirke,
> Go to Kirke when thou may, and let for no rayne,
> And ther shall thou fare the bet, when thou God has sayn:
> Full well may they thrive
> That serven God in their live,
> My leve dere child. (Stanza 2)

In contrast, the headings of the *Mothers Counsell* include the following: "1. That you keepe a narrow watch over your heart, words, and deedes continually. . . . 8. That you prepare your self to beare the Crosse, by what meanes soever it shall please God to exercise you . . . " (p. 2). Learning per se is not stressed by M. R., but her remarks assume both mature sense and a prior acquaintance with and understanding of Christian doctrine on the part of her daughter: "Chastity is the Seale of Grace, the staffe of Devotion, the marke of the just, the crowne of Virginity, the glory of life, and a comfort in martyrdom" (p. 3). It can be said that the *Mothers Counsell*, like the other tracts addressed to daughters by Renaissance English mothers, embodies an acceptance of the religious precepts and social and familial roles advocated by the Renaissance theorists.

The remainder of the tracts on motherhood by English Renaissance mothers are addressed to sons; nevertheless, they throw considerable light on both Renaissance mothers and daughters.

The earliest of these tracts is by a Catholic, Elizabeth Grymeston (d. 1603), who was the daughter of Martin Bernye of Gunton, Norfolk, and the wife of Christopher Grymeston of Yorkshire. Her work, addressed to her only son, Bernye, was first printed after her death. It is an outstanding specimen of a counselling tract to a child which portrays the writer very clearly, and it is a transparent medium for the concern which motivated her to write: "My dearest sonne, there is nothing so strong as the force of love; there is no love so forcible as the love of an affectionate mother to hir naturall childe: there is no mother can either more affectionately shew hir nature, or more naturally manifest hir affection, than in advising hir children out of hir owne experience, to eschue evill, and encline them to do that which is good."[15]

Some of Grymeston's advice could be addressed equally to either a son or a daughter: "When thou risest, let thy thoughts ascend, that grace may descend: and if thou canst not weepe for thy sinnes, then weepe, because thou canst not weepe" (sig. B2). But other reflections would be less suited to a woman who is confined to a private life than to a man whose affairs take him into the wider world: "Labour in youth gives strong hope of rest in olde age." And, "the whole world is as an house of exchange in which Fortune is the nurse that breeds alteration" (sig. N1). Grymeston is almost certainly the greatest writer among the mothers considered here; indeed, Charlotte Kohler believes that this eloquent tract is similar to Burton's *Anatomy*, on a smaller scale.[16]

The solicitude which prompted Mrs. Grymeston to write was responsible also for the composition of the *Mothers Blessing* by Dorothy Leigh (no dates), a woman unknown outside this work,[17] and unlisted in the *DNB*. The tract is intended as counsel for her sons whose father had died and it treats many of the subjects of the religious reformers. Mrs. Leigh explains that she is writing to teach her sons religion, to inspire her sons to write when they are older, and to inspire other women to be careful mothers. She defends the writing of her tract as a fulfillment of her duty to her sons: "Setting aside all feare, I have adventured to shew my imperfections to the view of the world, not regarding what censure for this shall bee laid upon me so that herein I may shew myselfe a loving Mother and a dutifull wife."[18]

Mrs. Leigh is intrepid enough to write that women should "not be ashamed to shew their infirmities, but . . . give men the first and chiefe place: yet let us labor to come in the second." She expresses a hope that at least some of her sons will enter the clergy—if, that is, they will undertake that grave trust properly. Although she advocates the teaching of both young boys and girls, she separates the boys and the girls in advocating professional training for males only. The contrast between this distinction and Mrs. Leigh's defense of her own decision to write shows an awareness of the different restrictions on men and women of the period; there is no basis, however, for claiming even an unconscious resentment of these restrictions on Mrs. Leigh's part.

The last[19] of the tracts, the *Mothers legacie to her unborn childe* by Elizabeth Joceline (1596–1622), is perhaps the most moving and illuminating of the entire group. Mrs. Joceline, who was called by Myra Reynolds "one of the most notable young women of the time of James I,"[20] died in 1622, after six years of marriage to Towrell Joceline of Cambridgeshire, and just a few days after her only child was born. To this anticipated child of unknown sex she left her tract as a legacy. Her work begins with a letter addressed to her husband in which she expresses both her joy at the prospect of bearing and raising his child (thereby inadvertently revealing the exquisite closeness of their relationship), and her fear of dying in childbirth (an unfortunately realistic fear for the period, and one which proved prophetic). She explains that she has realized that she can leave written instructions for their child, even if she does not survive its birth.[21]

The body of the work (which is addressed to the child) is Mrs. Joceline's legacy. Her instructions are primarily spiritual; here is another mother imbued with an acceptance of the duty to instruct her children in religion:

> . . . the time now drawing on, which I hope . . . appointed to give thee to me: It drew me into a consideration both wherefore I so earnestly desired thee, and (having found that the true cause was to make thee happy) how I might compasse this happinesse for thee . . . .
>
> I never aimed at so poore an inheritance for thee as the whole world: . . .the true reason I have so often kneeled to God for thee, is, that thou mightest bee an inheritour of the Kingdome of Heaven. (pp. 1–4)

Mrs. Joceline offers different advice to her unborn son or daughter. To a son she writes, "I humbly beseech Almightie God . . . that thou maist serve him as his Minister, if he make thee a man" (p. 4). To her husband, she makes rather ambivalent comments on an unborn daughter:

> I desire her bringing up may bee learning the Bible, as my sisters doe, good housewifery, writing, and good workes: other learning a woman needs not: though I admire it in those whom God hath blest with discretion, yet I desired not much in my owne, having seene that sometimes women have greater portions of learning than wisdome, . . . But where learning and wisdome meet in a vertuous disposed woman she is the fittest closet for all goodnesse . . . . Yet I leave it to thy will . . . . If thou desirest a learned daughter, I pray God give her a wise and religious heart, that she may use it to his glory, thy comfort, and her owne salvation. (sig. B4–B5)

One may legitimately surmise that it was on the basis of her own experience that the learned Elizabeth Joceline wished to protect her unborn daughter from a potentially difficult and uncomfortable life style. In any case, the reader can certainly appreciate the aptness of Reynolds' comment that the Joceline tract was "deservedly popular because it was so genuine in its forecast of sorrow, so pathetically eager in plans and hopes for her husband and child."[22]

The fact that all these tracts on child rearing are expressive of deep feelings, clearly voiced, is beyond question. And the basis for this strong emotion would seem to lie in the integration of natural maternal feeling with the religious and intellectual development of women advanced through the theory of the new mother. Because educated English mothers of the Renaissance were theoretically restricted to the outlets of child nurture and private religion, there was a potential of incompatibility and conflict between the sense of maternal duty and the need for submission. This conflict is realized by the writers of tracts on child rearing only in the sense that they wrote their tracts, even though they knew that they overstepped themselves by writing. Certainly there are only slight suggestions of unease to be detected in the tracts of Dorothy Leigh and Elizabeth Joceline, and these are the only mothers who clarify distinctions for children of the two sexes. None of the other mothers suggest any dissatisfaction with the different limits placed on the two sexes within the period.

As literature, the quality of these materials varies. There are sections detailing minutiae of religious observance and fine theological distinctions which are tedious to the modern reader of literature. There are also portions which are eloquent, fervent, and touching; the roll of phrase and command of language in these sections are impressive. Indeed, these sections raise the tracts above the literary level of those by the men who inspired them, perhaps by virtue of the fact that the writings of the mothers are more intimate creations, each of which is addressed directly and warmly to a reader with whom the mother felt a special closeness.

Such writers as Charlotte Kohler failed to see the intimate connection made in the period between the development of woman's spirituality and her application of her increased spiritual resources to her domestic and particularly to her maternal role. Kohler dismisses the writers of the tracts on the family as "the least important and for the most part most uninteresting of the Elizabethan women of letters as figures of literature. Their literary activities are tangential; necessary for any solution of the problem in general, but not for an exposition of the basic moods and causes."[23]

On the contrary, these tracts, few in number as those which have survived may be, represent the essence of the thinking of the new mother, who was the most liberated female developed in the English Renaissance, in what was still a family-centered, religiously oriented time.

Notes

[1] Juan Luis Vives, *A very frutefull and pleasant boke called the instruction of a Christen woman made fyrst in Laten and dedicated unto the quenes good grace by the right famous clerke mayster Lewes Vives and turned out of Laten into Englysshe by Rycharde Hyrd* (London: Thomas Berthelet, 1529), II, p. 105. The importance ascribed to proper child-nurture by Vives is indicated by the following statement: "Of the woman who accustometh her children unto vertue, the maister of the pagannes Saynct Paule, speketh in this maner: The woman hath gone out of the waye by transgression, howe be it she shall be saved [obtain salvation] by bryngynge forthe of chyldren, if she contynewe in fayther, charite, and holynes with chastitie." (II, 120)

[2] See Vives, *The Office and duetie of an husband* . . . (London: John Cawood, 1550); Sir Thomas Elyot, *The defence of good women* . . . (London: T. Bertheleti, 1545); Desiderius Erasmus, the marriage group of colloquies, rpt. in *Colloquies of Erasmus*, translated by Craig Thompson (Chicago: University of Chicago Press, 1965). The term "new mother" is appropriated from the title of one of these colloquies. Foster Watson (*Vives and the Renaissance Education of Women*, London, 1912) gives selections from all the members of the circle.

[3] Bartholomaeus Batty, *Christian mans closet* . . . (London, 1581), f. 52B. The reformers differed from the humanists chiefly in limiting their educational program to a more practical level. See also Thomas Becon, *A new catechisme* . . . in *Worckes of Thomas Becon* . . . (London, 1564); William Gouge, *Of Domesticall Duties, Eight Treatises* (London: John Haviland, 1622); Richard Brathwaite, *The English Gentlewoman* . . . (London, 1631). In his definitive study of the genre, Chilton Powell, in *English Domestic Relations, 1485–1653* (New York, 1971), notes the strong similarity among the religious tracts.

[4] Eleanor C. McLaughlin, "Equality of Souls, Inequality of Sexes: Women in Medieval Theology," in *Religion and Sexism, Images of Woman in the Jewish and Christian Traditions*, ed. Rosemary Ruether (New York: Simon and Schuster, 1974), p. 222. McLaughlin

states: "Thomas . . . emphasises that the responsibility for the education of the children lies with the father, who alone possesses the force and authority deemed necessary for instruction."

[5] Watson mentions that a comprehensive study by Alice Hentsch, *De la Litterature Didactique du Moyen Age s'addressant specialement aux Femmes* (Cahors, 1903), cites only seven works written in England, and only four in English, throughout the Middle Ages.

[6] With only slight variations in stanza order, the text of the *Northern Mothers Blessing*, rpt. in *Certaine worthye manuscript poems of great antiquitie . . .* (London for R. D., 1597), is identical with that of the work called *How the good Wiif taughte hir Doughtir*, rpt. by Charles Hindley, *The Old Book Collector's Miscellany* (London, 1871), I, 2–17. Subsequent quotations from *Northern Mothers Blessing* are also taken from this text.

[7] Dorothy Gardiner, *English Girlhood at School* (London: Oxford University Press, 1929), pp. 169–193.

[8] For information about Lady Mildmay and large excerpts from her journal (the whole of which has never been published) see Rachel Wiegall, "An Elizabethan Gentlewoman," *QR*, 215 (1911), pp. 119–135.

[9] Elizabeth Clinton, Countess of Lincoln, *The Countesse of Lincolnes Nurserie* (Oxford: John Lichfield and James Short, 1622), p. 1. All quotations from the text are from this edition.

[10] Breast feeding by the natural mother had been advocated with fervor by humanists and reformers alike. Their claim was that the child was influenced by the nature of the milk it imbibed. See especially Erasmus, "The New Mother" (Basel, 1524); rpt. by Thompson, trans., *Colloquies . . . (1965)*.

[11] Christine W. Sizemore, "Early Seventeenth-Century Advice Books: The Female Viewpoint," *SAB* (Jan., 1976), pp. 41–48. Sizemore fails to see any significant distinction between the writings of male and female writers of advice books.

[12] Other, less personalized materials were preserved by Thomas Bentley in his anthology, *The Monument of Matrones* (London: H. Denham, 1582). These are prayers or instructions composed by mothers and intended for daughters, but addressed to God rather than to the child; therefore, they reflect the concern with their daughters of several Renaissance mothers, but differ in focus from the works considered in this essay.

[13] M. R., *The Mothers Counsell, or Live within Compasse. Being the last Will and Testament to her dearest Daughter, which may serve for a worthy Legacie to all the Women in the World, which desire good report from men in this world, and grace from Christ Jesus in the last day* (London: John Wright, 1630 [?]). All citations from the text are from this editon.

[14] On page 13 and page 19, *F.Q.* V, v, 25; on page 11, *F.Q.* II, ix, 1.

[15] Elizabeth Grymeston, *Miscelanea, Meditations, Memoratives* (London: Printed by M. Bradwood for F. Norton, 1604), p. 1. All citations from the text are from this edition.

[16] Charlotte Kohler, "Elizabethan Woman of Letters, the Extent of her literary activities," Diss., University of Virginia, 1936, p. 296. Kohler calls the tract "the first autobiography of an Elizabethan woman's mind" (p. 300).

[17] At the end of Mrs. Leigh's tract, some information, extracted from an undated issue of *Notes and Queries*, is appended: Mrs. Leigh was from an Essex family, and married a gentleman from Sussex named Ralph Leigh; intense piety of both husband and wife was in accord with the spirit of their neighborhood.

[18] Dorothy Leigh, *The Mothers Blessing: or the godly counsaile of a gentlewoman, not long deceased, left behind her for her children: contayning many good exhortations, and godly admonitions profitable for all parents, to leave as a legacy for their children* (London: for John Budge, 1616), pp. 9–10. All citations from the tract are from this edition.

[19] There is a tract by Ez. W., entitled *The Answere of a Mother Unto hir seduced sonnes letter* (Amsterdam, 1627), which purports to be the correspondence between a Protestant mother and her son, who has converted to Roman Catholicism. Since the

correspondence is a remonstrance after the fact, rather than instruction, however, it cannot be considered altogether similar to the other materials considered in this essay.

[20] Myra Reynolds, *The Learned Lady in England, 1650–1760* (Boston: Houghton-Mifflin Co., 1920), p. 29.

[21] Elizabeth Joceline, "Epistle, " *The Mothers Legacie to her unborn childe* (London: John Haviland, 1624), n.p.n. "I thought," Mrs. Joceline states, "there was some good office I might doe for my childe more than only to bring it forth." She reminds the child to pray, to guard against sloth and pride, etc. She even appends a daily schedule of religious observances. All citations from the text are from the 1624 edition.

[22] Reynolds, p. 30.

[23] Kohler, p. 418.

The Great Unwritten Story:
Mothers and Daughters in Shakespeare

There is a certain shock of recognition when as women scholars we look anew at the plays of Shakespeare from the vantage of our own womanhood. Tradition tells us that Shakespeare dramatizes the full range of human feeling; even Virginia Woolf idealized him as "androgynous," awake to the womanly part of himself and to the intricate passions of the female, as well as the male, psyche.[1] The Elizabethan convention of boy actors in female roles set the psychic stage for a Portia, Rosalind, or Viola to pass from one sexual identity to another with a change of costume; and if a boy playing a girl playing a boy who pretends to be a girl—the situation of Rosalind in *As You Like It*—is not evidence of the playwright's androgynous vision, what could be?[2] The value that Shakespeare attributed to the feminine seems evident, too, when we consider that it is the rejected or lost woman—particularly as daughter—who symbolizes, or is necessary to, the redemption of the hero. Cordelia, of course, is the most notable example; when Lear awakens from his madness, he envisions her as his "soul in bliss," his *anima*, the female portion of his own psyche which, in its kindly aspect, he was unable throughout the play to feel. In *The Winter's Tale*, the forgiveness of Leontes is conditional upon the return of Perdita, the daughter his fit of insanity caused him to lose.

Yet the roles of Portia, Rosalind, and Viola are inconceivable without Shakespeare's reliance upon sexual stereotypes. These women must change their costumes if they are to express sentiments otherwise unfitting for a heroine. They must pretend to be men to reveal their wisdom or to show a happy aggressiveness in the courting game. Without the manly disguise or the mask of comedy, women who express "masculine" traits are unequivocally threatening. Lady Macbeth is willing to murder her infant even at the price of her own sanity; Regan, to burn out the "other" eye of Gloucester. In the tragedies after *Troilus and Cressida*, as Joel Fineman has pointed out, "men become men by being poised against, opposed to, a feminity that . . . so grotesquely partakes of its opposite."[3] And Antony's donning of the "tires and mantles" of Cleopatra while she wears his "sword Philippan" has an ominous ring to it in the context of the play; a hero cannot wear the garb of a woman and still be a hero. Most important of all is that on the vast Shakespearean stage only one kind of parent-child relationship is virtually missing. Sons and their fathers are there, as are sons and their mothers, and fathers and daughters.[4] But where is the mother of Jessica? Desdemona? Ophelia? What woman carried in her womb Regan, Goneril, *and* Cordelia? What happened to the Duchess of Milan after Miranda was born? Did all of these shadowy, unnamed women die in childbirth? In plays where woman-as-daughter is so essential to the meaning of the drama, what does this absence of the mothers imply?

Adrienne Rich has movingly called the "cathexis between mother and daughter" the "great unwritten story." We acknowledge *King Lear*, obsessed with the "father-daughter split" and *Hamlet*, with the split between "son and mother," "as great embodiments of the human tragedy," she writes. But "there is no presently enduring recognition of mother-daughter passion and rapture."[5]

But just as *The Winter's Tale* cannot close until "that which is lost is found," so the meaning of a work of literature may pivot on what is left out as much as on what is there. We need to ask ourselves what the absence of mother-daughter cathexes in Shakespearean drama implies. This is particularly true of the plays from *King Lear* onwards, for the themes so brutally enacted in that tragedy emerge, as it were, from the womb of the absent mother and reappear, transformed, in the works that follow.[6] Uneven though it is, *Pericles* is important as a transition between the misogynistic *Lear* and *The Winter's Tale*, where the mythic and psychic significance of the mother-daughter bond is at last acknowledged. But it is found only to be lost again; *The Tempest* serves as a kind of retraction, and the mother again disappears.

The Motherless World

In *King Lear*, as in *Macbeth*, woman is portrayed as possessing a power terrifying in its capacity for cruelty, deception, and destruction. In both plays, the nurturant aspect of the feminine is denied; Cordelia and Lady Macduff, the only potential bearers of that aspect, are slaughtered. In a world where a beneficent female principle is suppressed, masculinity, too, turns grotesque. Goneril attacks Albany as a "milk-livered man" when he reacts in horror to her barbarity; for her, the moral man is an unmanly fool, and the more monstrous she becomes the more effeminate she perceives him to be ("Marry your manhood, mew!"). As Joel Fineman points out, Lady Macbeth as an "annihilating Mother"—her stated readiness to pluck from her breast "the babe that milks me" and dash "his brains out"—defines for Macbeth the "very principle of masculinity":

> Bring forth men-children only,
> For thy undaunted mettle should compose
> Nothing but males. (I. vii. 73–75)[7]

Although heroism is restored in *Macbeth*, there is no parallel redemption of womanhood. The cruelty of Macbeth is overcome by a man who leaves his wife at home when he ventures into the world of men, a man—crucially—who is not "of woman born." From his mother's womb "Untimely ripped," Macduff can bid "the tree/Unfix his earthbound root," and bring Birnam Wood to Dunsinane; for he is a technologist of nature, not her son (and therefore, in such a psychology, not her victim). Undaunted by the power of the feminine, Macduff subdues nature, pressing her into the service of the masculine heroic ideal, symbolically releasing manhood itself from the "witches's" grip.

Even more profoundly and problematically than in *Macbeth*, Nature in *King Lear* is made to bear the burden of male fears of the feminine archetype. In a conflation of fury and despair, Lear—so accustomed to giving orders—fantasizes himself able to command her:

> Hear, Nature, hear! dear Goddess, hear!
> Suspend they purpose, if thou didst intend
> To make this creature fruitful!
> Into her womb convey sterility!
> Dry up in her the organs of increase,
> And from her derogate body never spring
> A babe to honour her! (I. iv. 284–290)

The "dear Goddess" of Lear's fantasy is no less cruel, blinding, or derogate than Regan and Goneril prove themselves to be; Lear's view of nature is an extension of his abhorrence toward the whole of the female sex. But that view is also a projection of his own powerlessness, of the terrible impotence it is unbearable for him to face. No wonder, then, that as Nature pelts him with her thunder and he "Strives in his little world of man to out-storm/ The to-and-fro-conflicting wind and rain," he is tortured by images of woman's faithlessness. Earlier he had even been ready to distrust his dead wife. "I am glad to see your highness," Regan had said, to which her father responded:

> Regan, I think you are; I know what reason
> I have to think so: if thou shouldst not be glad,
> I would divorce me from thy mother's tomb,
> Sepulchring an adult'ress. (II. iv. 130–133)

His subsequent madness allows him to vent his revulsion without constraint:

> Behold yond simp'ring dame,
> Whose face between her forks presages snow;
> That minces virtue, and does shake the head
> To hear of pleasure's name;
> The fitchew nor the soiled horse goes to't
> With a more riotous appetite.
> Down from the waist they are Centaurs,
> Though women all above;
> But to the girdle do the Gods inherit,
> Beneath is all the fiend's: there's hell, there's darkness,
> There is the sulphurous pit—burning, scalding,
> Stench, consumption; fie, fie, fie! pah, pah!
> (IV. vi. 120–131)

The fathomless well of disgust toward female sexuality that informs *King Lear*, and the play's obsession with adultery and lust, are psychologically incomprehensible until we perceive that the universe depicted is inherently awry. Joyce Carol Oates—who has anticipated my view— has called attention to the "one-sidedness of a kingdom ruled only by a king"; she notes that "a psychology that has as its model a balance of male-female, or 'masculine-feminine' characteristics, might have speculated that 'tragedy' issued from such one-sided development, in both the individual and in culture."[8] Focusing on the "masculine predicament of kingship and fatherhood," the *Lear* world presents us with daughters but predicates itself on the absence of their mother, the absence of a Queen, the absence of a feminine principle to act as symbolic and psychological counterbalance to male authority. As Oates points out, the play enacts the devastating consequences of her exclusion, for by denying her a role in the world or in consciousness, the suppressed female assumes an inflated and terrifying form, an "uncanny power" for the dissolution and harm, until she threatens to "crowd out consciousness altogether." The "unspoken imperative" of the patriarch, *"away from the unconscious, away from the mother,"* creates an image of woman as deadly.[9]

But if Lear is driven "away from the unconscious, away from the mother," at the risk of madness, inadmissible desires must fester within him. The "pride" that forbids Cordelia to express—or, more accurately, to feel—an exclusive love for her father is a pride in her own womanhood and in her separate sexual being. "Why have my sisters husbands," she asks, "if they say/ They love you all?":

> Happily, when I shall wed,
> That lord whose hand must take my plight shall carry
> Half my love with him, half my care and duty:
> Sure I shall never marry like my sisters,
> To love my father all. (I. i. 100–104)

"But goes your heart with this?" her father retorts, as if hoping that his daughter's desire to love another man divides her against herself. Acting more like a "fiery, imperious suitor" than a father,[10] the man who "madst [his] daughters [his] mothers," demands a love from them that is by its nature at once Oedipal and incestuous. It is as if Lear's old age has aroused within him a need for a maternal Eros for whom he can be both son and lover; he is the "Dragon" pursuing the woman crowned with stars.[11] Regan and Goneril, willing to pander to the perversities of their father's psyche, are psychologically trapped by them. They turn into Terrible Devourers for whom, like Lear, sexuality is lust and is inextricable from violence. Only Cordelia is able to free herself from her family's twisted dynamic by refusing to be her father's Queen or his mother; she is thus able to become a Queen—of another country, as all Daughters should—in her own right. The tragedy of *King Lear* is that events—history—force her to return:

> For thee, oppressed King, I am cast down;
> Myself could else out-frown false Fortune's frown.
> Shall we not see these daughters and these sisters?
> (V. iii. 5–7)

As the syntax of the last line suggests, Lear and Cordelia *are* coupled at the end, despite herself. "Come," Lear begs her now, "let's away to prison;/ We two alone will sing like birds i'th'cage":

> Have I caught thee?
> He that parts us shall bring a brand from heaven,
> And fire us hence like foxes. (V. iii. 21–23)

He has "caught" her indeed. Cordelia is sacrificed at the altar of Lear's desperately undifferentiated need for the feminine and by the forces that need has set into motion. The final words of the play belong to the chaste Edgar, for whom sex is an "act of darkness" and an unmarried woman's womb "a dark and vicious place,"[12] a man who admits sexual desire only when he feigns insanity and who believes in retribution for sexual indulgence. In the great Romances that follow, Shakespeare wards off the power of the consolidated feminine archetype by doing what Lear could not. He separates her into mother and daughter and— aided by the conventions of Romance—keeps the two carefully apart.

Demeter and Persephone

The separation of mother and daughter, as embodied in the myth of the Korè with its seasonal associations, is a living part of Shakespeare's late Romances. But the significance of that myth, and its incorporation into male psychic awareness, cannot be realized without a transitional stage: the fear of incestuous desire haunting *King Lear* and the concomitant revulsion toward female sexuality, must first be acknowledged and then overcome. *Pericles* is Shakespeare's attempt to do both, and the play is unsatisfying not only because it is poorly written—probably a collaboration—but also because it touches upon these awesome themes only to skirt them in the end.

The fear of incest between father and daughter lurks behind the arras in *Pericles* and shadows all the actions of the Prince of Tyre. The elaborate circumnavigations of the play are both dramatic and psychological; they are designed to enable Pericles to avoid reenacting the sin he alone had perceived in Antioch, where he had unravelled the riddle that had cost so many young men's lives:

> He's father, son, and husband mild:
> I mother, wife, and yet his child. (I. i. 68–69)

Like Jonah, Pericles flees from a knowledge of sin and is punished by the sea (which Erich Neumann associates with the Great Goddess).[13] The kingdom of Antiochus, like that of Lear, is contingent upon the absence of a wife/mother/queen and the usurpation of her function by the daughter. Pericles must establish a new society—a new psychic constellation—which, by including yet disentangling mother and daughter, differentiates the functions of the feminine but allows the male to retain control (Divide and Rule). If the primordial relation of mother and daughter is to be overcome, however, it must, at some level, be admitted, and that entails a subtle retelling of the ancient myth of the Korè.

In the original mysteries, according to Neumann, the *heuresis* of the daughter by the mother, the "finding again" of Persephone by Demeter, signified the reestablishment of the mother/daughter bond by annulling the danger posed by male incursion into the female world.[14] In its Shakespearean context, however, this mother-daughter "passion and rapture" is modified, reconceived *sub species paternitatis*. Mother and daughter are now both purged of the threatening aspects of the feminine that so obsessed the heroes of the tragedies.[15] The mother, Thaisa, seems to die in childbirth and is lowered into the womb/tomb of the sea for whom her daughter Marina is named. Thaisa revives, but is not of woman reborn; rather, woman's power to bear life is annihilated by having the mother herself brought to life through the art of a male, the paraclete Cerimon. Appropriately, Thaisa afterwards takes a vow of celibacy. The power of a young woman's blossoming sexuality is nipped in the bud by showing Marina—nearly killed, like Imogen, by the wicked witch of a foster mother—defend her virginity with fervor in a graphically depicted, repellent brothel. Only after mother and daughter have "purified" their respective types is the family reunited. But Demeter doesn't find Persephone in this new version; the father-husband is the agent of *heuresis*.

Pericles discovers his daughter, rescued from the Hades of the brothel by the Governor of Mytilene. At the Temple of Diana he discovers his wife. By the end of the play, both women are contained by the masculine, embodied in men who are mirror images of one another: Pericles married the mother and fathered the daughter, Cerimon fathered the mother—brought her to life—and now weds the daughter. No sooner is Marina reunited with her mother than her nuptials are announced. The sexlessness of her match with Cerimon makes the green world of *Pericles* seem scarcely very green after all.

Yet Shakespeare returns to the myth of the Korè; the relationship of Thaisa and Marina foreshadows the more fully realized and symbolically rich relationship of Hermione and Perdita. Although, like Thaisa, and unlike Demeter, Hermione is incapable of rescuing her daughter, *The Winter's Tale* remains the most "maternal" of all of Shakespeare's plays. In no other play do we experience with such intensity the truth that "every mother contains her daughter within herself and every daughter her mother."[16] In *The Winter's Tale*, the banished daughter must be returned before the Queen/Mother can be restored, and the rejuvenation of the King/Father—and the kingdom as a whole—depends upon both events. As the myth of the Korè tells us, upon the mother-daughter cathexis depends the renewal of the world.[17]

The dramatic and psychological conflicts of *The Winter's Tale* are caused—as so often in Shakespeare—by male fears of woman's sexual power. But whereas in *Pericles* those fears were unstated, and in the tragedies they were the determiners of fate, in *The Winter's Tale* they are both explicit and revealed as unjust. Leontes, the King of Sicily, is passing through a climacteric; his sexual identity is threatened on all sides. Nothing he says manages to convince his friend Polixenes to stay on with him in Sicily, and with the impending departure of the Bohemian King would go the memories of boyhood and of sinless—prepubescent and womanless—days. Ironically, it is his wife who succeeds in retaining Polixenes. Leontes' hegemony over boyhood (and, in a different sense, over his own kingdom) is undermined in yet another way as the play opens, for he sees his own prepubescent life assumed in his son:

> Looking on the lines
> Of my boy's face, methoughts I did recoil
> Twenty-three years, and saw myself unbreeched,
> In my green velvet coat, my dagger muzzled
> Lest it should bite its master and so prove,
> As ornaments oft do, too dangerous. (I. ii. 153–158)

It is not mere coincidence that Leontes recalls himself unable to control his own "weapon." Alongside him on the stage is his ripely pregnant wife Hermione, a living symbol of the primacy of the female as the source of life, as an agent and organ of transformation, and as a tacit reminder of human mortality.[18] Like all fathers (before the advent of modern medicine), Leontes cannot authenticate his own paternal-generative role, and beside the power of the creating female, what is the power of a king? Like Lear before him, the King of Sicily is flooded by barely suppressed feelings of the limits of masculine power.

But *King Lear* repudiates the feminine, condemning the Goddess Nature and the cycle of human life as demonic and grotesque. In the tragic universe, nature can be conquered, never redeemed. *The Winter's Tale* is the dialectical opposite of *Lear*; it celebrates the natural world and hence embraces the female mysteries as essential to the renewal of the male as well. Once again mother and daughter, now Hermione and Perdita, are separated by the forcible intervention of the male. But no brothel scene ensues, for the only underworld in *The Winter's Tale* is that of the mad fantasies of Leontes himself, and it is the males—Leontes first, but afterwards Polixenes as well—who in this play must be "purified."

Longing to possess the flowers of Persephone, Perdita allies herself with "great creating nature," resisting man-made art as artifice and awakening to her sexuality in harmony with the natural cycle. Significantly, her choice of nature over art involves her in a debate with her future father-in-law in which she reveals herself as a woman with a mind of her own, unintimidated by paternal advice. In rejecting the hybrid "gillyvors," she rejects, too, an artificial femininity:

> I'll not put
> The dibble in the earth to set one slip of them,
> No more than, were I painted, I would wish
> This youth should say 'twere well, and only therefore
> Desire to breed by me. (IV. iv. 99–103)

Perdita perceives the seasons as corresponding to the stages of life: flowers of "middle summer" are given to "men of middle age," and "flowers o'th'spring" to youth. The nature she celebrates is that which "yearly confronts us with the miracle of renewed life," as Northrop Frye has written.[19] It is a miracle embodied at the opening of the play by Hermione, pregnant with Perdita, and at the close by Hermione reemerging into life. But the miraculous is rejected by reason, whose demonic form is the destructive irrationality of Leontes convinced of the faithlessness of his wife, just as earlier it was the madness of Lear and his brutal misogyny. Not until Leontes again finds Perdita, and what she, as young woman, symbolizes, is he psychologically prepared to reembrace his wife, to accept his own nature—his own stage of life—and to learn that that which is "monstrous to our human reason" need not be monstrous at all.

In the ancient myth, it is not enough that Hermes fetch Persephone from Hades; she must be met by her mother. In *The Winter's Tale*, the "finding again" of Perdita by Leontes, through the agency of Florizel, is but a preparation for the more encompassing Reconciliation enacted as a female mystery affirming the bond between mother and daughter, woman and woman, woman and nature, and woman and miracle. In place of a Cerimon, there is the loyal Paulina, symbolically reenacting the miracle of motherhood by bringing Hermione back to life. She shows us the triumph of nature over art—Julio Romano's, the supposed sculptor of the "statue" of Hermione, or anyone else's. Restoring Hermione to Perdita, and both, finally, to Leontes, Paulina shows us too that true art is the feminine, that of "great creating nature" after all.

Leontes is the only Shakespearean male to embrace woman-as-mother in a life-enhancing way, and *The Winter's Tale* the only play in which the restoration of the mother-daughter cathexis is perceived as necessary for male psychic health and welcomed in all of its power. *The Winter's Tale* is thus also the only play in which Shakespeare verges on a truly androgynous vision, and one can imagine it being followed by another centered in "great creating nature" with Demeter and Persephone in the lead roles. But it is followed by no such thing. Rather, the shadow of Cerimon—temporarily eclipsed by Paulina—reasserts itself again in the guise of Prospero, wifeless father, sole educator of his daughter, magician whose books teach him control of the natural world. "Nature without nurture," which might have described the flowers of Perdita, is used to condemn Caliban instead.

Notes
[1] In *A Room Of One's Own* (New York: Harcourt Brace, 1929; rpt. 1957), p. 102.
[2] See, for example, Carolyn Heilbrun's argument in *Toward a Recognition of Androgyny* (New York: Knopf, 1973), pp. 28–34, and Juliet Dusinberre, *Shakespeare and the Nature of Women* (London: Macmillan, 1975), chapter IV.
[3] In "Fratricide and Cuckoldry: Shakespeare's Doubles," *The Psychoanalytic Review* (Fall 1977), p. 448.
[4] Indeed, fathers and sons appear in 16 of Shakespeare's plays; sons and mothers in 12, but the most frequent relationship is that of fathers and daughters.
[5] In *Of Woman Born: Motherhood as Experience and Institution* (New York: Bantam, 1977), pp. 226, 240.
[6] It would be interesting to speculate whether Ophelia would have gone mad if she had had a mother, especially a strong one (*not* a Lady Capulet) who would have supported her love for Hamlet and his for her. Imagine if Hamlet, obsessed with disgust at his mother's behavior, could have turned to Ophelia's mother for solace and advice. On the other hand, what robustly sane and kind woman could have put up with Polonius?
[7] Fineman, p. 449.
[8] In "'Is This the Promised End?': The Tragedy of King Lear," *Journal of Aesthetics and Art Criticism*, 75 (1974), p. 27.
[9] Oates, pp. 29–30.
[10] Arpad Paunex, "Psychopathology of Shakespeare's *King Lear*," *American Imago* (1952), p. 60. See also John Donnelly, "Incest, Ingratitude and Insanity: Aspects of the Psychopathology of *King Lear*," *Psychoanalytic Review*, 40 (1953), 149–155.

¹¹ Carl G. Jung, "Aion: Phenomenology of the Self," in *The Portable Jung*, ed. Joseph Campbell (New York: Viking, 1971), p. 150; and note Lear's reference to himself as the "Dragon."

¹² Oates, p. 26.

¹³ Erich Neumann, *The Great Mother: An Analysis of the Archetype*, tr. Ralph Manheim (New York: Bollingen/Pantheon, 1955), p. 162.

¹⁴ Neumann, pp. 307–308.

¹⁵ See Otto Rank's discussion of male attitudes toward woman's capacity to give birth in *Beyond Psychology* (New York: Dover, 1958) (first published 1941), particularly chapters six and seven.

¹⁶ Carl G. Jung, "The Psychological Aspects of the Kore," *The Collected Works of C. G. Jung*, vol. 9, part 1 (Princeton: Princeton Univ. Press, 1968), p. 188.

¹⁷ Interestingly, the abduction of Persephone is said by some to have taken place in Sicily.

¹⁸ Rank, chapters six and seven passim; Neumann, p. 31.

¹⁹ Northrop Frye, "Recognition in *The Winter's Tale*," in *Fables of Identity* (New York: Harcourt, 1963), p. 118.

Part Two
DAUGHTERS OF THE PATRIARCHY

Introduction

The advice from the nursery in the high Renaissance became the cult of motherhood in the nineteenth century. The fiction of the time commonly revolved around the hearth, affirming the patriarchal values of the culture and insisting that woman's place was in the home. The early Victorian women's novel was thus primarily domestic, but with a difference. In order for the plot to unfold, the heroine had to act independently. She could not do so when chaperoned by a Victorian mother. So the heroine made her solitary pilgrimage to maturity but typically returned, with ending or epilogue, to the domestic circle.

As Professor Susan Peck MacDonald argues, "the good, supportive mother is potentially so powerful a figure as to prevent her daughter's . . . self-assertion and maturation." Hence mothers in nineteenth-century fiction, in large part, are "dead or absent or weak and in need of help themselves." In Jane Austen's novels, dead mothers are the most numerous. This, says MacDonald, is also true for Burney, Eliot, the Brontës, and other Victorian women writers. When a mother does appear, such as Mrs. Bennet in *Pride and Prejudice*, her presence creates more problems than would her absence.

Although the novels were primarily domestic, Professor Mitzi Myers begins her essay: "We have very little of correctly detailed domestic history." The mystique of motherhood often obscured the reality. Partly to remedy a lack of knowledge about how the private endeavors affected the public lives of nineteenth-century women, Myers looks at the life of Harriet Martineau, a feminist and radical reformer. Myers finds that "the key details in Harriet's early domestic history were fear, emotional deprivation, remorse, and lack of self-respect." From a large family, Martineau conceived of herself as unmothered.

In fact, Martineau's relationship to her mother underscores the relationship between the fictional heroine and her absent or intrusive mother. On the one hand, Martineau needed a mother who was more supportive. On the other hand, she rebelled against the concept of a Victorian mother who ruled through authority, made domesticity suffocating, and substituted discipline for tenderness.

George Eliot, writes Professor Bonnie Zimmerman, sought "the meaning of motherhood in her novels, " but she also sought a "definition applicable to her own life." Like Austen, Eliot portrayed a number of motherless heroines. Nor were her heroines mothers themselves. Zimmerman suggests, "the heroines cannot be mothers because society provides no realistic model for healthy motherhood."

In contrast, Mrs. Gaskell provides "a myriad of mothers: old and young, rich and poor, aristocratic and humble, natural and adoptive, strong and weak, English and French, caring and uncaring." Professor Jacqueline Berke and her daughter Laura Berke have together explored the mother-daughter constellations in Gaskell's *Wives and Daughters*. They find that "mothering as a concept—and as an experience for both mother and daughter" preoccupied Gaskell "in her later years." Gaskell's novels suggest that "stability in the community at large and in society as a whole can exist only if a foundation is laid at the family level." At the same time, Gaskell portrays Molly Gibson who succeeds without a mother and Cynthia Kirkpatrick who fails because of the intervention of an inept and selfish mother.

As we see in each of these essays and in the works they discuss, we do not have a heritage passed on from the Victorian mother to her daughter. The mother insists; the daughter resists. Or, the daughter attempts to make her way alone in hope of avoiding her mother's fate, but ends by choosing the same destiny. It is a surprising and significant paradox that in a culture that stressed the mother's importance, we have a literature of motherhood which is, at best, ambiguous. Mother is on a pedestal and yet devested of her ancient prowess. Instead, we have matriarchy without matrilineage and motherhood without matriarchy.

E.M.B.
C.N.D.

Jane Austen and the Tradition of the Absent Mother

Toward the end of *Emma* as Mrs. Weston contemplates the forthcoming happy marriage of Emma to Mr. Knightley, Jane Austen uses an image of happiness rare in her own novels and those of her greatest nineteenth-century women successors: "Mrs. Weston, with her baby on her knee, indulging in such reflections as these, was one of the happiest women in the world."[1] The women novelists of the period from Fanny Burney to Mrs. Gaskell and George Eliot create very few positive images of motherhood. They for the most part concern themselves with young women during the crucial transition period from adolescence, through courtship, up to marriage, and their young heroines—Evelina, Elizabeth Bennet, Jane Eyre, Catherine Earnshaw, Maggie Tulliver, Dorothea Brooke, and so on—do not have strong supportive mothers. Their mothers may be dead or absent or weak and in need of help themselves, so that while the heroines sometimes receive help from other strong, supportive women, they rarely receive help from their own mothers.

This literary phenomenon might, superficially, seem to imply that mothers are fairly unnecessary, expendable items in their daughters' passage to maturity, but tribute is paid to motherhood both in explicit comments characters make and in the relationships they have to motherly women who are not their own mothers. The absence of mothers, then, seems to me to derive not from the impotence or unimportance of mothers, but from the almost excessive power of motherhood; the good, supportive mother is potentially so powerful a figure as to prevent her daughter's trials from occurring, to shield her from the process of maturation, and thus to disrupt the focus and equilibrium of the novel. But if she is dead or absent, the good mother can remain an ideal without her presence disrupting or preventing the necessary drama of the novel. If the mother is to be present during her daughter's maturation, the mother must be flawed in some way, so that instead of preventing her daughter's trials, she contributes to them. The nurturing that we usually associate with motherhood, then seems to have to be withdrawn or denied in order to goad the daughter into self-assertion and maturation.

The particular kind of mothering abstractly required by these adolescent heroines is made clear within the social contexts of the novels. The heroine's task is to survive the perils of "coming out." She must move out of the private (perhaps even tomboyish) world of her family into the social world where she will take her place as a woman—ready to marry and mother in her turn. Her mother's task, abstractly seen, is to ease the transition from the private and individualistic world of adolescence into the social and therefore somewhat conventionalized world of maturity. The mother does not aid this transition alone, for the father must provide his daughters with enough money to attract appropriate suitors. But the mother has three, perhaps more crucial, tasks: she must handle her daughter's social contacts; she must insist upon propriety; and she must prevent the wrong suitors from gaining her daughter's affections. We see that these are the mother's tasks, not because they are performed properly by the absent or inadequate mothers of these novels, but because they are not performed properly. The daughter is thus left to handle some or all of these tasks herself and, in so doing, to make mistakes and encounter difficulties. The strength she gains in emerging from her trials is the proof that her mother's failure was beneficial. Since this process perhaps is clearest and most interesting in Jane Austen's novels, I will concentrate on its manifestations in Austen, but I will begin first with a look at her eighteenth-century predecessor, Fanny Burney.

Austen's ironic narrator in *Northanger Abbey* shows that Austen saw the absent mother tradition as a literary convention traditional to her predecessors. In initially describing her heroine, Catherine Morland, Austen writes, "Her mother was a woman of useful plain sense, with a good constitution. She had three sons before Catherine was born; and instead of dying in bringing the latter into the world, *as anybody might expect*, she still lived on—lived to have six children more—to see them growing up around her, and to enjoy excellent health herself" (p. 13, italics mine). Fanny Burney's *Evelina* (1778) is probably representative of the novels Austen's narrator has in mind in which the absence of the heroine's mother generates the heroine's trials. Evelina's problem is social; although she has matured morally under her guardian (a clergyman) in the country, such male guidance is insufficient for launching her socially in London. She can only be accepted into society if she learns how to act properly there and if she removes the doubts surrounding her birth. Ostensibly the critical decisions are being made by men; men decide whether to dance with or marry her, and men (her father and her future husband) determine her name and thus her status. But only ostensibly, for behind their conscious decisions a system of mother figures is responsible for Evelina's social acceptance.

Evelina first must learn how to behave at balls, to recognize the proper young men and women, to know what to wear to the opera, and so forth. She is aided in these tasks by a series of three chaperones, all women and all inadequate substitutes for her own mother. Her first chaperone, Mrs. Mirvan, though a model of propriety, is prevented from thoroughly supporting Evelina by her duty to an eccentric husband and by her lack of natural authority to resist the claims of Evelina's vulgar grandmother, Madame Duval. But Evelina internalizes enough of Mrs. Mirvan's good direction so that when she is forced to leave Mrs. Mirvan's protection for Madame Duval's, she is able to dispense with the support her grandmother cannot offer and to neutralize the latter's vulgarity. Had Mrs. Mirvan or Madame Duval been able to protect Evelina fully, the latter would never have had to learn by herself how to fend off the wrong suitors and appear all she should in the eyes of Lord Orville, her eventual husband. Her third chaperone, Mrs. Selwyn, has the kind of "masculine" intellect and force of character which makes her useful in negotiations with Evelina's father, but she is otherwise portrayed as Evelina's inferior in feminine grace and refinement, so that Evelina manages to reach the point of marriage with less and less nurturing from other women.

Burney's absent mother pattern, then, contains several displacements. The mother is absent and so, seemingly, powerless. The mother substitutes nurture their charge imperfectly and thereby fail to prevent her distress. The men, on the other hand, provide money and status and have the power to cause distress or prevent it; Sir Clement's attempted seductions, Mr. Smith's forcing Evelina to go to the Hampstead assembly, and Lord Orville's repeated rescues of Evelina all demonstrate this male power. But the women *have* succeeded; by withdrawing support from Evelina, they force her to act for herself so that Lord Orville is drawn to her partly by the poignancy of her distress and partly by the strength of character it produces in her. Evelina's father, Sir John Belmont, seems to control the power of social acceptance; he has cruelly disowned his dead wife and in so doing deprived his daughter of the name, the money, and the social respect that should be hers. But his power is somewhat illusory. A letter from Mr. Macartney's dead mother forces Sir John to acknowledge the latter as his natural son, the young woman he has always considered his daughter turns out to be the daughter of a servant woman who has duped him, and finally the memory of Evelina's dead mother forces him to recognize Evelina. Sir John does not seek these revelations; they are forced upon him by women. In Evelina's case Sir John is stunned by the sight of her and says, "My God! does Caroline Evelyn still live! . . . lift up thy head, thou image of my long lost Caroline! . . . I see thou art her child! She lives—she breathes,—she is present to my view!"[2] So the final rewards of the novel—money and social recognition, both seemingly within the father's power to bestow—come to Evelina partly by the hand of her dead mother, because she is her mother recreated. At the moment that she passes the threshold from adolescence to womanhood, her mother's power is symbolically extended to her from the grave to confer social acceptance upon her.

Despite the mocking comments of Austen's narrator in *Northanger Abbey*, Austen's novels continue the pattern we have seen in *Evelina*. There are three kinds of mothers in Austen's novels—dead mothers, absent mothers, and flawed (perhaps even obnoxious) mothers. The dead mothers are by far the most numerous. Among the young men and women eligible for marriage, the following have dead mothers: the Tilneys in *Northanger Abbey*; Willoughby in *Sense and Sensibility*; Darcy, the Bingleys, and Wickham in *Pride and Prejudice*; the Crawfords in *Mansfield Park*; Emma, Knightley, Jane Fairfax, Frank Churchill, and Harriet Smith in *Emma*; and the Elliots and Captain Wentworth in *Persuasion*. The heroines of Austen's first four novels—Catherine Morland, the Dashwoods, the Bennets, and Fanny Price—have living mothers, but their mothers are either absent or flawed. A few of the minor characters have mothers on the scene, but they share with the heroines' mothers one trait in common: they contribute no very positive support to the processes of maturation and marriage which form the backbone of the plot.

Northanger Abbey, Austen's first novel, shows the absent mother tradition in a form not very different from that of *Evelina*. Despite

Austen's narrative irony about the absent mother, the heroine, Catherine Morland, must go through her formative experiences at Bath and Northanger alone, without her parents' help. Her parents are alive, but Catherine's coming of age occurs only when she leaves home to go to Bath, chaperoned by her neighbors, the Allens. Mrs. Allen's task is to launch Catherine into Bath society, but she is an inadequate chaperone. The narrator even jests about the literary tradition of chaperones like Mme. Duval: "It is now expedient to give some description of Mrs. Allen, that the reader may be able to judge in what manner her actions will hereafter tend to promote the general distress of the work, and how she will, probably, contribute to reduce poor Catherine to all the desperate wretchedness of which a last volume is capable—whether by her imprudence, vulgarity, or jealousy—whether by intercepting her letters, ruining her character, or turning her out of doors" (pp. 19–20). Just as in the contrast between Catherine's Gothic fantasies about General Tilney and the latter's real, but rather prosaic cruelty, the narrator's comments on the inadequate chaperone figure are directed only against its melodramatic trappings, not against its psychological substance, for Mrs. Allen's inadequacies do cause Catherine distress. Her only qualification for introducing Catherine to society is a fondness for going places and an obsession with dress (p. 20). But after three or four days of helping Catherine to dress appropriately, Mrs. Allen takes Catherine to the Upper Rooms and is powerless to introduce her to anyone. She spends several days wishing that she could get Catherine a partner and other acquaintances until finally the master of ceremonies introduces Henry Tilney to Catherine and Mrs. Thorpe introduces herself to Mrs. Allen. Provided with acquaintances, however, Mrs. Allen is still powerless to direct Catherine in handling competing social claims with propriety. On the three occasions that the Thorpes and Catherine's brother ask Catherine to go for an outing, Mrs. Allen simply advises her to do as she pleases, even though the second outing prevents her honoring a prior commitment to the Tilneys. On the third occasion when Catherine is once again already committed to a walk with the Tilneys, Catherine shows that she has learned to stand up to John, Isabella, and James without help from anyone, even though their entreaties are made more forcefully than ever. Thus Catherine, like Evelina, has been forced to learn how to act for herself because there is no one to act for her.

In the meantime the men of the novel have ambiguous roles. Mr. Allen, for instance, has the principles and intellect his wife lacks, but since he is never present to help Catherine when she needs help, he is ineffectual. Similarly Catherine's father hardly exists, except for his power to distribute money to his marriageable children, and even then he hasn't enough money to assure James of marrying Isabella Thorpe or Catherine of marrying Henry Tilney. General Tilney seems more powerful—almost the embodiment of patriarchal power. But the General cannot ultimately keep his son from marrying Catherine. Furthermore, the power of motherhood in the abstract is again indirectly attested to at Northanger Abbey by Catherine's preoccupation with the dead Mrs. Tilney.

Having learned to survive socially without Mrs. Allen, Catherine is next ready to do without a female chaperone altogether in visiting the motherless Tilney household. Ostensibly Catherine needs at this point to come to an understanding of General Tilney's power, but since Catherine's imagination is preoccupied with Mrs. Tilney—with the General's treatment of his wife and with Mrs. Tilney's room—the General's power is somewhat overshadowed by his wife's. Catherine's coming of age is paralleled by her coming to understand the mother's place within the Tilney household.

Catherine's coming of age coincides with her return to her own mother. Mrs. Morland intends to resume her supportive role, cautioning her daughter against being "spoilt for home by great acquaintance" (p. 241). But Catherine has outgrown her mother's advice: "Catherine's feelings contradicted almost every position her mother advanced" (p. 239). And while her mother is upstairs looking for a "clever essay" to console and instruct Catherine, the latter's problems are being solved downstairs by the arrival of her suitor Henry Tilney.

Mrs. Morland herself provides the reader with a final judgment of Catherine's experience when she says to the latter: "I am glad I did not know of your journey at the time; but now it is all over, perhaps there is no great harm done. It is always good for young people to be put upon exerting themselves; and you know, my dear Catherine, you always were a sad little shatter-brained creature; but now you must have been forced to have your wits about you, with so much changing of chaises and so forth; and I hope it will appear that you have not left anything behind you in any of the pockets" (pp. 234–5). Similarly, she says to Mrs. Allen, "and it is a great comfort to find that she is not a poor helpless creature, but can shift very well for herself" (p. 237). So, the introductory irony about the absent mother tradition seems directed only at the melodramatic excesses of the tradition, for Catherine has come of age, not by encountering the threats of would-be seducers and villains, but by learning to see and act for herself without help from her mother.

As with Burney's use of Evelina's dead mother, there are hints of unusual fascination with the mother figure in Catherine's preoccupation with Mrs. Tilney, but otherwise *Northanger Abbey* contains the absent mother tradition in a fairly straightforward form. Some separation from the nurturing mother is necessary for the daughter's maturation, and instead of a psychological rift between the mother and her daughter, physical separation and an inadequate chaperone provide the necessary hardships. But in *Pride and Prejudice* the heroines mature through a psychological rift from their mother.

Mrs. Bennet's function in *Pride and Prejudice* is complementary to that of the absent mother; the latter figure creates obstacles—and learning experiences—for her daughter simply by her absence, while Mrs. Bennet creates obstacles by her presence. The social world of *Pride and Prejudice* suffers from too much of the wrong kind of mothering. With the novel's focus upon the economic realities of the marriage market for young women without a good fortune, the mother's function in *Pride and Prejudice* is to facilitate her daughter's social coming of age in the usual ways, with a particular emphasis upon economics—providing social contacts who have money and preventing suitors who haven't money. Yet Mrs. Bennet and her like exacerbate the ugliness of the marriage market by their competition for suitors for their daughters. Mrs. Bennet uses every opportunity to denigrate Charlotte Lucas as an eligible young woman, and there is a recurring drama in which Mrs. Bennet lords it over Lady Lucas whenever Jane seems likely to marry well. Then Lady Lucas lords it over Mrs. Bennet when Charlotte does well and Jane seems likely to be disappointed.

Mrs. Bennet's improprieties and the blatancy of her schemes initially have effects opposite those she intends. Elizabeth and Jane reject their mother's competitive desire to corner young men, instead choosing to be sisterly and cooperative with each other and with friends like Charlotte Lucas. Elizabeth also refuses to choose men for their money, as her mother would have her, and so refuses two financially eligible suitors—Collins and Darcy. Furthermore, Mrs. Bennet's schemes affect the suitors negatively; both Bingley and Darcy are slowed in their courting by their disapproval of Mrs. Bennet, and it is only Elizabeth's trips away from her home that allow Darcy's first proposal, Darcy's and Elizabeth's better understanding at Pemberley, the reunion of Bingley and Jane, and ultimately the two sisters' marriage.

But in a perverse way Mrs. Bennet has succeeded in achieving her ends with Jane and Elizabeth, as their sister Lydia's role helps to show. Lydia's relation to their mother is different; she is her mother's favorite, the one most like the girl Mrs. Bennet once was. Mrs. Bennet greatly regrets being separated from Lydia—either during the latter's trip to Brighton or after her marriage—and Lydia has no desire to leave her mother. So, Lydia comes closer than the other daughters to being a recreation of Mrs. Bennet, and yet if Mrs. Bennet's fondest desire is to have a daughter well married, Lydia is her greatest failure. Elizabeth and Jane, seemingly so unlike their mother, fulfill Mrs. Bennet's dreams much more satisfactorily, and their mother deserves at least some credit for their success. She has goaded Elizabeth and Jane into exemplary behavior so as to differentiate themselves from her, and in so doing she has helped her daughters to mature and gain, not just the husbands they deserve, but particularly rich and eligible husbands, the very sort of men she has desired for her daughters. In this way *Pride and Prejudice* implies that the mother's power is perhaps greatest, not when she replicates herself (as with Lydia), but when some psychological or physical separation forces her daughters into independence from their mother. Lest daughters become too proud of their success and scornful of their mothers' failures, however, the plot of *Pride and Prejudice* subtly reminds us that even in rebelling against our mothers we may be doing no more than achieving the goals they have set for us.

In *Persuasion* once again the heroine Anne Elliot's mother is dead, but she was an estimable woman whose loss is still felt. *Persuasion* repeats the earlier pattern of the absent mother. Mrs. Elliot's dear friend, Lady Russell, has tried to take the place of Anne's mother in the courtship process, and the resultant doubling of the motherly role allows the mother herself—and Motherhood—not to be denigrated while at the same time Anne must reject her substitute mother's view of who Anne should marry. The plot revolves around Anne's regret that she was formerly persuaded by Lady Russell to give up Captain Wentworth and her renewed encouragement of him under less fortunate and more trying circumstances—when he is angry at her for her former refusal and when she has lost some of her youthful bloom. Thus Anne is like the other Austen heroines who become stronger from having to struggle either without their mother's help or in spite of obstacles caused by a mother or her substitute.

But implicit in *Persuasion* is a second aspect of the absent mother theme that suggests a more sociobiological dimension of the theme. Since the strength of genetic diversity throughout human evolution has been to create diverse individuals to adapt to varying environments, the mother might be said to be strongest not when she simply replicates herself but when she creates a daughter both like and unlike herself. After all, no society can afford to have too many essentially similar individuals trying to do exactly the same thing. Diversity is a form of strength, as we have already seen implied in *Pride and Prejudice*. In *Persuasion* Anne has the choice of accepting an inferior way of life which superficially would repeat her mother's life or creating a somewhat new way of life for herself. Anne's loss of her mother is then a central part of this novel about loss. *Persuasion* begins by contrasting what was with what is; Anne once had a loved and respected parent (her mother), she once loved and was loved by Captain Wentworth, and there are glimpses of a more perfect past social order in which land, conventions of gentility, and social cohesiveness helped support and sustain the individual within a meaningful social context. Unlike the other Austen heroines, Anne has already matured as an individual, but she needs to *recreate* a version of all that she has lost.[3] She cannot either regain her mother or alter the socioeconomic forces which are elevating the navy men of the novel and declassing her father, but she can and does arrive at a sort of private recreation in which she becomes a wife and (potentially) a mother—like her own mother but not a copy of her mother. She is momentarily tempted by the image of becoming a second Lady Elliot, and thus replicating her mother through marriage to her cousin:

> [Lady Russell said,] "I own that to be able to regard you as the future mistress of Kellynch, the future Lady Elliot—to look forward and see you occupying your dear mother's place, succeeding to all her rights, and all her popularity, as well as to all her virtues, would be the highest possible gratification to me.—You are your mother's self in countenance and disposition; and if I might be allowed to fancy you such as she was, in situation, and name, and home, presiding and blessing in the same spot, and only superior to her in being more highly valued! My dearest Anne, it would give me more delight than is often felt at my time of life!"
>
> Anne was obliged to turn away, to rise . . . and try to subdue the feelings this picture excited. For a few moments her imagination and her heart were bewitched. The idea of becoming what her mother had been . . . was a charm which she should not immediately resist. (pp. 159–160)

But when Anne thinks of Mr. Elliot she knows she cannot marry him.

Lady Russell's inadequacy as a mother substitute is just this—that she would have Anne slavishly copy the past. But Anne creates a new and different life for herself and in doing so manages to recapture the best that is possible of the past while averting the sorrow that befell her own mother in marrying a man who was her inferior.

This pattern in *Persuasion* may explain a good deal about the relation of mother to daughter in novelists from Burney to Eliot. The pattern is basically paradoxical: on the one hand, nurturing is withdrawn and replaced by psychological or physical separation so that the daughter can develop her own strength and autonomy. But on the other hand, the mother remains a powerful ideal, and the daughter must, despite or because of their separation, recreate a version of her mother without simply copying her mother. We have seen how Evelina recreated her mother's life without her mother's sorrows and how Elizabeth Bennet arrives at an end which her mother would have wished for her if her mother's vision had not been so faulty.

The tradition is also carried on by Austen's successors, even those like Charlotte Brontë, who thought she had little in common with Austen. In Emily Brontë's *Wuthering Heights* all the mothers die either before their children mature or before they marry so that most of the children are raised in part by Nelly Dean, another inadequate mother substitute. The central event is Catherine Earnshaw's death when she becomes a mother. Without Catherine's death Hindley, Edgar, Isabella, and, most important, her daughter Cathy would have been protected to some extent from Heathcliff's vengeance. However one interprets the younger Cathy's story, Cathy has to relive her mother's life in reverse, becoming first Cathy Linton, then Cathy Heathcliff, and finally Cathy Earnshaw. In the end she has her mother's eyes and her mother's name. In Cathy the conflicts of her mother's life are finally worked out, but they can be so only by Cathy's repeating, to some extent, her mother's trials without her mother's protection.

Charlotte Brontë's heroines usually have no mothers either. Early in *Jane Eyre*, Jane contrasts her own isolation to the closeness Mrs. Reed enjoys with her children: "The said Eliza, John, and Georgiana were now clustered round their mama in the drawing-room: she lay reclined on a sofa by the fire-side, and with her darlings about her . . . looked perfectly happy."[4] But later events demonstrate the weakness of this nurturing closeness; the Reed children all turn out poorly while the independent Jane prospers. And rather oddly, at the major crisis in Jane's development—when she must decide whether to remain with

Rochester as his mistress—Jane sees a vision of her dead mother in a dream warning her to leave Rochester. The visionary woman says, "My daughter, flee temptation!"—and replying "Mother, I will," Jane leaves Thornfield (p. 281).

George Eliot, too, uses variations of the absent mother. Maggie Tulliver in *The Mill on the Floss* has a mother so weak that Maggie must mature either without her mother's help or in spite of her mother. In *Daniel Deronda* Gwendolen Harleth initially feels different from her mother, thinking that her mother might have been better in control of her own happiness. But acting for herself, Gwendolen marries as unhappily as her mother, and after she has undergone the moral and emotional education her marriage forces upon her, Gwendolen returns home to support and understand her mother in ways she could not have done before.

On the surface the mother in Austen and in these other women novelists seems rather a negative figure, usually absent, dead, weak, or otherwise flawed, but I think we would be mistaken in assuming either that these writers were neurotic or that mothers themselves are in general negative influences. The negativity seems to have its psychological source, instead, in the demands of adolescence. As Patricia Meyer Spacks writes:

> If conflict is the essence of fiction, adolescence provides rich material . . . . To discover the right relation between the individual consciousness and the world outside, a problem by no means confined to the female sex, may be especially difficult for girls because of the pressures women in Western society endure to orient themselves towards the needs of others; a denial rather than a resolution of conflict.[5]

In order for these girls to mature as successfully independent adults— and in order for the novels to focus centrally upon them—the most powerful outside personality, the person who could best facilitate the adolescent's social rites of passage, but who could in doing so upset the balance of the adolescent's precariously sought selfhood, the Mother must be kept at some sort of distance. By this distancing the daughter is allowed to fulfill the potential passed along to her by her mother; she recreates her mother's life, preserving what is best in it and avoiding its failures. While the absence or failure of her mother appears to threaten the daughter, the stronger, hidden threat is that she will become too like her mother and not a strong enough individual in her own right. She must therefore be distanced either physically or psychologically in order to create herself and in so doing to fulfill her inheritance from her mother.

Notes

[1] *Emma*, p. 468, in *The Novels of Jane Austen*, ed. R. W. Chapman, 3rd ed. (London, 1934). All further references to Jane Austen's novels are to this edition and page references to each appear in parentheses in my text.

[2] *Evelina* (New York: W. W. Norton & Co., Inc., 1965), p. 354.

[3] William Walling discusses the theme of recreation in *Persuasion* but without relating it to Anne's mother as I do; see "The Glorious Anxiety of Motion: Jane Austen's *Persuasion*," *Wordsworth Circle*, 7 (1976), p. 336.

[4] *Jane Eyre*, ed. Richard J. Dunn (New York: W. W. Norton & Co., Inc., 1971), p. 5. References in my text are to this edition.

[5] *The Female Imagination* (New York: Avon Books, 1972), p. 146.

Unmothered Daughter and Radical Reformer: Harriet Martineau's Career

"We have very little of correctly detailed domestic history, the most valuable of all as it would enable us to make comparisons. . . ."[1]

Francis Place's remark anticipates a key concern of the new social historians, a concern of particular relevance to women, so much of whose history has hitherto been invisible because, until recently, it has consisted mostly of those female activists and writers who succeeded outside the home. However, careful exploration of the world of domestic experience not only illuminates the lives of ordinary women, but also places in a fresh perspective the achievement of those who made it in a man's world. Harriet Martineau, nineteenth-century feminist and radical reformer, provides a good example of how subtly and complexly family relationships affect public endeavors. This essay seeks to connect Martineau's private experience with her public achievement, both exploring formative familial circumstances and sketching some public consequences of those private factors. Domestic history, in this view, is the nexus between past and future, the link between the formation of individual character and the evolution of social change.

The key details in Harriet's early domestic history were fear, emotional deprivation, remorse, and lack of self-respect. The main cause of these miseries was, in her opinion, her mother's mishandling. Martineau's extraordinarily vivid reminiscences recognize that she was a difficult and rebellious child but also insist that she need not have been so. Though outwardly bold and obstinate, she was a sickly, painfully sensitive little girl, subject to irrationally paralyzing fears of almost everything, from the starlight sky to magic lanterns. At her birth in 1802, she was put out to nurse and almost starved before her wet nurse's dereliction was discovered. The milk-diet her mother subsequently decreed gave her years of awful indigestion, hallucinations, and nightmares, probably the result of a severe allergy. She recalled that she had scarely any respite from terror throughout her childhood. The first person she remembered not being afraid of was an aunt who won her heart and confidence when she was sixteen. Scared and isolated in the midst of a large family, she kept her miseries to herself, but she thought in later years that closer observation and "a little more of that cheerful tenderness which was in those days thought bad for children, would have saved me from my worst faults, and from a world of suffering."[2] Harriet's difficulties in communicating frankly with her mother persisted throughout her life, and so did her great need for her mother's love and approval.

The chief resource of the emotionally deprived child was God. She hoped to find in religion the love and justice lacking in her little world and frequently planned suicide to get to heaven:

> I had a devouring passion for justice;—justice, first to my own precious self, and then to other oppressed people. Justice was precisely what was least understood in our house, in regard to servants and children. Now and then I desperately poured out my complaints; but in general I brooded over my injuries, and those of others who dared not speak. . . . It seems to me now that [my temper] was downright devilish, except for a placability which used to annoy me sadly. My temper might have been early made a thoroughly good one, by the slightest indulgence shown to my natural affections, and any rational dealing with my faults: but I was almost the youngest of a large family, and subject, not only to the rule of severity to which all were liable, but also to the rough and contemptuous treatment of the elder children. . . . I had no self-respect, and an unbounded need of approbation and affection. My capacity for jealousy was something frightful. . . . Nobody dreamed of all this; and the "taking down" system was pursued with me as with the rest, issuing in the assumed doggedness and wilfulness which made me desperately disagreeable during my youth, to every body at home. The least word or tone of kindness melted me instantly, in spite of the strongest predeterminations to be hard and offensive. Two occasions stand out especially in my memory, as indeed almost the only instances of the enjoyment of tenderness manifested to myself individually. (I, 14–15)

Only one of these involved her mother. Though no orphan, Martineau clearly perceived herself as an unmothered child, deprived of female nurturance and comprehending sympathy, yet subject to capricious and arbitrary external authority. (There is little mention of Martineau's father in her *Autobiography*, and that little shows him a gentle, supportive parent.) Harriet summarized the experience of her childhood as "a painful and incessant longing for the future . . . a longing for strength of body and of mind, for independence of action—for an escape, in short, from the conditions of childhood."[3]

The central fact of Martineau's mature public history was the realization of that independence in a long, productive career, shaping, and often shocking, public opinion. Famous at thirty for her *Illustrations of Political Economy* (1832–34), she was an outstanding female achiever in areas where nineteenth-century Englishwomen often feared to tread (politics, economics, philosophy, history), as well as in more conventionally acceptable fields (fiction, education, household management, travel). R. K. Webb, author of a comprehensive intellectual biography of Martineau, subtitles his study "a radical Victorian," and he makes a good case, noting that reading her calls to mind Karl Marx. Webb's analysis is valuable, but he is primarily concerned with public history, both of his subject and of her society. Intellectual stances and political events are his métier. He is not much interested in Martineau's feminism and related issues or in the personal factors which predisposed her to embrace so early and with such fervor the intellectual heritage he describes. Yet Martineau's philosophical obsession with individual autonomy and rational self-governance was clearly fueled by private suffering and revolt. Webb is insensitive to Martineau's difficulties as a nineteenth-century daughter and woman, and dismisses the impact of such difficulties on her thought and achievement. Harriet's profound ambivalence toward her mother and the debate of his biographical predecessors over it have caused far too much fuss, Webb asserts. He sees Martineau as "latently homosexual" (hence her many intense friendships with women and her negative attitude toward marriage), with an "essentially masculine nature" (hence her achievements in unorthodox fields, one suspects).[4] It would be simplistic to attribute Martineau's stresses and successes solely to a difficult mother-daughter relationship, but it is equally so to see her as an eccentric, the cultural context of whose gender is irrelevant.

Martineau was of course a highly atypical Victorian woman. Her deafness, her liberal Unitarian background, and her career all set her apart from the conventional female image. But her experience is also quite different from the pattern Barbara Welter describes as typical of many nineteenth-century American women reformists:

An interesting family pattern emerges in the lives of woman suffragists. . . . The father assumes direction of his daughter's education
and character, while the mother is relegated to the role of invalid or
nurse-housekeeper for younger children. The girl and her father develop
an extraordinarily close relationship. . . . In later life these women, who
achieved much more than most of their contemporaries, look back on
their father with some ambivalence, and see their mother's role as that
of a silent martyr. They both blame and credit their fathers with their
own desire for achievement, which, in nineteenth-century values, was
not a desirable quality in a woman. Many of these women choose weak
husbands . . . and they themselves are preoccupied, in their reforms or
their writings, with finding a suitable definition of woman's nature and
role.

In a rather different formulation, Alicia C. Percival tries to find some
common denominators in the early years of eminent Victorian Englishwomen. She too finds frequent male mentors, but she also notes the
influence or obstruction of far from negligible mothers and suggests that
mothers seem to have withstood their daughters' plans more often than
fathers did.[5] It is, after all, mothers who first enforce cultural com-
mands. Images of womanhood, embodiments of both love and discipline, they provide for their daughters initial patterns of possibility or
limitation. Whether the girl internalizes her mother's ideals, steels herself to reject them, or works out some kind of compromise, she must
come to terms with those ideals. Martineau's case history, so unusual
in many ways, is very conventional in others.

The chief document in that case history is Martineau's *Autobiography*,
a developmental record of both her character and her philosophy, written at breakneck speed in 1855 when she believed herself about to die;
the volumes were printed and stored unaltered for more than twenty
years, since she proved a long-lived invalid. Their publication in 1877
precipitated a furor, one focus of which was her depiction of her mother.
Margaret Oliphant's shocked response to Martineau's "desecration" of
Victorian pieties surrounding home and motherhood is a good example.
She accuses Harriet of overemphasizing her childhood miseries, instead
of being properly grateful for the excellence of her education. Many
admirers (and some later biographers) disliked the book. One contemporary male lecturer announced that Martineau should have maintained
"a manly reticence. The woman who has got rid of the customary
mental sterility of her sex" ought to have dismissed "unhealthy, foolish
brooding—acrid dribblings of her private pen." The apparent discrep-
ancy between the autobiographer's internal view and the "healthy truth"

of her public image was just too great for him to encompass, though to Martineau and to the discerning modern reader continuities of character and purpose seem clear. Maria Weston Chapman's *Memorials*, published with the *Autobiography* and crammed with private miscellanea, also distressed Victorian decorum, particularly since Chapman—American feminist, abolitionist, and passionate friend of Martineau—sentimentalized her materials into a model of heroic rebellion. Following the 1884 publication of Mrs. F. Fenwick Miller's biography, Harriet's once beloved younger brother James (a Unitarian leader and philosopher of considerable note) sprang to his mother's defense. He too admitted to a cheerless childhood, but to him his mother was a saint, albeit a sharp-tempered one.[6]

Much energy has been expended on whether Harriet or James was "right." (No one seems to have noticed that a talented son's view might well be very different from a daughter's.) Biographers have suggested both that Mrs. Martineau was an exceptional woman with no outlets for her abilities except her family, and that she was simply a too ordinary one—that she and Harriet could never get on either because they were of radically different temperaments, or because they were just too much alike. Such limited controversies miss interconnections, most of which Martineau herself was acutely aware of. Like the body of her work, the story of her life is a study of human experience in transition to modernity, a movement from imprisonment in old intellectual and social structures to new and difficult freedoms and integrations. Martineau had long felt it a duty, a moral obligation, to relate her life-history, planning it in her twenties before she had any success story to tell. Its inception was probably to help others by analyzing the "early unfavorable influences" (II, 106) of her youth and suggesting more innovative and sympathetic modes of rearing children (a project accomplished in her highly personal *Household Education* of 1849). But the completed *Autobiography*, though it reiterates these points, is a far more complex document: it and the *Memorials* show how Martineau transmuted private female frustrations into public achievements through an intricate process of rebellion against and incorporation of the female role models and family patterns her mother provided. Martineau wanted to tell her readers "how I found my way out" (I, 33), but her works also suggest how much baggage she carried with her.

Harriet's family background was thoroughly middle class. She was born and reared in the provincial center of Norwich. Her father, descendant of a Huguenot family, was a manufacturer; her mother, the daughter of a grocer and sugar-refiner. Neither was very well educated. All accounts agree that the father was unaggressive and the mother decidedly the dominant figure. Having "great energy and quickness of resource," wrote James, "she naturally played the chief part in the government of the household, though always supported by the authority and admiration of her husband." She was also his confidante and adviser in business matters. She set goals for and administered a household of eight children—Harriet was the sixth—on an uncertain income. She was a busy woman, with an impatient, decided way of doing things herself and a sarcastic tongue when children and servants could not meet her high standards. Harriet, who was so much afraid of her that she habitually lied to her in childhood, was not the only one she scared. Other youthful acquaintances testified to her way of ordering "every thing and every body right and left" and her *"setting-down way"* (II, 147). Intelligent, with a strong will and an undeviating sense of duty, she had a great taste for literature. The youngest daughter, Ellen, described her father as a plain businessman and her almost wholly self-educated mother as the instigator of the family literary culture: "snatches of reading must have carried her through many trials . . . the anxieties of rearing a large family by means of a fluctuating and finally ruinous business."[7]

Decidedly ambitious for her children, Mrs. Martineau trained them with a firm hand and perfect confidence in her methods. The girls, like the boys, received a solid classical education. In many ways, Mrs. Martineau's goals were forward-looking and antitraditional; she tried to prepare her daughters for independence. The girls were expected to learn anything that boys could and were brought up to be self-supporting, if necessary. Extremely fond of reading herself, Mrs. Martineau let Harriet sneak away from the family dinner table early to gorge herself on poetry and newspapers instead of dessert. At the same time, she was strongly averse to open bluestockingism, with a sharp eye for feminine propriety and good manners. Her daughters could never be seen in public with pen in hand, so that Harriet had to rise before dawn or work very late to carry on her private studies: "If ever I shut myself into my own room for an hour of solitude, I knew it was at the risk of being sent for to join the sewing-circle, or to read aloud" (I, 78). The girls were expected to be proficient in all aspects of domestic management, everything from ironing and cooking to the prodigious amounts of sewing that the mature Harriet recalled with horror and pride. Painfully unhandy at first, she used to wonder what would become of her if her mother left home or she herself should marry, but she eventually became the extraordinarily capable household adept that Charlotte Brontë viewed with awe, and she frequently claimed that every girl has an innate longing and natural faculty for domestic arts.[8]

By both precept and example, then, Mrs. Martineau clearly offered a complex female role model, with significant consequences for Harriet's personal emotional and intellectual development, as well as for her public stances on feminism and such related issues as female education and employment. Harriet's brand of feminism is strenuously heroic: "Whatever a woman proves herself able to do, society will be thankful to see her do,—just as if she were a man. . . . I judge by my own case" (I, 302–03). While criticizing the absurdity of society's rules, Martineau showed a woman could succeed in a man's vocation through determined hard work. At the same time, she had internalized almost impossibly high standards of woman's vocation as wife and mother—so much so that she felt herself personally incapable of living up to them, fit only for a single life. She makes it quite plain that her unorthodox achievements were not the result of an essentially masculine nature (as Webb would have it), but rather the hard-won fruits of a damaged personality.

The young Harriet tried hard to be a dutiful daughter, though she continually felt herself a failure. She evolved a number of strategies for dealing with her difficulties. Though crying daily for years and constantly reproaching herself with faults, she would never own herself wrong. Always "pretending entire complacency and assurance" (I, 17), she was both imitating her mother and evolving the stance which would serve her well against the criticism she handled with such seeming aplomb throughout her public career. She also elaborately mothered James and Ellen, pouring out on them the love she felt herself deprived of. The force of her personal misery generated in her very early the desire to understand her situation so as to be able to change it and, by extension, that of "others who dared not speak." Her lifelong pursuit of objective principles and laws (first, moral and religious; later, scientific—she wound up a notorious atheist) began in childhood in response to the subjective injustice by which she felt ruled. Burying herself in books and religion, she fantasized about a martyrdom in which she would demonstrate that she was the good girl she wanted to be and win the praise she craved. But in religion, as at home, she found her passionate longing for sympathy and justice balked. All she heard was the duties of inferiors to superiors, a doctrine of passive obedience. She used to thirst for some notice of the oppression which servants and children had to endure and was especially tormented by her mother's highhanded treatment of the maids and by the favoritism shown to her sister Rachel. Outwardly obedient, she seethed with hidden rage. In one striking scene, she describes how she nerved herself to revolt. Her mother told her to pray God for forgiveness, for she did not know that *she* could ever forgive her daughter. Mrs. Martineau subsequently treated the girls with scrupulous impartiality, but Harriet never got the frank reassurance of love she really sought.

From such childhood troubles eventually germinated the themes of Martineau's public career. Her radical views of society were learned at her mother's knee, so to speak. Her early concrete experiences evolved into a conceptual model of the extant social power structure, her sense of familial injustice developing into a critique of the aristocratic spirit pervading English society. Her own period of growing up coincided with an era of repression and increasing need for change in the country, generating her radical ideology and her very consciously-conceived mission. In her case, generational conflict offered a model for other forms of conflict, suggesting how personal family contentions can be turned by the reformer into useful patterns for analyzing other modes of social relationships. The key elements of Martineau's struggle with her mother, as in the Rachel episode, are mirrored in her mature work, from the demand for equality of treatment to the conviction that communication between, mutual education of, inferiors and superiors is the key to progress. She was very much aware of how her childhood had shaped her career. In a letter of 1844, she calls herself a "pioneer in the regions of pain" to make the way easier to those who come after: "what a continued series of disappointments & troubles my life has been, & how directly whatever I have been able to do has arisen out of this. . . . So do we stumble & grope onwards . . . to the clear issues of our lives!"[9] The clear issues of Martineau's life and career everywhere inform her *Autobiography:* her lifelong hatred of irresponsible power, her pervasive interest in education and all forms of human development, her obsession with justice for all—workers, servants, children, women, slaves, the poor.

Martineau transmuted her youthful wilfulness and need for approval into a social mission which united personal emotional compensations with an urgent sense of vocation—to be the teacher, the mother, of a new society. But her escape from dependence and achievement of autonomy involved a lengthy, arduous apprenticeship, which seems at times almost a parable of the modern woman's struggle to reconcile the conflicting claims of family and career. She had male mentors and some encouragement from her mother and brothers. She also searched for female models: her first published essays were on female writers and female education. Reading the earliest in 1822, her eldest brother said, "(calling me dear for the first time) 'Now, dear, leave it to the other women to make shirts and darn stockings; and do you devote yourself to this.' I went home in a sort of dream. . . . That evening made me authoress" (I, 92). But it was ten years before she could escape the domestic duties of Norwich to realize her dream publicly in London. Harriet was by this time in the second stage of her relationship with her mother. As her daughter's intelligence matured, Mrs. Martineau became much more supportive and affectionate, though she frequently nagged Harriet about overwork on her numerous and unremunerative essays. At the same time, Harriet still had to obey all family rules as to hours, sewing, and so on. It is not surprising that she felt the failure of the old manufactory in which all the women's money had been placed after the father's death to be a great blessing. Having lost her "gentility" (I, 108), she set down rules for her career in June 1829 (II, 165–68) and made plans for London. Eventually, she secured employment:

> But, to my disappointment,—I might almost say, horror,—my mother sent me peremptory orders to go home. . . . I rather wonder that, being seven and twenty years old, I did not assert my independence, and refuse to return,—so clear as was, in my eyes, the injustice of remanding me to a position of helplessness and dependence, when a career of action and independence was opening before me. . . . The instinct and habit of old obedience prevailed, and I went home, with some resentment, but far more grief and desolation in my heart. (I, 113)

The letter to her mother which Chapman prints (II, 176–78) shows the persistence of childhood patterns: Harriet is placatory, yet determined to reserve options. Her female relatives recommended needlework as a vocation, but the very day after her return to Norwich, Harriet set to work for three essay prizes which the Unitarian Association was offering. She was determined to prove to her mother in open competition that she could write. She won all three, to the astonishment of competing male ministers.

Yet only after the political economy tales became an undoubted success did Martineau convince her mother that residence in London was necessary. Her mother was enormously gratified by her daughter's achievement, but Harriet's meticulously detailed letters back to Norwich were no substitute for the active participation and power her mother expected. Harriet, recognizing the inevitable, tried to reconcile her duty as a daughter with what she saw as her duty to society:

> If we at once begin with the change of habits which our change of position renders necessary, I fully expect that both you and I shall occasionally feel as if I did not discharge a daughter's duty, but we shall both remind ourselves that I am now as much a citizen of the world as any professional *son* of yours could be. . . . You know exactly under what feelings I say "Come." (II, 218)

But the ground rules did not work. Harriet soon found herself being urged to take a larger house and cultivate aristocratic acquaintances when she very self-consciously viewed herself as a radical. Moreover, she still had to do all her own sewing and mending since her mother refused to let her hire someone else to do it. Harriet loved and respected her mother, and her journals of the period show how hard she tried to satisfy conflicting needs. But her two-year trip to America was as much a respite from her mother as from overwork. It was there that she met Chapman and became actively involved in abolitionism. Having found a cause and a sense of female solidarity with other women reformers, Martineau wanted to emigrate, but her mother and her own illness intervened. Harriet stated plainly that her breakdown was a response to domestic stress. She also noted that for months after her retreat to Tynemouth, she "rarely slept without starting from a dream that my mother had fallen from a precipice, or over the bannisters, or from a cathedral spire; and that it was my fault" (I, 422). Whatever her guilt or relief, Harriet spent five years in solitary invalidism before the mesmeric cure which alienated her mother. Long after she had built her own house (notably well managed, with devoted nieces and servants as surrogates for the family she felt every woman needed) and securely established her career and philosophy, she suffered such anxieties during her mother's last illness that she was unable to work—an unheard-of event—from watching for the post. Martineau never really succeeded in coming to terms with her mother, but she did succeed in coming to terms with herself. In a sense, she ultimately made herself into the mother she had always wanted to have—sympathetic, confident, just, and serene. Her complex experience richly illustrates both the strengths and weaknesses of Victorian mother-and-daughter relationships.

Notes

1. *The Autobiography of Francis Place*, ed. Mary Thale (Cambridge: Cambridge University Press, 1972), p. 91. Place, the self-educated London tailor and reformer, was a correspondent of Martineau's.

2. *Harriet Martineau's Autobiography*, ed. Maria Weston Chapman (Boston: James R. Osgood, 1877), I, 8–9. Page references subsequently incorporated in the text refer to this edition.

3. *Life in the Sick-Room: Essays by an Invalid*, 3rd ed. (1844; rpt. London: Edward Moxon, 1849), pp. 168–69.

4. R. K. Webb, *Harriet Martineau: A Radical Victorian* (New York: Columbia University Press, 1960), pp. 90, 45, 51, 26.

5. Barbara Welter, *Dimity Convictions: The American Woman in the Nineteenth Century* (Athens: Ohio University Press, 1976), pp. 6–7; Alicia C. Percival, *The English Miss To-Day & Yesterday: Ideas, Methods and Personalities in the Education and Upbringing of Girls During the Last Hundred Years* (London: George G. Harrap, 1939), pp. 50–51.

6. [Margaret Oliphant], "Harriet Martineau," *Blackwood's Edinburgh Magazine*, 121 (April 1877), 472–96; Lord Russell, quoted in Vera Wheatley, *The Life and Work of Harriet Martineau* (Fair Lawn, New Jersey: Essential Books, 1957), p. 26; James's "The Early Days of Harriet Martineau" was published as a letter to the *Daily News*, 30 December 1884; it is reprinted in Theodora Bosanquet, *Harriet Martineau: An Essay in Comprehension* (London: Frederick Etchells and Hugh Macdonald, 1927), pp. 218–41.

7. James's "Biographical Memoranda" are quoted in James Drummond and C. B. Upton, *Life and Letters of James Martineau, D.D.* (London: James Nisbet, 1902), I, 4. Drummond prints several other contemporary estimates of Mrs. Martineau, including Ellen's, I, 8–9.

8. "Female Industry," *Edinburgh Review*, 109 (April 1859), 316; *Household Education* (London: Edward Moxon, 1849), p. 306; "Middle-Class Education in England: Girls," *Cornhill Magazine*, 10 (1864), 564. In the last, Martineau discusses the main difference between girls' and boys' training—"the claim of the household arts as an essential part of education. Boys have two things to divide their days between: study and play. Girls have three: study, the domestic arts, and play." Girls simply have *more* to do, but Martineau always expresses perfect confidence in their ability to master everything from the "Differential Calculus" to a "good batch of bread and pies."

9. Quoted in Webb, pp. 206–07.

"The Mother's History" in George Eliot's Life, Literature and Political Ideology

Christiana Pearson Evans is the most enigmatic character flitting across the rich stage of George Eliot's life. In the only letter remaining from the period before her mother's death, the young Mary Ann Evans betrays little emotion over her serious illness, nor does she ever mention her again. One or two comments from old family friends do nothing to focus the hazy blur surrounding George Eliot's mother. We know for fact that Mary Ann was Christiana's third child, that the birth of short-lived twins two years later left the mother forever ailing, that all the children were sent to boarding schools at very young ages, and that Christiana died when her youngest daughter was sixteen. Most other biographical information has been gleaned from her novels, particularly *Adam Bede* and *The Mill on the Floss*. The available portrait is a mere sketch, but ingenious psychological sleuthing (especially by Ruby Redinger in a recent interpretative biography) has added the detail necessary for a convincing if sometimes overdrawn picture.[1]

There is little doubt that Mary Ann was not mother's pet. Her older sister seems to have been a model girl, and the only son, as one might expect, was his mother's favorite. Mary Ann turned to her father for approval and protection. The dynamics of the Tulliver family in *The Mill on the Floss* are, therefore, generally considered to be autobiographical. The actual character of Christiana Evans is less certain. Rather than resembling the fluttering, ineffectual Mrs. Tulliver, she seems to have been more like the capable, sharp-tongued Mrs. Poyser in *Adam Bede*. Redinger suggests that as a mother Mrs. Poyser is "a woman who dominates through verbal criticism . . . [who is] over-anxious about her children . . . [upon   whom]   the   mother   role   seems   to   weigh heavily . . . [who is] motherly toward neither Dinah nor Hetty" (pp. 40–1). From this Redinger postulates, I believe correctly, that Christiana's attitude toward her youngest daughter was characterized by withdrawal, disapproval and rejection—however subtle—and that this marked Mary Ann's passage through life: "she [George Eliot] did not easily come to terms with her unresolved feelings for her mother. But her attempt to do so may well have been a motivating, although untraceable, force in the private quest that led her from novel to novel once she was free to write fiction" (p. 43).

I cannot agree, however, that George Eliot's unresolved feeling for her mother is an untraceable force in her novels and in her life. Redinger, like all other biographers and critics, turns away from Christiana Evans because of the more rewarding material that illuminates Mary Ann's relationship with her father and her brother. But although Robert Evans directly influenced *Adam Bede*, and Isaac Evans powerfully motivated *The Mill on the Floss*, I believe that Christiana was a more enduring leaven throughout her daughter's life and career. The dynamics of motherhood and daughterhood permeate every novel, because George Eliot's novels are preeminently about being a woman in the nineteenth century. Not only did George Eliot search for the meaning of motherhood in her novels, but she sought a definition applicable to her own life. And, furthermore, motherhood was a *political* concept to her, as it was to the nineteenth century in general. Christiana Pearson Evans was, therefore, a prism refracting her daughter's light in multiple directions: literary, personal, and political.

II

The Victorian heroine, it has been said, is motherless, and George Eliot certainly conforms to this maxim. Caterina, Hetty and Dinah, Effie and Nancy Lammeter, Romola, Esther Lyon, Fedalma, Dorothea, and Mirah all lack mothers.[2] Maggie, Rosamond, and Gwendolen have weak mothers who often act like children to their own daughters. Only one of George Eliot's protagonists—the proud and destructive sexual sinner, Mrs. Transome—is herself a mature woman and a mother. Nevertheless, all of the novels incorporate a process by which her motherless heroines do or do not themselves become mothers. For there are two categories of George Eliot heroines: the productive and the sterile. Rather than being a literary convention, the inability or unwillingness to bear children is a moral and political principle by which George Eliot criticizes or punishes her heroines. Janet Dempster, driven to alcoholism by a brutal husband, is childless until she repents; she then mothers the consumptive minister who converted her. Hetty Sorrel, George Eliot's most autistic heroine, murders her illegitimate child. Maggie Tulliver, although more sinned against than sinning, returns to the conforting womb of the river before she can herself pass from childhood to motherhood. Nancy Lammeter pays for her husband's sins with her own sterility. Mrs. Transome rejoices in the death of one son and is drawn to her ruin by the illegitimate issue of her adultery. Rosamond miscarries when she goes riding in defiance of her husband's advice, an obvious metaphor for her remorseless egoism. And Gwendolen Harleth, the most tragic heroine of all, is "reduced to dread lest she should become a mother," because she knows that the man she married to satisfy her taste for freedom and luxury already had a common law wife and children (chap. 54).

A striking pattern emerges from these examples. Women who step beyond the social and biological limitations of womankind, who desire to transcend the ordinary "lot of woman" by any means no matter how admirable, who defy sexual standards, who rebel rather than submit: these women are visited with the curse of sterility. Those women who do not rebel—or, more typically, who suffer and then submit—are blessed for their womanly wisdom by becoming the radiating center of a quasi-mystical family circle. Dinah Morris takes the place of the murderous Hetty and, surrounded by children and family, brings *Adam Bede* to its close. Lucy visits Maggie's grave, leaning on the arm of the tall male who will no doubt become the father of her many children. Romola, sterile until she learns to submit, ends as the nonbiological mother of her husband's children by his innocent mistress. Dorothea learns the ways of womanhood in her childless marriage with Casaubon, and then closes the "home epic" of *Middlemarch* as the contented mother of Will Ladislaw's children. Daniel and Mirah sail off to Palestine, with many little Zionists in their future, and even Gwendolen is allowed the vague possibility of motherhood in some distant Garden of Eden.

George Eliot's heroines cannot *be* mothers because society provides no realistic model for healthy motherhood, which, in the words of *Felix Holt*, would incorporate "a fact perhaps kept a little too much in the background, that mothers have a self larger than their maternity" (chap. 8). But motherhood in the nineteenth century was fearfully oppressive, destroying both mother and child. The "bland, adoring, and gently tearful women" most immersed in motherhood are actually trapped in the repetitive, numbing rhythm of femininity: cleaning, cooking, and childbearing. So frightening did George Eliot find this image—personified by Lisbeth Bede, Mrs. Tulliver, Mrs. Holt, and even the sympathetic Milly Barton and Gritty Moss—that she created an opposing idealization of motherhood as "an expansion of the animal existence [which] enlarges the imagined range for self to move in" when accompanied "by much suppression of self, and power of living in the experience of another" (*Felix Holt*, chap. 1). Mrs. Poyser and Mrs. Garth are nostalgic fantasies of what a mother should be and might have been in some golden age before industrialization and modernism disrupted the balance of nature. Mrs. Meyrick extends this wish-fantasy into the urban present. They provide models for George Eliot's heroines, being women perfectly satisfied with the domestic ideal.

But George Eliot was not herself this kind of woman; she consciously rejected this future for herself, symbolized by the drowning of her alternative self, Maggie Tulliver (a woman yearning for poetry and beauty who escapes provincial ugliness through death, not literature). Beneath the pious longings, the novels sizzle with anger and resentment. One might say, then, that the recurrence of women who destroy their own children points to the real George Eliot also. The two most powerful destroyers, Mrs. Transome and the Alcharisi, speak with George Eliot's own voice. Having found themselves in a hateful role, they hate, reject, and destroy in their turn. If George Eliot turned Romola and Dorothea into figures of the Virgin Mary, then she was equally capable of turning Mrs. Transome and the Alcharisi into variations of Lilith or Kali. We might even find the supreme example of wish fulfillment to be Rosamond, who never retreats one step from her plan to control everything around her, and yet ends up triumphant—with money, positions, *and* daughters.

III

George Eliot, failing to discover a viable maternal role model in her own life or in her society, demanded an impossible ideal in her novels. But, in a curious way, she also lived that family ideal. Over the years, she created herself first as a daughter, then as a sister, and finally as a mother figure for countless younger women (and men). The young girl found something of a mother substitute (or, even more, an older sister) in her teacher Maria Lewis, and then in her lifelong friends Cara Bray and Sara Hennell. Many of the men she met in the intellectual communities of Coventry and London were more adequate brothers than Isaac Evans; one of them, George Henry Lewes, became her husband and companion. As an older woman, she became a "spiritual mother" to several young women and one younger man, John Walter Cross (whom she eventually married). Only during the early 1850s, before she met Lewes, did she create friendships outside this family model. As a part of London's radical intelligentsia, she met the active feminists—Bessie Raynor Parkes, Clementia Taylor, Jane Elizabeth Senior, and particularly Barbara Bodichon—who never became mothers, daughters, or even sisters, but simply friends and equals.

In 1856, Marian Evans made the courageous decision to live with George Henry Lewes even though he is still legally married and the father of three sons. In doing so, she chose to give up her respectability, her old family ties (and, for a time, some of her old friendships), and the possibility of having children of her own. One result of this liaison was the birth of George Eliot the novelist. Lewes adored Evans as a person and worshipped her as a writer. He propped up her constantly flagging self-confidence by creating a cult that bestowed upon her a holy, maternal aura. He called her "Mother" and "Mutter" to the family (as she called him "Pater") and often "Madonna" to close friends. Adopting the conceit of books as children, he wrote to publisher John Blackwood that she "will rock the cradle of the new 'little stranger' with fresh maternal vigour" (*GEL* III, 117). Later, George Eliot herself comments that *Felix Holt* "has been growing slowly like a sickly child" (*GEL* IV, 236).

Bookbirth, to borrow from a nineteenth century reviewer, was not the only result of George Eliot's liaison with Lewes. Family ties grew sanctified to the ostracized woman, both in her own life and in the organization of society as a whole. Marian Evans the reviewer and critic had been sharply and wittily radical; George Eliot the wife and novelist is now guardedly conservative. One example of this conversion can be seen in her changing concept of motherhood. The only reference to mothers I have found in her letters before 1856 caustically refers to "Mother nature" as "an old lady with some bad habits of her own" (*GEL* I, 272). But after 1856, references to mothers abound. She exults in Rubens' paintings because "the women [are] such real mothers" (*GEL* II, 451). She praises Gaskell's *Life of Charlotte Brontë* as "a bit of the true religion of the home" (*GEL* II, 315). "I like to think of you as a happy wife and mother," she writes to an old friend (*GEL* II, 343). In Italy she exclaims over the vista of "a madonna and child at every third or fourth upper window. . . ." (*GEL* III, 288).

This idealization of motherhood and the domestic model of life intensifies throughout the 1860s until reaching a peak during her final decade. In 1869 she writes to Robert Browning that "the getting older brings some new satisfactions, and among these I find the growth of a maternal feeling towards both men and women who are much younger than myself" (*GEL* V, 5). She defers to Harriet Beecher Stowe as both novelist and woman, for "you have had longer experience than I as a writer, and fuller experience as a woman, since you have borne children and known the mother's history from the beginning" (*GEL* V, 31). The topic seems to have obsessed her in 1869, for she also writes that "in proportion as I profoundly rejoice that I never brought a child into a world, I am conscious of having an unused stock of motherly tenderness, which sometimes overflows, but not without discrimination" (*GEL* V, 52).

George Eliot came to a resolution over this "unused stock" by adopting the persona of the "spiritual mother," the wise Sibyl, the all-knowing and all-nurturing mother goddess. Age was certainly one factor in this conversion, but Adrienne Rich offers a psychological clue: ". . . the 'motherless' woman may also react by denying her own vulnerability, denying she has felt any loss or absence of mothering. She may spend her life proving her strength in the 'mothering' of others—as with Mrs. Ramsay, mothering men, whose weakness makes her feel strong, or mothering in the role of teacher, doctor, political activist, psychotherapist."[3] George Eliot considered herself an "aesthetic teacher" and in her relationships with younger people she often seems to adopt the role of psychotherapist. And there were certainly numerous women around in need of her "mothering."

If Lewes commenced the transformation of George Eliot into a Great Mother and her books into their children, then an enthusiastic younger generation finished the job. Women had always been drawn to Marian Evans. As a very young girl at boarding school, she was called by the older girls "'little Mamma' . . . a proof that already something was to be seen of the maternal air which characterized her in later years, and perhaps more especially in intercourse with her own sex."[4] She and Sara Hennell wrote to each other in the language of lovers: "my Sara, thou art very dear to me and I sometimes talk to you in my soul as lovingly as Solomon's Song" (*GEL* I, 279).[5] In London, Eliza Lynn, another "literary lady," tells her "she was 'never so attracted to a woman before as to me'—I am 'such a loveable person'" (*GEL* I, 337). (As Mrs. Lynn Linton, she became one of George Eliot's most vicious detractors.) Bessie Parkes and Barbara Bodichon echoed her sentiments (see, for example, *GEL* III, 128).

These were the women to whom she related as an equal. But when Marian Evans was first "rolled up, mashed, absorbed in the Lewesian magnificence" (*GEL* III, 65) and then transformed into the sage George Eliot, some way of incorporating new relationships into her changed life became necessary. With Lewes as companion, mentor and protector, there was no place for a new "Geliebte" or even a "sort of flesh-and-blood sisterly feeling" (*GEL* II, 19). Marian Evans had always been uneasy about the feelings she inspired in women and turned to friendships with men in apparent relief.[6] I would hesitate to say whether it was the insufficiency of these female friendships that disturbed her, or their oversufficient emotionalism. In either case, George Eliot made no new reciprocal friendships with women after 1856. Instead, she gradually created a comfortable new role for herself as a "spiritual mother" to an eager generation of younger women.

IV

"The influence of one woman's life on the lot of other women is getting greater and greater with the quickening spread of all influences," George Eliot wrote to Jane Elizabeth Senior in 1873 (*GEL* V, 372). The influence of great women who break through the barriers of patriarchal society has hardly been touched upon in feminist criticism. In the nineteenth century, which saw the growth of the most widespread feminist movement in history, only Florence Nightingale caught the imagination of women as thoroughly as did George Eliot. Aware of her "influence" on her readers, she relished her responsibilities as the "aesthetic teacher" of universal moral truths. The *content* of these truths will be discussed in the next section, but here I want to bring out the equally important *form* George Eliot adopted as woman and teacher. By 1873, Lewes had successfully completed the beautification of George Eliot. Anna Thackerey Ritchie writes that "the Shrine was so serene and kind that this authoress felt like a wretch for having refused to worship there before."[7] She is not always so charitable, however, as when she complains to Lewes's son Charles that "it was better to be genuine than to have influence, and that I didn't suppose she [George Eliot] imagined herself inspired, though her clique did. It rather shocked him, and he mumbled a good deal" (180–1). Other observations from outside—an acidly detached one by Emily Davies and a frankly libellous one by Eliza Lynn Linton—further deflate the carefully created goddess image.[8]

But her circle cherished the sibylline image. One of her fiercest worshippers, the remarkable Edith Simcox, recorded her grand passion for the older woman in a spell-binding autobiography.[9] To Simcox, George Eliot *was* her mother: "I am unspeakably thankful for her goodness—for the future hope that she will accept a daughter's duty at one's hands" (p. 96). In her turn, George Eliot fostered the relationship by calling Simcox "a thoughtful child" and "a silly child" (pp. 95, 97). Simcox writes, "she has often signed her letters 'M' and with my wonted stupidity, I have been shy to conclude whether it stood for her name or 'Mother'—though she has often signed that too" (p. 103). George Eliot later became uneasy over Simcox's passionate attraction and discouraged her use of "mother" although other spiritual daughters received the cherished signature: Maria Congreve, Georgiana Burne-Jones, Mrs. Mark Pattison, Mary Ponsonby, and Elma Stuart, whose grave next to George Eliot's identified her as she "whom for 8½ blessed years George Eliot called by the sweet name of 'Daughter.'"

In her eulogy of George Eliot, Edith Simcox wrote that she "was the object of much passionate and romantic worship [because of] the attractive force of this rare character, in which tenderness and strength were blended together and as it were transfused with something that was all her own—the genius of sweet goodness" (p. 784). Liberation is a hard struggle in any age, and I would suggest that one reason women were attracted to George Eliot was that they recognized in her the shattering of sexual stereotypes. She proved that it was possible for a woman to be both tender *and* strong; to demonstrate all the comfortable, conventional qualities of femininity *and* the power of intellect traditionally reserved for men.[10] They saw in her a woman both outstanding in her career and fulfilled in her domestic life. In other words, George Eliot provided women struggling for identity with a transitional role model, one that was both challenging and safe, far-reaching yet cautious. How were these women or George Eliot herself to envision this fountain of strength and gentleness? Without exception, the image of Mother rushed to their minds, the one example of female power available in a patriarchy, especially since George Eliot's nurturing and affectionate personality encouraged the association. This seems to be Simcox's astute although groping analysis: "So you see darling that I can only love you three lawful ways, idolatrously as Frater the Virgin Mary, in romance wise as Petrarch, Laura, or with a child's fondness for the mother one leans on notwithstanding the irreverence of one's longing to pet and take care of her" (p. 108). George Eliot gave women what Rich calls "courageous mothering": "The most notable fact that culture imprints on women is the sense of our limits. The most important thing one woman can do for another is to illuminate and expand her sense of actual possibilities" (p. 250). George Eliot's influence came not merely from the doctrines and noble sentiments scattered through her novels, but every bit as much from the exemplary statement of her life.

Her followers eagerly drank in every word and gesture. Few were as passionately devoted as Edith Simcox, who bathed her goddess's feet with tears and kisses, but many wrote for comfort and advice or simply in gratitude. Mrs. Frederick Lehmann wrote her husband, "It is impossible to be with that noble creature without feeling *better*" (*GEL* IV, 336). Lewes, a fertile source of goddess lore, writes in his diary, "I saw a lady gazing very devoutly at Polly and then quietly as if unobserved stroke the back of her cloak and person" (*GEL* VII, 376). Another woman writes that she had "copied passages from *Romola* into her New Testament" which Lewes observes is "a strong measure from an English woman" (*GEL* V, 376). At a party George Eliot is "surrounded by adoring women, and a crowd of others all waiting their turn to say a word. She compared it to a flock of birds waiting each to have a peck at her" (*GEL* V, 84). Men such as Charles Lewes and "Johnny" Cross also admired her, but only women became the passionate, inspired, even erotic worshippers: women like Simcox, Elma Stuart, Maria Congreve (who, Simcox says, "also loved my darling lover-wise") and the nameless young lady who "helped Polly on with her cloak and kissed her hand and then her cheek" (*GEL* VII, 16). As a final example, consider Mrs. Charles Sanders Peirce, who, in 1869, composed a trembling liturgy to her goddess:

> Don't answer this, dearest. I don't require you to think of me as anything more than the evening breeze that sometimes kisses your cheek. I *love* you, you are so love-worthy. And once in a long time I *love* to say so to you. But I would not have it burden you with the weight of a rose leaf.[11]

V

I have so far argued that it was George Eliot's example as a courageous and creative woman that inspired the worship of her spiritual daughters.

However, to George Eliot herself it was her message that mattered. The message was conveyed both through the moral choices made by her protagonists and through the didactic passages spoken by the omniscient, maternal narrator that George Eliot brought to such perfection. Before turning to the novels themselves, however, it is worthwhile looking back to the young Mary Ann Evans, still under the influence of evangelical Christianity and the domestic ideology of the early nineteenth century.

In 1840, Mary Ann, like many other women of her generation, was "electrified" by *The Education of Mothers; or the Civilization of Mankind by Women*, a grandiloquent vindication of Woman as Mother of the Race by Louis Aimé Martin (*GEL* I, 70). She had already become acquainted with his ideas through an anonymous translation of exerpts called *Woman's Mission*, which she found "the most philosophical and masterly [book] on the subject I ever read or glanced over" (*GEL* I, 66). The 1830s and 40s provided her with a multitude of female guidebooks to read and glance over. Many were little more than expanded etiquette books, but others, like the famous works of Mrs. Sarah Ellis, purported to advise women about their societal functions as wives, mothers, and daughters. Aimé Martin went even further. He wrote a philosophical paean to civilization nestled in the lap of Woman as Mother. "It is upon maternal love that the future destiny of the human race depends," he claimed.[12] But *The Education of Mothers* did more than appeal to nostalgic sentiment. With messianic fervor, Aimé Martin tells women that "I come to reveal to you your rights, your power, your sovereignty" (p. 41). He strongly reinforced an ideology, already current at the time, demanding the elevation of woman's status and influence for the good of the children she bore and educated:

> Oh, women! could you but have a glimpse of the wonders promised to maternal influence, with what noble pride would you enter upon this career, which nature has generously opened to you during so many ages! . . . Young girls, young wives, young mothers, you hold the sceptre; in your souls much more than in the laws of legislators, now repose the futurity of Europe, the world, and the destinies of the human race (p. 303).

The tone is foreign to Mrs. Ellis and the ladies magazines, but the sentiment is exactly the same.

Thus, the "female influence" ideology that George Eliot maintained throughout her life had its roots in these nineteenth-century versions of

Ann Landers. What could have been so appealing to a thinker as profound as George Eliot? One answer is that "female influence" provided a way for her, like countless of her contemporaries, to reconcile power and powerlessness. The "liberation" of women through their unique biological condition provided the meeting ground for feminism and tradition. The ideology of "female influence" or "woman's mission" was certainly used to maintain patriarchical authority, but it was also used subversively to increase woman's power by expanding her sphere of influence. Shattering the dichotomy of home and world was one way to increase power in the nineteenth century. Extending the home to *encompass* the world was another, and far more common, way. Rather than shaking up the social order through demands for the franchise, expanded work opportunities or legal reforms, women, it was argued, ought to concentrate on influencing their husbands toward right actions and educating their children to be good citizens. Here they have unlimited possibilities to uplift themselves and society "by the simple fulfillment of their duties as wives and mothers of families" (Aimé Martin, p. 61). Thus, George Eliot unequivocally supported expanded education, for how were women to take on this important responsibility without adequate knowledge? She certainly wanted to see women take their place in the gradual improvement of the human race, and that to her was irrevocably rooted in "sweet family affection" (*GEL* V, 33).

Keeping Aimé Martin's philosophical evocation of motherhood in mind, I think we might be more charitable toward the underlying domesticity of George Eliot's great final novels. It is true that a fine line exists between the "Mother of the Race" and the "Angel in the House," but George Eliot does not lightly condemn her villainesses to sterility and her heroines to motherhood. *Middlemarch* is a "home epic": the domestic community she carefully creates through four volumes is also a microcosm of England. The glue that holds the nation together is provided by women like Dorothea, who accept the possibilities inherent in their limited role, and because of whom "things are not so ill with you and me as they might have been" (Finale). *Daniel Deronda* carries the message of *Middlemarch* further into the very modern world in which she wrote. There, established values have already begun to erode and thus the younger generation must search for new mothers, since the binding ties of home and society are found in the "maternal transference of self" that transcends all other social relations (chap. 40). Mrs. Meyrick, one of George Eliot's exemplary mother figures, explains: "It is easier to find an old mother than an old friend. Friendships begin with liking or gratitude—roots that can be pulled up. Mother's love begins deeper down" (chap. 32).

Thus, in her last novel, George Eliot returns to the family roots of both the individual and England as a nation. Mirah, for example, leaves her corrupted father to search for the mother associated with her earliest memories ("I think my life began with waking up and loving my mother's face"—chap. 20). Daniel, haunted by his rootlessness, searches Europe for his mother, eventually finding her in a curious idealization of Judaism as the "heart of mankind," the "core of affection," the "well of mercy": all receptive, passive, "inner space" metaphors for the tender, nurturing mother. What little hope is left for England after Daniel, representing heroic energy, leaves, lies in Gwendolen's discovery of the mother in herself. For, although she never becomes a real mother in the novel, she finally learns what it means to be the "best of women" (chap. 65). In her most direct polemic, George Eliot declaims: "What in the midst of that mighty drama are girls and their blind visions? They are the Yea or Nay of that good for which men are enduring and fighting. In these delicate vessels is borne onward through the ages the treasure of human affections" (chap. 11). In Gwendolen Harleth, therefore, the biological and metaphorical aspects of motherhood become one.

VI

The conclusion of *Daniel Deronda*, at once George Eliot's most conservative and most modern novel, may seem disappointing unless we see it as the culmination of an entire life's search for the Mother. In her life, she created herself as a mother to younger women. In her novels, she expounded an ideology of motherhood that she hoped would satisfy "woman's diseased, unsatisfied longings" while leaving undisturbed the family base of society (*GEL* III, 403). This was not George Eliot's individual weakness. Her quest was that of the nineteenth century, to stem the female drive for authority by offering them traditional forms of power. We can certainly say that George Eliot faltered in not keeping female relationships as flexible as they in fact were in the nineteenth century, and indeed as male/female relationships were in her own life. She was, after all, able to treat John Cross as friend, son, brother, and husband. Her sense of "uncanniness" with women perhaps cut off many of her options. It is also true that in offering a solution for the future she did not really see existing in the present, she idealized individual mothers and the institution of motherhood. She had no way of truly reconciling the reality of being a mother with the ideology of mother-hood, and thus her solution is always posed in the windup, two pages from the end. But I do not think she should be faulted for that. Adrienne Rich has written, "we are, none of us, 'either' mothers or daughters; to our amazement, confusion, and greater complexity, we are both" (p. 257). George Eliot found motherhood and daughterhood—indeed, the complete cycle of womanhood—to be an ever deepening mystery throughout her life. The greatest tribute we can pay to her is to recognize that so complex and confusing did she find womanhood, she was unable ever to define it.

Notes

[1] Redinger, *George Eliot: The Emergent Self* (New York: Alfred Knopf, 1975). The best biographical work is undoubtedly *The George Eliot Letters*, ed. Gordon S. Haight (New Haven: Yale University Press, 1954), in seven volumes (hereafter *GEL*). A point about George Eliot's several names must be made. She went from Mary Anne to Mary Ann to Marian Evans, then became Mrs. Lewes and Mrs. Cross (as she is *still* known in some indexing systems). I will call her Mary Ann as a young girl and Marian as a mature woman and, of course, George Eliot as the novelist.

[2] Since most readers are familiar with only some of the novels, I will provide a key to the characters: *Scenes from Clerical Life* (Milly Barton, Caterina, Janet Dempster); *Adam Bede* (Hetty Sorrel, Dinah Morris, Mrs. Poyser, Lisbeth Bede); *The Mill on the Floss* (Maggie Tulliver, Lucy Deane, Mrs. Tulliver, Gritty Moss); *Silas Marner* (Effie, Nancy Lammeter); *Romola* (Romola); *Felix Holt* (Esther Lyon, Mrs. Transome, Mrs. Holt); *The Spanish Gypsy* (Fedalma); *Middlemarch* (Dorothea Brooke, Rosamond Vincy, Mrs. Garth); and *Daniel Deronda* (Gwendolen Harleth, Mirah, Mrs. Meyrick, the Alcharisi).

[3] Adrienne Rich, *Of Woman Born* (New York: Bantam Books, 1977), p. 246.

[4] Edith Simcox, "George Eliot," *The Nineteenth Century*, LI (May 1881), 779.

[5] See also *GEL* I, 146–7, 150, and 275. The framework for understanding this classically Victorian "female friendship" (and the intense, even sexual, emotion generated by her "spiritual daughters" as I discuss) is given in Carroll Smith-Rosenberg, "The Female World of Love and Ritual," *Signs* I, 1 (Autumn 1975), 1–29.

[6] She told Edith Simcox that "she had never all her life cared very much for women—it must seem monstrous to me . . . when she was young, girls and women seemed to look on her as somehow 'uncanny' while men were always kind." K. A. McKenzie, *Edith Simcox and George Eliot* (London: Oxford University Press, 1961), p. 97.

[7] Letters of *Anna Thackerey Ritchie*, ed. Hester Ritchie (London: John Murray, 1924), p. 151.

[8] For Davies, see *GEL* VI, 287. Linton, in her autobiography, wrote that: "She grew to be artificial, *posée*, pretentious, unreal. She lived an unreal life all through, both mentally and socially; and in her endeavour to harmonize two irreconcilables—to be at once conventional and insurgent—the upholder of the sanctity of marriage while living as the wife of a married man—the self-reliant lawbreaker and the eager postulant of the recognition granted only to the covenanted—she lost every trace of that finer freedom and whole-heartedness which had been so remarkable in the beginning of her connection with Lewes. She was a made woman—not in the French sense—but

made by self-manipulation, as one makes a statue or a vase." This account quite frankly reeks of envy and spite. Yet I, for one, am inclined to sympathize with Linton's further assertion that "never for one instant did she [George Eliot] forget her self-created Self—never did she throw aside the trappings or the airs of the benign Sibyl." *My Literary Life* (London: Holder and Stoughton, 1899), pp. 98–99.

[9] Discussed in McKenzie, *op. cit.* The "Autobiography of a Shirt Maker" is due to be published in its entirety, I have been told, in the eighth volume of the *GEL*.

[10] This position should not be confused with the sexist one praising George Eliot's "androgyny." Many writers—mostly men—in her own day commented on her "feminine" personality and "masculine" mind (see *GEL* V, 464 and VII, 242.)

[11] Quoted in Haight's introduction to McKenzie, p. xiv.

[12] 1st American edition, reprinted from the London edition (Philadelphia: Lea & Blanchard, 1843), p. xxxii.

JACQUELINE BERKE
LAURA BERKE

Mothers and Daughters in Wives and Daughters: A Study of Elizabeth Gaskell's Last Novel

Psychologist Erich Fromm has said of the child that he must grow until he becomes his own father. Presumably we may extrapolate from this that the girl-child similarly must grow until she becomes her own mother. This metaphor, so highly suggestive of what the maturation process is all about, strikes at the very center of Elizabeth Gaskell's *Wives and Daughters,* for the novel written in 1864–66, concerns two young women, Molly and Cynthia, undergoing the pleasures and pains of growing up, separating themselves from family dependencies and becoming, as it were, their own parents.

In one sense we have here a typical English provincial novel of the nineteenth century in that the setting is a small country village back in those still faintly feudal days before "new fangled railways" had threaded their way through the English countryside, and the plot line follows—roughly—the lives of two young women until their respective marriages.[1] But Mrs. Gaskell, always an acute observer of human nature, was not satisfied with a leisurely stroll through a provincial town; she opted instead for a profound psychological journey through the complicated psyches and contrasting careers of her two heroines: Molly in whom we see healthy ongoing development under the loving, protective wing of a devoted father and a whole constellation of deeply concerned, warmly affectionate mother-surrogates; as against the arrested development of Cynthia in whom we see the drying up of tender feeling under the long strain of deprivation: no father, and an envious mother who regards her daughter—right up to and including the final scenes of the novel—as an "encumbrance" (p. 650), if not a threat.

In a much-needed and long-overdue reassessment of Mrs. Gaskell, published in 1965 (and designed as corrective to a traditionally patronizing view of the author of *Cranford* as a charming *minor* novelist), Edgar Wright points out that in no novelist is the impact of family upbringing stressed more strongly or dramatized more vividly. For in Gaskell's view, "stability of character is . . . linked with emotional stability and social stability in the family unit."[2] More than that—as Gaskell believed—stability in the community at large and in society as a whole can exist only if a foundation is laid at the family level. When individual parents fail to provide such a foundation—when they withhold affection, or even sufficient protection; when they are themselves poor and unprincipled models of adulthood—then the character of the offspring must suffer, perhaps irrevocably. The apple, alas, will not—cannot—fall very far from the tree.

We shall address ourselves here specifically to mothers and daughters in *Wives and Daughters*, limiting our consideration to the major women characters but hoping at least to suggest thereby the remarkable richness of this novel, particularly the fascinating and intricate constellation of mother/daughter relationships. It is clear that Mrs. Gaskell, "the heroine," as Showalter calls her "of a new school of 'motherly fiction,' "[3] is pointing in this novel to the crucial and determining influence of mothering in each of her protagonist's lives.

Daughters

Elizabeth Gaskell opens *Wives and Daughters* in an atmosphere of sun, warmth, light, and pleasure—with the expectation of more pleasure to come for twelve-year-old Molly Gibson. Indeed, Chapter One, entitled "The Dawn of a Gala Day," begins with the old and perennially delightful "rigmarole of childhood":

> In a country there was a shire, and in that shire there was a town, and in that town there was a house, and in that house there was a room, and in that room there was a bed, and in that bed, there lay a little girl . . . It was a June morning, and early as it was, the room was full of sunny warmth and light. On the drawers opposite to the little white dimity bed in which Molly Gibson lay was a primitive kind of bonnet stand on which was hung a bonnet . . . the bonnet; the pledge of the gay bright day to come. (p. 35)

But on the very next page Mrs. Gaskell refers to Molly as "Poor child!" What can be wrong in the life of this young girl, joyously awaiting her trip to the large Towers Estate for its annual party? Molly, the happy "quintessence of a young girlhood,"[4] is snugly settled in a well-ordered, affectionate community with a loving father—the reputable country doctor, Mr. Gibson. But, as we learn on the second page of the novel, Molly, at a very early age, lost her mother, an event "which was a jar to the whole tenour of her life" (p. 36). Yet we need not weep for Molly; at the time of this trauma, she was, Mrs. Gaskell assures us, "too young to be conscious of it" (p. 36). Certainly this early blow has not significantly scarred young Molly for whom several dawns announce many gala days—days of love and friendship, stability and security.

Wives and Daughters relates this heroine's growth from young, naive daughter to adult mature wife-to-be. She makes this transition from child to woman because, Gaskell strongly suggests, she has had a good, loving upbringing, an upbringing which enables her to become, as one critic perceptively points out, the "summation of the qualities that Mrs. Gaskell admired . . . [she] is affectionate, self-reliant, honest and natural, with vitality . . . intelligence . . . eagerness, energy, strong emotions balanced by . . . self-control, unselfishness."[5]

But if we return to that reliable rigmarole of childhood, we find a startling contrast in Gaskell's second heroine, the remarkably beautiful, languid, psychically maimed Cynthia Kirkpatrick, "a fatherless girl," as her shallow, hypocritical, self-centered mother labels her. With such a mother as Hyacinth Clare Kirkpatrick, how could the novel's second daughter-character enjoy even one "gala" June day?

Indeed, on that same bright, sunny, June morning, Cynthia wakes up alone in the boarding school she has attended since the age of four. Her mother, flitting about Hollingford, has no thought of her daughter, no awareness that she feels deprived and lonely—as the later brief confrontation between mother and daughter amply testifies: "Mama, I've my feelings too," Cynthia wails. "Nonsense, child!" (p. 443) replies the heartless Clare.

Thus if Molly Gibson's childhood is filled with the love and attention of her father and a variety of motherly townsfolk, the key word of Cynthia's early childhood is *neglect*:

> Oh, Molly, you don't know how I was neglected just at a time when I wanted friends most. Mamma does not know it; it is not in her to know what I might have been if I had only fallen into wise, good hands. (p. 486)

But just as Molly has always had "wise good hands" to support her, so

Cynthia receives guidance too late in her development—after her flawed but luminous character is formed.

At seventeen Molly and Cynthia become half-sisters; each has experienced early love; each will respond differently to her new parent; each will walk a different road to maturation and matrimony. As we have already contrasted their June mornings, so we must continue to contrast these loving sisters, always keeping in mind what Gaskell is telling us: that Molly's steady progress towards adult happiness is possible because of her early stable home, and that Cynthia's chequered flight towards pained womanhood is the result of early deprivation.

We shall consider first Molly's adolescence and its effect on her father. Mr. Gibson, foolishly and precipitously—in a moment of panic—marries Mrs. Kirkpatrick, convinced that an adolescent girl *must* have a mother. Disregarding the essentially excellent mothering he himself has given his daughter, he wrongly reasons that only a woman can deal with the confusion, if not catastrophe, caused by early adolescent romance. So upset and bewildered is Mr. Gibson when Molly receives an ardent love note from nineteen-year-old, perennially blushing Mr. Coxe, that Gibson throws a parental tantrum and ships Molly out to neighbors, the Hamleys. Blind to the possibility of romance with one of the Hamley sons, the befuddled father then marries Mrs. Kirkpatrick to insure his present complacency—Molly is now safe with the Hamleys and with a new mother.

When Mr. Gibson visits Molly at the Hamley estate to tell her of his upcoming marriage, Molly, in her anguish, turns to the sensitive Roger Hamley whose affectionate counsel sparks the first genuine flicker of love in her young woman's heart.

Cynthia's initial reaction to her mother's wedding is unrecorded, in fact unknown, since she is discreetly—vindictively—not invited; after all, Mrs. Kirkpatrick (now to be called Gibson) reasons, it would be disagreeable "to her to have her young daughter flashing out her beauty by the side of the faded bride" (p. 156). Once again mother has failed daughter during the crucial years of adolescence.

Cynthia, alone and unloved, without the guidance or concern of a fatherly (motherly) Mr. Gibson or even of a neighboring Hamley family, finds herself with no money, only with sparkling goods to sell—herself. Thus, at the same age as Molly is when she begins to admire Roger, Cynthia foolishly engages herself to the rakish, unscrupulous Mr. Preston. When Cynthia later describes the situation to Molly, we realize fully the striking differences in their adolescent backgrounds:

> The worry about money made me sick of my life [Cynthia explains] . . . but I would have stinted and starved if mamma and I had got on as happily together as we might have done—as you and Mr. Gibson do. It was not the poverty; it was that she never seemed to care to have me with her. (p. 518)

Utterly lacking love, Cynthia understandably not only finds herself incapable of loving, but obsessed by an inordinate need for and compulsion to gather love around her. Thus she continually insinuates herself into the affections of others:

> Cynthia had an unconscious power of fascination . . . A woman will have this charm not only over men but over her own sex; it cannot be defined, or rather it is so delicate a mixture of many gifts and qualities that it is impossible to decide on the proportions of each. Perhaps it is incompatible with very high principle. (p. 254)

Gaskell is not saying here that Cynthia is utterly cynical or manipulative, but rather that warm-hearted, witty, and vitally alive as she is, she is *not* a young woman of high principle—as she herself admits:

> I am not good, and I shall never be . . . . Perhaps I might be a heroine still, but I shall never be a good woman, I know . . . . I'm capable of a great jerk, an effort, and then a relaxation—but steady, every-day goodness is beyond me. I must be a moral kangaroo. (p. 258)

Having traced the careers of solid, stable Molly and the "moral kangaroo" Cynthia, we must proceed with the natural Victorian plot—marrying them off. For each the process is fraught with difficulty, pain, and crisis—and yet how differently each moves from the role of daughter to that of prospective wife: one with measure, increasing control, and ongoing affection; the other with irresponsible, near promiscuous disregard for the feelings of others. As might be expected, then, Cynthia—unloved but eternally needing love—receives in the course of the novel four proposals of marriage; Molly one, and at that a Cynthia-reject.

Cynthia not only engages herself to Molly's Roger (while Cynthia is still engaged to Preston) but she additionally trifles with the affections of still a third suitor, blushing Mr. Coxe. She explains:

> I knew he liked me, and I like to be liked; it's born in me to try to make everyone I come near fond of me. (p. 453)

Despite Cynthia's somewhat cavalier attitude, she is deeply wounded when Mr. Gibson accuses her of being "a flirt and a jilt" (p. 596–7).

"I've never lived with people with such a high standard of conduct before; and I don't quite know how to behave," she later moans (p. 456).

Cynthia tries to live up to the Gibson standards, one prerequisite of which is not to "use" people. Nevertheless on her visit to the Kirkpatrick family in London, she elicits still another proposal, this one from a distinguished young lawyer, Mr. Henderson.

But the largest crisis, and the one Cynthia most fears, is the presence and persistence of Mr. Preston. For Preston has in his possession letters from Cynthia which contain not only evidence of her previous passion for him but also numerous unkind references to her mother (herself rumored to have been involved at one time with Preston). Threatened almost daily by Preston, Cynthia cannot handle the crisis or possible scandal that will of necessity ensue. Thus she regresses, as it were, to a child; while Molly, adult and mature enacts a mother's role, rushes off to meet Mr. Preston in a hideaway spot (a compromising situation for any Victorian heroine) and demands the letters.

In this critical episode Molly emerges as a far tougher heroine than many critics have recognized—a sharp contrast again to Cynthia who is not really tough, only brittle and perhaps a bit jaded. For in the remarkably subtle delineation of character, Cynthia is seen as pathetically vulnerable and ultimately incapable of handling adult problems. Of course, once the letters are returned and the danger averted, Cynthia reverts to her old lightly affectionate ways, taking herself off for another jaunt to London.

Meanwhile Molly is forced to bear the brunt of a scandal rightfully belonging to Cynthia. For Molly has been spotted with Preston, and the town gossips have had a field day. Although in true Victorian fashion Molly's reputation is finally saved, her heart is near to breaking. For long months she has endured the pain of seeing the man she loves (Roger) engaged to someone who does not truly love him (Cynthia). This sad spectacle, combined with fresh tragedy in the Hamley family (Osborne Hamley's death), causes Molly's physical collapse, victim of that elusive Victorian malady which inevitably lays up even the goodliest and grandest of heroines. Characteristically, however, Molly, like the resilient character she is, turns knock into boost, acquiring during her illness a new maternal and adult sweetness.

Cynthia, having already broken off her engagement to Roger and accepted Mr. Henderson, spontaneously rushes home to the ill Molly, thereby and finally winning the approval of Mr. Gibson who warmly declares, "Sometimes one likes foolish people for their folly, better than wise people for their wisdom" (p. 640).

The novel's end was predictable from the beginning. Roger, recognizing at last the value and beauty of a grown-up Molly, asks Mr. Gibson for her hand, and chastizes himself for ever choosing Cynthia, a "false duessa," he calls her (p. 699). "Come, come," says Gibson, in a line which ultimately sums up Cynthia's character, "Cynthia isn't so bad as that. She's a very fascinating, faulty creature" (pp. 699–700).

Molly, one of the most admirable and lovable of Gaskell's heroines, has successfully passed from childhood to adulthood, not without pain or stress but always relying on her own inner resources, seeded and cultivated throughout her childhood by loving counselors, family, and friends—all mother-surrogates. No wonder that Molly lives, as we may infer, happily ever after.

The enigmatic Cynthia, one of Gaskell's greatest creations, also lives her life in what we may assume to be relative ease and happiness. That she achieves and sustains a suitable marriage, we may speculate, is due to the Gibson influence, coming though it did so late in her life. Yet we are left wondering about Cynthia, for Gaskell tells us that "often in after years, when it was too late, she wondered and strove to penetrate the inscrutable mystery of 'what would have been.'" (p. 602).

What would have been indeed! It appears that what *has* happened *had* to happen to both of these daughters. Their mothering was so different: in one case so helpful, in another so hopeless.

Mothers

Certainly it is mothering as a concept—and as an experience for both mother and daughter—that preoccupied Gaskell in her later years. Just before she began to write *Wives and Daughters*, she set aside a manuscript she had been working on, titled *Two Mothers*. *Wives and Daughters* gives us more than two—indeed a myriad of mothers: old and young, rich and poor, aristocratic and humble, natural and adoptive, strong and weak, English and French, caring and uncaring. The novel abounds in all types, acting in scenes that range from genuine pathos to the mildly even wildly amusing. For like Jane Austen to whom she is often compared (both, says one critic, "begin in excellence" and proceed to "greatness"),[6] Gaskell has the gift of gentle, sometimes devastating irony.

Let us focus for the moment on the novel's main mother, Hyacinth Clare Kirkpatrick Gibson, whose story runs parallel to that of her daughter Cynthia and her stepdaughter Molly, and whose life inter-penetrates theirs in ways that range from the merely annoying to the damaging and destructive.

"Superficial and flimsy" (p. 175) as she is, and as callously as she behaves toward her own daughter and later on toward her stepdaughter, Clare is—ultimately—a comic figure. Here to be sure are shades of Jane Austen, specifically of the flighty Mrs. Bennet: always good for a laugh, though she never understands the joke of which she has made herself the inadvertent butt. Mrs. Gibson is cut from the same mold: she is a woman with no insight into herself, no sensitivity toward others, little common decency, and certainly no common sense. She is steeped in platitudes and stereotypes. Can such a woman avoid recurrently casting herself as "fool"? And can we blame the long-neglected Cynthia for taking a grim pleasure in pricking the bubbles of her mother's self delusion? To see this dynamic in progress, we need only turn to the following scene: On returning suddenly from London where she has visited prosperous relatives and where her mother hopes she has snagged the successful lawyer, Mr. Henderson, Cynthia silently and coolly eats her lunch while Mrs. Gibson, beside herself with curiosity, plies her with questions:

> "And how is your aunt, how is her cold? And Helen, quite strong again? Margaretta as pretty as ever? The boys are at Harrow, I suppose? And my old favourite, Mr. Henderson?" She could not manage to slip in this last inquiry naturally; in spite of herself, there was a change in tone, an accent of eagerness. Cynthia did not reply on the instant; she poured herself out some water with great deliberation and then said—
>
> "My aunt is quite well; Helen is as strong as she ever is, and Margaretta very pretty. The boys are at Harrow, and I conclude that Mr. Henderson is enjoying his usual health, for he was to dine at my uncle's tomorrow." (p. 639–40)

And again—for examples are many—we watch Clare at the Charity Ball, trying to emulate the awesomely aristocratic Lady Cumnor, a direct descendant, surely, of Austen's Lady Catherine de Brough, and a match in arrogance, as we can judge from Lady Cumnor's disdainful remark: "I never think whether a land-agent is handsome or not. They don't belong to a class of people whose appearance I notice" (p. 128).

One of Gaskell's cleverest creations, Clare is "the acme of the ridiculous":[7] pretentious, affected, fuzzy-minded, patently incapable of coherent thought, utterly inept, and when thrust into the world on her own, pathetically helpless. "She went and married a poor curate," Lady

Cumnor disparagingly says of Clare in Chapter One:

> . . . and became a stupid Mrs. Kirkpatrick; but we always kept on
> calling her 'Clare.' And now he's dead, and left her a widow, and she
> is staying here; and we are racking our brains to find out some way of
> helping her to a livelihood without parting her from her child. (p. 42)

The truth is, of course, that Clare has already parted herself from
her child, shipped her out of the country to a school in France, an
unprecedented and callous move, given the provincial community and
social class in which Clare is rooted. Since London is viewed "as a
center of dissipation, a sort of moral pitch, which few could touch and
not be defiled" (pp. 500–01), imagine how much more distrustful the
Hollingford villagers are of a foreign country. When Mr. Gibson, in an
uncharacteristic but monumental act of misjudgment, solves Lady Cumnor's problem of what to do with "poor Clare" by marrying the witless
woman, we hear the gossipy Mrs. Goodenough (later referred to caustically as Mrs. Badenough) deplore the union for Molly's sake, if no
other:

> I don't like saying so to the doctor, but I shouldn't like having my
> daughter, if I was him, so cheek-by-jowl with a girl as was brought up
> in a country where Robespierre and Bonyparte was born. (pp. 465–66)

No matter that Mrs. Goodenough is reminded that "Bonyparte" was a
Corsican: she knows that "a travelled young lady" like Cynthia is "a
risk . . . a great risk" (p. 464).

In terms then of this "little straggling town" (p. 36) of Hollingford,
Clare has compromised her daughter irrevocably by sending her abroad.
This mother is so indifferent to her daughter's reputation and welfare,
however, that she remains oblivious to all dangers. Later she becomes
so oppressively interfering in her stepdaughter's affairs that Molly begins to feel at age nineteen, as Cynthia must long have felt, "too old to
feel pleasure, much less happiness again" (p. 485). That this mother
(described by Rosamund Lehmann as "just this side of wickedness")[8]
should be depicted with compassion is a tribute to Gaskell's "wise
sympathy towards those who are victims of their own nature and environment."[9] "In a censorious age," as Gaskell's recent biographer,
Winifred Gerin, points out, "Mrs. Gaskell was singularly uncenso-
rious."[10] Moreover, her charity extended beyond her fiction to her own
life as a motherless child and to the failure of her stepmother (to whom
Mrs. Gibson bears striking resemblance) to provide any compensating
warmth or affection. "Her sense of deprivation of maternal love in-

creased rather than diminished with the years," Gerin notes, citing as evidence a letter written when Gaskell was close to forty years of age: "I think no one but one so unfortunate as to be early motherless can enter into the craving one has after the lost mother."[11]

Only thirteen months old when her own mother died, Gaskell was obviously too young to remember her. Molly Gibson, on the other hand, has a few concrete and comforting memories of her own mother, memories which intermittently surface in her mind to serve as soothing balm to the abuses and obtuseness of her stepmother. We see an example of this when Mrs. Gibson, in her typically cloying manner, fusses over Molly's dark curly hair: "It's worse than ever," she complains at one point. "Can't you drench it in water to take those untidy twists and twirls out of it?":

> "It only makes it curl more and more when it gets dry," said Molly, sudden tears coming into her eyes as a recollection came before her like a picture seen long ago and forgotten for years—a young mother washing and dressing her little girl; placing the half-naked darling on her knee, and twining the wet rings of dark hair fondly round her fingers, and then, in an ecstasy of fondness, kissing the little curly head. (p. 496)

It is interesting to note that Gaskell provides Molly, but not Cynthia, with a very significant resource missing in Gaskell's own life—a continuing relationship with her father. Cynthia's father has of course died, a loss which her narcissistic mother views as an inconvenience and affront, for as Gaskell tells us, "whenever anything went wrong, poor Mr. Kirkpatrick was regretted and mourned over, nay almost blamed, as if, had he only given himself the trouble of living, he could have helped it" (p. 495). Gaskell's own father lived to marry again and raise a second family, leaving the infant Elizabeth to be raised by her mother's relatives and seeing her occasionally, only after she had already grown up. According to Gerin, Gaskell's lifelong sense of deprivation of maternal love "was further intensified . . . by the failure not only of the second Mrs. Stevenson but of her own father to fill the void."[12]

In sharp contrast, then, to both Gaskell herself and to the fatherless Cynthia, Molly during the first sixteen years of her life enjoys an idyllic relationship with her father, perhaps too idyllic in the eyes of the modern reader inclined to see in their closeness an Oedipal attachment. And rightly so, for it is only when he becomes aware that Molly has become a young woman attractive to his medical apprentice that Mr. Gibson seeks "a protectress and guide for his daughter" (p. 570). He has been as devoted a mother as any father can be, but he himself—as suggested earlier—suddenly feels inadequate to meet the demands and possible complications of romantic relationships. A young woman needs another woman at such times—a protec*tress* rather than protec*tor*. So Mr. Gibson views the situation and so we may infer Gaskell herself viewed it: that at certain stages of a young woman's development she must be in close touch with the female principle—or, to put it another way, beyond a certain point mothering can be provided only by a proper mother or mother-surrogate, i.e., by a woman.

"A young daughter is a great charge," Clare coyly points out to Mr. Gibson, "especially when there is only one parent to look after her" (p. 141). What Clare really means is "especially when the young daughter has no mother." The warning, of course, is fraught with irony, for Clare herself—though she is yearning to become Mrs. Gibson—is looking forward to finding a husband and provider who will relieve her of the necessity of earning her own living; Clare has no maternal impulses whatsoever. Nor does Molly need a stepmother at this time in her life. Gaskell has provided her with a whole constellation of substitute mothers, each of whom plays a distinctive and crucial role in her growing up. Indeed the novel itself, as Patricia Spacks aptly described it, is concerned with Molly Gibson's "learning how to be a woman—a hard lesson," as we see, but in Molly's case made easier by the "number of different models available to her."[13] In the absence of a real mother, Gaskell appears to be telling us, a young girl's needs may be met by surrogates—even as the beloved Aunt Lumb, in whose home Gaskell spent twelve years of her childhood, served as model and mother-surrogate after Gaskell's own mother had died. "Oh! there will never be one like her," Gaskell would later write of her aunt.[14]

The earliest of Molly's mother substitutes is described in Chapter One as "an unseen presence in the next room . . . a certain Betty whose slumbers must not be disturbed until six o'clock, when she awakened of herself 'as sure as clockwork' and left the household very little peace afterward" (p. 35). Faithful Betty, bustling and officious, sometimes (though always affectionately) called "the Dragon," feeds and clothes her little charge, ministering to her many needs, physical and emotional. Mrs. Gibson will later capriciously dismiss Betty from the household, causing Molly genuine grief but in no way damaging the character that has already been molded in part by this "live-in housekeeper." In truth Betty is more of a primal mother in the Gibson household, the earliest nurturing substitute for the natural mother who has died.

Nature and nurture: Gaskell builds the novel on the dynamic interaction between the two, tracing their mutual influence on the contrasting heroines. When Cynthia wistfully yet very wisely observes: "I don't think love for one's mother comes quite by nature" (p. 257), she is pointing an accusing finger at her own biologically natural mother, an "unnatural" mother in that she refuses to nurture her own offspring. No wonder that Cynthia will remain, even as an adult, forever dependent on the image reflected back from other people's eyes.

Molly provides a stark contrast, for she thrives under the loving ministrations of such dedicated mother substitutes as the comic Browning sisters and the sorrowful Mrs. Hamley of Hamley Hall (to cite only three main mother figures in the novel: there are many others too numerous to mention). The Miss Brownings are two fluttery maiden ladies, friends of the first Mrs. Gibson, who transfer their affection and loyalty to her daughter, "poor Mary's child," as they repeatedly refer to her, as if the phrase were a one-word synonym for Molly's proper name. When Miss Phoebe, the younger of the two (who once secretly envisioned herself as successor to "poor Mary" and thereby stepmother to Molly) tells her sister that, scandal is abroad: "Molly Gibson has lost her character" (p. 560), the elder Miss Browning soundly boxes her sister's ear (for sisters these two may be by nature, but mother and child they are by practice): "How dare you repeat such stories about poor Mary's child?" Miss Browning asks indignantly. When a neighbor assures her that the story is told on good authority, Miss Browning is crushed. "I'm very sorry I've lived till this day," she says, "it's a blow to me just as if I had heard of such goings on in my own flesh and blood" (p. 562).

In many ways these two Cranfordian ladies represent the gamut of motherly concern, ranging from the very tender to the equally tough. Tenderhearted Miss Phoebe treats socially ostracized Molly "with even more than her former tenderness" (p. 573) at a time when everyone else in town "was civil to her; no one was cordial" (p. 573). Tough-minded Miss Browning treats Molly "with chilling dignity and much reserve" (p. 573), grudgingly conceding to her father that "I shall always love Molly for her mother's sake" (p. 566), to which Mr. Gibson makes a loyal parental reply, "You ought to love her for her own" (p. 566). Miss Browning finally agrees: "I'll be her guardian angel, in spite of herself," she says (p. 493).

Yes, in spite of herself: Molly attracts guardian angels as if she were born to provide daughterhood to those in need. And none more needy than the frail invalid. Mrs. Hanley, mother of two sons and wife of Squire Hamley whose ancient lineage goes back to the Conquest—or in Mrs. Goodenough's claim . . . "there were Hamleys of Hamley afore the time of the pagans" (p. 72).

"The darling, I'm beginning to love her already," Mrs. Hamley tells Mr. Gibson when he proposes the visit that will remove Molly from the menacing Mr. Coxe. The two women will in fact become the greatest of friends, right up to the time of Mrs. Hamley's death, described by Gaskell with biblical simplicity: "The quiet waves closed over her, and her place knew her no more" (p. 256). Molly is bereaved, experiencing for a second time, in a sense, the loss of a well-loved mother-figure.

Molly will make frequent references to Mrs. Hamley in the months following her death, as with the Squire and his sons, all of them reiterating the fact that Mrs. Hamley had regarded Molly as a daughter. Interestingly, however, Molly never reverses the terms of the relationship by saying, "Mrs. Hamley was like a mother to me," for indeed though innocent and unworldly, Molly was a basically secure young woman, a considerable person in her own right, by the time her path crossed that of the Hamleys. Thus she was able to minister to the gentle invalid with countless acts of kindness and service. "You're a blessing to mothers, child," Mrs. Hamley tells Molly gratefully (p. 118). Mrs. Hamley will try to reciprocate Molly's kindness by providing motherly counsel when she sees how upset Molly is about her father's remarriage:

> Now, dear child, tell me all; it's no breach of confidence, for I shan't mention it again, and I shan't be here long. How does it all go on—the new mother, the good resolutions? Let me help you if I can. I think with a girl I could have been of use . . . (p. 226)

But Molly maintains a stoic silence; out of loyalty to her father she will not speak her sorrow. Only once, when Mr. Gibson had first announced his intentions, had Molly broken down, thrown herself like a child on Mrs. Hamley's maternal breast and sobbed (p. 154).

In this essay, we have dealt only with major mothers and daughters in *Wives and Daughters*, not even mentioning the relationship of minor characters, nor such fascinating aberrations as the reversal within the Cumnor family in which three sensible daughters serve as "keepers," as it were, of their persistently petulant and childlike mother. Nor have we indicated the larger patterns and deeper intricacies of other family relationships explored in this inexhaustible novel: mother-father, father-son, husband-wife, brother-brother, brother-sister, grandmother-grand-child, and so forth—and all this set against the still larger and equally intricate social and political structure of a community barely beginning to bestir itself out of its provincial comforts and complacencies.

For if the individual child must eventually become his or her own parent, so must adults collectively become determiners of their own destiny. The novel—set in the 1820s—is a retrospective view. Times are changing within the years spanned by the novel itself; they had already changed radically by the year 1865 when Gaskell was writing it. Who changes and grows? And who fixates at the child's level, unable to accept the responsibilities—personal and social—of adulthood? There are no easy or final answers, but Gaskell certainly suggests that early nurturing and training, a goodly dose of mothering in particular—whether from mother herself or from mother-surrogates—are crucial determiners. In the body of her work Gaskell has given us a vision of struggling humanity seeking to make the most of itself. That not every-one can do so is understood and—in the compassionate view of Gas-kell—forgiven. "Poor old Clare" (p. 399), as even Clare jokingly refers to herself, pointing as most jokes do, to a kernel of sober truth. Really, as the old song puts it, she is more to be pitied than censured. Indeed it is significant, as Gaskell tells us, that Molly sympathizes with her father's plight in having such a wife as Clare and at the same time pities Clare herself, "feeling acutely for both and certainly more than Mrs. Gibson felt for herself" (p. 458).

As for the two daughters, flawed Cynthia and nearly flawless Molly, Gaskell does not polarize here either. On the contrary, as Gerin con-cludes, "Mrs. Gaskell seems prepared to say that even in very lovable girls there can, given her upbringing, lurk a Cynthia."[15] One might add that, given the proper "mothering," within even a Cynthia can lurk a Molly, too.

Notes
[1] Elizabeth Gaskell, *Wives and Daughters* (Harmondsworth: Penguin Books, 1969), p. 616. Future references to this edition will be made parenthetically within the text.
[2] Edgar Wright, *Mrs. Gaskell: The Basis for Reassessment* (London: Oxford University Press, 1965), p. 55.
[3] Elaine Showalter, *A Literature of Their Own* (Princeton: Princeton University Press, 1977), p. 71.
[4] Winifred Gerin, *Elizabeth Gaskell: A Biography* (Oxford: The Clarendon Press, 1976), p. 288.

5 Wright, p. 223.

6 W. A. Craik, *Elizabeth Gaskell and the English Provincial Novel* (London: Methuen, 1975), p. 266.

7 A. B. Hopkins, *Elizabeth Gaskell: Her Life and Work* (London: John Lehmann, 1952), p. 283.

8 Rosamund Lehmann, "Introduction," *Wives and Daughters* (London: John Lehmann, 1948), p. 14.

9 Craik, p. 25.

10 Gerin, p. 276.

11 Ibid., p. 276.

12 Ibid., p. 17.

13 Patricia Meyer Spacks, *The Female Imagination* (New York: Avon Books, 1976), p. 113.

14 Gerin, p. 10.

15 Ibid., p. 276.

Part Three
COLUMBIA'S DAUGHTERS

Introduction

Christopher Columbus may have discovered the continent, but it was Columbia, the feminine personification of the new United States, who perpetuated it. The popular fiction written after the American Revolution was invariably dedicated to the "Daughters of United Columbia," those daughters who would become mothers of the next generations of Americans. Professor Cathy N. Davidson states that the popular fiction, specifically what we now call "sentimental fiction," was primarily instructive, a "warning to a rootless young nation." Columbia's daughters were to be respectable, unlike their Mother England, that "profligate lady, the matron turned madam," whom we see in Revolutionary political cartoons.

Like the English heroine of women's fiction, the American daughter was typically motherless: "unguided, uneducated, unprotected, but also unencumbered." But the message of her motherlessness is different. Whereas the British daughter succeeds on her own (if only to become a mother herself), America's motherless daughters were unable to "establish themselves as stable individuals or capable mothers." Many died in childbirth, bearing daughters of questionable paternity. But if the motherless daughter symbolized America's uncertainty as a nation, the good Republican mother with her pure, chaste daughter became a national icon, a new Madonna and Child. She affirmed the "powers of pious procreation" in a nation unsure of its own legitimacy. Thus, it is the fate of the daughter (the new nation), not the missing mother (Great Britain) that preoccupied the popular novelist.

It is not a far jump from the absent mother to mother as servant, another American prototype. Professor Barbara Ann Clarke Mossberg describes the mother of Emily Dickinson, a typical midnineteenth-century American mother, a "servant of her family . . . dominated, disregarded, weak, passive, dull, occupied with petty charity and housework, and conventionally pious." When she died, her death caused barely a "ripple."

Because Dickinson's mother did not instruct, the daughter, as poet, omits her from her work, mocks her, and, finally, reconstructs her. But the daughter feels the loss. The product of a nonnurturing household, she ends up "mother-hungry." Sleuthing in letters and poems for psycholinguistic clues, Mossberg finds food imagery which suggests the ways Emily Dickinson's poetry expresses the needs of the hungry, unsatisfied, unnurtured daughter.

Dickinson, like Harriet Martineau, is here described as having no adequate mother-models and is, therefore, "locked by default into a limbo of perpetual daughterhood." Where the English Victorian daughters suffered from the same destiny as their fictional mothers, Mossberg states, "Dickinson is forced to dispossess herself of her biological mother in order to circumvent her mother's destiny."

In the novels of Ellen Glasgow, we continue to see the mother who exists mostly as a shadow cast over her daughter's promise. Professor Linda W. Wagner notes that "the chief role of these sanctified wives and mothers . . . is to provide stability for their less complacent daughters. . . . They are never role models; they serve rather as specters of the expected female."

Like the earlier American foremothers of our first popular literature, the women in Glasgow's fiction have but one choice available to them—marriage. Spinsterhood is a chasm, and failed marriage, says Wagner, is desolation and even disaster: "desperate acceptance of desolation . . . somehow more tragic than death or willed violence." In Glasgow's books, the daughters try to free themselves from the romantic notions about life and love that their mothers uphold. The novelist, whose works have been too long ignored, ultimately justifies the daughters' yearnings for a different way.

"The strained relations between mothers and daughters is one of Edith Wharton's persistent themes in her late novels," says Ms. Adeline Tintner. Tintner observes that the later books of Wharton should be reevaluated in terms of that intense relationship. The shadowy advisor or the perfect mother gives way to the woman of ambiguous role who even competes with her daughter for the same lover. Both mother and daughter struggle for a place in society or against society.

Wharton's later novels, written after World War I, still were influenced by the British nineteenth-century writer Grace Aguilar. Aguilar's books were among the many "how to's"—how to be the perfect mother, how to form the daughter. These guide books descend from the Renaissance advice tracts. What Wharton does in writing a novel dedicated to Aguilar, even with the same title—*The Mother's Recompense*—is to negate that earlier teaching. There are no "how to's." The mother must create her own role separated from marriage and mothering. And so must the daughter.

In this new age, says Tintner, Wharton examined the mother-daughter relationship as the "most dramatic as well as the most personally touching representation" of the changing roles of women. But, as we see in Wharton's novels, the freedom of the daughter was sometimes earned at the expense of the mother. Shackled by outworn concepts of the proper maiden and the married matron, Columbia's daughters and Society's mothers often achieved only an impasse.

E.M.B.
C.N.D.

10

Mothers and Daughters in the Fiction of the New Republic

> Compared with maternal influence, the combined authority of laws and armies and public sentiment are little things.
>
> —*Parent's Magazine* (October, 1840)

One lesson the contemporary mother should teach her daughter is that throughout history there have been women dedicated to bettering the lot of their sisters. In America, for example, the first significant women's movement began soon after the nation itself established its independence. At that time, a number of prominent women such as Abigail Adams, Eliza Southgate, and Judith Sargent Murray advocated better female education and women's greater "independence" in both public and domestic arenas. Their arguments bore some fruit. New Jersey women were briefly enfranchised after the Revolution. Women began to speak up in church and civic meetings. In New England, women's academies were founded in such numbers that Murray could enthusiastically proclaim, "I expect to see our young women forming a new era in female history."[1] A language of liberation also began to appear. Thus, in terms remarkably contemporary, an anonymous poet wrote in "Rights of Women, by a Lady," published in *The Philadelphia Minerva* of October 17, 1795:

> Man boasts the noble cause
> Nor yields supine to laws
> Tyrants ordain;

Author's Note: I wish to thank the Newberry Library for awarding me a Resident Fellowship which allowed me to complete the research for this study. An earlier version of this paper was presented at the Canadian Association of American Studies on October 27, 1978, in Montreal.

> Let Woman have a share
> Nor yield to slavish fear,
> Her equal rights declare,
> And Well Maintain.

However, just as the later suffragist movement largely ended after women were granted the vote but long before they achieved real political equality, the late eighteenth-century movement also declined far short of its highest goals. "Wollstonecraftism," as it was often called in the last decades of the eighteenth century, passed away soon after Mary Wollstonecraft herself died. Serious debate about the political role and status of women gave way to a somewhat more restrictive "cult of domesticity." But even cloistered physically and psychologically within their homes, women still managed to communicate with other women. The most public form of their communication was the sentimental novel. Written frequently by women, primarily for women, and always about women, the sentimental tales of America's late eighteenth and early nineteenth centuries show how a pervasive rhetoric of motherhood was conjoined with a submerged language of feminism. These novels themselves therefore partially demonstrate the manner in which the political zeal of our founding mothers could be transformed into the quieter female collectivity of their nineteenth-century daughters and granddaughters—who, of course, were to be the mothers and grand-mothers of suffragists.[2]

Many factors drew early nineteenth-century women away from the political arena and consigned them to the narrower circle of their private homes. One of the more obvious influences was the change in the intellectual climate of the time. In both England and the new United States, political thinkers substantially renounced radical theories after France fell into a chaos that ostensibly justified reactionary views. Proponents of political reform who had advocated female rights in the 1770s and 1780s quickly retrenched and returned to a more conservative view of woman.[3] Furthermore, retrenchment was cloaked in a new and particularly effective rhetoric, a rhetoric that has persisted into our own time. I refer now to the language of "Motherhood," the insistence that woman, rather than man, was intellectually, spiritually, and emotionally fitted for parenthood. This position reversed earlier denigrations of women. Long after the Middle Ages—in Puritan America, for example, and even in post-Revolutionary France—the "second sex" was still seen as innately licentious, impulsive, and irrational. Women were suppos-edly men's intellectual and moral inferiors and were not to be trusted with such a crucial task as raising the children. As Ruth H. Bloch has amply documented, the vast majority of Puritan and neo-Puritan tracts on child rearing emphasized the responsibility of the father, not the mother. But by the 1800s in America, such tracts addressed the mother. The wife was now deemed "innately" capable and solely responsible for rearing the next generation for life in the new Republic.[4]

This novel concept of motherhood not only removed women from public life, it also rationalized that removal. If mothers were the true force behind the nation, were not women's attempts toward political emancipation and legal reform trivial and irrelevant? Why worry about a few votes when you already run the country? The new theory was convenient in another way too. After the Revolution, rapid changes in the American economy more and more took the father into the business world. But he could justify leaving his family because the responsibility for tending the family, as opposed to supporting it, had been passed on to his wife. She had been so definitively placed within the home that modern proponents of that nineteenth-century dicta, "Woman's Place is in the Home," can insist that she has been housed there eternally.

Even radical thinkers, including Mary Wollstonecraft herself, embraced the ideal of motherhood. For one thing, it did give women more credit than did the older paternalistic theories of parenting. Furthermore, the new rhetoric particularly allowed middle-class women some status. Despite changes in labor patterns, the wife still had one most significant role to play. No longer burdened with farm chores or cottage industries, the women of the middle class could become the moral and intellectual tutors of small children. Moreover, the rising middle class required tokens of its newly achieved status. This task also was generally assumed by the wife, for the husband was already fully occupied in the world of commerce. One consequence of both factors was the demand for genteel female education. A mother needed to be literate in order to educate her children; a wife needed to be cultured to prove her husband's affluence.

By the early nineteenth century, then, some American women had made definite gains, a consideration that was both a tribute to and an argument against the early equalitarian feminists. The ideal woman— always a wife—was better educated, hyperbolically respected, and somewhat sovereign within her limited sphere. She also had more leisure time than previously and needed some kind of daytime diversion. The sentimental novel filled that purpose, so much so that it soon became the primary literary form in the new nation. In fact, "the first American novel," *The Power of Sympathy* (1789) was a sentimental novel as were approximately two-thirds of the some two hundred tales that were published in America during the succeeding thirty years.[5] These novels were the soap operas and the Harlequin romances of their time.

They were also something more. As I shall subsequently argue, sentimental novels, for all their swoons and sighs, spoke more directly to the real concerns and justifiable fears of their readers than do contemporary equivalents, which are often little more than exercises in fantasy and escape. What especially distinguishes these early novels is their unremitting concern with the process of female generation. There is almost an obsession with the proper (and improper) means by which a daughter might pass into motherhood. Such was not only a theme and focus in this fiction, it was also its *raison d'être*. Literally dozens of these books were dedicated to the "Daughters of United Columbia." Prefatory remarks regularly assured the female reader that what she read would educate her socially and morally, if not intellectually, and would prepare her for the crucial function she was to fulfill.

Although sentimental novels were produced by writers whose politics varied widely, the social views promulgated in the genre as a whole might best be termed ambivalently conservative. The Prefaces were unquestionably conservative, advocating nothing more revolutionary than feminine chastity and maternal propriety. But by implication the novels themselves affirmed that women and woman's sphere were at least worthy subjects for literature. Furthermore, the heroines, for all their well-timed swoons, often acted independently and capably overcame seemingly superior adversaries, who were usually male. More to the point, by suggesting that society, not frail womanhood, was to blame for social inequities, numerous sentimental fictions covertly attacked the very morality editorally espoused. Prefatory pieties may, indeed, have been intended largely to placate various censors who found women's novels inherently suspect.[6] In fact, the rewards and punishments doled out at the end (in seeming fulfillment of prefatory promises about "virtue being rewarded" and so forth) did not always erase a different picture which often emerged from the story itself. Stripped of their moral rhetoric, these books could sometimes elaborate eloquently upon the social, economic, and legal plight of the single woman—a real problem after frontier expansionism and the Revolutionary War depleted the male population in New England cities and towns.[7] The spector of unwanted pregnancy, for example, loomed large in the books just as it did in a society that, unlike French society of the same time, simply did not condone birth control but did condone the conduct of the "rake." The horrors of childbirth, the stigma of illegitimacy, and the economic helplessness of the unwed mother were all overworked plot devices in sentimental fiction. Such bugaboos, however, were not foreign to the lives of women during America's first century as a nation.

The sentimental novel in its bleaker aspects could suggest the dark possibilities of life for America's potential mothers. But these same novels also reflected the new romantic obsession with motherhood. Insuring the continuation of a nation newly born and affirming the powers of pious procreation in a country only too recently devastated by a revolutionary war, the mother became almost a national symbol. In the fiction of the time, the virgin as heroine was often, paradoxically, metamorphosed into the mother as icon. A good daughter of the Republic would refuse to be swayed by the blandishments of a seducer who, like Montraville in the nation's first best-seller, *Charlotte Temple* (1794), was typically aristocratic and generally British (either by birth or aspiration). Instead, she would settle for the simpler homespun pleasures of connubial bliss and maternal satisfaction. Motherhood was thus meted out as both the reward for virtue and the punishment for vice.

The equation between domestic felicity and national destiny could be closely drawn. In certain novels of the early Republic, the transformation of man and woman into husband and wife and thus father and mother of future Americans corresponds implicitly and explicitly with the uniting of states into a flourishing new nation. Thus in Jessee Lynch Holman's *The Prisoners of Niagara, or Errors of Education* (1810) the marriage of heroine and hero occurs at the same time that a treaty is signed assuring America's independence as a nation. Or in Royall Tyler's *The Algerine Captive* (1797), a picaresque novel with a sentimental ending, the hero lectures the reader on the necessity of "uniting" all the diverse elements in the country to form a strong "United States" immediately after promising to "unite himself" in matrimony to an amiable and chaste wife.[8]

The reverse of the proper marriage was the improper affair. And here too a major theme in sentimental novels, the problem of illegitimacy, had an obvious social relevance. In a nation unsure of its own birthright, questions of parentage could well be asked. A country that had only recently broken from a reviled mother-country might wonder who the real mother was, England or the revolution? There was surely a covert nationalistic appeal in such books as Susanna Haswell Rowson's *The Fille de Chambre* (1794), the anonymous *Moreland Vale* (1801), or

Rebecca Rush's *Kelroy* (1812), all of which featured an evil or profligate mother-figure whose machinations the daughter had to actively resist. It is also of some possible psychosocial significance that there are dozens of sentimental novels in which the heroine's mother is killed off before the daughter reaches maturity, sometimes even before the first page of the novel. A motherless daughter is unguided, uneducated, unprotected, but also unencumbered. While a few unmothered daughters, such as Rachel in Rowson's *Reuben and Rachel* (1798) or Rosa in the anonymous 1810 novel of the same title, managed to survive a series of traumatic trials, many others—such as the heroines of *The Power of Sympathy* (1789), *The Hapless Orphan; or Innocent Victim of Revenge* (1793), *Amelia; or, The Faithless Briton* (1798), and *Lucinda, or the Mountain Mourner* (1807)—were unable to establish themselves as stable individuals or capable mothers. Of course, many novels written by women and about women in nineteenth-century America and England also featured motherless heroines, but in the later novels the motherless daughter succeeds alone. That is not the case in the fiction of the early Republic. These novels, on one level, seem to be a warning to a rootless young nation.

The equation of the heroines of popular fiction with the nation is also demonstrated by a pervasive iconography. In any number of eighteenth-century American political cartoons, England was portrayed as a profligate lady, the matron turned madam.[9] More crudely, she was the bitch mindless of her whelps, and thus the equivalent of such characters as the British Clara in Rowson's *Trials of the Heart* (1795) who would rather have affairs with young men than tend her children. Other characters like Mrs. T———n in Gilbert Imlay's *The Emigrants, or The History of an Expatriated Family* (1793) also exemplified Old World corruptness, as was especially indicated by that mother's lax rearing of her equally corrupt daughter, Mary.[10] In contrast to popular images of England as the bad mother, we see America as the virginal Liberty—the young, lovely "Daughter of Columbia," pictured in chaste white flowing robes, pure but also rather vulnerable, the archetypal sentimental heroine and an incongruously desexualized bearer of the American nation. Such a figure equally represented the new nation, the innocent heroine of the sentimental tale, and Columbia's daughters to whom those books were often dedicated—the female reader who was to learn from the books how her virtue could be rewarded by marriage, her weakness punished by pregnancy, abandonment, or death. As Linda K. Kerber has argued in detail, the pure and chaste Republican Mother symbolised the new country.[11] As the sentimental novel stressed, the daughter had to be carefully instructed in order to fill her maternal role, for more was at stake than the heroine's personal happiness. Even as the epigraph to this essay attests, there was an increasing emphasis placed on the relationship between the individual woman's virtue and the well-being of the nation. As young ladies of the time were dubiously told:

> The solidity and stability of the liberties of your country rest with you; since Liberty is never sure, 'till Virtue reigns triumphant . . . it rests with you to make this retreat [from European values] doubly peaceful, doubly happy, by banishing . . . those crimes and corruptions, which have never yet failed of giving rise to tyranny, or anarchy. While you thus keep our country virtuous, you maintain its independence.[12]

The virtuous woman was an icon in America's early years. But the American sentimental version of the Madonna and Child was mother and daughter, not mother and son. Although a few early novels do center on mothers and sons—Samuel Woodworth's *The Champions of Freedom, or the Mysterious Chief* (1816) and "Guy Mannering's" *Rosalvo Delmonmort* (1818), come immediately to mind—most sentimental novels concern themselves with the female members of the family.[13] Also interesting, in most of the novels the focus is on the daughter as potential mother and not on the woman who is already the actual biological mother. Except for a few works such as Ann Eliza Bleecker's *The History of Maria Kittle* (1793) or Samuel Relf's *Infidelity, or the Victims of Sentiment* (1797), sentimental books tell of the daughter's growth from late adolescence into adulthood. The mother can serve as a foil or a model, but it is the daughter's fate which holds our attention.

The pattern can clearly be seen in Hannah Webster Foster's best-selling novel, *The Coquette; or, the History of Eliza Wharton* (1797).[14] In this novel, the protagonist's mother tries to raise her daughter properly to prepare her for wifehood and motherhood. But Eliza proclaims that, for a while, she must sow her "wild oats" (Letter 34). She soon reaps the predictable harvest: seduction, abandonment, the stillborn delivery of a child, death in childbirth. Eliza's mother was right. Yet her reward for being right, for being a good mother, is the death of her daughter. The sin of the daughter is visited not only on her mother but on her stillborn child too. With the devastation of three generations, this tale of seduction becomes an effective warning to successive female generations about the necessary consequences of improper generation. Mother and daughter were conjoined in the plot of the book and the moral it would teach, just as were the many mothers and daughters who together read these tales and received from them their primary literary education.[15]

The Coquette, however, can also illustrate the ambivalence many American women felt during the transitional years following the Revolutionary War. Those women who read, on the one hand, reformers like Mary Wollstonecroft, William Godwin, Thomas Paine, and Mary Hays, and, on the other, such conservative writers as James Fordyce, William Beloe, Elizabeth Hamilton, and Hannah More, could well be uncertain of where they stood, as were many others in reactionary, post-Revolutionary American society.[16] In *The Coquette*, we have, for example, a clear case of vice being punished—a conventional proof of the conventional morality. But Foster also capably portrays a female protagonist who engages our sympathies despite her actions, largely because she has no other viable alternatives. She must drift into a complacent marriage to the insufferably boring Reverend Boyer, or live alone. Foster takes pains to show that this second alternative, the life of the single woman, is hardly an enviable one. Eliza, unwed at thirty-seven years of age, finds herself a social misfit, begins to think of herself as an outcast, and, after losing all self-respect, finally allows herself to be seduced by Major Sanford—who, according to type, is a would-be aristocrat and a total misogynist. Eliza and her mother suffer, partly because of the daughter's fall. Yet some of the blame surely lies elsewhere. The novel depicts a society that educates one-half of its population only in "coquettry" and other such frivolous, unproductive behavior. The novel demonstrates the unfair workings of the double standard. Eliza Wharton's story—a story historically founded—both confirms a conservative ethos and also questions it.

The genre as a whole exhibits the same ambivalence. Again and again sentimental novels claim to illustrate the disastrous, and supposedly fully deserved, consequences of the loss of chastity. But by the very way in which these novels elicit sympathy for their female protagonists, they also make it impossible for the reader to condemn completely those imperfect "daughters of Columbia" who do finally succumb to temptation. A similar ambivalence is seen in the way sentimental fictions regularly argue for better female education. The guilty heroine should be partly exonerated by virtue of her inexperience. Yet she cannot be at all forgiven, for her fate must provide vicarious experience for the reader—must teach the reader the lesson the hapless heroine learns too late. Accordingly, except in a few novels like William

Hill Brown's satirical *Ira and Isabella; or the Natural Children* (1807) where the seductress Lucinda lives happily ever after or Leonora Sansay's more serious *Laura* (1807) where a "fallen woman" is allowed to rise again (after watching her lover die in her arms and experiencing temporary insanity), almost all sentimental tales plead extenuating circumstances but then fully insist on the "evil consequences of seduction"— for the woman.

Yet what was the alternative? As implausible as these books may seem to the modern reader, they were realistic enough to ring true for the majority of readers of the time. Critics today rightly mock the sensationalism of the plots and the extravagance of the emotions the characters exhibit, but who can deny that the unwed mother probably would have been abandoned by her family, her church, and her society? "The Female Advocate" (1801) could argue that women should have all the rights allowed to men. But even tentative claims for sexual equality were far too extreme for early nineteenth-century Americans and elicited general ridicule.[17] The average middle-class New England woman lived her life to be married and to raise a family. She knew very well that her chastity would be an important factor in finding a husband. The sentimental tale, for all its histrionics, was not so far removed from the daily life of many American women.

Certainly the case of Mary Wollstonecraft demonstrated the way in which, for all its dire predictions regarding the necessary consequences of vice, the sentimental novel still imitated life, which is to say that Wollstonecraft's life finally imitated sentimental fiction. Wollstonecraft had been widely read in America. *A Vindication of the Rights of Woman* (1792) went through two American editions by 1794 and "Wollstonecraftism" had become a standard term for even the American feminist movement of the time. But Godwin's publication of Wollstonecraft's memoirs—which appeared in the United States as *Memoirs of Mary Wollstonecraft, Author of "A Vindication of the Rights of Woman" (1799)*— discredited Wollstonecraft as a person and a thinker, dealt a severe blow to feminism, and, in a peculiar way, vindicated the vision of the most reactionary of the sentimental tales, such as Helena Wells's *Constantia Neville; or The West Indian* (1800), Sarah Wood's *Dorval, or the Speculator* (1801), and Benjamin Silliman's *Letters of Shahcoolen, a Hindu Philosopher, Residing in Philadelphia* (1802), all of which attacked Wollstonecraft directly and by name. Various commentators have noted the dismay that many readers felt when they read the personal history of the admired advocate of female rights.[18] That dismay was justified. After the publication of the *Memoirs*, proponents of the "Rights of Woman" were generally seen as "shameless" advocates of free love—just like Mary Wollstonecraft. After 1800, the term "Wollstonecraftism" was used with derision. But I would suggest that Wollstonecraft's biography struck another chord in the average, middle-class reader. For anyone who wavered on the women's rights issue, the *Memoirs* must have seemed proof that women really did not have any options and that "Motherhood," after all, was at least a secure and socially respected occupation.

Wollstonecraft herself became, for readers of sentimental fiction, simply another sentimental heroine, a woman who had loved badly and lost. Like many a fictional protagonist on the downward path to disgrace, Wollstonecraft had left her mother's side and aspired to freer actions. She fit other patterns too. Like the heroine of *Amelia; or, The Faithless Briton* (1798), Wollstonecraft not only bore a child out of wedlock but tried to kill herself (twice) when the lover—who, incidentally, was Gilbert Imlay, the American sentimental novelist—abandoned both mother and daughter. Saved from suicide and temporary insanity, Wollstonecraft went to live with another man. Here there was some departure from the standard formula—for Godwin married Wollstonecraft after conceiving a child with her and in the *Memoirs* painted a rosy (although apparently false) picture of their life together. However, the *Memoirs* ran true to type again when Wollstonecraft—like Amelia Blyfield, like Eliza Wharton, like Charlotte Temple, and like a whole host of other major and minor characters in sentimental plots—died in childbirth, bearing the child conceived outside of matrimony. Furthermore, another generation would see that Wollstonecraft's sentimental story did not end with her death but with the suicide of her daughter, Fanny Imlay. One is reminded not only of *The Coquette* but also of the sequel to *Charlotte Temple, Charlotte's Daughter* (1828), in which seemingly because of her illegitimate birth, Lucy Blakeney (the product of the illicit relationship between Charlotte and Montraville) is denied any chance of personal happiness. But at least Charlotte's daughter was ultimately allowed a life of self-denial, an existence dedicated solely to serving others. Fanny Imlay's career was not even that fortunate. She took her own life in 1816, leaving only a note to the world in which she described herself as "one whose birth was unfortunate"—as sentimental an epilogue to a sentimental tale as anything a Mrs. Rowson or a Mrs. Foster could ever conceive.[19]

Mary Wollstonecraft, as a philosopher and a feminist, argued for radical revisions in the society of the time. As merely another fallen woman, her life seemed mostly a depressing vindication of the status quo. If even a brilliant activist for women's rights faced the various "consequences of seduction"—heartache, abandonment, temporary insanity, attempted suicide, death in childbirth, infamy, and the suicide of an illegitimate daughter—how could the average middle-class wife hope for a different life? Maybe the sentimental formula was right after all. At least as the glorified, be-pedestalled, pre-Victorian "MOTHER" a woman earned a modicum of respect—more than was paid the poor, dead namesake of "Wollstonecraftism."

The theme of the fallen woman was, I would suggest, so prevalent in America's first popular fiction precisely because it was so true. At a time when women had neither control over their own bodies nor the vocational skills to allow them to exist independently (as single women or mothers raising children alone), "seduction" was to be feared. The good mother warned her daughter against it—lest her daughter share the fate of so many fictional heroines. But as Helen Waite Papashvily has argued, *Lucinda* (1807) by Mrs. P. D. Manvill, was one of the last books in early America to center on the consequences of seduction. After the first decades of the nineteenth century, the fallen woman had a relatively minor role in American fiction (with Hester Prynne serving as one notable exception to that general rule).[20] The obsessive interest in the daughter's process of becoming a mother gave way to more obvious fantasies of female adventure. Perhaps coincidentally, after about 1810 relatively few women publicly championed "women's rights," as Wollstonecraft and other eighteenth-century feminists would have used the term. With noted exceptions such as Margaret Fuller, most women accepted the notion that woman's sphere was the home—and the first woman's *movement* was but a memory.

The public cry for women's political rights would not be heard again for another generation when the suffragists would assert women's claims to political and social equality. Significantly, it was also in the late nineteenth century, coincident with the height of the second women's movement, that the fallen woman reappeared as a major literary character. In the popular literature of the late nineteenth century and especially in the "working girl" novels of writers like "Bertha M. Clay" or Laura Jean Libbey, seduction again was the issue and death the price for licentiousness. Even more serious fiction—*The Awakening, Sister Carrie, Maggie*—would concern itself with the price a woman paid (or did not pay) for her lost "virtue." The rhetoric may have changed in the intervening years (as it has in our own decade, with *Fear of Flying* or *Looking for Mr. Goodbar*) but the focus once more was woman's sexuality, her procreative powers, her initiation into maturity, her path to motherhood: anatomy as destiny.

It is as if each time women have argued for equality in America, politics has been reduced to biology and motherhood offered as the consolation prize. The first women's movement did not take full apprizal of this situation. Mary Wollstonecraft insisted on living her life as an intellectually and sexually free woman, but, at the same time, she praised motherhood as woman's highest goal and abhorred birth control. As we have seen, in her personal life she had to face the same degradations with which sentimental heroines unsuccessfully contended and she died no differently than did a hundred of those heroines. Of course, in Kate Chopin's *The Awakening* (1899), Edna Pontellier, a feminist heroine of the suffragist era, goes to a self-inflicted death, at least partly to solve the conflicting claims of motherhood on the one hand and her desire for fuller self-expression on the other. It is not surprising, in view of such a history, that the contemporary women's movement has sought to resolve this problem passed down to us from America's earliest novelists. By attempting to *reinvolve* fathers in parenthood, by insisting that women should be in control of their own bodies, and by looking again at the special relationship that does bind mother to daughter and daughter to mother, the contemporary feminist movement has attempted to solve a dilemma that our nation's founding mothers could pose but could not answer. We are our mothers' daughters, and one torch that has come down to us from our revolutionary foremothers is not the torch of liberty but the continuing task of finding possible modes of liberty.

Notes

[1] Judith Sargent Murray, *The Gleaner: A Miscellaneous Production by "Constantia"* (Boston, 1798), III, 189.

[2] Many scholars in recent years have debated whether the nineteenth-century emphasis on domesticity meant an elevation or a devaluation of woman's status. For a concise summary of the various arguments, see Nancy F. Cott, *The Bonds of Womanhood: "Woman's Sphere" in New England, 1780–1835* (New Haven, 1977), pp. 197–206.

[3] Throughout *The Life and Death of Mary Wollstonecraft* (New York, 1974), Claire Tomalin stresses the changing political climate in late eighteenth-century England, France, and the United States. See especially chapters 13 and 19.

[4] "American Feminine Ideals in Transition: The Rise of the Moral Mother, 1785–1815," *Feminist Studies*, 4, no. 2 (1978), 101–26.

[5] Much debate has surrounded the title, "first American novel," but in recent years the honor has gone to *The Power of Sympathy* which was written by a native born American,

in America, and about America. William S. Kable, in his edition of *The Power of Sympathy* (Columbus, Ohio, 1969), xi–xvii, lists other major contenders.

[6] Cf. G. Harrison Orians, "Censure of Fiction in American Romances and Magazines, 1789–1810," *PMLA*, 52 (1937), 195–214.

[7] Some of the most reliable census information is presented and analyzed by Alexander Keyssar, "Widowhood in Eighteenth-century Massachusetts: A Problem in the History of the Family," *Perspectives in American History*, 8 (1974), 83–119.

[8] Tyler uses different forms of the verb "to unite" four times on the last page of *The Algerine Captive; or, The Life and Adventures of Doctor Updike Underhill* (Walpole, N. H., 1797). The final sentence of the book is, "BY UNITING WE STAND, BY DIVIDING WE FALL."

[9] Philip Young, in *Revolutionary Ladies* (New York, 1977), pp. 175ff., notes that British cartoonists during the war pictured the colonies as a very scantily dressed (often topless) young white woman. Of course, American cartoonists portrayed England as the "loose" woman—considerably older and more obviously promiscuous than the women portrayed in the English cartoons. Young also notes that, after the War, Americans began to picture their country as a somewhat older woman—more maternal, less vulnerable than the pre-Revolutionary "Liberty."

[10] See Henri Petter, *The Early American Novel* (Columbus, Ohio, 1971), pp. 216–17.

[11] "Daughters of Columbia: Educating Women for the Republic, 1787–1805," in *Hofstadter Aegis*, ed. Eric L. McKitrick and Stanley M. Elkins (New York, 1974), pp. 36–59; and "The Republican Mother: Women and the Enlightenment—An American Perspective," *American Quarterly*, 28 (1976), 187–205.

[12] A commencement address delivered at Columbia College, this speech was published as "Female Influence" in *New York Magazine* (May 1795), 301–5. A portion of the speech is quoted in Kerber, "Daughters of Columbia," p. 57.

[13] *Rosalvo Delmonmort* is a rarity in that its protagonist is an illegitimate *son* and much of the plot centers on his ambiguous birth and motherless upbringing. Another reversal of the usual plot occurs in *The Champions of Freedom* where we see a motherless *son* seduced (but it is his seductress who is eventually punished).

[14] Only two American novels, *The Coquette* and *Charlotte Temple*, enjoyed the kind of success that English imports such as *Pamela* had. Both *Charlotte Temple* and *The Coquette* went through dozens of editions in the eighteenth and nineteenth centuries and each is currently available in a College and University Press (New Haven) paperback edition.

[15] Many eighteenth-century educational reformers lamented the fact that most middle-class American women read little more than sentimental novels. One excellent early American novel, Tabitha Tenney's *Female Quixotism: Exhibited in the Romantic Opinions and Extravagant Adventures of Dorcasina Sheldon* (Boston, 1801), satirized this tendency and railed against a society that educated women only to read romantic fiction.

[16] See David Lundberg and Henry F. May, "The Enlightened Reader in America," *American Quarterly*, 28 (1976), 262–71 and appendix.

[17] For example, see Hannah Mather Crocker's *Observations on the Real Rights of Women* (Boston, 1818).

[18] Cf. "The Creation of the American Eve: The Cultural Dialogue on the Nature and Role of Women in Late-Eighteenth-Century America," *Early American Literature*, 9 (1975), 252–66, in which Patricia Jewell McAlexander also draws the connection between the *Memoirs* and sentimental fiction; and R. M. Janes, "On the Reception of Mary Wollstonecraft's *A Vindication of the Rights of Woman*," *Journal of the History of Ideas*, 39 (1978), 293–302.

[19] Tomalin, p. 243.

[20] *All the Happy Endings* (New York, 1956), pp. 31–32.

Reconstruction in the House of Art: Emily Dickinson's "I Never Had A Mother"

Long before the age of the airbrush, Emily Dickinson practiced the art of erasing once-prominent figures out of group portraits. She strategically edited out of her poems and letters a person presumably instrumental in her development: Emily Norcross Dickinson, her mother.

Scholars have always found Dickinson's achievement as a poet incredible—one of the most inexplicable, if not unlikely, events in literary history. To hear Dickinson tell it, her development was indeed miraculous, for she states, "I never had a mother."[1] The truth is that her mother lived until Dickinson was fifty-one, and was the one with whom she shared the most intimate contact of her adult daily life. But for some reason Dickinson cannot admit this. Instead, as if to prove her motherlessness, she covers up any evidence that her mother really existed for her. Thus, in her poetry, we see no mother at all. The persona relates a gothic-type childhood, complete with midnight terror, imprisonment, torture, starvation, and neglect. Because an omniscient, oppressive father-figure dominates the poetry, literary critics seek a real-life villain in Edward Dickinson; the mother is so completely absent, in concept, theme, name, metaphor, or image, that Emily Norcross does not even rate being stopped for questioning. In the letters, she fares no better. We glimpse her only occasionally as the butt of jokes or complaints. She is patronized as the mouther of clichés, one who does not "care for thought" (*L.*, II, p. 404). But most interestingly, even though we see Emily Dickinson describing her mother as totally inconsequential, she also describes her, paradoxically, as absent. We see explicit denials of her existence at all: "I never had a mother" (*L.*, II, p. 475); "I always ran Home to Awe when a Child, if anything befell me. He was an awful mother, but better than none" (*L.*, II, pp. 517–18); she has no one but her sister to dress her, to tell her right from wrong (*L.*, II, p. 508); she even asks an editor she has never met to advise her "how to grow" since she has "none to ask" (*L.*, II, p. 403, 404); and she complains to her brother, "how to grow up I don't know" (*L.*, I, p. 241).

It is not surprising, then, that since Mrs. Dickinson has been effectively removed in Dickinson's reconstruction of her life through her poems and letters, and the father cast into the limelight, that the majority of studies accordingly dismiss Dickinson's mother as irrelevant to her daughter's development as a poet. So cleverly does Dickinson cover up her mother's role—and the cover-up operation itself—that scholars poring over her work for clues to the mystery of her development have come up with every other conceivable influence for the poetry: gene pool, schooling, magazine subscriptions, health, friends, lovers, father, family history, sister-in-law, brother, editor, church attendance, books read, sermons heard, and so on. Only John Cody, a psychiatrist, has dealt with Mrs. Emily Dickinson as a significant figure, and his approach is hypothetical—from the viewpoint of an analyst to whom Emily Dickinson has presumably come for help with her psychosexual psychoses.[2] Certainly, in the light of what we now know about the significance of the mother in any person's development, especially a woman's, we should not take someone at her word when she says she never had a mother.

In spite of all the intensive study made about Dickinson's life and poetry, we still confront a puzzle. In 1860, poets wore beards; the woman who aspired to be more than a minor "poetess" was a self-styled freak. Yet shy little Emily Dickinson with her baking pans and white dress, afraid to leave home lest it displease her father (*L.*, II, p. 337, 450, 453), dared no less than to be Emerson's great Poet and devoted her life to this ambition. The poetry of Dickinson's contemporaries was strictly rhymed and metered, formal, romantic, and patriotic (only Walt Whitman broke the taboo on form and rhyme, and Dickinson was told he was "disgraceful"). Yet Dickinson wrote original short stanzas with questionable rhymes, shockingly unorthodox—if not heretical—views on sacred subjects including God, the state, the Bible, clergymen, society women, "wild nights," madness, fame, faith, and female sexuality. How did such poetry emerge from a life she herself described as "too stern and austere . . . to embarrass any?" (*L.*, II, p. 460).

Dickinson claims that her life is beyond reproach, but in her own day she was a topic of wild rumor and speculation, a living "Myth." Why did she withdraw from the world and retreat to her upstairs bedroom, never to reemerge? Why did she begin writing hundreds of poems, sometimes several a day, and keep them secret? Why are her poems so startlingly unconventional? Emily Dickinson's life and poetry veer dramatically from a conventional female orbit for nineteenth-century America, and the explanations returned to again and again to account for this divergence from tradition revolve about a love affair. Such theories may be logical, considering the many poems and letters about love, but these explanations have not proved satisfying, particularly since no one can quite agree on who these lovers are and just how they influence the life and poetry.[3] The reason is that Emily Dickinson's themes, concerns, attitudes, and use of language do not evolve after she begins writing. Because her literary style is fully fashioned at age fifteen, later events cannot substantively affect Dickinson's art. The key to her radical departures from convention is her experience *before* she begins writing: her childhood. Therefore, I would suggest that the real influence in Emily Dickinson's life is her mother, the person who exerts a crucial influence on a woman's development.

This supposition about Emily Dickinson's mother is substantiated by another curcumstance: Dickinson appears to be using her mother's absence and insignificance as part of some aesthetic strategy. As Dickinson herself reveals to an editor, she believes that art must do a lot of feigning: "Nature is a Haunted House—but Art—a House that tries to be haunted" (*L.,* II, p. 554). Dickinson is trying to effect a past of ghosts to produce her art. The fact that in her tour of her haunted house of art, our poet-guide displays her father on every landing and never takes us upstairs to meet her mother does not mean her mother is not important: it only makes us wonder what Dickinson is trying to hide. Finally, although Emily Dickinson strived throughout her life to deny any maternal influence, her attempt to make her readers believe she is both motherless and mothered by a fool only serves to arouse suspicion: in one version, the mother is profoundly important—when she is absent; in the other, she does not matter at all—when she is there. As a matter of fact, both versions can be true in that they reflect a child's ambivalence to a parent who cannot win. But the contradictions inherent in these conflicting versions denote a complex relationship which is important enough to Dickinson to make her try to cover it up. Our problem is to discover why: how airbrushing Mrs. Dickinson out of the picture fits in with Dickinson's aesthetic strategy to haunt her house of art and become a Poet, and insofar as possible, to determine the nature of the actual mother-daughter relationship as it is manifested in the poems, life, and letters—specifically, why her mother was so important to Dickinson, and why poets cannot have mothers. A thematic and psycholinguistic analysis of the poems and letters, a summary of which follows below, reveals the degree to which Dickinson's development as a poet is a function of her relationship with her mother: how it is the mother who motivates her daughter's radically unique life-style far beyond the more visible influences of father, lover, editor, and others whose places in the family portrait were left intact or even highlighted.

Emily Dickinson's development as a poet begins and ends with her identity as a daughter. The "daughter" is the female who relates to others and conceives of herself in terms of her relationship to her parents. Typically, this identity is temporary, only the first in a series of identities that the woman will adopt, adapt to, or incorporate into her self-image as she matures. Subsequent identities are a function of the breaking away from the parents to acknowledge the primacy of friends, lovers, spouses, children, work, or religion, when the dominant self-image as daughter becomes submerged or eclipsed. But Emily Dickinson never transacts another identity than her primary one as daughter, functioning in reference to parents: she never leaves home ("my Father's house"); she retains her adolescent dress, hairstyle, behavior, mannerisms, and attitudes; she never develops a significant relationship which will take her away from her parent-child matrix. The question of course is why.

The inability or lack of motivation to transcend the daughter role is actually due to several different circumstances: her experience as a daughter is so secure and idyllic that she cannot bear to leave home; she harbors an antipathy for other culturally acceptable identities for women such as wife, mother, or Sister of Charity and is therefore trapped in her original identity as daughter by default; the original relationship between the daughter and the parents is not satisfactory in an elemental way, and the unfulfilled daughter tries to recreate or project this primary relationship onto other people to give her the parental nurture she craves. In this last case, she expresses her ambivalence to her parents by remaining a daughter but refusing to be dutiful, and instead rebelling against social, sexual, and religious expectations. Dickinson freely uses versions of all three accounts to explain herself in the letters and poetry. The contradictions these theories present apply especially to Dickinson's mother.

Dickinson's first recorded words at age two-and-a-half occur when she is leaving home for the first time, in the midst of a lightning storm: "Do take me to my mother."[4] But she is being sent away by her mother. When her mother dies, Dickinson speaks of her "sorrowing gluttony," and utters, "To have *had* a Mother—how mighty!" and "Mother: what a name!" (*L.*, III, p. 892, 747, 748). Coming at the beginning and ending of her life as they do, these statements constitute a kind of frame for Dickinson's relationship with her mother, indicating that a "mother" is essential to her and that she is deprived of maternal nurture. This view is supported in her poetry, where she equates food and love, and complains of being starved ("I had been hungry all the years," "Deprived of other banquet," "It would have starved a gnat"). Words take on the function of food for her as a way to love and nourish herself, and in this way Dickinson becomes a mother to herself as poet. Her persona is the unsatisfied daughter, the oppressed and hungry child who uses her hunger to stimulate her literary talents: "Deprived of other Banquet/ I entertained Myself." Therefore, being mother-hungry is actually a requisite for writing poems because the need for nurture promotes the making of words. Psychologists would be tempted to claim that Dickinson experiences maternal rejection, but as Erik Erikson admits, their "occupational prejudice is the rejecting mother . . . 'Mom' . . . is blamed for everything."[5] A failure on Mrs. Dickinson's part is neither a necessary nor accurate interpretation of Dickinson's poems about starvation and maternal neglect. Dickinson can be seen doing the actual rejecting by projecting this attitude onto her mother to provide the necessary stimulus and motivation to write poetry.

Dickinson's rejection surfaces in another form as well. The mother is a crucial figure in a child's development, as Dickinson is only too aware. Not only is she dependent upon her mother for nurture and guidance, but as daughter she is expected to identify with her mother in physical, social, and sexual ways. While her brother can anticipate emulating a man who is somebody in the eyes of the world, a local and national public figure (Edward Dickinson was a U.S. Congressman, prominent in the affairs of Amherst College, town and state), Dickinson's same-sex role model is a nobody, perceived by Dickinson as an "anxious-dependent" servant of her family who is dominated, disregarded, weak, passive, dull, occupied with petty charity and housework, and conventionally pious. Friends describe her making pies, too busy for letters, fluttering, timid, meek, and plaintive (*L.*, I, p. 82). The apparently only times she displays "decision of character" and the "air of authority and *independence*," her husband reports it to the world, "with amusement" (*L.*, I, p. 77). Knowing that the growing daughter cannot help but identify with her mother in at least physical and emotional ways, we must try to conceive of the pain it causes the daughter to see her mother as a physical and emotional invalid, whose life is so insignificant that her death, her son reports, causes barely a "ripple."[6] Following conventional nineteenth-century standards, Dickinson's mother is a "perfect" wife; but Emily Dickinson sees the world's contempt for this dutiful woman. She confronts the paradox that although her mother is society's ideal nineteenth-century woman, "it was in the bosom of her family that she was most unappreciated,"[7] since she was neglected by her husband and ridiculed by her children.

What, then is Emily Dickinson going to be, and who is she to identify with, if not this self-same wife and mother who society, church, parents, and school are all training her to become? When Dickinson wrote, "how to grow up, I don't know" (*L.*, I, p. 241), she was expressing the dilemma resulting from her refusal to grow up dutifully as the conventional woman. She rejects one orbital path but there is no other available to her, and therefore she is locked by default into a limbo of perpetual daughterhood. In this way she rejects her mother by not becoming her, and Dickinson's mourning a mother is seen in a larger perspective.

We see Emily Dickinson's efforts to escape the fate of her mother through her writing and the way she lived her life. She engages in a verbal struggle throughout her letters to dissociate herself from her mother. The mother is largely absent from Dickinson's accounts of her intellectual, spiritual, and even mundane daily life. When she does include her, it is with ironic detachment and she records and makes fun of her mother's use of clichés: cold as ice, like a bird, turn over a new leaf ("I call that the Foliage Admonition," *L.*, II, p. 622)—as if to assert her independence and disapproval of her mother's limited mental and moral conventionality. Her own poetic sensibility is juxtaposed against her mother's common piety, so that the reader can discern the intellectual and artistic difference between these two Emily Dickinsons (*L.*, II, p. 454; I, p. 116; I, pp. 137–138). Mocking her mother's narrow intellect, she will tell her correspondents of sophisticated and witty conversations she has had which her mother considers "very improper" (*L.*, III, p. 675). She claims to deplore the time spent on "Mother's dear little wants" which consume her whole day: "I have hardly said 'Good-morning, Mother,' when I hear myself saying, 'Mother, good-night'"

(L., III, p. 675). Dickinson is fifty when she writes this latter complaint, and fifty-one when she complains of her "Gymnastic Destiny" in taking care of her mother (L., III. p. 687). The fact that she is still rebelling as a daughter at an age when her contemporaries are grandmothers, suggests that Dickinson considers her mother an important—if negative—part of her life.

Dickinson tries to make her correspondents think her mother means little to her, as when her mother dies, for example, and she makes witty remarks about her mother's ascent to heaven ("like a bird"). But she now continues: "We were never intimate Mother and Children while she was our Mother—but Mines in the same Ground meet by tunneling and when she became our Child, the Affection came—" (L., III, pp. 754–755). Dickinson does not specify whose love finally came. The ambiguity suggests that mother and daughter are unable to love each other *as* mother and daughter: it is only when Mrs. Dickinson is paralyzed out of the role of mother that she "achieves . . . sweetness" and becomes "larger" with tenderness to her daughter. The mother is now the child and is no longer seen as threatening. Also, perhaps the role that Mrs. Dickinson had felt duty-bound to play as perfect wife makes her "small" by not allowing her to be sweet or tender.

What is important is that Dickinson's references to her mother before her mother's death are ironic records of the mother's disapproval of her and her inability to mature, while the references afterwards try to come to terms with the mother as a human being. It is apparently safe to acknowledge the mother-daughter relationship once the mother is dead and her threat is removed; before that, she must artificially separate herself from her mother in people's eyes. Perhaps Dickinson actually feels they are too close: her public rejection of her mother, in word and deed, is extremely complex. Dickinson mourns her mother even though she denied having one and mocked the one she had. Her mourning can make sense if we understand that she has been deprived of a mother who can give her the emotional support and guidance she needs to become "somebody," not just now that her mother is deceased but before, while she was growing up. Dickinson clearly wants to become somebody, and writing poetry is her way to do it (L., II, p. 315; I, p. 195; I, p. 146; I, pp. 276–277; II, p. 421). After she had written a poem and discussed its prospects of publication with her sister-in-law, she once wrote: "Could I make you and Austin [her brother]—proud—sometime—a great way off—'twould give me taller feet" (L., II, p. 380). Emily Dickinson feels chronically "small" in the eyes of the world in terms of importance. She cannot turn to her mother for a role-model or even ask her how to become larger, because her mother is small herself; she does not know how to become somebody "taller," and what is more, does not even share her daughter's aspiration to be something other than a "lowly" dutiful wife and mother. In this way Dickinson *is* deprived of a mother, and consequently turns to a masculine editor of an important literary journal to ask *him* "how to grow" to get those "taller feet" (*L.*, II, p. 404). Thomas Wentworth Higginson of *The Atlantic Monthly* functions, then, as a kind of substitute literary mother figure; because he has the power to identify her as a poet by publishing her, he effects her growth and stature. Dickinson does want to grow up. She simply does not regard becoming what her mother is as "growing." Dickinson's strategy seems to stem from her feeling that she must assure Higginson that she does not have a real mother. This provides a rationale for her request for his guidance and nurture. If she proclaims herself an orphan to him ("I never had a mother"), she is not being unfair so much as she is describing her dilemma as an ambitious woman without a role model or a mother adequate to her needs.

Emily Dickinson is forced to dispossess herself of her biological mother in order to circumvent her mother's destiny. Outwardly, she conforms to being a dutiful daughter par excellence by staying home to take complete care of her mother and bake her father's daily bread. This feeds her anger and rebellion, which provides the tension necessary to produce her art—and she knows it. Her rebellion must be subtle, because an open break would resolve the tension and dry up the source of her art. Therefore, her rebellious poetry is kept secret and private, where she describes the awful effects of an internalized mother-daughter conflict. In her own life, she refuses to convert and accept Christ as her savior in spite of her mother's fervent urgings and in spite of the fact that she knows she is damning herself. Saying "yes" to Christ is to say "yes" to the oppressive maternal matrix; and besides, Dickinson does not need any reminders of how precious the Son is to the Father. When puberty looms, we find Dickinson on the edge of psychoses, probably because her physical maturity is too immediate a threat to her identity as a would-be poet.

Emily Dickinson's letters illustrate another form of rebellion from what her mother stands for. She is not only alienated from religion in her need to demonstrate how she does not fit into the woman's world, but from other aspects of the woman's domain as well, including marriage, housework, good works, and sewing societies. These are only obstacles in the way of Dickinson's determination to be somebody. There is no way that she can escape her duties, but she can distance herself from her dutiful role and retain her integrity by complaining about it. She creates a synthesis of duty and rebellion, acting dutifully but rebelling through her letters. David Higgins, a critic of Dickinson's poetry, finds that tracing Dickinson's poetic development is so difficult because her early letters do not give him many glimpses of the "poet-to-be."[8] On the contrary, Dickinson's letters give us a portrait of the artist at odds with tradition: there is nothing in her letters that is not intended to turn her reader's attention to the fact that she is outwardly doing work and living a life for which she is manifestly unsuited—that she is a poet who is being temporarily eclipsed by society's mistaken conviction that she is just another woman who will do when the real mother is taken out of commission. When her mother is sick, for example, and Dickinson takes up the "culinary arts" which she has "always neglected" as being particularly "prickly," she goes "cheerfully around my work" pleasing her father and brother who "clamor for food." But lest the reader think *she* enjoys being eclipsed as this maternal figure, she confesses that she is actually miserable, and "cries with all my might," convinced she is "much abused." She is careful in giving these renditions to express herself very poetically so that the reader is convinced that she is not her mother. At one point, she writes that "twin loaves of bread have just been born into the world under my auspices— fine children—the image of their mother . . . " (*L.*, I, pp. 97–100). To emphasize that making bread is a specifically feminine duty which has been imposed on her, she relates the activity in the sexual terminology of giving birth (certainly a feminine duty).

A major reason for her rejection of her maternal matrix, then, is that Dickinson perceives her mother's normal functions as veritable martyrdom that keeps her from being a poet : "Wouldn't you love to see me in these bonds of great despair, looking around my kitchen, and praying for kind deliverance . . . *My* kitchen I think I called it, God forbid that it was or shall be my own—God keep me from what they call households." Writing will give her status; household chores keep her from writing, and make her angry. She gives her attitudes towards the feminine ideal in a letter to a friend:

> . . . my time of so little account—and my writing so *very* needless—and really I came to the conclusion that I should be a villain unparalleled if I took but an inch of time for so unholy a purpose as writing a friendly letter . . . mind the house—and the food—*sweep*, if the spirits were

low—nothing like exercise to invigorate . . . and for society what neigh-borhood is so full as my own? The halt—the lame—and the blind—the old—the infirm—the bed-ridden—and superannuated—the ugly, and disagreeable—the perfectly hateful to me—and *these* to see, and be seen by—an opportunity for cultivating meekness—and patience—and sub-mission— . . . . The path of duty looks very ugly indeed (*L.*, I, pp. 81–85).[9]

This letter is as open as Dickinson is ever to be about her feelings as a daughter in her family and community: her hostility and resentment against her family, her scorn for the precepts of church, school, and home; her feelings of being imposed upon and misunderstood; her rejection of the Christian Puritan work ethic, especially as it applies to women. Religious submission is equated with housework: in Dickinson's mind, church, family, and society are conspired in league against her to prevent her from becoming "great." The most intense antagonism is leveled against the mother, who is bedridden and lame: ugly, disagree-able, and hateful to her. The qualities that her mother embodies are the Christian virtues of meekness, patience, and submission, but these are attributes Dickinson feels to be deserving of contempt. Dickinson ex-tends her rejection of her mother and the maternal world to any con-vention which she, as a woman, is expected to submit to: courtship, marriage, children.

When astronomers chart a star whose orbital behavior seems inex-plicably erratic, they presume that the star is not alone, but rather, is locked in a tango with a partner it eclipses. The star is only properly understood in the context of the dual-star system to which it is bound by gravitational force. Similarly, when we ponder the meaning of Emily Dickinson's off-course literary and social behavior, we should under-stand that Dickinson is functioning as part of a mother-daughter con-figuration, even though the mother is eclipsed by Dickinson's back-and-forth movements. If we perceive that Dickinson is acting throughout her life as a daughter in reference to an invisible but omniscient mother, then her ambivalence towards her feminine identity, poetry, patriarchal society, God, church, politics—which have heretofore so puzzled her critics—makes significant and coherent sense. For Dickinson, the House of Art is not a "household"—"God forbid"—and cannot be established by a woman unless she is one of those who "never had a mother" to teach her a woman's proper place.

Notes

1 *The Letters of Emily Dickinson*, ed. Thomas H. Johnson, 3 vols. (Cambridge, Mass.: The Belknap Press of Harvard University Press, 1958), II, p. 475. Subsequent passages from the letters are from this edition, hereafter cited in parenthesis in the text by *L.*, followed by volume and page number.

2 Millicent Todd Bingham, *Emily Dickinson's Home* (New York: Harper, 1955), discusses the significance of Mrs. Dickinson's "tremulous fear of death," p. 4; George Whicher, *This Was A Poet: A Critical Biography of Emily Dickinson* (New York: Charles Scribner's Sons, 1938), mentions her on her husband's arm as they stroll down the street, p. 6, and gives her a paragraph in which he says she is insignificant, pp. 28–29; David Higgins, *Portrait of Emily Dickinson* (New Brunswick, New Jersey: Rutgers University Press, 1967), cites Mrs. Dickinson as a background figure in the life of her family: "pious, quiet, dutiful," p. 30; Klaus Lubbers, *Emily Dickinson: The Critical Revolution* (Ann Arbor: The University of Michigan Press, 1968), cites Dickinson's father, sister-in-law, brother and sister in his index to the kind of work that has been done on her, and makes no reference to any approach to Dickinson which would make her mother important enough to be mentioned, p. 328. On the other hand, Whicher discusses the importance of Edward Dickinson, and Clark Griffith's *The Long Shadow: Emily Dickinson's Tragic Poetry* (Princeton, N.J.: Princeton University Press, 1964) is premised on the dark role the father played in Dickinson's life; Richard B. Sewall, in his two-volume biography, *The Life of Emily Dickinson* (New York: Farrar, Straus, and Giroux, 1974), notes: "Tradition has it that Emily Dickinson's home was dominated by her father," p. 44. John Cody's *After Great Pain: The Inner Life of Emily Dickinson* (Cambridge, Mass.: The Belknap Press of Harvard University Press, 1971), is the first full-scale study of the role Emily Norcross Dickinson played in her daughter's life and poetry. Following this work, we have Jean Mudge, *Emily Dickinson and the Image of Home* (Amherst: University of Massachusetts Press, 1975), which discusses Mrs. Dickinson at more length in the study of Dickinson's sense of "place."

3 For example, Millicent Todd Bingham offers evidence for Judge Otis Lord; David Higgins makes a case for Samuel Bowles; Rebecca Patterson, *The Riddle of Emily Dickinson* (Boston: Houghton, Mifflin, 1951) argues that Dickinson loved Catherine Scott Anthon; Josephine Pollitt, *Emily Dickinson: The Human Background of her Poetry* (New York; Harper, 1930), claims that the lover is Major Edward Hunt; Genevieve Taggard, *The Life and Mind of Emily Dickinson* (New York: Scribner's, 1938) writes that Dickinson loved George Gould; George Whicher and Thomas Johnson, *Emily Dickinson: An Interpretive Biography* (Cambridge, Mass.: The Belknap Press of Harvard University Press, 1955) are inclined to favor Rev. Charles Wadsworth. John Cody feels that Dickinson loved both her sister-in-law and her brother. As George Whicher remarked in 1938, all of these theories cannot be true, p. 18 ff.

4 Jay Leyda, *The Years and Hours of Emily Dickinson*, 2 vols. (New Haven, Connecticut: Yale University Press, 1960), I, p. 21.

5 Cody, p. 2; Erik Erikson, *Childhood and Society*, 2 ed. (New York: W. W. Norton & Co., Inc., 1967), p. 288.

6 Mabel Loomis Todd writes, from what she gathered from Austin Dickinson, that the mother died "without giving a perceptible ripple on the surface of anyone's life, or giving concern to any of her family." MSS Todd-Bingham Archive, in Sewall, p. 287.

7 Mudge, p. 29.

8 Higgins, p. 27.

9 See also I, p. 90, II, p. 453, and I, p. 238.

Ellen Glasgow: Daughter as Justified

> The most important thing one woman can do for another is to illuminate and expand her sense of actual possibilities. . . . *To refuse to be a victim* . . . . As daughters we need mothers who want their own freedom and ours.[1]

Adrienne Rich's 1976 statement could serve as summary for Glasgow's developing perspective during her forty years of writing fiction. Once Ellen Glasgow began writing novels in the 1890s, the premises of her education as a privileged Southern woman became all too evident. The type of women characters she chose to write about, as well as her treatment of them, clearly revealed the conflict between her own ideal woman—and that woman's place in her culture—and the feminine ideal of the traditional Virginian society in which Glasgow lived and wrote.

The ideal Southern woman was to be deferential to the patriarch of the family, and in his absence, to any other male—uncle, brother, even nephew. If she challenged that male direction, she was only acting on the whimsical impulse that sometimes ruled women. As a deviant, she could be scolded, cajoled, or humored; but any serious breach in conduct (that usually related to morality or family honor) could mean ostracism.

Glasgow's early novels are filled with worn women whose lives have been poured out on the altar of that deference. The pale shadows like Mrs. Pendleton and Mrs. Carr, seemingly blessed in their marriage, progeny, and eventual widowhood, are in Glasgow's presentation bereft of any individual spirit. As she had described such women in her 1898 novel, *Phases of an Inferior Planet*, they were among "that numerous army of women who fulfil life as they fulfil an appointment at the dentist's—

with a desperate sense of duty and shaken nerves. . . . The saints of old, who were sanctified by fire and sword, might well shrink from the martyrdom sustained, smiling, by many who have endured the rack of daily despair."[2]

The chief role of these sanctified wives and mothers in Glasgow's early fiction is to provide stability for their less complacent daughters, the willful "modern" women—Mariana, Eugenia, Virginia, Gabriella. Mothers give love and fearful wisdom; their dialogues convey vividly the social and familial expectations for the heroines. But as Glasgow presents these mature women, they are never role models; they serve rather as specters of the expected female. By slanting her readers against women characters who should be beloved and respected, by allowing these women to glimpse the promise lost, Glasgow establishes sympathy with those female characters who are trying to move against the rigid traditions: she justifies the rebellious daughters.

Glasgow's most complete statement of the dichotomy between "received" opinion about women's role and their need to create that role occurs in the 1913 novel *Virginia*. As she said in a 1916 interview:

> In *Virginia* I wanted to do the biography of a woman, representative of the old system of chivalry and showing her relation to that system and the changing order. Virginia's education . . . was designed to paralyze her reasoning faculties and to eliminate all danger of mental unsettling. Virginia was the passive and helpless victim of the ideal of feminine self-sacrifice. The circumstances of her life first molded then dominated her.[3]

The first third of the novel contains more description of Lucy Pendleton, Virginia's mother, than of Virginia herself, partly because Glasgow recognized the importance of a mother's example to developing women; partly because selfhood, in the Southern culture, had to depend on "the larger tyranny of tradition."[4] Virginia's story is, in fact, told by following her mother's exemplary life—her "pathetic cheerfulness" and her willingness to erase herself into oblivion. All sacrifice is reasonable because she has been happily married for thirty years to that rarest of species, a devoted husband. "Love is the only thing that really matters, isn't it, mother?" asks Virginia; and her mother's answer is the *reductio ad absurdum* for the twentieth-century daughter: "A pure and noble love, darling. It is a woman's life. God meant it so."[5]

Virginia's mother had earlier instructed her, "Your first duty now, of course, is to your husband. Remember, we have always taught you that a woman's strength lies in her gentleness. His will must be yours now, and wherever your ideas cross, it is your duty to give up, darling. It is the woman's part to sacrifice herself" (p. 152). Repeatedly in *Virginia* Glasgow discusses the myth of romantic love, always in relation to the options open to modern woman. Virginia sees the completed Lucy Pendleton at one extreme; at the other, Miss Willy Whitlow, the spinster seamstress. There is no center to her vision, and her traditional mind-set only signals the beginning of her personal tragedy. Notice how clearly Glasgow images Virginia's lack of choice:

> Leaning there from the window, with her face lifted to the stars, and her mother's adoring gaze on her back, she thought of the "happiness" which would be hers in the future: and this "happiness" meant to her only the solitary experience of love. Like all the women of her race, she had played gallantly and staked her world upon a single chance. Whereas a man might have missed love and still have retained life, with a woman love and life were interchangeable terms. This one emotion represented not only her sole opportunity of joy, it constituted as well her single field of activity. The chasm between marriage and spinsterhood was as wide as the one between children and pickles. . . . Every girl born into the world was destined for a heritage of love or of barrenness (p. 113).

The impossible weight resting on such a fragile human relationship was doomed to crush it, and Virginia was only one of several Glasgow heroines who had to face the loss of that absorbing love, and continue living without it. Their stoic if desperate acceptance of desolation is somehow more tragic than death or willed violence would have been. As Glasgow describes Virginia once Oliver has asked for a divorce, "There was no rebellion in her thoughts, merely a dulled consciousness of pain, like the consciousness of one who is partly under an anaesthetic" (p. 381).

Glasgow's portrayal of the adventuresome Gabriella Carr in her 1916 novel, *Life and Gabriella*, is meant to contrast that of the unquestioning Virginia Pendleton. Gabriella has as role model a mother who has enjoyed widowhood for sixteen years ("a beautiful grief"[6]), a woman completely dependent on relatives for all of life's necessities. She rejects that dependence, along with a largely romantic view of life, opting for both independence and realism. Her refusal to lead the "sheltered life" her family would prefer makes her a maverick, and such she remains throughout the book. Glasgow's emphasis early in *Life and Gabriella* falls on her mother's ineptitude to be any kind of mentor, her reversal in fact of the parental role so that Gabriella must assume responsibility for her. This somewhat different picture of maternal influence leads to the same result, however: Gabriella as daughter must reject the traditional feminine values. Again, the mother's role seems chiefly to implement the force of established beliefs. Any rebellious daughter was also doomed to disappoint a loving mother.

Dorinda Oakley, in the 1925 *Barren Ground,* is one of Glasgow's hardiest and most independent heroines, but her education early in the book echoes that of Virginia Pendleton. Dorinda longs for romantic love, and does give all to her passion for the young doctor, Jason Greylock. She admires her own self-sacrificing mother and the fragile, dying friend, Rose Emily Pedlar; but she also questions the sterility of their lives ("Dorinda sighed. Was this life?/ 'I don't see how you keep it up, Ma,' she said, with weary compassion."[7]) Dorinda reacts against the "morbid unselfishness" of her mother's perpetual, hysterical work; but she does turn to her when she wants answers to her questions about love and marriage. Glasgow's 1925 heroine was already aware that her only accurate information would come from another woman. Contrasted with the dialogue about marriage between Virginia and Lucy Pendleton, in the 1913 *Virginia,* Dorinda's exchange with Mrs. Oakley is a bleak deflation of any notion of "romance." Mrs. Oakley minces no words:

> "Grandfather used to say that when a woman got ready to fall in love the man didn't matter, because she could drape her feeling over a scarecrow and pretend he was handsome. . . . The way I've worked it out is that with most women, when it seems pure foolishness, it ain't really that. It's just the struggle to get away from things as they are" (p. 81).

To emphasize the accuracy of Mrs. Oakley's comment, Glasgow underlines it by showing Dorinda's surprised chagrin: "To get away from things as they are! Was this all there was in her feeling for Jason; the struggle to escape from the endless captivity of things as they are? In the bleak dawn of reason her dreams withered like flowers that are blighted by frost."

It is important that the stunting of Dorinda's dreams occurs here, long before she knows she has been betrayed, with the loss of her fantasy. Dorinda's real betrayal is more than Jason's abandonment; it is as ageless as history, and stems from people's failure to create lives of promise for their daughters. When Dorinda questions her mother further, Mrs. Oakley speaks directly to the point of self-actualization, feminine independence:

> "Marriage is the Lord's own institution, and I s'pose it's a good thing

as far as it goes. Only," she added wisely, "it ain't ever going as far as most women try to make it. You'll be all right married, daughter, if you just make up your mind that whatever happens, you ain't going to let any man spoil your life."

The tendency of women to let their lives be shaped, damaged, and even destroyed by their husbands (fathers, sons) is so common that Mrs. Oakley does not elaborate on it. Yet one of the ironies of *Barren Ground* is that, after burying her own gentle husband, Mrs. Oakley *does* allow her life to be destroyed by her careless young son, Rufus. When Rufus is accused of the murder of a townsman, Mrs. Oakley perjures herself to give him an alibi:

> ". . . Rufus was right here with me the whole evening."
>
> When she had finished speaking, she reached for a chair and sat down suddenly, as if her legs had failed her. Rufus broke into a nervous laugh which had an indecent sound, Dorinda thought, and Mr. Wigfall heaved a loud sigh of relief.
>
> "Wall, you jest come over tomorrow and tell that to the magistrate," he said effusively. "I don't reckon there could be a better witness for anybody. Thar ain't nobody round Pedlar's Mill that would be likely to dispute yo' word" (p. 248).

Mrs. Oakley never recovers from the shock of Rufus' crime, and from her own betrayal of basic moral values. Her love for her son has cost her her integrity and, soon, her life.

Dorinda's reaction to her mother's sacrifice shows a great deal about Glasgow's position on the role of woman, and especially mother. "'I couldn't have done it,' Dorinda thinks, judging the act a waste: "She was shocked; she was unsympathetic; she was curiously exasperated. Her mother's attitude to Rufus impressed her as sentimental rather than unselfish; and she saw in this painful occurrence merely one of the first fruits of that long weakness. . . . 'I'm not made that way,' Dorinda decided; 'There's something deep down in me that I value more than love or happiness or anything outside myself'" (p. 251).

The primary story line of *Barren Ground,* which is the account of Dorinda's life after Jason has jilted her, illustrates the scarcity of options for women intent on getting away from things as they are. It also brings Dorinda into frequent contrast with her mother, so that as she develops strength after strength, her mother fades more and more rapidly into the background of our interest. "There were times when it seemed to Dorinda that she could not breathe within the stark limitations of her mother's point of view" (p. 235). The eventual triumph of Dorinda's struggle may have resulted as much from the conflict with her mother as from her own pride—or so the pattern of the novel suggests.

In *Barren Ground*, Glasgow successfully breaks open the stereotypes of "romance." As a betrayed woman carrying her illegitimate child, Dorinda should either repent or seek vengeance. Narrowly missing the opportunity for the latter, she does neither; instead she looks for a new kind of life. She uses her talent in ways her culture does not approve for a woman. Wearing borrowed overalls, Dorinda withdraws from the society that would shame her until she has regained her reputation in the man's world of farming. Only when she is successful does she return to wearing women's clothes, and to the church that symbolizes the stern morality that would have banished her a decade before. But her life after Jason's betrayal has been prompted by bitterness, and it takes many more years before she can learn the compassion that marks the woman as woman. Glasgow's story in *Barren Ground* is not so much an account of the way a woman learns to know the land, but so much more, the story of the way a woman learns to know herself.

What is most masterful in this novel, contrasted with *Virginia* and *Life and Gabriella*, is that Glasgow conveys her theme through a subtle overlay of imagery most appropriate to Dorinda's absorption in farming, that of which vegetation covers the land. The whole novel hinges upon the reader's definition of "barren," and various levels of irony. Dorinda has never been a barren woman; she has known passion and given birth in the earliest of her female cycles. What she wrests from the generally unyielding land is success, promise for the future, the opposite of barrenness. As the title phrase is used early in the novel,

> Almost everybody is poor at Pedlar's Mill. The Ellgoods are the only people who have prospered. The rest of us have had to wring whatever we've had out of barren ground (p. 182).

"That's what life is for most people, I reckon. . . . Just barren ground where they have to struggle to make anything grow," Dorinda observes as she runs away to New York, pregnant and frightened (p. 150).

Glasgow structures the novel into three parts to emphasize the kind of vegetation growing on the gradually reclaimed land, a pattern which parallels the stages of Dorinda's own personal growth. Part I, "The Broomsedge," shows the striking if flighty romantic girl, wearing her orange shawl, determined to find some beauty in life through the easiest path: escape through sensual excitement. Glasgow uses the life of Jason's bride, Geneva Greylock, to contrast Dorinda's: her use of coercion and duplicity to marry Jason, her disappointment when the marriage fails and there are no children, her own mental illness when this single source of meaning in her life crumbles. Geneva never comes to know what Dorinda understands early, that life has some value "so long as she could rule her own mind" (p. 199). This recognition is the subject of Part II, "Pine," and Part III, "Life-everlasting," in which she learns the value of complete dedication: "For the next few years she gave herself completely to Five Oaks. Only by giving herself completely, only by enriching the land with her abundant vitality, could she hope to restore the farm" (p. 317). Dorinda's life has confirmed the promise she had made to herself in New York, that she would fill her years "with something better than broomsedge. That's the first thing that puts out on barren soil, just broomsedge. Then that goes and pines come to stay—pines and life-everlasting" (p. 184).

The novels that followed *Barren Ground* continued to portray women who had made important personal choices, who were not coerced by convention into lives unsuited for them; unfortunately, these women too saw their mothers as forces acting for the society which was in place, rather than being allies for their full development. Perhaps because Glasgow had found some answers to the conventional life pictured so vividly in *Virginia*, *Barren Ground* remained her favorite book. "It is the best book I have written"; "the one of my books I like best"; "putting my whole heart into a book in which I believe"[8]—Glasgow's enthusiasm for the novel never diminished; in 1932 she spoke again of her love for it: "In reading this book over again, after seven years, I felt, as I had felt when I was writing it, that it is the truest novel ever written . . . a perfectly honest interpretation of experience, without illusion, without evasion."[9]

Some readers have connected *Barren Ground* with Glasgow's own failure to marry, and with the end of her engagement to Henry Anderson in 1919.[10] As she had written in 1928 about the novel, "A novel like that grows slowly. For ten years I had carried that idea in my mind, and I gave three years to the actual writing."[11] Her statements about the Anderson engagement, and its end, in *The Woman Within*, also parallel the kind of resolution Dorinda was able to achieve fictionally:

> Nothing, apparently, had changed—nothing, except that I was free. The obscure instinct that had warned me, in my early life, against marriage, was a sound instinct . . . . I was free from chains. I belonged to myself. . . . After more than twenty-one years, I was at last free. If

falling in love could be bliss, I discovered, presently, that falling out of love could be blissful tranquillity. I had walked from a narrow over-heated place out into the bracing autumnal light of the world. Earth wore, yet once again, its true colors. . . . Gradually, as this grasp weakened and relaxed, all the other parts of my nature, all that was vital and constructive, returned to life. Creative energy flooded my mind, and I felt, with some infallible intuition, that my best work was ahead of me. I wrote *Barren Ground,* and immediately I knew I had found myself.[12]

"I was free from chains. I belonged to myself," wrote Glasgow; "To refuse to be a victim," echoes Rich. And the mother figures of Glasgow's novels bow their heads somberly and mutter in chorus, "Your first duty now is to your husband." "It is the woman's part to sacrifice herself." The brilliance in Glasgow's portrayal as novelist is that we watch these lives of "repressed and hungry devotion" with compassion, not resent-ment; that we take warning from them; and that we—hopefully—learn to find our own path to life-everlasting.

Notes
[1] Adrienne Rich, *Of Woman Born* (New York: W. W. Norton, 1976), p. 246.
[2] Ellen Glasgow, *Phases of an Inferior Planet* (New York: Harper Brothers, 1898), p. 88.
[3] Grant M. Overton, *The Women Who Make Our Novels* (New York: Moffat, Yard and Company, 1922), p. 32.
[4] Ellen Glasgow, *Virginia*, Preface (New York: Charles Scribner's Sons, 1938), xii.
[5] Virginia, p. 154. See also p. 33 for a description of her husband's "love" for her.
[6] Ellen Glasgow, *Life and Gabriella* (New York: Charles Scribner's Sons, 1938), p. 7.
[7] ———, *Barren Ground* (New York: Hill and Wang, 1957), p. 39.
[8] *Letters of Ellen Glasgow,* ed. Blair Rouse (New York: Harcourt, Brace and Co., 1958), pp. 74, 107, and 69.
[9] *Letters,* p. 118.
[10] E. Stanly Godbold, Jr., finds the novel an attack on the relationship, a defensive face-saving diatribe; internal evidence of the novel itself would seem to contradict that view (*Ellen Glasglow and the Woman Within*, Baton Rouge, Louisianna State Univ. Press, 1972, pp. 107–63 ff).
[11] *Letters,* p. 90.
[12] Ellen Glasgow, *The Woman Within* (New York: Harcourt, Brace and Company, 1954), pp. 245, 244, and 243.

Mothers, Daughters, and Incest in the Late Novels of Edith Wharton

The strained relationship between mothers and daughters is one of Edith Wharton's persistent themes in her late novels. Concealed within is the struggle for the father, a struggle that wounds their relationship.

Lewis[1] and Wolff[2] have pointed out in their recent studies of the life and work of Edith Wharton how the relations between parents and children which contain the theme of incest obsessed the American novelist in her later years. The existence of the pornographic fragment, "Beatrice Palmato," highlights Wharton's interest in introducing into her fiction an explicit account of the sexual act between father and daughter. This motif emerges in the fiction written in her sixties in a concentrated form in mother and daughter relations.

By this time Wharton had rejected the role of wife, had finished her role as lover, and her yearning for biological children could now never be satisfied. Her progeny were her books; in letters to her friends she called her literary productions her "children." Her own deprivations as a mother encouraged her fantasies in this direction. During the war years her maternal feelings were directed to a few young men, especially to one who lost his life early in the war and whom she memorialized in *A Son at the Front*.

The three novels, *The Old Maid*, *The Mother's Recompense*, and *Twilight Sleep*, published from 1924 until 1927, project the drama between mothers and daughters. The intensity of Wharton's feelings invested in these stories make them very good indeed and their excellence belies the generally accepted view that her late novels are her worst. These particular ones are compelling to read, and their plots are well organized. They leave us with tremendous respect for a woman who was trying to climb out of her class, out of the nineteenth century, and out of the box, that "convenient box, with nice glass sides, so that we can see out" from which Verena Tarrant implores men to release women in James's *The Bostonians*. In fact, it is the plot of James's short story, "The Chaperon"[3] that we see behind the plot of *The Mother's Recompense*.

A Son at the Front[4] (1923) had begun Edith Wharton's parent-child dramas. It is concerned with a painter who, alienated from his son, allowed him to be raised by his wife's second husband because his own deep concern was with his art. After the young man's death in the war, the father is left with the portrait he had made of his son, and a commission for a monument in his memory. So he incorporates his son into the art for which he had rejected him. In this way Wharton masks her own persona and her own concentration on her work in the portrayal of John Campton, the father.

The next year *The Old Maid*[5] (1924) presents two mothers, neither of whom have a claim on Tina, the daughter—the real mother, Chatty Lovell, who has to conceal her true motherhood of the child conceived out of wedlock, and the adoptive mother, Delia Ralston, who takes care of the girl because she is the offspring of a man Delia loved. Delia's own biological offspring never means what this girl means to her, and the problem of the book is, will the real mother divulge to the girl her true parentage?

The story is placed in the 'Fifties in New York when "dark destinies coiled under the safe surface of life" (OM, p. 120) and "the blind forces of life were groping and crying underfoot" (OM, p. 129). In it Wharton showed that a mother could have no relation to her illegitimate daughter in a society that knew but would not accept such a relationship. In this way she denigrates the value of biological motherhood. Delia says to Chatty, "You . . . sacrifice her to your desire for mastery?" (OM, p. 155). It can do no good for Tina to know Chatty is her mother. Delia, her mother surrogate, satisfies the girl in relation to the society which determines her happiness. In fact, the point of view in the story is that of the adoptive mother, Delia, not of the real mother. Wharton, in addition to making plausible her own role as an adoptive mother, a role she played in regard to her friend's children late in her life, is also making a statement about families. Natural families are not the families of our choice, and children will turn to those who appeal to them through their personalities and satisfy certain needs, not to their biological parents. Wharton anticipated the point of view of our modern youth who have in so many cases surmounted the traditional guilt that children feel for their parents and have chosen other parent figures. Wharton's ambivalent feelings for her own mother show how close to home this point of view was. When the question in *The Old Maid* is asked, "Which of us is the mother?" the answer is not readily available. Sometimes a child needs more than one mother, and here two mothers join in their love for Tina. In this novel Wharton has removed the mother role from its biological determinants.

Wharton's novelistic situations flushed out after World War I pertained to the changing role of women. Having moved into the world as artist or war worker, her roles as mother, wife, and lover were breaking out of their nineteenth century molds. Kate Clephane's difficulty in *The Mother's Recompense*[6] (1925) was going back to something she had really elevated herself out of, even though it had been considered by her society twenty years before as a fall from grace. Wharton, of course, left her unhappy marriage for a life abroad as a writer. This parallels in some ways Kate Clephane's situation in the novel. Having abandoned her husband and infant daughter, Anne, for a life of love affairs abroad, Kate finds that the price she must pay for her restoration and rehabilitation in New York society is acceptance of the knowledge that Anne's fiancé is her own last, much younger, former lover.

Kate Clephane's accomplishment was, Wharton seems to conclude, a breaking down of old containments which would never again be erected around this particular woman. She is conscious of her decision of twenty years before to give up the traditional roles of wife and mother and to take on the role as lover. Now having outgrown that role she has a new identity, the woman *without* a traditional role. She is faced with the task of finding a new one. She is not Edith Wharton, a woman with a career. But Kate remains firm in her conviction that old roles are out. At the end of *The Mother's Recompense*, Kate's recompense is knowledge about herself gained from hard experience. However, her notion of what her recompense should be has changed during the time of the book.

Wharton's *The Mother's Recompense* relates to the James story, "The Chaperon" in its initial situation, the return of the prodigal mother and the presentation back to her old role, only for Wharton the role is not her role in society; it is her role as mother, the center of the emotional life of a child deprived of her mother early in life, and the mother deprived of a full expression of her maternal feelings. Kate Clephane is brought back by her daughter Anne to a society that accepts her willingly enough and forgives her earlier betrayal of her family. All goes well until she discovers that her younger lover, who has appealed to her partly because there was an incestuous element in his extreme youth, is about to marry Anne. The agony of the story becomes Sophoclean and the horror Kate faces is the realization that her role as mother and her role as lover can never be united in the same person. She cannot play both roles at once.

The impossibility of her tolerating the situation gives the book a clear-cut dazzling intensity, although from the facts of the situation as presented this is clearly absurd. Why should a mother in 1925 living for the past two decades in the most sophisticated society in Europe regard her daughter's marrying her former lover as so horrifying? It can only be because Mrs. Clephane views the lover as a husband and the coupling of her daughter and the man who represents the husband-figure becomes an incestuous act. The father, as it were, cohabits with his own child. Such a situation therefore can produce the kind of emotional pain and intense horror which Kate Clephane feels. Wharton has presented the same pattern of the discovery of incest and consequent horror shown by Oedipus.

In fact, it does not seem to me to be forcing the issue if we see the three novels, *The Old Maid*, *The Mother's Recompense*, and *Twilight Sleep*[7] (1927) as Wharton's Sophoclean trilogy. Given her addiction to classical literature and Greek myths it is not too hard to believe she may even have consciously modeled them on their classical predecessors. *The Mother's Recompense* is a novel reflecting the horror and the insupportability felt by a woman when she learns that her daughter is to marry the young man she herself has been in love with. But the horror is so incommensurate with her realistic situation, that we realize it emerges, not from the situation in the book but from another situation that we know from Edith Wharton's life, which operated both in her unconscious and conscious fantasy. This situation has been revealed by a posthumous fragment—"Beatrice Palmato" published by R. W. B. Lewis in his biography of Wharton. Her horror really stems from the fact that her lover is having sexual relations with her daughter, as if the daughter were his own child. We see the horror of the situation in this novel, but we see the pleasure in the fragment. In the fragment, the daughter is enjoying the act of sexual intercourse with her father. In the novel the mother experiences horror when she learns of the possible sexual intercourse of the "father" with their daughter. And the horror comes out with tremendous creative and artistic force. The placing of Beatrice Cenci's picture in *The Mother's Recompense* gives us the clue, but what takes place in the novel is not really horrendous, especially since Edith Wharton had read Balzac's *Comédie Humaine* where there are a number of situations in which mothers and daughters share the same lovers. Diane de Maufrigneuse, in "A Princess's Secrets," tells her lover that her marriage is unhappy because her mother married her to her own lover so she could go on having her relation with him. We know that *The American* by Henry James bases its dramatic core on the fact that Madame de Bellegarde had married off her daughter to her lover so she "could go on herself all the same," an actual quotation from the novel. This was a traditional pattern of behavior in French society. Why Kate Clephane could get into such a turmoil is that her anxiety is really based on another situation not in the novel, but back of the horror in Edith Wharton's mind. This explains why the ending is so factitious and so unreal. The key statement in *The Mother's Recompense* is the following quotation: "Jealous? Was she jealous of her daughter? Was she physically jealous? Was that the real secret of her repugnance, her instinctive revulsion? Was that why she had felt from the first as if some *incestuous horror* [my emphasis] hung between them? She did not know; it was impossible to analyze her anguish." Lewis thinks that *The Mother's Recompense* shows an attempt on the part of Wharton to reestablish some kind of contact with the American authors of the new generation and their new ways of doing things. He also tells us that it was around this time that she began a little diary in which she hoped to render a truer account of her inner nature than that attempted in reviews and comments about her. She

> commented to Berenson on a story by Moravia that in her view contained an inadequate treatment of the always interesting theme of incest. "Faulkner and Céline did it *first*," she remarked, "and did it *nastier*." She added that she herself had an "incest *donnée* up my sleeve that would make them all look like nursery rhymes," but that business was too poor and attitudes too prudish for her to risk trying to sell it. The *donnée* referred to, in all probability, was "Beatrice Palmato." (L, p. 524).

In Wharton's novel the mother's final recompense was that she gets back just what she had put in. She goes back to the life that she had made for herself, a life divorced from all aspects of her marriage, both the motherly aspects and the wifely aspects. Her recompense is that she is given back her own life, the one she had chosen to create when she left John Clephane and Anne. The definition of the word "recompense" is that we are given back something which has been taken away from us. But nothing had been taken way from her, for Mrs. Clephane had *thrown* it away.

The meaning of the book, then, suggested by its title, is that the recompense that the mother gets is her own identity in repudiating her husband and child. Once she has created it, she is committed to it. She has become an individual, divorced from the role of mother, of wife, and of lover. Her recompense is the restitution of her own personality which confirms an existence beyond her relation to a husband or a child. In this sense Wharton is a woman of the second-half of the twentieth century.

This brings us to the dedicatory paragraph with which Wharton prefaces her book: "My excuses are due to the decorous shade of Grace Aguilar, loved by our grandmothers, for deliberately appropriating, and applying to uses so different, the title of one of the most admired of her tales." Grace Aguilar wrote two novels about life with mother in 1847 which became the "how to do it" books for mothers with daughters and with problems of keeping them under their influence. The first, concerned with the raising of small children, was called *Home Influence*.[8] The second, and the more popular, was *The Mother's Recompense* whose title Wharton appropriated for her own novel. In Aguilar's novel, getting the girls safely launched into society and finally married is accomplished through the "confidence" they have in their mother.

Grace Aguilar seems to have had a very satisfactory and comforting relationship with her own mother who survived her. The daughter of a Sephardic Jewish merchant who emigrated from Spain to England, Grace Aguilar wrote about a dozen books, among them explications of the Jewish faith: *The Perez Family*, *Women's Friendship*, and *The Vale of Cedars*. The books that were most popular were the didactic novels, advising mothers and daughters how to get along. A successful mother had to answer these questions: was her daughter properly introduced into society, did she behave herself well, and did she finally make the proper marriage? In Aguilar's *The Mother's Recompense*, the mother, Mrs. Hamilton, intervenes in her daughters' lives to the extent that she reads their mail and inserts advisory comments. Her second daughter, Caroline, has been influenced by a young girl with a poor relationship with her own sick and lazy mother who has lost control over her own daughters. One of the girls takes on Mrs. Hamilton as a model foster mother and does well, but the other weans Caroline away from her mother, and encourages her to flirt with a young earl in order to throw him over. Just as she is about to elope with a man with a bad reputation, she goes back to her mother, to whom her chaperone puts it, "It was the recollection of your untiring care . . . that made her pause ere it was too late and she regains your confidence." The daughter concludes, "My mother was right." Mrs. Hamilton states her "recompense" very clearly as seeing "my children, as I do now around me, walking in that path which alone can lead to eternal life, and leading their offspring with them . . . and yet lavishing on me, as on their father, the love and duty of former years. . . . Is not this a precious recompense for all which for them I may have done or borne?" Mr. Hamilton ends the edifying book by saying, "long, long may you feel as you think on your mother, my beloved children, and teach your offspring to venerate her memory, that the path of the just is indeed as a shining light which shineth more and more unto the perfect day." The ending justifies working hard over raising children, for the mother will be remembered forever.[9]

This is the kind of lesson that Edith's grandmother and other women of her generation in New York, as late as the 1870s, were given as to the proper attitude and the proper relationship between mothers and daughters. Daughters were to listen to their mothers and to respect them, especially when it came to making the big decisions of their life. Since Mrs. Hamilton devoted all her time and all her concern to the happiness of her children, she received her recompense. They all gave her blessings and were grateful that she had kept them from disorder and disaster.

Wharton apologized in her prefatory note to "the decorous shade of Grace Aguilar." However, she makes no apologies for nor even indicates her obligation in imitating very closely that same book in her next novel, *Twilight Sleep* (1927), for even though the customs of the New Yorkers of the 1920s which she writes about bear no relation to those of the Hamiltons of the 1830s in England, there are striking similarities in both books.

It is astonishing how Mrs. Manford, the mother in *Twilight Sleep*, mimics Aguilar's Mrs. Hamilton in exerting the same kind of control over her children—daughter, son, daughter-in-law, and two husbands. We see in the same kind of family circle the mother who sets standards for her family, although the standards are handled ironically because they are all wrong. The name *Twilight Sleep* is taken from the name of the drugs which at this time were popular among the rich for painless childbirth. The elimination of pain is the aim of this upper middle class New York society. Anxiety must be avoided at all costs; everything must be made easy, so everyone in pain must be drugged.

Mrs. Pauline Manford, like Mrs. Hamilton in Aguilar's novel, had an "iron rule" in her home and conducted "the clockwork routine of . . . a perfect establishment." Nona, her daughter, is very affectionate to her mother only they never talk to each other. Although Aguilar's book was based on the confidence one puts in one's mother and the restoration of that confidence, Nona and Mrs. Manford have no confidence in each other at all. Nona knows her mother covers everything over. Mrs. Manford has trained her butler to save the honor of the family by covering up an attempted murder by her first husband, who wishes to punish the couple involved in an incestuous affair. The family circle in this book certainly reminds one of Mrs. Hamilton's circle where the mother does everything she can to keep the *status quo*, but in Wharton's novel, much is hypocrisy.

Pauline Manford's activities include being the Chairman of the Mother's Day Association and a speaker at the Birth Control Banquet, and her daughter Nona is very amused to see that her mother can reconcile such contradictions. Like Mrs. Hamilton of the Aguilar novel she is the ideal mother, since she respects everybody's point of view, and in this sense, too, she plays a role like Mrs. Hamilton's. "True, in Nona's case there had been Pauline's influence. Pauline, who whatever her faults was always good-humoured and usually wise with her children. The proof was that while they laughed at her, they adored her. They had to do her that justice." Here, as in Aguilar's book, there is a rich relationship between mother and daughter, as well as between the various people whom she brings into her circle, because she has energy and consequently a strong influence on people around her.

In the Aguilar book one was expected to behave ethically, to marry, to produce children and to increase the harmony in a family circle. So, too, in the Wharton book one is expected to live in harmony, to avoid pain, and to have life go on with the machinery unimpaired. But the ironical Wharton sees that this can only be done by self-delusion and the payment of a great price. The self-delusion must be continued from beginning to end.

Nona is a daughter who follows her mother's precepts and helps cover everything up, but marriage has been ruined for her. Wharton's book is like Aguilar's because the mother has lived in a certain way and has trained her family for their own good. The good is not religious as in the Aguilar novel, but it is moral. As in the Aguilar book, there had been one daughter for a while who rebelled. In Wharton's book even the rebellious characters follow the family necessity of hushing up everything. In Aguilar's story the family that greets life's problems with uncontrolled behavior is made to go on the rocks. Edith Wharton is showing in her book as Aguilar had shown before that an authoritative mother is the essential factor in a family's success. At the same time, the mother—like "twilight sleep"—represents the masking of pains which, even when unfelt, remain. The attempted murder and the incest, even when covered up, do not entirely fade away. There are no real illnesses in this American financially facilitated world. Nervous tension is controlled by soothsayers, hypnotists and psychic fadists.

Cynthia Wolff, in *A Feast of Words*, gives a very good explanation for the incestuous pattern in Edith Wharton's work, manifested in mother-daughter relations. Her emotional past had created a voracious need for affection, and as she grew older she carried it "into her attachment to her father and that crisis too was incompletely resolved." Wolff continues:

> However, one thing is worth recalling. A woman who has such a past can never completely eradicate its effects. Despite the resolute determination with which she attacked the impending remnants of her early failures, Edith Wharton would always carry certain emotional habits with her: an inevitable residuum from those early traumas remained to complicate the dilemmas of adult life. . . . Given that the implications of incest touched so many elements in Wharton's life, it is scarcely surprising to discover that the theme of incest was integrated into the apparatus of her fiction.[10]

Whether these psychological interpretations of Edith Wharton's early emotional life are correct in part or in whole, the point I have been trying to make in this study is that for Edith Wharton the struggle between mother and daughter projected so insistently in these late novels is the struggle for the father. Nor is it unworthy of comment that although she was a daughter but never a mother these novels are written from the point of view of the mother, not of the daughter. Thus she remains a lineal—if rebellious—descendant of Grace Aguilar, the very name of whose book she has made her own. Wharton's interest in Greek drama stemmed from her belief that the basic turmoil of life was best expressed for Western civilization in the Greek myths. For this reason, in her novels all the relationships within the family are archetypically expressed. I believe that Edith Wharton wished to do the Sophoclean thing for the bewildering twentieth century, the period of her maturity, in which the form of the family itself reflected world changes. Since women's roles were most "shook up" by these changes, she found in the relations between mothers and daughters the most dramatic as well as the most personally touching representation of these changes.

Notes
[1] R. W. B. Lewis, *Edith Wharton: A Biography* (New York: Harper and Row, 1975). When quotations are made from this volume page numbers are given, preceded by "L".
[2] Cynthia Griffin Wolff, *A Feast of Words* (New York: Oxford University Press, 1977).
[3] Henry James, "The Chaperon," *The Complete Tales of Henry James* (Philadelphia and NY: Lippincott, 1963), pp. 71–118.
[4] Edith Wharton, *A Son at the Front* (New York: Scribner's, 1923).
[5] Edith Wharton, *Old New York: The Old Maid* (The Fifties) (New York: Appleton, 1924). Future references in the text are indicated by "OM" plus the page number.
[6] Edith Wharton, *The Mother's Recompense* (New York: Appleton, 1925).
[7] Edith Wharton, *Twilight Sleep* (New York: Appleton, 1927).
[8] Grace Aguilar, *Home Influence* (New York: D. Appleton & Co., 1870).
[9] Grace Aguilar, *The Mother's Recompense* (New York: D. Appleton, 1864), p. 499.
[10] Wolff, p. 379.

Part Four
A TRINITY OF MOTHERS

Introduction

As we have seen, in medieval times the mother Eve was orphaned of her daughters. Then, in the eighteenth and nineteenth centuries, daughters were orphaned of their mothers. As Professor Jane Lilienfeld notes, the mothers of Mary Wollstonecraft, the Brontës, George Eliot, and Elizabeth Gaskell wore themselves out with childbearing and died prematurely, two of them in childbirth.

But a number of women of the early twentieth century—writers such as Willa Cather, Colette, and Virginia Woolf—were "born into famil[ies] of strong women." Mary Virginia Cather, Sido (Colette's mother), and Julia Stephens (mother of Virginia Woolf) ran complex households, in two cases had difficult husbands, or in the case of Julia Stephens, "matchmade . . . nursed . . . organized."

But Woolf's mother did not "give herself to anyone deeply—or not to her daughter," says Lilienfeld. Woolf, like Cather and Colette, thus saw her mother from a distant perspective. Woolf writes of her loss: "Can I remember ever being alone with her for more than a few minutes? Someone was always interrupting." At the same time that the three daughters were separated from their mothers, they also saw their mothers as paradigms: managing mother, active mother, independent mother. Unlike nineteenth-century mothers, the mothers of these famous early twentieth-century writers were neither obsessive nor felt a need to dominate their daughters' lives.

Not surprisingly, all three writers wrote about strong women. And all of these writers maintained close, physical relationships with women. The nineteenth-century world of women's friendship—as shown in Professor Zimmerman's essay on the attitudes and language of Eliot's friends, or as one might find in the intense friendships Margaret Fuller established with her women friends—is continued by Cather, Woolf, Colette. Now there is a degree of "physical intimacy" as well as "spiritual intimacy," says Lilienfeld, and "Virginia Stephens in London, Willa Cather in New York, and Colette in Paris achieved and helped create for others an alternative female culture of action and vision." That vision was nurtured by the triumverate of mothers. And the novels by their daughters render unto them "a just and thankful applause."

The second essay in this section continues the applause but in a different vein. In this essay, we have another trinity of mothers: a scholar-mother, Professor Irene G. Dash, and her daughters, Deena Dash Kushner and Deborah Dash Moore, engage in a subtle trialogue, inspired by Woolf's *To The Lighthouse*. Writes Professor Dash: "My daughters and I have sought to combine the role of mother with that of professional person." They write from a personal as well as a professional perspective, conjoining the fiction read with the reality of their remembered lives. The mood and message of each of the two essays in this section is the same, however, as we see in Professor Dash's final comment to her daughters: "We have been challenged although we have not found the dream, the promise, and the inspiration of *A Room of One's Own*. Thank you for joining me. Thank you for the treasures you are— communicating daughters." If the daughter-authors Colette, Cather, and Woolf write partly to thank their mothers for a legacy of strength and hope, this second essay completes the cycle: mother thanking daughters who, by their participation in the very process of criticism, are a tribute to the legacy of a scholar-mother.

E.M.B.
C.N.D.

Reentering Paradise: Cather, Colette, Woolf and Their Mothers

In their books of the 1920s, Willa Cather, Colette, and Virginia Woolf wrought a great change in the literature of a mother-daughter relations. When we think of their predecessors in the novel, we think of women whose mothers died prematurely, of circumscribed conditions. Mary Wollstonecraft's mother had six children in ten years; Charlotte Brontë's mother had six children in seven years, the birth of the last causing her death; Elizabeth Gaskell's mother bore eight children, only the first and last of whom lived, while she herself died on the anniversary of the eighth child's birth. How could these daughters see their mothers as fully heroic, sacrificed as they had been? Betrayed by the facts, the daughters could not admit to themselves the implications of their mothers' bravery which nevertheless shone in the fire of the daughters' lives.[1] "We think back through our mothers if we are women," which, Virginia Woolf said in 1928, can only be said by a woman whose womanhood is no longer an accusation against her of biological and mental inferiority.

The generation of Cather, Colette, and Woolf reaped the benefits of radical change in women's position and consciousness which their nineteenth-century sisters had achieved in Europe and America. In England, for instance, in 1882, the year of Woolf's birth, The Married Women's Property Act enabled women to sue and be sued, to inherit, bequeath, and own property. Such women as the great radical Mona Caird published articles in prestigious periodicals entitled "Marriage as Failure." Emily Davies had opened Newnham and Girton College for Women; Elizabeth Blackwell had fought successfully to enter and complete medical school. Jobs other than governess were increasingly available. "Life has changed completely," chortled Lily Briscoe to the ghost of Mrs. Ramsay in 1919.[2]

By the time Cather, Colette, and Woolf wrote of their mothers, it appeared that with the vote, and wider educational and job options, women were men's equals. Alas, we now know that institutional change must coalesce with a change of heart, for those in power will not relinquish it. But Cather, Colette, and Woolf grew into their forties and fifties during a time when it still seemed possible that by their sisterhood, intelligence, and united efforts, women could forge new, free lives.

Willa Cather was born into a family of strong women. Mary Virginia Cather, the mother whom Willa resembled but with whom she did not get along, "dominated" the household.[3] For relief from the intensity with her mother, the young girl turned to her father, Charles Cather, a kind, patient, soft-spoken man. The mother of seven children, Mary Virginia Cather needed the help she received from her own mother who lived with them until her death in 1893. Rachel Seibert Boak endeared herself to her granddaughter Willa by taking charge of her education generally, and reading and telling her her favorite stories.[4] Thus, for Willa Cather, snug in deep family feelings, pleasure and prose came to be associated with her secure relation to a maternal figure.

The meaning of the intertwined lives of Mary Virginia, Rachel Seibert Boak, and Willa Cather the author could only explore at her mother's death in 1928, in "Old Mrs. Harris."[5] As Mrs. Victoria Templeton, Mary Cather appears deeply selfish, yet her use of her mother Mrs. Harris to shoulder all the household and child-care tasks leaves her free to be openhandedly generous, and to use her beauty to increase her own and her children's joy in life. Old Mrs. Harris freely gives her life for her daughter and grandchildren, and gains selfhood from what others see as her daughter's abuse of her. Vicki, the young woman of the third generation, oblivious to the complexities of her mother's and grandmother's lives, goes on her way to adulthood, "unknowing."[6]

The will and power of Mrs. Templeton defined the mother in the daughter's eyes, and recreate Willa Cather's adolescent feelings for her mother. At this time of boundary problems between mother and daughter, puberty,[7] the women divided sharply over the issues of femininity. Willa Cather at fifteen cut her hair to her ears and signed her name Willie Cather, M.D.[8] With Mrs. Cather's illness, Willa had had to manage her abundant hair, and perhaps because she took this as a rejection of her own femininity, or because she refused any longer to fulfill her mother's image of her, Cather sacrificed her hair.

No one could have accused Mary Virginia Cather, that "determined Southern belle,"[9] of Mrs. Templeton's stupid selfishness. Though Mr. Cather wanted Willa to work before college, Mrs. Cather insisted she go immediately after high school graduation,[10] thus insuring her daughter a life the mother had not received. To prove her support of her daughter, the mother kept Willa's attic room locked in her absence, though that space must have been sorely needed in a house full of other children. (This private nook of an attic haunts many of Cather's fictional characters.[11])

Many teenaged girls search for surrogate mothers to help them establish a selfhood beyond the bounds of their mothers. Willa Cather turned to the mothers of the Old World Immigrants, like her, immigrants to Nebraska. Seated in these women's kitchens, taking in their generous harvests, Cather revelled in their nourishing her. Perhaps her love for old fashioned American values found its fount in these early passionate associations with mothers whose skins she longed to share.[12]

The search to find the meaning of other persons led Cather first to professional theatre criticism and then to fiction. It was in a Pittsburgh actress's dressing room that Cather met the woman whom Woodress describes as "the one great romance of her life,"[13] Isabelle McClung, the young daughter of a socially prominent judge, beautiful and wealthy, who had inherited her father's imperious will. As Cather came to know her, Isabelle McClung clearly resembled Mary Virginia Cather as she might have been had she had an easy and luxurious life.[14]

Isabelle McClung threatened to move out of her father's house if Cather were not allowed to move in, and so began the five happiest years of Cather's life. Cautiously Woodress hints that the womens' deep attachment had a physical analogue, remarking, "It seems perfectly clear that Cather had no need of heterosexual relationships."[15] The women shared a bedroom.

McClung was generous in her love and support of Cather's writing— to great effect. Such were Cather's achievements in the short story, that reading them McClure offered Cather an immediate editing job in New York. Isabelle McClung apparently chose not to accompany the writer, perhaps unable to leave the father whom she so resembled. Soon after her move to New York, Cather began sharing an apartment with Edith Lewis, a New York colleague. The pain of intense involvement with one woman still flourishing as another deep love was being established,[16] is clear in Cather's actions: she spent Christmas of 1911 with McClung, to comfort her at Mrs. McClung's death, but returned to her apartment shared with Edith Lewis. Even though she lived with Edith Lewis for forty years, Cather never relinquished Isabelle McClung; the bitterness of losing her to Jan Hambourg in 1917 still rankled ten years later.[17] Perhaps Edith Lewis gave Cather the unconditional love she could not accept from Mrs. Cather, a love she lost when Isabelle married.

In nineteenth-century America, close ties between women found symbolic enactment in ritual, action, language, and love. The active meetings about politics and world events of women in America and Europe, the changed attitude possible for women to take toward themselves, and the intense friendships coalescing under the pressure of jointly shared oppression, created "a female world of love and ritual."[18] Virginia Stephen in London, Willa Cather in New York, and Colette in Paris achieved and helped create for others an alternative female culture of action and vision.

In a world of spiritual intimacy, physical intimacy may bloom. All of us raised on pop Freudianism know the word regression has been judgmentally foisted on lesbianism. Adrienne Rich's superb work *Of Woman Born* cleanses that onus away, as she shows that sexual relations between women enable women to accept their physical selfhood and that of the body that bore them. "It is most clear during lovemaking, when the separation of everyday life lifts for a while, when I kiss, and stroke, and enter my lover, I am also a child reentering my mother . . . So, I . . . return to the mystery of my mother, and of the world as it must have been when motherhood was exalted."[19] In the exalted world rich in the body of the returned mother, Cather, Colette, and Woolf found life support.

Willa Cather did not openly celebrate in her novels her sexual ties to other women. Thus it may have been harder for her than for Colette and Woolf to support the burden of being a woman identified woman: "By indoctrination, training, and practical experience, women learned to accept and internalize the beliefs that kept them 'adjusted' to living in subordinate status in a Patriarchal world. The final brick in the wall enclosing women within the world of domesticity was her horror of deviance . . . "[20] Perhaps Cather bore her situation by claiming her motherly inheritance in the lives of women she loved and women she imagined into being.

One can argue that the central issue fusing and separating Cather and her mother had been power, and it is power around which Cather constellated her last finished novel, *Sapphira and the Slave Girl*.[21] Sapphire

Colbert looks on the surface to be the power in her family, but Sapphira's power, like that of Mrs. Ramsay, is entirely indirect, as women's power has usually been, for in order to take any action, the physically crippled Sapphira must force men to do her bidding.

In this novel Cather fictionalized and thus worked through the patterns of dominance, rivalry, anger, and annoyance that had comprised her relations to Mary Virginia Cather. All the mother-daughter relations in the novel grow from these "tangled strands."[22] Sapphira opposes her own daughter Rachel and vies with Rachel for the primary loyalty of Rachel's two little daughters. Sapphira's slave, Til's daughter Nancy, is, however, loyal to the Rachel who helps her escape from the rapist intent encouraged by Sapphira in her nephew Martin Colbert. An ironic echo of the slave mother and daughter's failed sisterhood, itself a comment on the failure of Rachel's and Sapphira's love, is that of the kitchen slaves Bluebell and Lizzie. Their true mother-daughter partnership is solidly based on their subversion of their slave status.

Throughout the novel, the major mother-daughter relationship being studied through this shifting kaleidoscope of possibilities is Cather's relation to her mother. The peace achieved at last between Rachel and Sapphira and Nancy and Til was first enacted before the young Willa as she lay with a cold in her mother's bed: for before her five-year-old eyes,[23] the real life counterparts of Nancy and Til were reunited in their old age, the daughter having successfully escaped to Canada, as Cather has Rachel enable Nancy to so free herself from her own mother and her mother's owner. Til is old, and Nancy is herself a mother, but the divisions caused by their enslavement under patriarchy are embedded now in a mature view, one of the other, and an acceptance of the mother's failure to free herself, for in *Sapphira and the Slave Girl*, Cather has at last intermingled into artistic synthesis, her many feelings for her mother.

Colette has chronicled her life in literature, incorporating reality into an imagined world so beautiful that one accepts its veracity while doubting its perfections. Her childhood with her mother Colette was embowered in a magic garden, so enclosed in bloom that for many the theme of sensual delight in the organic world summarizes both Colette's mother's personality and her daughter's writings.[24]

The small garden where Colette spent her first sixteen years was in Saint-Sauveur, Puisaye, a village "so remote that even today only rare country coaches link it to Auxerre."[25] Sido, Colette's mother, loved the children of that garden exhaustively, yet she remained slightly remote from them and their fathers (for she had Juliette and Achille by her first husband, and Colette and Leo by her second, Jules Joseph Colette). There is no doubt that the second husband adored his wife. She once said, after his death, that he had spent his life serving her. "He prefered to think only of me, to torment himself for me, and that I found inexcusable."[26] So speaks the voice of a woman so complex and sane that only a Colette could do her justice.

Sido ran the house, baked, cooked, and cared for increasing groups of cats, dogs, swallows, spiders, caterpillars.[27] Her garden burgeoned with life, the flowers so perfectly tended they resembled those of Eden. "The presence of plants acted on her like a restorative, and she had a curious way of lifting roses by the chin to look them full in the face."[28] Capturing her mother, Colette said, "Her voice spoke words that had always the same meaning. 'That child must have proper care. Can't we save that woman? Have those people got enough to eat? I can hardly kill the creature.' "[29] Once Sido told Colette the heart-rending story of the starving summer wolf which had followed her "Victoria for five hours. 'If only I had known what to give him to eat,' " she had said, still hurt for his suffering after all those years.[30]

Colette's diamond, Sido, is so faceted, that sometimes her sparkle blinds us. Drawing out implications Colette herself embedded in her portrait of her mother, Crosland argues that Sido's aloof but overwhelming love imprisoned her children, and prevented Colette from accepting or giving complete love.[31] Perhaps Sido's very detachment did not cripple Colette so much as it deepened her own self-sufficiency. Yet, in discussing giving up her mother, Colette implicates as she exonerates.

To leave Sido cost Colette's elder sister Juliette her life. Juliette had been a withdrawn child, and at her marriage engaged in a law suit demanding a complete break with Sido. Next door to the daughter locked away from her by law, Sido mimicked all night Juliette's struggle to give birth to her first child. Observing her mother from her window,[32] Colette painted the price of leaving Sido, for Juliette, unable either to break free or remain tied, killed herself.

Colette's battle was to accept her mother's independence, Sido's life outside her children. Colette's victory shines from her comments on what is justly one of the most famous letters in French literature:

> Sir, You ask me to come and spend a week with you, which means I would be near my daughter, whom I adore. You who live with her know how rarely I see her, how much her presence delights me, and I'm touched that you should ask me to come see her. All the same I'm

not going to accept your kind invitation, for the time being at any rate. The reason is that my pink cactus is probably going to flower. It's a very rare plant I've been given, and I'm told that in our climate it flowers only once every four years. Now, I'm already a very old woman, and if I went away when my pink cactus is about to flower, I am certain I shouldn't see it flower again . . . [33]

Colette's commentary on the love in this letter, so justly revelatory of her mother, is equally famous. Far from seeing her mother's independent life as a rejection of her, Colette accepts that her mother's involvement with her own life grows out of the soil of such health, that Sido inspired her daughter's greatest resilience and courage. The note of exultant celebration bursts forth in the song Colette forges for her mother: "I am the daughter of a woman who . . . " she incants, "waiting for the possible bursting into bloom of a tropical flower held everything up and silenced even her heart, made for love."[34]

Indomitable, but dominating, loving, but powerful, fascinating, hard to resist, Sido comes to us in a complexity inseparable from the daughter's powers. Sido's nature was the perfect resource for her daughter, whose own abilities developed from the subtlety of capturing throughout her life in prose a mother whose fascination embowers her selfhood with the ambiguous essence of fragrance.

The encircling garden the mother had wrought was defiled when Jules Joseph Colette lost the mother's fortune. Forced to move for a few years to Achille's home for refuge, Colette fell into love with Willy, Henri Gauthier-Villars, himself created as complexly in Colette's writing as Sido. Marrying Willy, Colette described herself forty-two years after the event as losing a mother rather than gaining a husband—an astute observation more women believe in than speak of.[35] Willy trapped Colette in his sordid life of plagiarism even as he gave her the key to unlock her prison door.

Willy kept a "stable" of hungry writers around him to put into language plots, dialogue, characterization that he invented but could not imbue with written life. Thinking Colette's early years as a teenager blooming with her mother's flesh might make him some money, Willy encouraged Colette to write what made him famous overnight and rich very soon, for under his name were issued the Claudine novels,[36] the *succès d'estime* based on Colette's early years.

Like Colette's myths about Sido, the story of Willy locking Colette for hours in a dark room where she miserably eked out her novels has something in it of an enabling archetype. Like the myth of Rumpelstilskin and the story of George Henry Lewes urging George Eliot into authorship, in each case there is a woman faced with the-most-wished-for but the-most-impossible task. Her only apparent motive for turning the straw into gold, the pain into life, the words into print—for she cannot admit to herself her own aggression for fame and success as a writer—is to ascribe this to a man. George Eliot created herself, just as Colette did. Lewes and Willy could not and did not write the works they encouraged or supervised. Colette and Eliot unlocked their own doors, and entered a world where imagination made possible a language of freedom.[37]

Earlier, when Colette's illness revealed that her failure at marriage to Willy had stripped her will to live, Colette rejected the easy return to her mother who came to Paris to care for her. Now without Willy "hour by hour I fought my unutterable yearning to go back to her."[38] Rather than a fear she would be eaten alive by her mother, Colette's wish for autonomy grew from the very resources Sido's independence had planted in her daughter. A quick irony of self-sufficiency now tinged Colette's language as it always does that of Sido.

In Colette's growing free, a woman played the same part a woman played in the lives of Cather and Woolf. Perhaps Colette's "amitie amoreuse" for the Marquise of Morny or Belboeuf,[39] called Missy, is more famous than Woolf's intimacy with Violet Dickinson and Vita Sackville-West or Cather's with McClung or Lewis, because Colette's famous description of a night spent resisting intercourse rocks with the sexual tension that results only from deep passion. In "Nuit Blanche" Colette describes the women lovers, mounting tension into an unbearable dawn when only love-making can relieve them.[40] From Sido's enabling care to Missy's protection was a movement that Colette made natural by her mode of narrating the events. Loving Missy brought back to Colette the deepest feelings for her mother, and nurtured in her the regeneration and tenderness of her mother's garden that sustained her without the actual presence of her mother. Loving Missy, Colette became Sido tending herself and her garden, Missy. Loving Missy, Colette became wholly a daughter to a mother she was determined to resemble. Loving Missy made Colette's freedom and adulthood a reality. Loving Missy was, finally, for Colette, as similar unions were for Woolf, an interim during which Colette established a selfhood.

The sisterhood with Missy faded into a thirteen-year marriage of bitterness and loss to Henri de Jouvenal. After the pain of this, Colette turned for renewal to a younger man, Maurice Goudeket. Even here she incorporated her mother into herself. First she had married Willy, a man not able to come to terms with his desire to write—an exact replica, in this fear, of Colette's own father, Jules Joseph, at whose death the titled notebooks of his writing desk were found to contain blank pages.[41] Thus her first marriage came as near as possible to repeating Sido's relation to Jules Joseph. In her second marriage, Colette still followed the example of her mother who had also married twice. Supported by mother, friend, and husband, Colette by 1920 was recognized as one of France's greatest prose stylists.[42]

For contemporary women writers and readers, it is arguable that Colette's greatest bequest is not her depiction of male-female relationships, but her treatment of the relationships between mothers and daughters. Interwoven throughout her novels, stories, and autobiographical narratives is the thread of Colette's examining and accepting her mother's bequests which Colette forcibly made her own through writing about them. In writing about her own daughter Bel Gazou in *My Mother's House*, Colette grants the girl an independence she herself may not have received at Sido's musky hands. Fascinating, however, is the fact that Bel Gazou appears to Colette as Colette says she herself appeared to Sido.[43]

In 1928 Colette published *Break of Day*. Her second marriage ended, before she meets her third husband, Colette consciously travels her path through experience according to Sido's example and wisdom, these serving both as a mode of revelation and a mode of narration. Each section of the book begins with a letter from Sido, and each section culminates with Colette's meditating on the life choices the narrative itself presents her, in light of the mother's dicta and behavior.[44] Fully entered at last into her own life, Colette enriches it with her mother's selfhood. This example of a woman consciously turning to her mother's strengths as a source of her own is essential to the new vision contemporary women writers have forged of their relationships to their mothers. Colette is a great practitioner of meditation on the mother whose enabling example changed the course of women writers' visions of the mother in our time.

The magical beauty and the embowered garden of Colette's Sido enshrine Julia Jackson Duckworth Stephen, Virginia Woolf's mother, the original of Mrs. Ramsay. In *The Voyage Out*,[45] writing about Helen Ambrose, and in *To the Lighthouse*, writing about Mrs. Ramsay, Woolf went beyond Colette's subtle irony to show the harmful power of a too perfect and too applauded mother.[46] Julia Stephen was, like Sido, a brilliant manager of her own and others' lives. She matchmade, she nursed,[47] she organized cottagers' lives in St. Ives, Cornwall, her summer home, and she glittered, out of reach, to a daughter longing to be loved alone.

Julia Stephen was graced with breathtaking beauty, apparent now, in the photographs her aunt, the photographer Julia Margaret Cameron, took of her.[48] In those days, when looks were a woman's only economic security, Julia Stephen made two fine marriages, and used her beauty for the power it gave her. First she had married the wealthy barrister Herbert Duckworth, by whom she had three children. After mourning his loss for years, Julia Stephen married Leslie Stephen, by that time a famous man of letters. The marriage of these two complex people was itself complex. Julia's beauty automatically granted its possessor rights and privileges denied the more ordinary. Another factor, equally important, helped Julia in her marriage to the demanding Sir Leslie. She had enormous power in the domestic sphere, in those days, the only arena open to feminine talent and intelligence.[49] There was an added facet to Julia's domain, for Leslie Stephen did not have a job which removed him from the home. He wrote, read, entertained, studied, and made his living writing at home. Therefore, he was technically ensconced in the sphere over which she was allowed precedence. Moody, dependent, yet charming as only he could be were his needs assuaged, Leslie Stephen was nurtured under his wife's able hand. She ran the household, supervised the child care, controlled the finances, helped educate her daughters when the time came. She might have spoken the words Adrienne Rich attributes to the speaker in "From An Old House in America": "My power is brief and local, but I know my power."[50]

When Julia Stephen's daily mail was opened by her family after her death, they found letter after letter asking for emotional support, often from persons unknown to the rest of the family.[51] Her family's need for her was equally exhausting. She ran a home with eight children in it, three by her first marriage, Leslie's mentally defective daughter by his first marriage, and the four children Julia and Leslie had produced by their own union. She coped, according to Virginia Woolf, by not giving herself to anyone deeply—or not to her daughter: "I see now that a woman who had to keep all this in being and under control must have been a general presence rather than a particular person to a child of seven or eight. Can I remember ever being alone with her for more than a few mintues? Someone was always interrupting."[52] Woolf goes on in that paragraph to report that her mother loved her youngest child, a son, best. "Him she cherished separately; she called him 'My Joy.'" Equally one would assume, Julia cherished Leslie. Thus the picture of Mrs. Ramsay preferring James to Cam, stinting Minta Doyle in favor of Paul Rayley, and generally feeling men need to be protected, while women can take care of themselves, is apparently based on Julia's choice of whom to succor. She did not choose her daughter Virginia.

Her mother's sketchy attention, and then her desertion through death generated in Woolf an anger so deep she could never fully fathom it. Like Delia in *The Years*,[53] at her dying mother's beside she denied all feeling and repressed her rage. It can be argued, as Phyllis Rose does superbly,[54] that the rest of Virginia Woolf's life was an attempt to reconcile herself to the loss of a mother whom she felt she had never truly had, who had never given her the amount and kind of love she had given husbands or sons.

The only person in Woolf's life ever to begin to make up to her for her mother's loss was her sister Vanessa Bell. Ironically, Vanessa, like Julia, was competent with her hands, was managerial, practical, and coldly remote or joyfully present,[55] and she loomed as a flaming light to her sister Virginia. Quentin Bell's narrative of the years 1909–1910[56] implies what I believe to be true: that was the year in which Virginia Stephen tried to squeeze herself physically into every cranny of her married sister's life. If the Bells went for a vacation, Virginia took a room up the road. Finally the strain was so great that Vanessa resolved, as she put it to her best friend, "I have come to think in spite of all the drawbacks she had better marry."[57]

Feminist Woolf scholars have proved, furthermore, that the relation which was supposed to have eclipsed this imperious sisterhood has been vastly overrated.[58] Rather than the conclave of gangly young men called The Bloomsbury Group, Virginia Stephen's enabling cohorts were women. Especially prominent among them in these years was Violet Dickinson, the friend of Virginia Stephen's early twenties who got her her job reviewing for *The Times*, nurtured her writing talents, and nursed her when she was ill. Thus Violet Dickinson, like Isabelle McClung and Missy, gave to Virginia Stephen what she felt had slipped through the hands that had entreated her mother.

Violet Dickinson faded imperceptibly into Leonard Woolf. A balanced friendship, their marriage grew from his nurturing support, but this was as confining as it was freeing, much like Willy's hobbling of Colette. Leonard Woolf himself faded into the deepest love of Virginia Woolf's middle years, Vita Sackville-West. Turning to letter 1613 in

Volume 3 of Woolf's *Letters,* we find the passions pouring forth:

> Your letter from Trieste came this morning—But why do you think I
> don't feel, or that I make phrases. 'Lovely phrases' you always say
> which robs things of reality. Just the opposite. Always, always, always,
> I try to say what I feel. Will you then believe that after you went last
> Tuesday [for six weeks to Persia]—exactly a week ago . . . and ever
> since nothing important has happened—Somehow it's dull and damp.
> I have been dull; I have missed you. I do miss you. I shall miss you.
> And if you don't believe it, you're a longeared owl and ass. Lovely
> phrases? . . . Please tell me [everything]; you can't think how, being a
> clever woman, as we admit, I make every fragment you tell me bloom
> and blossom in my mind.[59]

The only letters comparable to this in intimacy, jokey passion, and
desperate intensity are those in the same volume to the cherished sister.
In this letter, Woolf pleads, plays, excuses herself, and subtly milks
love from her absent lover. Whether they made love twice, as Nicolson
first printed,[60] or twelve times, as he later named his count,[61] Woolf
and Vita Sackville-West built on the intimacy of women-identified-
women a sisterhood like others as we have seen. But the passionate
attachment Woolf felt in those years of the twenties for Vita Sackville-
West, as had Cather for McClung and Colette for Missy, enabled her
to reclaim the self given to the mother and sister.

One reason for this was that the Sackville-West love for Virginia
was unmixed with the condescension that Woolf herself half encouraged
from husband and sister. Leonard and Vanessa had known her well;
they knew her weaknesses, weaknesses that for a complex series of
reasons their very loving concern supported rather than changed. With
Sackville-West, Woolf had started anew, been born to a new selfhood.
Vita had no real vision of a Virginia Woolf other than the mature,
witty, complex, and iridescently successful writer and publisher of
1925. Furthermore, Vita was a Vanessa whom one might legally embrace. As Vanessa, Vita was Bohemian while socially prominent, rest-
less and promiscuous, but a mother, an artist, and a commandingly
magnetic physical presence. Perhaps in having a sexual relationship
with a woman similar to her sister, Virginia Stephen was acting out a
buried fantasy of a physical closeness to a sister who, like Julia, was
always just beyond her reach.[62] Thus, her love affair with Vita Sackville-West granted Woolf a new vantage from which to regard her past.

For one thing, she had attained a position in the world of letters as
experimental writer and publisher of other experimental writers at the

Hogarth Press by 1925 as powerful and prestigious as that her father had occupied at her birth in 1882. She thus may have felt herself Leslie's equal as adversary in a way she never had before. And, having captured the passions of Vita Sackville-West, had Woolf at last conquered an object as elusive as the radiant Julia Stephen? From her new position, Woolf was critical of her parents, critical in a way that made her fear for her very life;[63] and yet she sustained her anxieties and in *To the Lighthouse* rigorously subjected traditional marriage and traditional male-female roles to remorseless probing and reproval.[64] The light turned on Mr. and Mrs. Ramsay and their union is in each case a just but leveling one. It is the very mixture of feelings illuminating the mother as well as the father that give the novel its greatness as well as reveal how it was a therapeutic tool.[65] In the figure of the painter belittled by both Ramsays, Woolf has put herself. And at the triumphant Lily's easel, the last touch is put to a picture of a child who sustains her mother's loss, comes to work through that loss as an ability to reject her mother's limiting example, and goes on to live beyond her parents' life to achieve her own personhood.

Criticism of Mrs. Ramsay is, in the end, justly turned to constructive ways to move beyond her. Mrs. Ramsay had manipulated Minta Doyle into a mistaken marriage, and had almost forced the unwilling Lily to marry, too. Minta moves beyond the powerful mother woman to a social independence in which her broken marriage supports her (III, v, 257–60). For Lily, the task was equally difficult, but she comes to cherish in herself powers equal to but different from those of Mrs. Ramsay. An artist who lives, not by manipulating others' lives, but by her work itself, Lily moves beyond the narrow domestic sphere of action to a world of achievement in paint as well as deep friendships like that with Mr. Bankes (III, v, 264). It was imagining Lily's freedom from bondage to Mr. and Mrs. Ramsay that enabled Virginia Woolf, in her next four novels, to consolidate and transfigure the achievements of her earliest years. After *To the Lighthouse*, especially in *The Years*, Woolf's portraits of family life have a rich complexity which make them a critique of patriarchy, revealing it to be, not the special invention of one father, but a generalized imprisonment that we must all band together to reform.[66] In Woolf's final novel, *Between the Acts*, the hints about Lily's other sexual choice burst forth in "the dyke" Miss La Trobe, failed yet successful creator of the pageant (and the ending) of the book. Miss La Trobe's sexual preference for women, like the choices made at times in their lives by Cather, Colette, and Woolf, broadened the base of her art, and sustained her search for artistic fulfillment. Striving for a language to do justice to their visions, Cather, Colette, and Woolf forged novels whose greatness comes from the soil their mothers nurtured, novels which render to the mothers of the writers a just and thankful applause.

Notes

[1] Adrienne Rich, *Of Woman Born* (New York: Norton, 1975), pp. 224–25.

[2] Virginia Woolf, *To the Lighthouse* (New York: Harcourt, Brace and World, 1927), III, v, 260. Subsequent references will be included in the text, cited by book, chapter, and page.

[3] James Woodress, *Willa Cather: Her Life and Art* (Lincoln: University of Nebraska Press, 1970), pp. 22–23.

[4] Woodress, *Cather*, p. 4.

[5] Willa Cather, "Old Mrs. Harris," *Obscure Destinies* (New York: Knopf, 1932).

[6] Cather, "Harris," p. 190.

[7] Nancy Chodorow, *The Reproduction of Mothering: Psychoanalysis and the Sociology of Gender* (Berkeley: University of California Press, 1978). pp. 130–40, especially pp. 134–35.

[8] Mildred Bennett, *The World of Willa Cather*, A New Edition with Notes and Index (Lincoln: The University of Nebraska Press, 1974), caption to seventh picture, after p. 221.

[9] Woodress, *Cather*, pp. 22–23.

[10] Bennett, *Cather*, p. 30.

[11] See the use of the attic in Cather's *The Song of the Lark* and *The Professor's House*.

[12] Woodress, *Cather*, quotes her loving comments on these immigrant mothers, p. 33.

[13] Woodress, *Cather*, p. 86.

[14] Carol Matthews, "Willa Cather: Toward a Feminist Vision," M. A. Thesis, Goddard College, Cambridge, Mass. I have been fortunate to be able to discuss Cather with Ms. Matthews as she wrote this thesis.

[15] Woodress, *Cather*, p. 86.

[16] See Karen Vierneisel's fine discussion of this complexity in her unpublished dissertation, "Fugitive Matriarchy: Willa Cather's Life and Art," especially ch. 2, University of Chicago, 1977.

[17] Leon Edel, *Literary Biography* (Bloomington: Indiana University Press, 1959), pp. 115–22.

[18] Carroll Smith-Rosenberg, "The Female World of Love and Ritual," *Signs*, I (Autumn, 1975), pp. 1–29.

[19] Rich, *Woman*, pp. 232–33.

[20] Gerda Lerner, *The Female Experience: An American Documentary* (Indianapolis: Bobbs-Merrill, 1977), pp. xxxv–xxxvi.

[21] Willa Cather, *Sapphira and the Slave Girl* (New York: Vintage Books, 1975).

[22] I paraphrase the title of *Tangled Vines: A Collection of Mother & Daughter Poems*, ed. Lyn Lifshin (Boston: Beacon Press, 1978).

[23] Woodress, *Cather*, p. 25.

[24] Margaret Crosland, *Colette: The Difficulty of Loving: A Biography* (New York: Dell, 1975), p. 31.

[25] Crosland, *Difficulty*, p. 36.

Jane Lilienfeld

26 Colette, *Break of Day*, trans. Enid McLeod (New York: Farrar, Strauss & Giroux, 1961), p. 127.
27 Colette, *My Mother's House and Sido*, trans. U. V. Troubridge & E. McLeod (New York: Farrar, Straus & Giroux, 1953), pp. 47–53.
28 Colette, *Mother's*, p. 152.
29 Colette, *Mother's*, p. 53.
30 Colette, *Mother's*, p. 184.
31 This is the crux of Crosland's brilliant reworking of Colette's life, in *Difficulty*.
32 Colette, *Mother's*, pp. 78–9.
33 Colette, *Day*, p. 5.
34 Colette, *Day*, pp. 5–6.
35 See Crosland, *Difficulty*, p. 51, and Robert Phelps, ed. of *Colette: Earthly Paradise: Colette's Autobiography Drawn from the Writings of Her Lifetime*, trans. Briffault, Coltman, *et. al.* (New York: Farrar, Straus & Giroux, 1966). p. 88.
36 Crosland, *Difficulty*, pp. 70–1.
37 Colette, *Paradise*, p. 122.
38 Colette, *Paradise*, p. 114.
39 See Yvonne Mitchell, *Colette: A Taste for Life* (New York: Harcourt, Brace, Jovanovich, 1975), pp. 76–100.
40 Colette, *Paradise*, pp. 164–68.
41 Colette, *Paradise*, pp. 48–50; Crosland, *Difficulty*, p. 37.
42 Phelps, *Paradise*, p. xv.
43 Colette, *Mother's*, pp. 134–41.
44 For example, see Colette, *Day*, pp. 23–25.
45 Virginia Woolf, *The Voyage Out* (London: Hogarth Press, 1965).
46 See my " 'The Deceptiveness of Beauty:' Mother Love and Mother Hate in *To the Lighthouse*," *20th Century Literature*, 23 (October, 1977), 345–76.
47 Julia Stephen's *Notes From Sickrooms* (London: Smith & Elder, & Co., 1883). Available at Cambridge University Library, Cambridge, England. She loved the power that nursing gave her (see, for example, pp. 1, 2, 5) but showed extreme empathy for the helplessness of the patient (pp. 6, 14–5). See as well Sir Leslie Stephen's *The Mausoleum Book*, edited by Alan Bell (Oxford: Clarendon Press, 1977), pp. 34, 40–41, 64, 66–75, 82–83, 87–89.
48 See Woolf and Fry, eds., *Victorian Photographs of Famous Men and Fair Women by Julia Margaret Cameron* (Boston: Godine, 1973), plates 15, 16, and 30.
49 See especially John Ruskin, "Of Queen's Gardens," *Sesame and Lilies: Three Lectures* (New York & London: G P Putnam's Sons, n.d.).
50 Adrienne Rich, *Poems, 1950–74* (New York: Norton, 1975), p. 239.
51 Quentin Bell, *Virginia Woolf: A Biography* (New York: Harcourt, Brace, and Jovanovich, 1972), I, 38.
52 Virginia Woolf, "A Sketch of the Past," *Moments of Being, Unpublished Autobiographical Writings*, ed. Jeanne Schulkind (Sussex: University of Sussex Press, 1976), p. 83.
53 Woolf, "Sketch," p. 92.
54 Phyllis Rose, *Woman of Letters: A Life of Virginia Woolf* (New York: Oxford University Press, 1978).
55 Angelica Bell Garnett describes her mother Vanessa Bell in *Recollections of Virginia Woolf by Her Contemporaries*, ed. Joan Russell Noble (New York: Morrow & Co., 1972), pp. 83–6.
56 Bell, *Woolf*, I, pp. 141–70, especially p. 165.
57 Bell, *Woolf*, I, p. 144, letter to Marjorie Snowden.
58 See Ellen Hawkes, "The Magical Garden of Women: Virginia Woolf's Literary Sisters and Women Friends," forthcoming in Jane Marcus, ed. *Thinking Back Through Our Mothers*, London: Macmillan, 1979. See Jane Marcus, "Some Sources for *Between the Acts*," *The Virginia Woolf Miscellany* (Winter, 1977), pp. 1–3; and Marcus, "The

Years as Greek Drama, Domestic Novel, and Gotterdammerung," *BNYPL*, 80 (Winter, 1977), pp. 276–301.

[59] Virginia Woolf, *The Letters of Virginia Woolf, Vol. 3, 1923–1928*, ed. Nigel Nicolson and Joanne Trautmann (London: Hogarth Press, 1977), pp. 231–32.

[60] Nigel Nicolson, *Portrait of a Marriage* (New York: Atheneum, 1973), pp. 204–7.

[61] Nigel Nicolson, introduction to Woolf, *Letters, Vol. 3*, p. xxi.

[62] Is it possible these screen memories of brotherly incest are projections of a wished for sisterly attention? See Bell, *Woolf*, I, 42–43; Woolf, "22 Hyde Park Gate," in Schulkind, *Moments*, pp. 154–55.

[63] Jane Marcus, introduction to *Thinking Back Through Our Mothers*, forthcoming.

[64] See Jane Lilienfeld " ' Where the Spear Plants Grew Arm in Arm': The Ramsay's Marriage in *To the Lighthouse*," Marcus, ed., *Our Mothers*, forthcoming.

[65] Woolf, "Sketch," p. 81, says that the writing of *To the Lighthouse* enabled her to do "for myself what psycho-analysts do for their patients."

[66] See *BNYPL*, 80, (Winter, 1977), The Virginia Woolf Issue, on the later writings of the 1930's. See also Diane F. Gillespie, "Virginia Woolf's Miss La Trobe: The Artist's Last Struggle Against Masculine Values," *Women and Literature*, 5 (Spring, 1977), 38–46.

IRENE G. DASH
DEENA DASH KUSHNER
DEBORAH DASH MOORE

15

"How Light a Lighthouse for Today's Women?"

Because my daughters and I have sought to combine the role of mother with that of professional person, I suggested we read Virginia Woolf's *To the Lighthouse* for possible insights into our lives.[1] Dominated by two women—one a mother or mother-surrogate, the other an artist—the novel questions the options open to women. It also seems to challenge us to choose between being mothers and being artists—between mothering and having a career. Since Woolf understood the problems of woman as artist and made an important contribution to feminist thinking, her world could also provide a valuable focus for an interchange of ideas.

My proposal met a mixed response. Since one daughter is an American historian, she preferred an American writer. Because, however, Woolf was familiar to her from teaching a women's studies course, she finally agreed to read and comment on *To the Lighthouse*. The other daughter, who had majored in English and American literature in college and had loved Woolf's writing, agreed to the idea but wondered at the method. Now a resident of Georgia, she was troubled about communication; the potential for verbal exchange would be limited by distance. Promising to act as mediator, organizer, and final synthesizer, I volunteered to fill the mother-role again and to carry the major share of the work.

My method has been to present each of my daughters, Deborah and Deena, with the same set of questions on the novel and to follow this up with a taped discussion with each of them. The last conversation, that with Deena, was the most complete—partially because of its place in the sequence, but also because, loving literature, although now completing a Ph.D. in business administration, she had read and reread the novel, drawing, therefore, from a rich store of recollection for our talk. Nevertheless, there were weaknesses. We three had never actually met together on the subject although we had worked with each other's material. Another was a certain reticence, the difficulty of "baring the soul," of breaching the habit of confidentiality in a mother/daughter/sister relationship despite the professional level of this adventure.

Because I could so easily visualize us sitting together in the living room or, over a cup of tea in the kitchen, arguing, agreeing, and laughing—the problems of communication temporarily eradicated—I have brought us together again to one place, to one time, for this exchange. Although we concentrated on *To the Lighthouse* as a window into the lives of women as mothers and daughters, our final consideration was whether or not Woolf, the artist, had provided new understanding of the human condition. I believe that we have heard resonances of our own experiences as career women and mothers, listened anxiously to the problems daughters must face, and marveled at her insight into women's minds.

Turning to my daughters, I asked, "Do you think the novel offers any new perceptions of the relationship between mothers and daughters?"

"I don't think so," Deena answered. "I do not think the novel tells very much about the mother-daughter, parent-child relationship."

"And yet it opens with the scene between Mrs. Ramsay, the mother, and her youngest son, James, expanding to include all those people to whom Mrs. Ramsay represented different aspects of the mother figure. This includes not only her own eight children, but the guests in their home—and most of all Lily, the young artist who loved and yet resented Mrs. Ramsay," I reminded her.

"Nevertheless," continued Deena, "I believe Woolf is interested in something larger, woman's place in society, not just her role as a mother. Woolf is saying that the only way one can exist and cope is to have an outlet. But a woman's not allowed these outlets, whereas a man is."

"I agree with Deena," Deborah said. "I think that Woolf is presenting a false dichotomy, based on sex, each person speaking out of his or her own world and then retreating into the world of individual consciousness.".

"Have you noticed," Deena interrupted, "that just about every time Woolf mentions Mrs. Ramsay, her beauty is mentioned. And whenever Mr. Ramsay is mentioned, his thinking is mentioned. When Prue is mentioned, her beauty is mentioned. When Andrew is mentioned, his achievement is mentioned. And this is consistent. Women are valued for their beauty while men are valued for their intelligence. The women in the book are not permitted intelligent, serious thought. They are denied the privacy, the time, and the encouragment which, as Woolf emphasizes in *A Room of One's Own*, are essential to artistic expression. This denial pushes Mrs. Ramsay to the point of mental and emotional exhaustion.

"The only person who doesn't fit into this pattern is Lily, the artist, who acknowledges the values of society but rejects them. She remains free to express herself, albeit quietly, without sharing her experience with others. Through Mrs. Ramsay and Lily, the author shows how the values of female beauty and male intelligence trap women in a cycle of underachievement."

"Not only that," Deborah agreed, "but according to Woolf women's physicality and sensuality are tied up with their intellectual and emotional reactions. She describes Mrs. Ramsay as intuitively accurate. But she also suggests that the beautiful exterior which stimulates one type of reaction in men may conceal an interior tormented by inaccessible options."

"Both of you seem to find an absence of options for women pervasive in this work," I summarized. "How do you feel Mrs. Ramsay conforms to, or challenges your own definitions of mothering? What do you think her aim is as a mother?"

"I think Mrs. Ramsay aims to make a dent in the world, to assuage the poor," Deborah continued. "She also aims to create ineradicable images for her children who never forget. She desires beauty and peace, love and constancy. I don't see these aims as mine. I value solidarity and initiative, responsibility and freedom, individual quest and collective sharing."

"I disagree with you Deborah," Deena countered. "I think that Mrs. Ramsay's goal is not 'to make a dent in the world,' but to maintain the clearing in the forest—to keep the poor from becoming dissatisfied, and to keep the sickly from dying. It is much more depressing, as a woman, to hold back the forces of time than, as a man, to go out and conquer."

"Do you really think that holding back the forces of decay is a mother's role?" I queried.

"No, but in this novel Woolf argues that after the men take roles as thinkers and rulers, the women pick up the pieces as mothers and weave the fabric of society," Deena answered. "Ironically, mothers must wage the struggle against the decay of civilization, hence a struggle with life—the side of decay not of creation."

"Woolf's problem lies in her perception of commitment," Deborah interrupted. "Mrs. Ramsay has committed herself to Mr. Ramsay and his children, and this comes to represent an ideal of womanhood. Mr. Ramsay has committed his life to an ideal, too, although he engages in maudlin self-pity at times. As an artist, Woolf perceives commitment to an ideal as all-encompassing. But I doubt whether the transference of this definition of commitment to the role of mother is valid. Perhaps it truly represents the ideals of upper class Victorians.

"Living in the American tradition which is pragmatic and flexible, I see my life as one of constant adjustment. Moreover, I live in five year plans—occasionally interrupted—and I seek in each segment of time to construct a community around me and my children which leaves each of us a chance to grow. When we lived in New York City, I built a playgroup community around my son to sustain both of us and to free me to pursue my personal career."

"I'd like to return to Deena's reference to Mrs. Ramsay as holding back the tide rather than being creative. As a mother, I have never thought of creativity as defining my role," I said. "To me mothering was an intellectual challenge. These are very different concepts. Creativity is the process of bringing something to artistic life where before there was nothing. Children are never 'nothing.' "

Both daughters laughed in agreement.

"Even when helpless, new infants possess definite personalities," I continued, thinking of how Debby, my first child, had provided the perfect ego trip for a new inexperienced mother. Most frequently her eyes were closed in sleep. Her bladder too had helped build my confidence. I could boast of "training" her at a young age. Deena was born with her brown eyes flashing wide open. Curious, moving, looking, she had a different personality from her sister. Rarely could I complete a sketch of her. Two different children, they presented two challenges. "I treated childrearing as an intellectual challenge, not as a creative process. For me it never became confused with the two creative processes that meant the most in my life: writing and painting."

"Perhaps that's because as mothers and women who considered becoming artists, we know the difference between the two, Mom," Deborah asserted.

"Speaking of creativity and mothering, I am reminded of a conversation with my male art professor at Brandeis," Deena interjected. "He was discussing with a number of female art students the predominance of women majoring in art at the undergraduate level and the absence of women at the professional and graduate level. He threw out, half in jest, a comment he had heard accounting for the dearth of female artists by women's biological role of giving birth to children rather than to works of art."

"Attitudes towards women as artists take a long time to change, don't they?" Deena triggered my own recollections of wanting to become a painter and of the indulgent attitude of society to women as painters. They are—or perhaps were—considered dilettantes and dabblers unless they remained unmarried and committed to nothing else.

As if reading my thoughts but bringing us back to the novel, Deborah observed how ironic it was that Mrs. Ramsay, the woman who mothered everyone until "there was scarcely a shell of herself left for her to know herself by; all was so lavished and spent" (60), was probably most successful as the spiritual mother of Lily who chose never to mother anyone but became an artist.

"And yet," Deena commented, "marriage is Mrs. Ramsay's objective for all women—even Lily. Think of the section where, in a series of nonsequiturs, she describes Lily: 'With her little Chinese eyes and her puckered-up face, she would never marry; one could not take her painting very seriously' (29). What relevance did her painting have to the fact that she wouldn't marry, except in Mrs. Ramsay's mind? Marriage, not painting, is connected with people."

"Your observation that Lily is unsuccessful in Mrs. Ramsay's opinion is interesting because actually, this work is considered highly autobiographical and may reflect Woolf's sense of having disappointed her mother." I felt it necessary at this point to acquaint them with Woolf's background. "Parallels exist between Woolf's life—as recorded in her diaries, letters, and in Bell's *Biography*—and specific adventures or opinions expressed by characters in *To the Lighthouse*. For example, Mr. Ramsay resembles Woolf's father; and Cam's thoughts about her father as she observes him reading on the trip to the lighthouse sound much like Woolf's jottings in her diary of her reactions to her father—her mixture of love and hate, of admiration and antipathy. Lily, although an unmarried painter rather than a married writer, voices some of the problems Virginia Woolf faced as an artist.

"Probably the most meaningful parallel," I continued, "is that of Mrs. Ramsay to Woolf's mother. Since her mother, Julia Stephen, seemed like a tremendously overworked and emotionally drained woman, dying when Virginia was only thirteen, this portrait of the burdens of motherhood and of the great contribution of the mother to her daughter is perhaps romanticized here."

"Fascinating, Mom, because at the close of the book, Lily completes her painting," Deena noted. "Unlike Mr. or Mrs. Ramsay, she achieves what she sets out to do. And I wondered, 'Is this achievement of one's goal denied to Mrs. Ramsay because of Virginia Woolf's perception of motherhood? Is it a criticism of Mrs. Ramsay as a mother, or criticism of Mrs. Ramsay as a person, or criticism of the institution of marriage, that neither Mr. nor Mrs. Ramsay is ever going to be an artist?' "

"I think that Woolf is speaking to the problem facing women when they choose to have a career," I responded. "From the biographical material we learn that originally she wanted children but that eventually she and Leonard, on the advice of mental doctors, decided against becoming parents. You may remember that in *To the Lighthouse*, Woolf writes of Lily, 'She took shelter from the reverence which covered all women' (75), strongly identifying with her sex. On the other hand, Woolf writes of Mrs. Ramsay's thinking, 'An unmarried woman has missed the best of life' (77)."

"Lily Briscoe should strike me as real and evoke memories from my own life when I considered becoming an artist," Deborah thought aloud. "But there is a self-indulgent quality to her which I tend to see in my life as flourishing mainly during adolescence—that is, something to be outgrown and controlled. Certainly her perceptions of the problems of painting are accurate, albeit exaggerated."

I could remember painting in the outdoors, painting in the museum—trying to learn and hating to have people look over my shoulder, much as Lily feels. "The one inconsistency, I think, is Lily's intense involvement with the personality of her subject, Mrs. Ramsay, while painting her."

"But Mom," Deborah continued, "the struggle with space, the attempt to control forms, the difficulty in attaining an external vision which corresponded to the internal one, the desire for recognition and praise, these are all things I remember encountering when I had active pretensions to be an artist. But I also recall expressing my artistic frustrations verbally rather than turning inward. I would complain like a child, or eat some caloric treat, or give vent to the problem by ignoring it (and denying my serious interest in art). Obviously, Lily does none of these things since she is already a mature woman when we meet her."

Thinking of the imperfect parallel between Woolf and Lily, I speculated, "We know what Woolf achieved as an artist whereas you never feel that Lily will be a great artist or has the potential for greatness. That's what's so sad. If you had the feeling that she were on her way to becoming great—"

"But you're not meant to," Deena interrupted, "because of the whole position of women in the book. Although it is acceptable for Mr. Pauncefort to be an artist—and the implication is that he is less talented than Lily—it is not proper of her. Again, when William Bankes walks up to Lily and she's very involved in her art, what does he think about— her shoes, that they were 'excellent' (31). To everyone, she is the poor old maid; her choice of painting over marriage is never accepted."

I wondered aloud, "Do you think that there is a basic conflict, as this novel suggests, between being an artist and mothering?"

"To the extent that being an artist demands 'immature' self-absorption, self-indulgence," Deborah continued, "it is not compatible with motherhood. Having chosen the latter, I forfeited the former."

Deena felt that circumstances having to do with marriage and the concessions husbands and wives make for one another contributed to her decision to reject a career in art. Children and mothering were not involved.

"Certainly in the scene at the dinner table," I noted, "Woolf has Lily interacting with everyone to show her aloneness and inability to make contact. But the author also shows that Lily is willing to 'be dishonest' and join Paul in search of the brooch. She wants to be in contact with other human beings if she can be assured that she will be in a situation where she is not vulnerable."

"In some ways, Lily is fearful of the world," Deborah explained, "pursuing private images which will never be made public. In other ways, Lily represents a real alternative to Mrs. Ramsay the wave of the future perhaps. Lily is equally perceptive of social norms and relationships; she knows her own soul well and what she wants; and she stubbornly pursues her vision."

Still thinking of the choices Woolf seemed to be insisting on, I suggested, "By having Lily dominate that last section of the book, the author is saying that a woman must choose between children and a career. Lily's constant avoidance of Mr. Ramsay and of his demand for attention is in contrast with Mrs. Ramsay's attitude. It partially explains why Mrs. Ramsay did not, could not, pursue a life beyond that of family, wife, and mother." Again I wondered whether a woman could create paintings when she was bringing up children. Perhaps she could. In my case it wasn't possible. On the other hand, this may not have been a true ambition. I remember drawing my children when they were little; I remember attempting to paint them and having an interested three-year-old take the brush from my hand although she had been supplied with her own brush and paper. How much of the artistic mothering can be transferred to the daughters—the love of art, the ease with the medium? Despite evident potential skill, neither daughter chose to become an artist. Nor did I.

"But it is not simply a matter of becoming an artist or becoming a mother," Deena observed. "The women in the book are permitted neither to speak on issues nor to create paintings. That's what I started to say about life and art and creation. Lily is always made to feel ill at ease by Mr. Ramsay or just about anyone else whenever she is discovered painting, creating. Nobody, including Mrs. Ramsay, who tries to tell her to stop painting, accepts her as an artist."

"That's why I don't see this as a glorification of Mrs. Ramsay, even if you say it is Woolf's portrait of her mother," Deborah insisted. "Mrs. Ramsay has put her whole stock—all of her life—into her kids. Two of them die very young; the young ones never know her that well; she ends up at most having a maternal relationship with Lily who recalls her lost spirit."

"Oh no, I don't think that she wasted a whole book on her family," Deena concurred. "She's speaking of the ways women are denied the 'normal' channels of self-expression. They must keep everything under wraps; men need not. Look at the portrait of Charles Tansley. She's saying that just because Tansley (or any man) would help Lily out of the underground doesn't mean that that is equivalent to helping him express himself. Since he had already sneered, 'Oh, women can't paint, can't write,' an equal exchange of support doesn't exist. I think that the book centers more on the problem of woman as artist than on family. Otherwise, why have all those extra characters?"

"On the other hand, why have one third of the book centered around Mrs. Ramsay?" I challenged.

Were there no resonances familiar to them from their own lives as mothers as well as from their identification, if only slightly, with Lily as an artist? Certainly I had remembered the boredom at times, the fatigue, the desire to speak with intellectual equals rather than infants or even young children. I had remembered trying to pick up a book to read and being unable to concentrate on anything beyond the daily newspaper. I had remembered the long telephone conversations with friends equally housebound—in an effort to retain adult contact.

Deena had observed that "Woolf captures the fatigue in mothering, the constant attention to trivia, the expectation that a mother will run errands, see to the repair of the greenhouse, plan meals, maintain the flower garden, furnish the rooms with life, and, besides everything else, visit the sick, dying and poor."

Deborah took exception to Woolf's thesis as to the role of the mother. "In *A Room of One's Own*, Woolf shows that the reason women created a world for their family, as Mrs. Ramsay did, stemmed not from inner views of womanness but from the values imposed upon them by society and the economic constraints under which women operate. In other words, these patterns of mothering were initiated by the social, economic and political subservience of women; they did not derive from women's particular abilities."

"Before you analyze the social and political factors, Deb, I'd like to say, yes, there are resonances of my experiences in this novel. One occurs when Mrs. Ramsay wraps her shawl around the skull in the nursery. She hides the truth from Cam and creates the illusion of a beautiful mountain full of happy living things. However, James insists on maintaining the truth by feeling the skull under the shawl. To go through such a procedure as altering a story or covering a skull, Mrs. Ramsay must perceive clearly the truth and understand its impact on her children. This is a much more complex and difficult feat than never tampering with a fact.

"As a mother, I find the 'tampering' requires perception, clear thinking, and inventiveness. It is infinitely easier not to buffer one's children than to use reality in a constructive, albeit, not forthright manner," Deena asserted.

"In a way, this might be construed as a creative device," I conceded.

"That leads to my second point. I think that Mrs. Ramsay—and there are some Mrs. Ramsay's in this world—saw her role as a creator of children. When her youngest child, James, grows up, she will not be needed in the mothering role."

"You don't really think that childrearing is creative, like painting or writing, do you Deena?" Deborah asked.

"Not really. But I can understand the feeling. As a parent, I understand Mrs. Ramsay's protectiveness towards her children. It's very comforting to walk into your child's room and see her in a crib—and know that if you really want to pick her up, you may. There she is, just a bundle of humanity—and she's there for you to mold. Although you can imagine this in your mind, particularly before your child starts talking, ultimately you discover that she is not as malleable as you thought. If having and raising children is considered a creative process, it ends when the children reveal their own personalities. At that point the mother realizes that she is not creating sculpture from a piece of clay."

"Deena, I'd like to return to the mother-daughter relationship suggested by Mom's biographical reference, because I think I see a parallel to myself as daughter."

Ah, I thought, we are perhaps discovering the relevance of this work to our own lives.

"Now, in *To the Lighthouse*," Deborah continued, "Woolf suggests that Mrs. Ramsay's own inner strength and abilities make her mother all the individuals who enter her house. This attitude may be good when we reach the point of saying, 'Now we have an equal society and we can ignore social pressures.' But I wonder if Woolf is misreading Mrs. Ramsay because she is her mother. Woolf doesn't want to say, 'Look, this is what this woman was forced into doing, and she might have done otherwise had she not had eight children and been married to this particular man.' She turns a social fact—her mother's skill in mothering—into something that is creative, but in doing so, she obscures the social factors behind it.

"Now how else would a daughter react to her mother?" Deborah continued. "You know, you talk about your past in negative terms, at times, and yet if you were to ask me, I would say it was wonderful. I had a glorious childhood. From my perspective all the things you did as a mother for me paid off. I absorbed your ideals even if you felt conflict over mothering versus pursuing and independent career. I could write the same type of book, granted with a Jewish, New York setting instead of a Victorian one—that would glorify all the things that you did as part of your own initiative—which I don't think speaks to the situation of mothers in society. I think this spiritual indebtedness is inherent in a mother-daughter relationship especially if the daughter feels that she got something from her mother."

Mrs. Ramsay had thought, "For one's own children so often gave one's own perceptions a little thrust forward" (122). I too felt this way.

"I remember enjoying both of you very much—enjoying the activities we did together and the freedom that was involved. I think, however, there was the problem of later finding outlets for the skills that I as a mother developed."

"Do you think that the price is too high?"

"I don't think there need be a price. After all, Mrs. Ramsay had eight children and, as Deena implied, she died, perhaps because she felt her job was over," I continued.

"That's a dismal thought," noted Deborah.

"—especially since she had enough children to fill a lifetime of busyness. In our society, a woman who has two, three or even four children, has a long life ahead after the children are grown."

"You're speaking of the 'empty nest' syndrome, aren't you, Mom?" queried Deena.

"Yes, but I'm also saying that society has made no room for this woman for the skills developed during mothering. She is considered useless. Moreover, having functioned alone in a home, she frequently has become fearful of the outside world—a world from which she has too long been absent.

"Society still dictates what is expected of women. And men still find it difficult to accept role changes although verbally they agree that these changes should come about."

"Woolf captures this aspect of a woman's experience," Deena ruminated. "Whenever a woman steps over the boundary of her role and presents an opinion about anything other than children, she is laughed at. Mrs. Ramsay's concern over the political issue of milk is laughed off and Minta's opinion about people not enjoying Shakespeare's plays is ignored. Even worse, when Mrs. Ramsay picks up a book to read, her husband looks at her strangely."

"Mrs. Ramsay strikes me as conventionally victorian, but that conventionality is viewed through the eyes of a literary genius who endows it with timelessness, eternal validity," Deborah noted, explaining, "she talks of her daughters' futures as women, implying marriage, family, and the importance of good looks. Personality is merely a variation on a theme."

I agreed. "She did not for a moment consider that one of them might choose the path of a Lily Briscoe although she recognized the fact that Rose would 'suffer,' the implication being that Rose would suffer because she was intense and artistic. Mothering to me meant helping you to develop your full potential, to like yourselves as women, to be comfortable with yourselves, and to continue this growth in adulthood.

But a mother can never be certain of the message a daughter receives. Do you remember any kinds of pressures to marry or have children?"

"The pressure to marry came mostly from outside the family," Deena offered "—sociocultural expectations."

"Nor do I recall such pressures at home," Deborah said, "although I do recall yearning for romantic love, assuming marriage, and being uncertain about children. I'm sure such pressures existed in my life, however. I remember talk of trousseau when, during my senior year in high school, Gram gave me the silver candlesticks she made. Certainly I was not immune to the general pressures of society."

"The parental expectation was to achieve and find contentment in a profession other than homemaking," Deena suggested. "Preferably the career choice would require high intelligence and intellectual excitement."

Deborah concurred that the more important pressures were "to excel in artistic and intellectual endeavors."

"Well then, do you think the novel speaks to us?" I asked.

"Not as mothers, or even as daughters," Deborah answered, "but as women. I found it interesting to see most of the world through the eyes of two women. The book spends a great deal of time talking about women and women's perceptions, allowing you to go inside their heads whereas you spend very little time, relatively, in the heads of men."

"The first time I read it, the novel angered me as a portrait of a mother because of the eight children and the role of a mother as silent server or, to use Woolf's metaphor in *A Room of One's Own*, as 'magic mirror' in which men see themselves at twice their natural size. But on closer examination, one realizes that Woolf is hanging the father not the mother," I observed.

"*A Room* gives us a social context and an economic nexus for patriarchy and women's oppression," Deborah noted. "The psychosocial portrait of Mrs. Ramsay turns on itself and leads either to glorifying woman's intuition or rejecting motherhood and marriage."

"I don't think it's meant to be representative of the sex," Deena contended. "I think it's intended as the presentation of a certain type of woman. Mrs. Ramsay is no more a portrait of all women than is Lily Briscoe, or any of the other female characters in the book.

"The human values most central to the novel are friendship and love both between members of the opposite sex and between members of the same sex. The relationship between people is focused on in terms of giving and taking—sharing one's life and the price of such sharing."

Deborah conceded that although she did not like the novel, she heard a message. "The mother dies; an era ends. Lily Briscoe survives although she has no children. All she has are her paintings that are going to end up underneath the couch. But she points the way to the future for women."

"Maybe *To the Lighthouse* presents the mother as the 'historical' woman," Deena speculated, "the one who is a product of, and represents, all women in the past the way Woolf creates Mary Carmichael in *A Room* to be the product of all female authors. Although I love the novel, I do not agree with its conclusion about the limited options for a mother. If I did, I would not be participating in this analysis."

Nor would I. Although I think that the challenge is immense—to grow as a separate human being and to function as a mother—it must be faced by women. "I chose *To the Lighthouse* because I knew it would hold the potential for discussion. I think we have found expression of some of our problems as women; we have heard echoes of our conflicts as potential artists; we have heard the sometimes mocking, sometimes whining, sometimes autocratic voices of men. We have been challenged although we have not found the dream, the promise, and the inspiration of *A Room of One's Own*. Thank you for joining me. Thank you for the treasures you are—communicating daughters."

Notes

[1] Virginia Woolf, *To the Lighthouse* (New York: Harcourt, Brace & World, Inc., 1927). All references will be included in the text, indicated by page numbers enclosed in parentheses.

Part Five
THE MOTHER AS MEDUSA

Introduction

The applause has died. The thanks have given way to curses. The emancipation of an earlier time, that exuberant mood which energized the writers of the twenties, gives way to another mood, the power struggle of the contemporary author wrestling with her mother.

The women (like Sylvia Plath, for instance) who wrote during or about the 1950s, the years of the "feminine mystique," were reflected grotesquely in the chrome of their kitchens. In the sixties, when women were left out of the leftist revolt, they were forced into another version of the feminine mystique, a combination of flower child and earth mother. These women endured a kind of perpetual pregnancy, always in training for motherhood. The young woman who did not wish to fall into this mode of maternity often left home, wounded, without her mother's blessing. We see this in the novels of Doris Lessing. As Professor Katherine Fishburn shows, in Britain and in Canada, there is need for the "daughter to become something other than her mother." Yet, she continues, "Martha Quest is pressured . . . to become nothing more than a link in the chain of motherhood." Under such pressures, many writer-daughters rebel. Their protagonists feel, as Alice Munro writes, "the problem, the only problem is my mother." Or, as Margaret Laurence, another Canadian writes, mother's words stick "like burrs to the hair."

The mother has become monster. Margaret Atwood describes Joan Foster's mother in *Lady Oracle:* "She never let go of me because I never let go of her." The mother is monster because the daughter too much sees herself reflected in her mother's image, in her mother's life. The fear of all the daughters is that in looking at the mother they will also see themselves and turn to stone.

Medusa, of course, is a gorgon fair of face but with snake hair, the woman who turns to stone any who look upon her. Professor Karen Elias-Button, in her essay "The Muse as Medusa," uses this mythological figure as a metaphor for the contemporary author's mother-search and matrophobia. Medusa is the "dark side of the 'mother,'" the "grasping mother, representative of the entanglements mothers and daughters encounter." But Medusa is also powerful and thus becomes "a metaphor for powers previously hidden and denigrated, collective powers we are finally beginning to reaffirm and claim for ourselves."

In the four other essays in this section, we see variations of Medusa, the Good and Terrible Mother. Fishburn's essay on the "nightmare repetition of motherhood" in Lessing's *Children of Violence* series emphasizes the "poisonous influence of the mother." Martha Quest's mother is "an appropriate symbol of Martha's potential oppression and should be resisted." But we also see that Martha's view of her Terrible Mother is not the only one. When the mother tells her own story, she seems merely a "querulous old woman," hardly the mythological Medusa the daughter fears.

Sometimes the daughter sees herself mirrored in the mother but cannot distinguish her own features there. Sylvia and Aurelia Plath, says Professor Mary Lynn Broe, "both wasted so much time in handmaiden tasks, confusing intellectual curiosity for the most menial—and musial—duties. They confused creative identity with romantic involvement, yet neither recognized the crippling fact in the other." Plath, in her poetry about her mother, aims for "organic prepatriarchal power" but becomes instead "a stone . . . without dreams of any sort."

The only dreaming the Jewish women do, in Erika Duncan's study, is on their deathbeds. Song and joy come in memory and release one from a life of nurturing, of feeding others and of starving one's self. The Jewish mother-monster, that much maligned literary figure, is seen as "the all-engulfing nurturer who devours the very soul with every spoonful of hot chicken soup." But these mothers, "bread givers," are themselves "at once devourers and the devoured." They sacrifice themselves and yet are helpless to prevent the sacrifice of their daughters. When, rarely, the daughters do escape the pattern of their mother's life, they flee with bitterness, fears, guilts implanted by the past and by the stony stare of the mother. In a sense, then, the Jewish daughters are impregnated by their mothers with a model of powerlessness, of profound starvation. How can we abort these false pregnancies? By turning the monstrous vision, the hungry giantess, into the *artist*, into a Medusa of our own making. If the Jewish mother is the distorting mirror, the gorgon who is pregnant with us, then we, her progeny, must bear her truths.

Professor Lorna Irvine, in a more hopeful essay about Canadian women writers, describes a "coming to terms with the past." In fact, Canadian writers portray a past that, "for women, is peculiarly bound up with the mother." Unlike the women writers in the United States, Canadian women writers are creating "their country's fictional landscape," their names a laurel wreath of wisdom: Atwood, Engel, Fraser, Laurence, Munro, Shields. But there are stages we must journey through before we reach this pastoral, shared vision of a landscape. First, the daughter must negate the mother: "As the daughter grows stronger, the mother weakens." Then there is recognition, and, finally, reconciliation. Possibly there is in Canada a greater political openness, Irvine speculates, which makes the country hospitable to the woman writer. Perhaps the qualities of nonaggressiveness and of incorporation in the nation itself can be embodied in the outpourings of the Canadian daughters reconciling to their pioneering mothers.

Professor Elias-Button, who lays the theoretical groundwork for this section, speaks of the need to confront the "Terrible Mother in order to move beyond the entanglements of the mother/daughter relationship," to claim "her as metaphor for the sources of our own creative powers." Medusa's reflection is our own. We are, therefore, mothered by the mirror and, within it, we must seek a new mythology—a mother mythology. We must listen carefully to the wisdom of the hissing snakes; see the power flashing in the mother's eyes. We must shield her from those who would take her power. We must return her to autonomy.

The mothers in the previous section—Mary Virginia Cather, Sido, Julia Stephens—ruled in their own right, in their gardens and their homes. The mothers portrayed in this section too often trespass in their daughters' gardens, intrude in their daughters' lives. They seem to have little existence apart from their children and dread their daughters' independence as if it means their own death. The daughter who would mature must defeat her mother. Consequently, many mothers and daughters portrayed in contemporary literature are more embattled than loved. It is not until the last section of this book, "The New Matrilineage," that we shall witness their reconciliation.

E.M.B.
C.N.D.

16
The Muse as Medusa

It is significant that contemporary women's poetry is filled with Mothers: ourselves, our own, the dark, the gracious of the fields and seasons. For, as part of the process of women's self-discovery, we are finding it necessary to reexamine, in both personal and mythological terms, our relationship to the figure of the mother. No longer satisfied with the rigid role definitions which have traditionally been passed automatically from mothers to daughters, women are subjecting these restrictive assumptions to serious critical analysis. Some poets, therefore, examining the difficulties of this relationship, see it as the source of an emotional, or even literal, death. I treat the insights of these poets in the first part of this paper.

At the same time, however, perhaps because of the very nature of the mother/daughter relationship itself, others are reaffirming this connection by means of a complex process in which the current difficulties are transcended through a recovery of the mythological past. Thus, some contemporary poets have chosen to focus on the figure of the goddess, so prominent in prehistory, as part of a redemptive enterprise, involving not a relinquishment of ego development in the name of cyclicity and romantic unconsciousness but rather a reaching-back to the myths of the "mother" to find there the source of our own, specifically female, creative powers.

Interestingly, many of these poets have chosen the Terrible Mother, the goddess considered responsible during the Neolithic Age for the underside of creative renewal, to represent the potential source of female transformation. This dark side of the "mother," whose face is Medusa's own, functions in the poetry under discussion here in two ways: in the first section she is seen as the grasping mother, representative of the entanglements mothers and daughters encounter so often; in the second section she becomes a metaphor for powers previously hidden and denigrated, collective powers we are finally beginning to reaffirm and claim for ourselves. Medusa becomes for us, in a process that involves much more than simple inspiration, a muse.

Thus, by exploring the personal and mythological aspects of this intricate and inescapable mother/daughter bond, we are both realizing the need to define ourselves as "daughters" in new ways and, at the same time, rediscovering the roots of our shared woman's life in all its power and complexity. In her poem "Housewife" Anne Sexton states, "A woman *is* her mother./ That's the main thing"[1]: a simple story, true and not true, whose variations are still being invented and revealed.

* * *

In nineteenth-century America, according to Carroll Smith-Rosenberg, women were able to form emotionally satisfying relationships with one another based on shared biological and emotional experience. Because such experience could be counted on to remain constant, mothers and daughters participated in a system of apprenticeship by means of which accumulated female wisdom was passed from one generation of women to the next. "An intimate mother-daughter relationship lay at the heart of this female world." Daughters had few options: they accepted the mother's reality which, although restrictive, nevertheless afforded mutual support and understanding.[2]

Some contemporary poets, such as Margaret Walker, look back at such a time with nostalgia, sensing capacities for nurturance in the old way of life ("My grandmothers were strong. . . . They touched earth and grain grew."), capacities which seem today to have atrophied in spite of us ("Why am I not as they?").[3] But many express the idea that the mother's way of life, tidy sometimes to the point of sterility, is no longer satisfactory to use as a model in dealing with present complexities. Lucille Clifton, for example, imagines herself populating a room with her own chaotic yearnings, only to hear her mother's response:*

> if mama
> could talk

---

* The seven lines that follow are reprinted from *An Ordinary Woman* by Lucille Clifton, published by Random House, New York, and copyright © 1974 by Lucille Clifton.

> she would talk
> good girl
> good girl
> good girl
> clean up your room.[4]

This avoidance of the anarchic is also found in the mother's world in "Vierge ouvrante" by Miriam Palmer, combined here with a shallow, unthinking religiosity. Like the fifteenth-century French statue of the Virgin Mary by the same name, this mother's condition is also seen as hollow. She has never questioned her own life, accepting the role of wife and mother as a sacred, unshakable given, and now, with children gone, her body closes again, returning to its original impenetrable condition:

> She sits in Mother's rocker
> and sinks herself back
> to that just-beginning,
> that blessed virgin
> -ity, when the nuns
> made a dresden magic over everything.
> Flowers never died
> and never bloomed, there were no necessities,
> no demands
> from husband – children – strangers,
> her hands in their purity
> never trembled on the keys
> and the light
> always followed her to mass.[5]

Both poets depict the mother's narrow world in terms of a small room whose order must be maintained at all costs. But the daughters' realization that this future offers only extinguished possibility is not in itself enough to allow them to walk out the door. Leaving the old world behind is difficult not only because the traditions and conventions associated with the mother wield a heavy weight but also because this existence has held for us certain advantages. Although the speaker in Adrienne Rich's "Snapshots of a Daughter-in-Law," for example, recognizes the negative power of the traditional feminine role to induce madness, hysteria, obsessional neurosis and false hope, she also realizes that woman has been pampered, indulged, treated like a "precocious child, Time's precious chronic invalid. . . ." As long as we have been satisfied to remain within these limits, everything we have done, she says, becomes acceptable. Dare to defy these constraints, however, and we risk enforced estrangement, the terrors of the isolated life. Ending her poem with a vision of a new Aphrodite, who moves not by submitting herself to the current but by means of her own relentless courage and determination, Adrienne Rich claims that we can achieve this vision only by severing ourselves boldly from these easy comforts.[6]

While this effort requires persistence, however, it also involves a trust in the process itself, a belief that out of all our work growth and fruition will occur almost naturally, like a birth. In her "Raccoon Poem" Miriam Palmer imagines herself awakening in the spring, as an animal does from hibernation, and sees her final transformation as a natural result of the forces of renewal:

> I have been sleeping through a long cold
> in the hollow branch of my mother
> it is time now to splash through
> the thawed ice.[7]

If the traditional woman's role is no longer satisfactory, then the heritage passed between mothers and daughters is no longer an easy gift. In poem after poem, women watch as their daughters grow away from them, into their own realities. Anne Sexton, writing in "Little Girl, My String Bean, My Lovely Woman" of her daughter Linda as she approaches 12, wants her to enter her womanhood with pride. Having played the formative part in her daughter's first birth, the poet now assumes a more self-effacing posture, urging her daughter to accept her body in its second birth as a "garden," a "world of its own."[8]

But in spite of the mother's good intentions, the relationship often assumes formidable complexities. Audre Lorde discusses these intricate connections in "Progress Report," a poem in which the mother attempts to understand the necessities of her daughter's growth by remembering her own, but remains finally puzzled and uncertain. Worried that the loving relationship established with her daughter has begun to deteriorate, she tries to maintain perspective by recalling her own need to achieve independence by leaving her mother's house. Her daughter too, like a fish, must travel away from her, swimming "upstream to [her] final place of birth." But while realizing this, she is nevertheless forced to face the difficulties of the moment as her daughter, balanced between "history and obedience," both obeys her and at the same time begins to reflect the mother's own independent spirit, a process which, ironically, can only result in their alienation. At the end of the poem she is left standing outside her daughter's door, listening to pages rustle as the girl reads "under cover."[9]

In her poem "Mothers, Daughters" Shirley Kaufman also discusses this relationship in terms of reflection. Here the two seem to have become so thoroughly embedded in one another that the effect is suffocating. The daughter, in her efforts to assert herself as a separate person, merely becomes the mirror-image of the mother's own despair:

> She's cruel,
> as if my private meanness
> found a way to punish us.
> We gnaw at each other's
> skulls. Give me what's mine.
> I'd haul her back, choking
> myself in her, herself in me.

And by the end of the poem this mother too, willing to accept and support the daughter if only she would express her need for love, finds herself shut out. The girl has isolated herself in her own room where she shares her "thin bones with no one. / Only her shadow on the glass / waits like an older sister."[10]

The emphasis on reflection found in these poems is indicative of the difficulties women experience in attempting to establish identity. If mother and daughter can only become mirror-images of one another, where is a separate sense of self? In her article "Family Structure and Feminine Personality" Nancy Chodorow explores the effects of the mother/daughter relationship on female personality structure, finding problems involving boundary confusion inherent in the relationship itself. For both sexes, because child-rearing practices are centered primarily around the figure of the mother, this early relationship becomes centrally important in the development of personality. The male, whose primary identification must give way to a developing masculine gender identity, comes to define masculinity as "that which is not feminine or involved with women." This repudiation of the feminine appears in male mythology, interestingly, in the story of the hero who must overcome the Terrible Mother to achieve success. Perseus, as the developing consciousness in Neumann's view, must battle and defeat the fascination of the feminine unconscious, in the person of Medusa, in order to attain maturity.[11]

The female's gender identity, on the other hand, does not require rejection of the primary identification with the mother. The fact that feminine identity is, in a sense, rooted in this relationship provides the female, under favorable circumstances, with a healthy sense of security. But this relationship can also preclude differentiation, causing difficulties with

> boundary confusion or equation of self and other, for example, guilt and self-blame for the other's unhappiness; shame and embarrassment at the other's actions; daughters' 'discovery' that they are 'really' living out their mothers' lives in their choice of career; mothers' not completely conscious reactions to their daughters' bodies as their own (over-identification and therefore often unnecessary concern with supposed weight or skin problems, which the mother is really worried about in herself); etc.

Western daughters, according to Chodorow, are for various reasons highly susceptible to these problems and are, therefore, often caught up in difficulties having to do with infantile dependence.[12]
These problems seem especially acute during female adolescence, as we have seen from the poems. The difficulty of establishing identity for the daughter at this time arises, I believe, from the fact that the mother's body comes to represent to her two mutually exclusive things: the childhood she must move away from, as well as the adulthood she must journey toward and eventually accept. Anne Sexton, in her poem "Mother and Daughter," written to Linda at 18, reveals her understanding of this predicament, a situation painful for the daughter, and for the mother as well. Linda, she says, has inherited her "Mother & Co.," the problems and rewards of the adult woman, but while in one sense they are growing closer as the daughter enters adulthood, at the same time they now find themselves miles apart emotionally. In the transformation to adulthood, Linda has left her old body behind, the body of her childhood, but in this process the outworn body is equated with the mother herself who is also being forsaken ("and I am motherwarm and used, / just as your childhood is used"). And while the mother has been left "empty," the daughter remains oblivious, even hostile, intent on her own concerns:

> Question you about this
> and you will see my death
> drooling at these gray lips
> while you, my burglar, will eat
> fruit and pass the time of day.[13]

The entire body of Anne Sexton's work can be seen as her attempt to explore the negative aspects of the relationship with the mother in terms that are meant to be explicitly autobiographical. In an early poem, "The Double Image," she describes, brilliantly and painfully, the complexities of a mother/daughter relationship in which all three participants, her mother, her daughter, and herself, seem fated to reflect each other in cruel and almost disastrous ways. Feeling that her own dark side is as contagious as disease, the poet assumes the blame for her new daughter's illness, and just as the child regains her health, the poet turns toward death, attempts suicide, and is committed to a mental hospital. The idea that malady is passed on almost automatically from mother to daughter is applied here to the poet's mother as well. Feeling like a "partly mended thing, an outgrown child," the poet comes back from the hospital to live at her mother's house, and discovers that her mother has breast cancer:

> Only my mother grew ill.
> She turned from me, as if death were catching,
> as if death transferred,
> as if my dying had eaten inside of her.
>   . . .
> On the first of September she looked at me
> and said I gave her cancer.

This "double image" of mother and daughter is objectified in the poem by the set of portraits painted during this stay which are eventually hung opposite each other in the mother's house. The artist has captured the two faces just as they (like the mother and child found earlier in the poem) are about to turn away from each other, the mother's toward death and the poet's away from it. But the portraits remain, like their smiles, frozen in place. And although the poet realizes that she has burdened her daughter with her own feelings of unworthiness and encourages her in the poem to develop a well-grounded self-confidence, it is this sense of unremitting, almost haunting, paralysis which remains. The mother, like the figure of Medusa, continues to eye the poet from her "stony head of death," and the poet finds herself unable to break free:

> And this is the cave of the mirror,
> that double woman who stares
> at herself as if she were petrified
> in time—[14]

Anne Sexton continues to explore these difficulties in her later poetry. Unable to resolve the conflicts engendered by this relationship and suspecting increasingly that her own immense need for nourishment was somehow connected with her mother's (breast) cancer, the poet begins to equate nurturance with death. Seeing her body and her mother's as identical, the poet is unable to move beyond the ambivalence of this condition in which such embeddedness provides sustenance but also precludes separation. As the poetry progresses, she moves toward what begins to seem an almost inescapable fate with the deliberate intention of a hungry child.

Anne Sexton herself seems to have been aware of the deterministic nature of this maternal influence. During one of her hospitalizations for severe depression, she is reported to have looked around her at the young female patients and offered an explanation: "Because they couldn't break loose of their mothers."[15]

"Guilt and self-blame," "shame and embarrassment," entrapment and helplessness: these constitute, at least in part, the dark heritage passed between mothers and daughters in a recurrent cyclical process which can result in emotional impoverishment, paralysis, death. If I imply here, then, that, burdened with a childhood she was unable to shake off, Anne Sexton's relationship with her mother may have paved the way toward her suicide, I do so in order to suggest that it is this very relationship, seen now metaphorically rather than literally, which can herald another more positive journey. For women, as Robin Morgan writes to her mother in "Matrilineal Descent,"* are going beyond "the oasis of your curse, / even beyond that last mirage, your blessing" to claim the mother as the source of our woman's life: "Mother, in ways neither of us can understand, / I have come home."[16]

Maxine Kumin and Audre Lorde both discuss this process, in which a difficult, almost destructive relationship with the mother is transformed into something more positive, by using the image of a tree. In "A Voice from the Roses"† Maxine Kumin, making reference to the mythological story in which Athena, jealous of Arachne's creative powers, turns her into a spider, speaks of her mother's vengeance as the "thorn" out of which, like Arachne, she herself has spun her "messages" for thirty years. Now, though, perhaps because the poet has become

---

* From *Monster Poems* copyright © 1972 by Robin Morgan, published by Random House, New York.

† From *The Privilege* copyright© by Maxine Kumin, published by Harper and Row, New York.

receptive to her mother's own creative powers, the thorn has taken root and is "raising a tree inside me. / The buds of my mother's arbor / grow ripe in my sex."[17] And in "Black Mother Woman" Audre Lorde, too, makes use of mythological analogies to discuss this process. Just as many of the goddess figures of prehistory were turned to angry, chthonic powers and relegated to the underworld with the establishment of the Greek patriarchal pantheon, so the poet's mother, buried for years "in myths of no worth," has appeared to the poet as the fury-figure whose energies could be expressed only through a suffocating anger. Now, by working her way through this rage to the love at its center, the poet has discovered her mother's secret:

> and look mother
> I Am
> a dark temple where your true spirit rises
> beautiful
> and tough as chestnut. . . .[18]

The process of reclaiming the mother involves, in part, an historical reaching-back to the lives women have lived before us, to find there the sense that our experience is rooted in a strength which has managed to survive the centuries. Sharon Barba, in "A Cycle of Women," speaks of the heritage each woman senses as part of her own experience and suggests that every woman, when she is ready, will wake up to this reality and live it through again:

> Let her go from there, start over,
> live it again, until she knows who she is.
> Until she rises as though from the sea
> not on the half-shell this time
> nothing to laugh at
> and not as delicate as he imagined her:
> a woman big-hipped, beautiful, and fierce.[19]

Significantly, Sharon Barba uses the image of Aphrodite to end her poem, finding in the figure of this new Venus, rooted in the historical past and realized in the always-commencing present, a mythological equivalent. For women are searching not only for historical prototypes but also for mythological ones. As Barba and Chester state in their introduction to *Rising Tides*, "Women must learn the self-love, the self-idealizing, the self-mythologizing, that has made it possible for men to think of themselves as persons. The first step is to acknowledge that one is a woman and to begin discovering what that may mean."[20]

It is true that mythology can be considered a masculine construct, the shifting emphasis of its systems reflecting changes, both ontogenetic and phylogenetic, within the male psyche.[21] According to this view, the proliferation of goddess figures, which began as far back as the Upper Paleolithic and continued through the Neolithic Age, can be seen as an expression of the awe and even fascination with which the male viewed the all-powerful Mother, an attitude which was eventually replaced by dread and contempt. Others, however, see mythology as originally female: the world-view of the Magna Mater who ruled the cyclical forces of birth and death, renewal and decay. According to this view, it was only with the transition to patriarchy and the development of the heroic consciousness that this "matriarchal" world-view was obscured and distorted. By working to get beyond this stratum of patriarchal overlay, it is possible to discover the force and outline of these early, specifically female mythologies and, in the process, redeem them for our own use.

It is this process in which many contemporary women poets are currently engaged, finding in the figure of the goddess, specifically the Terrible Mother, a source of potential creative renewal. Medusa, probably the best exemplar of this figure, has come to represent, within male mythology and psychology, the grasping (female) unconscious whose power to fascinate, and ultimately castrate, must be permanently destroyed by the (male) hero. For women, however, the figure of Medusa takes on a more complex significance.

Women, too, in attempting to locate themselves in relation to the "mother," fear the threat of a potentially paralyzing entanglement. Medusa, then, as we have seen in the poems discussed in the first part of this paper, can take on the traditional significance for women as representative of the reflexive difficulties seemingly inherent in the mother/ daughter relationship. But, I would suggest, this figure only exerts a destructive effect on a woman when she is unable to resolve the confusion that results from seeing the mother's body as representative both of the childhood world and that of the adult. To move beyond this "cave of the mirror," to use Anne Sexton's phrase, involves, on the one hand, being able to define ourselves in new ways so that the process of becoming an adult and achieving maturity does not automatically mean becoming one's mother, retaining all the old connections, assuming automatically the outmoded roles. And, on the other hand, it involves not destruction of the "mother" but rather a confrontation with and an incorporation of those matriarchal powers which are both ancient and our own.

Thus, for women the confrontation with Medusa, though sometimes deadly, can turn out differently. Louise Bogan, Karen Lindsey, and May Sarton all speak in their poetry of the potential sense of renewal inherent in this encounter. In two thematically related poems, "Medusa" and "The Sleeping Fury," Louise Bogan wrote of coming to terms with her own "monster."[22] In "Medusa" she sees this figure in traditional terms. Here Medusa has a paralyzing effect not only on the speaker but also on her surroundings. What begins as a scene in which all the elements move in balanced, harmonious relationship becomes, with the vision of the "bare eyes" and "hissing hair," a stopped landscape in which movement remains suspended and the speaker sees herself as insubstantial in relation to this more powerful visionary reality.[23] The antagonist in "The Sleeping Fury," similar in appearance to Medusa, assumes the characteristics of a chthonic female power whom no sacrifice will appease. Remaining throughout by the speaker's side, she remorselessly reveals pretension, hypocrisy, and truths too painful to bear. And yet, by finally gathering enough courage to face her "hunter," the speaker achieves both a reconciliation and a new sense of her own strength:

> And now I may look upon you,
> Having once met your eyes. You lie in sleep and forget me.
> Alone and strong in my peace, I look upon you in yours.[24]

In a more contemporary "Medusa" poem Karen Lindsey realizes that only by facing this terrible figure, no matter how painful the experience proves to be, can we remain in touch with our life-giving forces:

> listen im telling you its
> every bit as ugly as you think it is
> ive seen it ive stared at it, it
> tears your stomach out you
> scream you claw the air the pain
> hold on, hold on, listen
> youre not imagining too much youre
> not imagining anything, believe me it
> burns your face off with its smile
> you scream believe me you
> scream you run you cry
> but the legends are wrong.
> it is those who do not look
> who turn to stone.[25]

Bearing witness to a similar experience, May Sarton speaks in her poem "The Muse as Medusa" of an encounter with the dark "mother" to which she came in fear, "as naked as any little fish / Prepared to be hooked, gutted, caught." Having looked Medusa "straight in the cold eye," however, she finds that instead of being turned to stone, she has been released into a "world of feeling / Where thoughts, those fishes, silent, feed and rove. . . ." And she realizes, at the end of the poem, that the "frozen rage" Medusa represents is really the necessary con-comitant of the world of creative feeling:

> I turn your face around! It is my face.
> That frozen rage is what I must explore—
> Oh secret, self-enclosed, and ravaged place!
> This is the gift I thank Medusa for.[26]

Here, as in the previous Medusa poems, the speaker is able to benefit from this confrontation because she has moved from the passive state of being looked at to the point where she can take the risks involved in a more *active* looking, a process in which perhaps she is asserting her own ability to perceive and experience the world. In addition, having confronted Medusa herself directly, she is able to understand that the powers she has feared are really her own and that, within the uncon-scious, darkness and light exist side by side, both necessary components of the creative imagination. It is significant, as well, that May Sarton speaks of release in terms of water imagery. As representative of a condition opposed absolutely to that of a stony paralysis, the water imagery we have seen so frequently in these poems signifies a freeing of the woman as a "solution" to the problems of the mother/daughter relationship. Thus, the figure of Aphrodite used by both Rich and Barba takes on additional significance as the image of the new woman advancing, with the force of the "mother's" rising tides, toward a birth which is both labored-after and a natural fruition.[27]

Medusa, as we have seen, has traditionally been used within the male system as a symbol of the castrating female, and perhaps part of women's obsession with her can be explained by the internalized gyn-ophobia we have come to recognize as part of our patriarchal "inherit-ance."[28] Women, though, are no longer finding it necessary to assume pleasing postures in order to undercut the threat and terror such a figure commonly invokes; rather, in an act of courage, we are turning toward the Terrible Mother to claim her as our own. Instead of focussing on her destruction, women are finding that our stance in relation to the "mother" is different from that assumed by the male. While the figure of Medusa, in her character as grasping mother, can come to represent for the female the potentially paralyzing effects of the mother/daughter relationship, she also embodies female creative energies which can be recovered for our own use. The darkness associated with this goddess is appropriate for two reasons. First, the energies embodied by her have been buried for so long that, to rediscover them, we have to be prepared to uncover our own righteous anger, an anger which can fuel our creativity if we can learn to let it. Second, the fact that the goddess figure of the Neolithic Age represented the forces of death and decay as well as those of birth and renewal reflects the wisdom of prehistory: the knowledge that every creative act is firmly rooted in the dark.

Thus, when we see women's development in its own terms and understand the active assumption of our creativity (in whatever form) as an incorporation of the forces of the dark "mother," then the enlargement of women's creative powers can be seen as a completely natural and, in fact, necessary process. As we have seen from these poems, then, the figure of Medusa can become the door, the way-in to the world not only of poetry but of a creative activity whose sources are fierce and powerful. For women, as we are discovering, these sources are already at hand. By confronting the Terrible Mother in order to move beyond the entanglements of the mother/daughter relationship, and by claiming her as metaphor for the sources of our own creative powers, women are creating new self-configurations in which the mother is no longer the necessary comfort but the seed of a new being, and in which we are no longer the protected child but the carriers of the new woman whose birth is our own.

Notes

[1] Anne Sexton, *All My Pretty Ones* (Boston: Houghton Mifflin, 1962), p. 48.

[2] Carroll Smith-Rosenberg, "The Female World of Love and Ritual: Relations Between Women in Nineteenth-Century America," *Signs*, 1 (Autumn 1975), 1–29.

[3] Florence Howe and Ellen Bass, eds., *No More Masks!: An Anthology of Poems by Women* (New York: Anchor Press, 1973), p. 110.

[4] Lucille Clifton, *An Ordinary Woman* (New York: Random House, 1974), p. 69.

[5] Howe and Bass, pp. 341–42.

[6] Adrienne Rich, *Snapshots of a Daughter-in-Law* (New York: Norton, 1956–1967), pp. 21–25.

[7] Howe and Bass, p. 340.

[8] Anne Sexton, *Live or Die* (Boston: Houghton Mifflin, 1966), pp. 62–65.

⁹ Audre Lorde, *From A Land Where Other People Live* (Detroit: Broadside Press, 1973), pp. 13–14.

¹⁰ Laura Chester and Sharon Barba, eds., *Rising Tides: 20th Century American Women Poets* (New York: Washington Square Press, 1973), pp. 129–30.

¹¹ Erich Neumann, *The Origins and History of Consciousness* (New York: Harper and Bros., 1954), pp. 54–95, *passim*.

¹² Nancy Chodorow, "Family Structure and Feminine Personality," in *Woman, Culture, and Society*, eds. Michelle Z. Rosaldo and Louise Lamphere (Stanford: Stanford University Press, 1974), pp. 43–66.

¹³ Anne Sexton, *The Book of Folly* (Boston: Houghton Mifflin, 1973), pp. 11–12.

¹⁴ Anne Sexton, *To Bedlam and Part Way Back* (Boston: Houghton Mifflin, 1960), pp. 53–61.

¹⁵ Barbara Kevles, "The Dying of a Poet," *The Village Voice*, 5 April 1976, pp. 47–50.

¹⁶ Robin Morgan, *Monster* (New York: Vintage, 1972), pp. 33–34.

¹⁷ Maxine Kumin, *The Privilege* (New York: Harper and Row, 1961–1965), pp. 37–38.

¹⁸ Lorde, p. 16.

¹⁹ Chester and Barba, pp. 356–57.

²⁰ Chester and Barba, p. xxvi.

²¹ See Neumann, *Origins*.

²² Although Louise Bogan's work predates the feminist movement, her insights are significant and worth including as part of this women's story.

²³ Louise Bogan, *The Blue Estuaries: Poems 1923–1968* (New York: Ecco Press, 1923–1968), p. 4.

²⁴ Bogan, pp. 78–79.

²⁵ Celia Gilbert and Pat Rabby, eds., *Women/Poems III* (Lexington, Mass.: Women/Poems Press, 1974), unpaginated.

²⁶ May Sarton, *Collected Poems (1930–1973)* (New York: Norton, 1974), p. 332.

²⁷ These insights were developed in conversation with Inez Alfors and Amy Kaminsky, colleagues at SUNY Oswego.

²⁸ See Annis Pratt, "Aunt Jennifer's Tigers: Notes Toward a Preliterary History of Women's Archetypes," *Feminist Studies*, 4, No. 1 (February 1978), 188. For the many ways in which negative attitudes toward women are "learned" preverbally by females as well as males, see also Dorothy Dinnerstein, *The Mermaid and The Minotaur: Sexual Arrangements and Human Malaise* (New York: Harper and Row, 1976).

The Nightmare Repetition: The Mother-Daughter Conflict in Doris Lessing's Children of Violence

In the past twenty-five years Doris Lessing has distinguished herself as a voice crying in the wilderness. Like the Old Testament prophets whose work she perpetuates, she warns the world of its impending doom. Because the bulk of her writing seems to consist of this inspired proselytizing, it is easy to overlook her concerns for humanity's more domestic problems. But even in the most overtly political of her novels, such as *The Grass Is Singing* (1950), *Retreat to Innocence* (1956), or *A Ripple From the Storm* (1958), Lessing uses the most intimate details of her characters' lives to enrich the meaning of her work. Like her contemporary, Margaret Drabble, who calls her "Cassandra in a World Under Seige,"[1] she finds the cause of our social problems to be in part attributable to our homelife. By concentrating as she does on the personal lives of her heroines, she is able, like both Drabble and Muriel Spark, another contemporary, to illustrate most convincingly her social and political theories. Unlike the proletarian novelists of the thirties, whose work she mocks in *The Golden Notebook* (1962), Lessing does not sacrifice her characters to her dogma. As a result, in all her fiction she has the power to strike responsive chords in her readers even when she foretells the decline and fall of western civilization.

In her masterwork, the five-part *Children of Violence* series, Lessing follows a single character, Martha Quest, from adolescence to old age and death, using her as both an example of and a foil to twentieth-century culture. In these books Lessing draws on the traditions of the past as they appear in nineteenth-century novels of manners and the psychic phenomenon of the future as they appear in the novels of such

writers as Robert Heinlein and Ursula LeGuin. Although not confined
to the nineteenth century, the technique of ironic distance Lessing uses
in *Martha Quest* (the first book) is strongly reflective of Jane Austen's
narration in *Emma*. More significantly, the two characters, Emma
Woodhouse and Martha Quest, even share a similar obsession: the
intention never to marry. What sets Martha apart from Emma, besides
a century and a continent (Martha is born in 1919 in what is now called
Southern Rhodesia, and what Lessing calls Zambesia in the series), is
her relationship to her mother, for Emma, like many nineteenth-century
heroines, loses her mother early in life. Not so Martha. In fact, in a
negative sense, Mrs. Quest is the major driving force in Martha's life.
It is the dialectics of the mother-daughter relationship in Martha's experience that give birth, for example, to her idealized vision of a four-
gated city. Throughout the series this utopian city functions as a symbol
of the world Martha seeks that is beyond domestic squabbles and political differences. One of its primary purposes, in her mind, would be
to keep out people like her mother, people who are neurotic, bigoted,
hopelessly old fashioned. To understand Martha's feelings toward her
mother, therefore, is to understand her politics—and, in turn, Lessing's.

The mother-daughter relationship in *Children of Violence*, as those in
the fiction of Margaret Drabble, reflects the needs of the daughter to
become something other than her mother. Dissatisfied with the demands
and limitations of motherhood, the adolescent Martha Quest has plans
to escape her sexual destiny by moving away from home. Finding few
role models for women other than that of mother in the paternalistic
society in which she lives, however, Martha has trouble defining herself
as anything other than nonmother and is continually asking others to
tell her who she is. The question her behavior raises is why this sensitive, intelligent girl becomes obsessed by her mother. Why does she
focus narrowly on her mother as the cause of all her problems, and the
object of all her fears and hatreds? I think the answer lies in the double
binds that Martha finds herself in—ones that seem peculiar to daughters.

Although both sons and daughters face the necessity of splitting
from their mothers, the sons seem to have the advantage here in that
they are not expected to, indeed cannot, become themselves mothers.
Their break, therefore, is enhanced by the fact that they will automatically free themselves to a certain degree simply by maturing and accepting their own sexuality. Their problem centers instead on not becoming their fathers.[2] On the other hand, daughters not only share their
mother's sex, which makes establishing an identity separate from their

mothers difficult, but they are not expected to become anything other than a mother. (A boy is hardly expected to become a father; rather a banker, teacher, or contractor.) At birth a girl is already what she is expected to be eighteen to twenty years hence: someone defined not in terms of what she can become but in terms of what she is to others. As a contemporary historian explains it, "A woman 'is'; a man is always in the process of becoming."[3] (If our teachers and scholars repeat such reactionary nonsense, is it any wonder an adolescent girl doubts her dreams?) In short, sons get jobs; daughters beget children. Herein lies Martha's problem. She is pressured by everyone to become nothing more than a link in the chain of motherhood. Compounding her problem is her relationship to her father, as what society requires of her is not that she assert her difference from her father but that she find a replacement for him—a man to whom she can submit and who will take care of her. In this situation she will recapitulate both her mother's sexual submission and her own daughterly subordination to her father. She will, in effect, become her mother.

One of the reasons for Martha's failure to find meaning on her own is that she has matured at a time when very few women worked outside the home, and those who did became primarily secretaries or beauticians. As a woman, Martha does not feel particularly pressured socially to choose a profession, as a man might. Nor, as a dreamer, does she feel particularly attracted to the options open to her in the business world.

Because of her hungers and continuing disappointments as a woman, it is not surprising that Martha's relationship to her mother is primarily antagonistic.[4] To the rebellious young Martha, Mrs. Quest represents the traditionally passive female role from which she is desperate to escape.[5] Their relationship, therefore, is less that of mother and daughter and more that of Mother and Daughter. In Erich Neumann's taxonomy, Martha represents the basic "male" drive toward consciousness and Mrs. Quest the archetypally "feminine" principle of the unconscious with which Martha, as she struggles for her own identity, is in eternal opposition.[6] Although Neumann's theories have been attacked for their potential for either pigeonholing women or reinforcing existing stereotypes,[7] I believe that his ideas can be useful if taken in a sociological rather than a psychological context. If we consider his findings to have a sociological validity, they can be viewed as legitimate historical accounts of social beliefs and behavior. This approach allows us to examine the symbolism of *Children of Violence* as it draws on tradition and myth,

it does not pretend to present any psychological "truths" about mothers
(or, for that matter, women).

What is important to note in this context is that both the narrator
and Martha herself describe Mrs. Quest as a symbolic figure, giving
credence to the fact that Martha's response to her mother, even though
it stems from her own "adolescent misery," is conceivably also that of
her creator.[8] From Martha's perspective—and also perhaps Lessing's—
Mrs. Quest literally is the Dark and Terrible Mother described by
Neumann as "the devouring womb of the grave and of death" (GM, p.
149).[9]

In resisting her mother, Martha seems to demonstrate "the dialectical
relation of the conscious to the unconscious" in an emergent ego, which
is, according to Neumann, "an archetypal experience of the whole
species, male and female alike" (GM, p. 148). When Mrs. Quest is
described as "the eternal mother, holding sleep and death in her twin
hands like a sweet and poisonous cloud of forgetfulness" (MQ, p. 24),
she is, therefore, mythologically speaking, "the hungry earth, which
devours its own children and fattens on their corpses" (GM, p. 149).
More specifically, she is the projection of Martha's inner turmoil, the
physical manifestation of Martha's archetypal fears. Although we might
question the accuracy of Martha's insistence that Mrs. Quest is a demon,
it is, I think, significant that Martha sees her mother and not her society
as the enemy of her growth and individuation. It becomes especially
ironic that the blame is misplaced when we realize that it is society
itself—in its language, literature, and popular culture—that has provided her with the traditional scapegoat: the myth of the evil mother.

Perpetuating the stereotype still further, Lessing, in her account of
the relationship between Martha and her mother, also illustrates what
Neumann calls the "two characters of the feminine": the elementary
and the transformative. The former he calls the "Great Round," which
"tends to hold fast to everything that springs from it and to surround
it like an eternal substance" (GM, p. 25). This is illustrated in the fact
that Mrs. Quest expects Martha to play the role of marriageable daughter. Again, this interpretation does not suggest any psychological truths
about Mrs. Quest; it simply reveals the social pressures that Martha is
heir to and that seem to her to be filtered through her mother's expectations. The second "character" Neumann describes as an "accent . . . on
the dynamic element of the psyche, which, in contrast to the conservative tendency of the elementary character, drives toward motion,
change, and, in a word, transformation" (GM, p. 29). This is illustrated

by the psychic use to which Martha puts her conflict with her mother. That is, as the Terrible Mother (metaphorically speaking), Mrs. Quest tries to control Martha's developing ego by enveloping her in the pattern of the "nightmare *repetition*" of marriage and childbirth.[10] But Martha is able to benefit psychologically from the conflict with this "Terrible Mother" by using the experience to strengthen her own will, her ego.

Because she is unable to accept the responsibility for her own short-comings, Martha accuses her mother of putting a "spell" on her after she has inexplicably failed to take her matric examination, the "simple passport" which would allow her to escape to "the outside world" (MQ, p. 23). Paralyzed by ennui, Martha seems incapable of acting rationally in her own interests; she is, rather, driven by a blind instinct to survive, which is nourished by her love of romance. The direction this instinct takes her is "through an ancient role" intended to separate her from the parents who have "destroyed her" (MQ, p. 70). Describing Martha's journey in these symbolic terms, the narrator seems to suggest an archetypal pattern here. In its development, however, Lessing is some-what inconsistent. On the one hand, when Martha responds to her mother's hypnotic murmuring by snapping, "I will *not* be tired . . . it's no good trying to make me tired," the narrator remarks that it is "extraordinary that Mrs. Quest [does] not question" what Martha has said, suggesting that, at least as far as Lessing is concerned, she may indeed be the "baneful figure" Martha perceives her to be (MQ, p. 24).

Because Martha is uncertain of her own identity, the plot of the entire *Children of Violence* series hinges on her quest for herself (a self different from that imposed upon her from without). Like a romance, it is composed of a series of adventures all leading to an ultimate epiphany in *The Four-Gated City.* What Martha does not know yet in *Martha Quest* is that her adventures should not only be outward-going but also inward-looking. Her movement in this book reflects her con-fusion and as a result is always away from and never toward. She is moving away from the one fate that she knows absolutely she would not choose given the chance: that of motherhood. She is terrified of repeating the pattern, of becoming her mother.

Inextricably intertwined with Martha's desire to assert her own identity is her relationship to her own body. Enamoured of her body's perfection, Martha perceives it as a symbol of her psychic integrity. She believes that if she can retain its beauty, and wholeness, she will retain her valued independence. When she sees the effects of childbirth in the varicose veins of Mrs. Van Rensberg, therefore, she is horrified by this certain evidence of the older woman's bondage (MQ, p. 3). Because of her radical fear of the effects of childbirth on a woman's body, one of the most poignant scenes in the entire series is the one in *A Proper Marriage* in which Martha lies in the bath examining her body which has become "heavy, unresponsive" and seems "to be pursuing ideas of its own" (PM, p. 63). Although she does not know it yet, her "flesh [is] uncomfortable on her bones" because she is pregnant (PM, p. 63). This scene is a far cry from an earlier one in *Martha Quest* where Martha with "frank adoration" falls "into a rite of self-love," worshipping her limbs as they lie "smooth and light in the water" (MQ, p. 146). By unintentionally becoming pregnant, she temporarily loses control of both her body and her life. In other words, when her body is "long, lean, and narrow" (MQ, p. 146), she is rather boyish-looking and as close as a woman can be physically to the supposed ideal figure of freedom: the young male. Coupled with her evident physical revulsion to even the touch of other women, including that of her own mother (MQ, p. 17, p. 142), her obsession with thinness seems to indicate a desire to pattern herself after and align herself with males, because of this sex's freedom of self-definition (MQ, p. 117).

Martha's view of the world is largely determined by her body. Although scholars and pyschologists alike continue to refute Freud's theory that the anatomy of a woman is her destiny, women remain sociologically bound to their bodies.[11] Unable to fulfill what could be liberating expectations for herself, such as her desire to remain unmarried, Martha rightfully fears her mother's body. Not that her mother or her mother's empty womb will, in fact, devour her, but that society will persist in seeing her as her mother. Thus when Martha's body corresponds to her idealized image of what an independent woman should look like, she is easy in it, and confident of her own possibilities for self-determination. When it betrays her by gaining weight and, worse, by becoming pregnant, she rejects it as an instrument of her oppression, despising both it and herself.

Convinced that the only way for her to break the pattern of the nightmare repetition is by having no children of her own, Martha's first response to the fact that she is expecting a baby is to deny it. When she can no longer ignore it, she tries, unsuccessfully, to redeem her body's integrity by aborting the fetus (PM, p. 100). Underneath her surface displeasure and confounding her by its implications runs a thread of elation, "as if she had wanted this damned baby all the time . . ." (PM, p. 102). Torn between her own individual needs to remain unviolated and those of her species to reproduce her kind,[12] Martha, not unrealist-ically, feels she has become the victim of a conspiracy that has channeled her from the moment of her birth into the role of motherhood. Feeling completely alienated from her body, she questions the point of trying to think or plan ("male" activities) when she is so obviously at the mercy of her emotions ("female" qualities) (PM, p. 103). Although it might be tempting to analyze Martha's feelings of alienation in pathological terms, I believe that she is simply expressing the helplessness of the female who has finally been confronted with her bodiliness.[13] Ironically, it is her most personal possession, her body, that is the agent of her feeling of otherness. But biology and the institution of motherhood (to borrow from Rich)[14] conspire to palliate her anger with joy. When she tries to disentangle these emotions, her mother offers her no help at all by offering the remark—which Martha finds incredible coming from Mrs. Quest—that having a baby is "the greatest experience in a woman's life" (PM, p. 102).

Nor do Martha's doubts disappear once the baby is born. Unable to enjoy her baby because to do so "would be a disloyalty and even a danger to herself" (PM, p. 201), she feels guilty—as, of course, she would be expected to feel by her society. Frightened by her potential to do Caroline psychological harm, she vows to send her away from her own "poisonous influence" as soon as possible (PM, p. 204). These are strong words the narrator is using to describe Martha's attitudes toward motherhood. That Martha, who has consciously set out to be different, finds herself as little fit for mothering as Mrs. Quest before her indicates that there are forces afoot that Martha has no control over. Whether these forces are inherited characteristics or learned behavior is a moot question. What is important is that Martha feels powerless before them.

Finally, in one last brave attempt to circumvent the pattern of history, Martha gives her husband, Douglas, custody of their child at their divorce. Although she questions her behavior six years later,[15] it isn't until she is in London that she realizes that what she has done was a mistake, that she was "mad" to let her daughter go.[16] The explanation she offers for deserting Caroline is not psychological but political. She claims that she left the child because at that time she and her communist friends believed that the family was the "source of [social] neurosis" (FC, p. 70).

Although her explanation makes sense, it seems to avoid her real motivation. While it is true that Martha is heavily involved in the Communist Party when she leaves Douglas, the contexts surrounding the descriptions of her relationship with her daughter are psychological and not political. It is her fear of being "sucked into the pattern" (PM, p. 251) of complacent motherhood that drives her to deny her own child. It is when her own body, "her female self" (PM, p. 251), tries to urge her into a second pregnancy that Martha finally determines once and for all to break away. In this decision she receives no support from the book's older women, as her mother-in-law longs for the announcement that Martha would "make the best of it" (PM, p. 336) and her own mother tells her it is a "woman's role to sacrifice herself, as she had done, for the sake of the children" (PM, p. 339).

Although Lessing confines most of the five book series to Martha's point of view, there are several sections in which she uses Mrs. Quest as the center of consciousness. Clearly she limits these sections so her readers will identify with Martha, who in many respects is less than admirable. That she includes them at all suggests she believes that Mrs. Quest is a victim of her time and society. In Martha's sections, as I have indicated, Mrs. Quest is not a person but a symbol of the Terrible Mother. In her own sections, however, Mrs. Quest is a querulous old woman who unintentionally but inevitably offends and annoys her daughter whose ways she cannot comprehend (MQ, p. 14, pp. 59–60; PM, pp. 107–110; L, p. 234, pp. 246–247; FC, pp. 247–286). In that Mrs. Quest tries to mold Martha into her own image of womanhood (that is, motherhood), she is an appropriate symbol of Martha's potential oppression and should be resisted. In that Mrs. Quest is herself a victim of romance (like Mrs. Talbot she mourns a lover who died in WWI; PM, p. 78; FC, p. 251), she is nothing more than a pawn of fate and should be pitied. For Martha the threat of the "nightmare repetition" is the only impetus she needs to keep moving until she can find her way out of the maze of history by awakening to a new reality. For her mother, less adventurous and more traditional, the nightmare ends only in the sleep of death. In *Children of Violence* "mothers and daughters" are not so much relatives as the fatal pattern of an ancient curse.

At the beginning of this essay, I suggested that there is a direct correlation between Lessing's politics and her portrayal of the mother-daughter relationship in *Children of Violence*. By politics I mean to include both Lessing's sexual politics and her social politics. What she is illustrating in the Quest family is the subordination of an individual to the powers of her superiors. What she is arguing is that this is a pernicious system that leads to alienation and lends itself only to extreme solutions.

In other words, the young daughter, Martha Quest, looks to her mother for guidance in establishing an identity for herself. Instead of finding a model that she wishes to emulate, she finds one she fears. She fears it because her mother is not free. Heir to a tradition in which women are supposed to be the passive and not the active members of the race, and unable to accept the fact that a truly integrated person can be both simultaneously, Martha fluctuates wildly between wanting to be independent and wanting to be cared for. Her independent spirit takes the form of her plans to remain single. Her desires for support take the form of her romantic yearnings for the perfect lover.

Unable to resolve her problem satisfactorily on the conscious level, she retreats to her unconscious. At this point in Martha's development (FC, pp. 497–525; pp. 535–553), Lessing incorporates her own brand of Sufism which, in brief, foretells a time in which humanity will have the psychic skills to communicate both verbally and pictorially without the aid of language or objects. Everyone will read everyone else's mind. This leap takes us a long way from the rather homely mother-daughter relationship which has been the focus of this essay.

In *Martha Quest* we see the adolescent Martha struggling with her dreams of selfhood and having them stunted by a patriarchal society that is so potent even her own mother betrays her. In *A Proper Marriage* we see the young mother Martha trying to overcome the crippling effects of the institution of motherhood, both as it affects her and her daughter. In the final three books of the series, *A Ripple From the Storm*, *Landlocked*, and *The Four-Gated City*, we see a maturing woman still haunted by her mother—driven, in fact, to actual illness upon the prospects of a visit from her. We also finally witness Lessing's ultimate solution to the politics of mother-daughter: eliminate the problem altogether by opening humanity's individual psyches to such an extent that no one would be able to control another person, nor would anyone want or feel the need to. Granted, her solution is virtually useless on a literal level. But on a metaphoric one she is calling for a time beyond both the sex war and the need for a concept of androgyny. She is asking not that we give up our bodies but that we learn to live more completely in them. In her cataclysmic conclusion to the series, she dramatically predicts that the power plays and oppression characteristics of the nightmare repetition of motherhood can lead not only to alienated women but to the end of the world.

Katherine Fishburn

Notes

Margaret Drabble, "Doris Lessing: Cassandra in a World Under Seige," *Ramparts*, 10 (February 1972), pp. 50–54.

A problem which is mitigated by the fact that a man's identity is based largely on his profession and not on his biological role in conception.

Page Smith, *Daughters of the Promised Land: Women in American History* (Little, Brown and Company, 1970), p. 318.

Lynn Sukenick calls her attitude "matrophobia"; see "Feeling and Reason in Doris Lessing's Fiction," *Contemporary Literature*, Vol. 14, no. 4. (Autumn 1973), p. 519. See also: Patricia Meyer Spacks, *The Female Imagination* (Avon Books, 1972, 1976), pp. 190–201; Sydney Janet Kaplan, *Feminine Consciousness in the Modern British Novel* (University of Illinois Press, 1975), pp. 136–172; and Linnea Aycock, "The Mother/ Daughter Relationship in the *Children of Violence* Series," *Anonymous: A Journal for the Woman Writer*, 1 (1974), pp. 48–55. (Although the latter is listed in the 1976 *MLA International Bibliography*, item #7222, I have been unable to obtain a copy of the article; nor can I or the Reference Library at Michigan State University find any publishing information on the journal in which it appears).

In *Of Woman Born* (Bantam Books, 1977), Adrienne Rich comments: "Many daughters live in rage at their mothers for having accepted, too readily and passively, 'whatever comes.' A mother's victimization does not merely humiliate her, it mutilates the daughter who watches her for clues as to what it means to be a woman" (pp. 246–247).

Erich Neumann, *The Great Mother: An Analysis of the Archetype*, trans., Ralph Manheim (Princeton University Press, Bollingen Series, 1955, 1972). Subsequent references appear in text abbreviated as GM.

See Rich, op cit., pp. 82–83.

Doris Lessing, *Martha Quest* (Plume Books, 1952, 1970), p. 7. Subsequent references appear in text abbreviated as MQ.

Of her mother and father Lessing says "We use our parents like recurring dreams, to be entered into when needed; they are always there for love or for hate . . ." ("My Father," in her collection of essays, *A Small Personal Voice* [Alfred A. Knopf, 1974], p. 83).

[10] Doris Lessing, *A Proper Marriage* (Plume Books, 1954, 1970), p. 77. Subsequent references appear in text abbreviated as PM.

[11] See, for example, Naomi Weisstein, "Psychology Constructs the Female," in *Woman in Sexist Society: Studies in Power and Powerlessness*, eds. Vivian Gornick and Barbara K. Moran (Basic Books, Inc., Publishers, 1971), pp. 133–146. In *The Second Sex*, trans. and ed. H. M. Parshley, (Bantam Books, 1949, 1961), Simone de Beauvoir, in discussing a woman's biological characteristics, remarks: "Woman, like man *is* her body: but her body is something other than herself" (p. 26). And later, of "biological facts": "I deny that they establish for her a fixed and inevitable destiny" (p. 29).

[12] See de Beauvoir, op. cit., p. 22.

[13] See Rich, op. cit., p. 268.

[14] *Ibid.*, pp. 15, 20–29.

[15] Doris Lessing, *Landlocked* (Plume Books, 1958, 1970), p. 239. Subsequent references appear in text abbreviated as L.

[16] Doris Lessing, *The Four-Gated City* (Bantam, 1969, 1970), pp. 69–70. Subsequent references appear in text abbreviated as FC.

A Subtle Psychic Bond:
The Mother Figure in Sylvia Plath's Poetry

Smarting from rigorous criticism in *The Bell Jar,* Aurelia Schober Plath collected her daughter's letters[1] to prove a kind of psychic bond between mother and daughter. Ironically, Sylvia did share the underlying pattern of her mother's life, but in a psychodrama between the lines that eludes the mother and, at the same time, discourages a full expression of the passionate bonding between mother and daughter that is the focus of much of the poetry.

The letters are introduced by Mrs. Plath's lengthy but unassuming family history, which hints that Sylvia fused parts of her life with her mother's. (The specific parts are not clarified.) We glimpse a pragmatic courtship, a prosaic student/professor coupling in which everything had to be sacrificed for his academic writing, the scientifically planned birth and rearing of two children according to Otto's prescription. The letters are replete with the mother's well-aimed directives, which had little relevance to Sylvia's continuing struggle to adjust to disillusionment, to calculate her energies so as to forge her present into future art. Those tidbits of advice only point up the intimate but misaligned portrait of mother and daughter that runs through the letters.

Charmed by the idealistic goal of strengthening the inner life and imprisoned in a social sycophancy, the mother fails to grasp the psychological and emotional roots of her daughter's creative development, a fact that figures prominently in Plath's later use of the mother figure, particularly in the *Crossing the Water* poems. Like two objects grazing each other but missing any real connection, mother and daughter are taken with their respective worldly tasks. For the same glittering princess who elaborated tales of taffeta debuts and Yale weekends for her mother's savoring also ambitiously calculated her literary career. She streamlined her stories for the big money glossies, ruthlessly criticized her own jingle verse, and all the while distinguished her authentic talents from the money-grubbing exercises. In intellectual and emotional events, Sylvia was always on a pendulous course between zest and paralysis, self-advertising brag and humble deprecation. Likewise, Aurelia Plath, who believed in ideals of self-education, that the poor and virtuous always triumph in rags-to-riches splendor, began her training as a businesswoman at the request of her father.

The overwhelmingly sad truth evident in *Letters Home* is that Sylvia and Aurelia Plath both wasted so much time in handmaiden tasks, confusing intellectual curiosity for the most menial—and muse-like—duties. They confused creative identity with romantic involvement, yet neither recognized the crippling fact in the other. We have been told that psychic interplay between mother and daughter, particularly in a patriarchal society, requires a strong sense of "self nurture" in the mother.[2] There is, to be sure, more than slight longing for that primordial mother/daughter passion throughout these letters, but whatever true psychic bonding might have connected mother and daughter has been diffused and deflected by the demands of Ted Hughes and Otto Plath.

At a certain point in her career, as the letters verify, Sylvia recycled her intellectual and creative talents as Muse. While she may have begun and ended her career as Pygmalion, Sylvia spent a great part of it as Galatea, confusing inextricably her poetic identity with the stimulation of romantic involvement. In one letter, for example, Plath talks of realizing the best in herself, yet at the same time she brags of Hughes that by working with her, he will help her to become a world-renowned women poet. Acting as Hughes' U.S. literary agent, Sylvia kept thirty manuscripts typed and circulating at all times. She scouted the Amherst job scene for him, cooked, kept house, prepared for her own Newnham honors exams and rigorously adhered to her own daily writing schedule. Love for him was absorbing her totally, she bluntly announced, and her conviction that he was always ahead of her in both his intellectual and his artistic life filled her with admiration and a strong sense of her feminity.

In similar fashion, Aurelia Plath enticed her children upstairs with fantasy fiction so as to spare Otto Plath all but one-half hour a day contact with his children. Once a week, on the night when he taught, Aurelia would make an elaborate drawing of his work materials spread out on the dining room table. She did this so that she might secretly have friends for dinner and then replace each book exactly as it was before Otto returned.

Aurelia became, in effect, a cartographer of her own fears, a map-maker of her emotional and intellectual vassalage. Yet as we review the recent Plath cult and its adulation of suicide as the privileged rite of femininity, it is curious to observe that it was Otto Plath who willfully sponsored his own destruction in this Plath history, not the mother. (Otto knew he was ill, refused medical care, and eventually died of the effects of advanced diabetes mellitus.) Aurelia Plath was a tenacious survivor, though one thwarted in finding adequate expression for the "passion of motherbonding." More precisely, it is in Sylvia's poetry, where Aurelia Plath least grasped her daughter's creative resources, yet where the daughter's talents most completely mimed the mother's modes of self-expression,[3] that we must look to recover a sense of filial passion. For Sylvia proclaimed her poetry to be the most vigorous female tribute yet to those creative natural forces shared by women. And Aurelia, announcing the dynastic link of psychic bonding between two genera-tions of mothers and daughters, found it sometimes a comfort and sometimes a burdensome intrusion on their privacy. Both women found it easier to write their feelings than to speak them.

A courageous struggle to trace a matrilineal bond and its effect on the daughter's separate vocation of poem-making runs throughout the poetry. Beginning with the comic women personae in the earliest Smith poems and continuing through Plath's praise for the small constructive-ness of motherhood (*Ariel* and *Winter Trees*), the persona of the poems carries on a continually changing dialogue with various woman figures. In the *Crossing the Water* poems, she explores and criticizes her own artistic development by using the myth that links voluntary and invol-untary creation; in later poems, Sylvia finds in her own passionately complex tribute to motherhood, both the limitations and separateness of children and some small protection against total effacement by the male world of papery abstracts.

Is this her way of exorcising matrophobia? Healing a womanly split? Sylvia's motherbond is more complex, more contradictory. The power of this bond is often denied, Adrienne Rich claims, "because it cracks consciousness, threatens at times to lead the daughter back into 'those secret chambers . . . becoming, like waters poured into one jar, inex-tricably the same, one with the object one adored' " (*R*, p. 236). The mother, who "stands for the victim in ourselves, the unfree woman, the martyr," with whom "our personalities seem dangerously to blur and overlap" (*R*, p. 231), must be purged. Yet the prepatriarchal biological mother not only produced and stabilized life, but exercised an active, transforming power: "What to many woman today may be experienced as a passive function, occurring beyond volition, once was felt to be transformative power and was associated . . . with other kinds of trans-formation, including reincarnation" (*R*, p. 101). In her several volumes Sylvia Plath offers surely one of the most moving records in modern poetry of a daughter's attempt to realize the complexity of the moth-erbond first introduced in *Letters Home*.

In the very earliest poems (those written before 1955 at Smith College), Plath's women are a host of campy public performers—crazy queens, aerialists, lion-tamers, fortune-tellers. Each of their narratives suggests the admonishing lesson about the hazards of indulging in ex-uberant love or the excesses of the imagination. In a neatly formalized series of technical pirouettes, each woman is schooled not to let her greedy reach exceed her grasp. Although Plath seems to mock those who do not risk loving, she nevertheless recognizes the inevitable pain and disillusionment that derive from participation in a love relationship and acceptance of its rules. Old Gerd the fortune-teller has mastered the art of bossing others' futures. But when she tries to "govern more sight than [is] given to a woman/ By wits alone" in her own love life, she finds only "gorgon-prospects." In "Snowman on the Moor," a young woman changes from a Joan of Arc to a patient Griselda as she bids for dominance and self-sufficiency in love. When she summons a "fire-blorting, fork-tailed demon" to help her subdue her "grisly-thewed helper," he turns out to be a far worse woman-hater than the man she sets out to trounce:

> . . . o she felt
> No love in his eye,
>
> Worse—saw dangling from that spike-studded belt
> Ladies' sheaved skulls;
> Mournfully the dry tongues clacked their guilt:
> "our wits made fools
>
> Of kings, unmanned kings' sons: our masteries
> Amused court halls;
> For that brag, we barnacle these iron thighs."[4]

Although the pursuing giant dissolves in smoke, she dutifully trots home, humbled by her moment of insight. Her illusions about love are ironically reversed by patriarchal values. How canny, then, is Plath's lament to Aurelia in *Letters Home* on the tedium of learning the boundaries of a woman's sphere. How appropriate, too, is Aurelia's handmaidenship that deferred her spunky will to the fiction of a happy home.

In *The Colossus* poems,[5] Plath idealizes several women figures from the realm of art and mythology. They nag her with their peculiar imaginative vision of simultaneity which unites qualities of both the practical and visionary realms in much the same curious way that Aurelia succinctly coupled the world of scientific childrearing and secretarial procedures with lessoned pieties that urged an idealistic inner life. Psychologically, these aesthetic women remain distanced, unreachable, perhaps even countervailing forces to the mother. Yet they are important for what they reveal about the poet's developing ambivalences regarding both the woman artist and the mother. The "Lorelei" trouble the face of quiet with their stony ambiguities. Still they embody qualities of a new imaginative life that tantalizes Plath throughout the volume. Their marble flux is an ideal concurrence of opposites. They float upward toward the poet, shapes light and fluid, but siren-like they also lure her downward ("hair heavier than sculpted marble") with their unusual Harmony:

> . . . They sing
> Of a world more full and clear
> Than can be. Sisters, your song
> Bears a burden too weighty
> For the whorled ear's listening . . . (*Col*, pp. 22–23)*

By the poem's end, Plath was moved from mere description of quiet, mythic sources to a plea for her own active involvement in a realm of frightening contradictions: "Stone, stone, ferry me down there."

Although Sylvia Plath defines this new imaginative world of contradictions throughout *The Colossus*, the Lorelei's realm remains one of oblivion, idealized but coldly elusive. Likewise the "bony mother Lucina" labors among the "socketed white stars," suggesting not the mother's, but the daughter's, alien metaphysics. The monumental "Lady of the Shipwrecked" ("Finisterre") is indifferent to all but the "beautiful formlessness of the sea." "Two Sisters of Persephone" play out their remote, unresolved "duet of light and shade." Dispassionately perfect, mythically or artistically removed, each woman figure fails to

---

* This and other quotations so identified are from *The Colossus and Other Poems*, copyright © 1957, 1958, 1959, 1960, 1961, 1962 by Sylvia Plath, published by Random House, New York.

show the poet "how far there is to go" in identifying with the powerful passion of the motherbond, the pain of the motherknot.

As the poet senses her own changes in *Crossing the Water*,[6] she appeals to a mother figure to resolve her undefined dramatic energy by assigning her a single identity. Repeatedly, by imagery of ingestion, she hopes to acquire that organic, prepatriarchal power from intimate union: "Mother, you are the one mouth / I would be a tongue to. Mother of otherness / Eat me." Cowering among dumb minerals and roots, at home among mouldering tubers and "wormy purple cabbageheads," her memory and dreams flattened paper thin, the poet finds comfort in diminution: "I am a root, a stone, an owl pellet, / Without dreams of any sort." If the essential female tragedy really is expressed by the Demeter-Kore myth—the loss of the daughter to the mother and vice versa—then the wish to remain small and enveloped is the poet's protective desire to get back: "If I am little, I can do no harm," or "I must remember this, being small." She wants nurturing protection from the "mother of otherness," that sometimes repudiating, but always compelling force. But despite her foot-stamping demands or imperious whining to be guided through her process of shape-shifting, she receives no response from the mother. In similar fashion, the letters reveal that the mother-daughter link was never vocal or emotional, merely a matter of Sylvia's underlining poignant passages in her mother's college texts; of her learning to think practically about a U.N. job, of her acquiring a few physical laws in order to lay a sound, rational foundation for her writing. The mother, in turn, lived vicariously through Sylvia's narratives, but broke filial bonding by never referring to Sylvia's previous confidences from one letter to the next.

Sylvia discovers her reality to be the continual, forceful changing for which she alone must find expressive form in art. She feels herself kin to God, fighting the destiny of classification and concentrating her energies on finding forms for dramatic metamorphosis that will enable her to shape her "early alien distinctness felt in childhood into the vocation of poetry":[7]

> Give me back my shape. I am ready to construe the days
> I coupled with dust in the shadow of a stone. My ankles
> brighten. Brightness ascends my thighs. I am lost,
> I am lost, in the robes of all this light. (*CW*, p. 53)*

---

* This and other selections so identified are taken from *Crossing the Water* by Sylvia Plath, copyright © 1971 by Ted Hughes, published by Harper & Row, New York.

Sylvia longs to capture the contours of the mind's own specificity: "the truth of the mental quirk of the moment, the individual feeling over the habitual one, the spontaneous over the rehearsed response, the fluctuations of consciousness rather than its rigidities."[8] Sheer imaginative power characterizes her equally energetic struggle to diminish the self to the palpable and domesticated, and then to reveal the self boisterously in the guise of various personae. While she is tiny and inert as a rice grain, she also explores the possibility of becoming "Mother of a white Nike and several bald-eyed Apollos."

Frequently the daughter recognizes the intrusion of—even catalysis by—some impersonal male force: "all mouth," "the bullman," a "fat sort," "Fido Littlesoul," the "bowel's familiar," "Mumblepaws," "Dogsbody." In "Maenad," the banal realm of the father functions as unlikely catalyst for her changes which will prove her anything *but* an ordinary woman poet. The boast of the willfully naive persona only prompts, by the poem's end, a greater dramatic awareness of her reluctant progress toward a more complex identity:

> Once I was ordinary:
> Sat by my father's bean tree
> Eating the fingers of wisdom.
> The birds made milk.
> When it thundered I hid under a flat stone.
> The mother of mouths didn't love me.
> The old man shrank to a doll. (*CW*, p. 51)

As the poet stops dissembling (the framework of a fairytale narrative) and shifts her power to a new linearity, she utters a direct imperative, stark statements of fact, and pointed a warning: "Mother, keep out of my barnyard, / I am becoming another" (*CW*, p. 51).

One poem in particular seems to summarize the entire *Letters Home* psychodrama between the lines. In "Disquieting Muses," it is the mother's world and the function of her female inheritance that prompt the daughter to accept her mission as a woman artist, suggesting again that powerful but unnoticed psychic bond between Sylvia and Aurelia: "I learned, I learned elsewhere / From muses unhired by you, dear mother." The intentionally naive voice that rehearses scenes from childhood and adolescence throughout the poem only exaggerates the intensity of the daughter's final recognition. Her singular talents cannot flourish by practicing arabesques and trills on the piano, or by "singing the glowworm song" in a twinkle dress:

> I woke one day to see you, mother,
> Floating above me in bluest air
> On a green balloon bright with a million
> Flowers and bluebirds that never were
> Never, never, found anywhere.
> But the little planet bobbed away
> Like a soap-bubble as you called: Come here!
> And I faced my traveling companions. (*Col*, p. 60)

The increasing muteness of the bald-headed muses—sinister figures borrowed from a deChirico painting[9]—assumes a growing authority over the made-to-order fairy tale world of the mother. Their active and macabre physical presence, yet their willful silence, starkly contrasts with the mother's chit-chat method of parrying or altogether avoiding the frightening moods in her daughter's life. At first they merely nod, "Mouthless, eyeless, with stitched bald head." Then, as the mother drums up her feeble chants to Thor, these "dismal-headed godmothers" smash the storm window panes with cavalier denial of the mother's polite fictions and "normalizing" explanations of pain. As their shadows lengthen, stretch and envelop the poet, they assume their permanent vigils, united with the poet as "travelling companions" in a timeless realm of stone. As the muses change from vengeful wedding furies to insistent guides, they act as touchstones against which the speaker can measure her emotional and artistic transformation.

The daughter's tragedy, however, is that while she has no use for the mother's Good Ship Lollipop world, she has no substitute reality of her own. She merely allows us to witness the whole range of emotions that accompany her developing consciousness, marking a gulf between the parent and child, but never specifying the actual difference between them. The final tonal ambiguity communicates precisely the poet's reluctance toward, yet need for, those unsavory muses who are at odds with Aurelia:[10] "And this is the kingdom you bore me to, / Mother, mother. But no frown of mine / will betray the company I keep" (*Col*, p. 60).

At times in the transitional *Crossing the Water* poems, the burden of consciousness is so rigorous that the poet would bluntly escape: "With no attachments, like a foetus in a bottle / the obsolete house, the sea, flattened to a picture / She has one too many dimensions to enter" (*CW*, p. 55). While she praises the warm inadvertence of the foetal state, Sylvia Plath hints that even involuntary creation demands further scrutiny by that voluntary and deliberate act of shaping words into poems:[11]

"I see by my own light . . . *I must make more maps*," she insists.

Throughout *Letters Home*, Sylvia Plath fails to recognize the similar plights of mother and daughter, the muse-like and handmaiden tooling, the compromises and self-recriminations, the gritty, practical bent of both mother and daughter, as well as their penchant for turning anything amorphous or unconscious into "daylight" polemics. It is significant that in poetic moments of ecstatic metamorphosis—whether she climbs to a bed of fire, flies through the candle like a singeless moth, or dissolves her selves like "old whore petticoats"—the poet asks the mother her soul-searching questions about the nature of the protean identity which she is experiencing. Her confrontation ranges from simple hope for dialogue; to frank questions; to yearning for passionate assimilation by the mother where all matrophobic concerns might be erased, but at the peril of the daughter's "otherness." Aurelia, the lover of Horatio Alger and Louisa May Alcott stories, utters only saccharinely optimistic wishes for her daughter. She fails to value and channel her magnificently vital performing energy expressed in "Years," "Getting There," "Fever 103," "Ariel," and "Lady Lazarus." At one point in the letters, Aurelia, always the cracker-barrel philosopher who finds kernels of practical wisdom in the most terrifying events, summarizes Sylvia's deep feelings of futility: she implies that the early development of Sylvia's tragic strain derived not only from her probing the dark secrets of self but ultimately from publication editors' advice that problem stories would sell best. As Sylvia dwells on the very energy of growth or change, she lacks the guidance or experience to define this process of transformation, to put her image, quite simply, into words. In the excitement of self-metamorphosis, Sylvia the daughter exposes to us the candor of her formlessness, the risk of nondefinition: "Is there no still place / Turning and turning in the middle air, / Untouched and untouchable."[12]

In her bee sequence,[13] Sylvia offers her most profound tribute to the ambivalence of motherhood, one that suggests by its powerful central symbol the curiously devalued and unrealized power of Aurelia in Sylvia's life, and at the same time Sylvia's separateness. In the apiary, the queen mother, with her tragic nuptial flight and her isolated existence, has a paradoxical power. In "Beekeeper's Daughter," the young girl discovers the complex interrelationship of life and death ("dark flesh, dark parings") in the queen's existence. Implied by the queenly "disconsolation" is a law of the apiary: the queen bee must suffer a uniquely regal motherhood, for she neither directs nor participates in any of her subjects' riches of cross-pollination, never sees daylight, has no bodily provisions for work. The realities of the queen's life and of adult sexuality—a thumbnail sketch of the Otto-Aurelia/Ted-Sylvia tangle—break over the young narrator of the poem: "Father, bridegroom . . . The queen bee marries the winter of your year."

The old queen bee appears only once in the sequence but controls functions of the apiary largely by her evasiveness. While she may be a physical pawn of the hive colony, sacrificing her life for future generations, she remains mentally untouched: " . . . She is very clever. / She is old, old, old, she must live another year, and she knows it." When the queen finally does appear in the central poem, "Stings," her elusive motherhood distinguishes her from the worker drudges, the "column of unmiraculous women," who are too easily deceived by their conscientious work ethic. To the queen, no one, nothing, is worth the sacrifice of one's life:

> They thought death was worth it, but I
> Have a self to recover, a queen,
> Is she dead, is she sleeping?
> Where has she been,
> With her lion-red body, her wings of glass?
>
> Now she is flying
> More terrible than she ever was, red
> Scar in the sky, red comet
> Over the mausoleum, the wax house.
> (*A*, pp. 66–67)*

The poetic record of this final "recovered self" measures Sylvia's distinctness as well as her matricidal rage.

Not until she writes her own poems to her children (Nicholas Farrar and Freida) in *Ariel* and *Winter Trees*, and artistically *becomes* her mother, does Plath offer the response unspoken by those idyllic women from art and mythology in *The Colossus*, by the solicited, silent mother in the poems of *Crossing the Water*, or by the resurrected queen bee. Faced with the unrecognized and undeveloped matrilineal bond between herself and Aurelia, she heals the split between those countervailing women figures and the unresponsive mother in these late poems. She portrays a mother's feeling of powerful love for, yet vulnerable separateness from, her children's lives:

* This and other selections so identified are from *Ariel* by Sylvia Plath, copyright © 1965 by Ted Hughes, published in London by Faber & Faber, in New York by Harper & Row. By permission of Olwyn Hughes.

All night I carpenter
A space for the thing I am given,
A love
Of two wet eyes and a screech.
White spit
Of indifference![14]

Plath's hopes for her children beg for "a life no higher than the grasstops / Or the hearts of sheep." Through the craft of her poetry, she feels her separateness from the motherbond, but actually by becoming *a* mother Sylvia becomes more like *her* mother whose always reasonable counsels saturate the letters. Miming the life of that efficient medical secretary, that cartographer of limited pleasures, Sylvia settles for a simple, factual existence where one is mirror-safe from the Grand Illusions (and consequent Grand Letdown) of the Power and the Glory; from the "bastard masturbating a glitter"; from the "heavy notion of Evil." "Is there no great love, only tenderness," she asks? She wants no "pietas," no "stains" from the great cathedrals; no baggage of false hopes loaded onto those who have been redeemed by the "dove's annihilation." Sylvia the mother cares not a whit for the rare or the exceptional. As a mother herself, what is important to her is a simple brass paperweight, the sun blooming like a geranium, the haloey glow of a single candle's power, or "what green stars can make it to our gate." These are the tangible realities tendered to her child by the mother-hierophant who "has seen": "Meaning leaks from the molecules / The heart has not stopped." Her hopes for her children reclaim these derided "woman preferences" that are cut from the domestic cloth. Now, however, they become positive wishes for clarity and precision, uncontaminated by the patrilineal world.

The father's world, accommodated in both Aurelia and Sylvia's lives, is poetically dismissed ("People with torsos of steel / Winged elbows and eyeholes"), a mere comic inferior to the small, immediate constructiveness of the motherworld ("In the lane I meet sheep and wagons, / Red earth, motherly blood"). In contrast to the patrilineal world inhabited by the buffoonish "Hogwallow" and "Mudsump," Sylvia describes the motherbond with tonal nuance, resonance, and lively variation. Repeatedly, Plath the mother asks for the remedy for seeing and feeling too much; for "having one too many dimensions to enter"; for totally "using" (i.e., "wasting") oneself in ill-starred idealism. "It is a terrible thing to be so open," she says in the radio drama *Three Women*: "How long can I be a wall keeping the wind off? / How long can I be gentling the sun with the shade of my hand, / Intercepting the blue bolts of a cold moon?"[15] Despite her tender wishes, the poet-mother does not impose on the child either her "hopes for grand and classical images," or her own terrible, hushed darkness. Rather, she creates room for various choices in life for her children, new options apart from the configuration of her own personality. A kind of rarified balance is achieved in the mother's loving surprise at the awesome separateness of her child. "Clean slate with your own face on," she says of the child, or "new statue / In a drafty museum, your nakedness / shadows our safety. We stand round blankly as walls."

Even the child's pain is relatively uncontaminated by mother Sylvia's despairing foreknowledge about the world the child must enter. In "Morning Song," for example, the mother's abstract perception of the world is run together in delicately timed balance with the child's simple particulars—the moth-breath, the nursery with pink wallpaper, the open mouth "clean as a cat," the heartbeat like a "fat, gold watch." In contrast, the mother's own existence, is found in the forming and dissolving elements of the universe, leaving her wistfully helpless in the face of the child's strange promise:

> I'm no more your mother
> Than the cloud that distils a mirror to reflect its own slow
> Effacement at the wind's hand . . .
> A far sea moves in my ear. (A, p. 11)

Yet by the poem's end, as the mother's "dull stars" are swallowed into blankness, the child offers her a momentary reprieve from the pain of inevitable effacement: "And now you try / Your handful of notes; / The clear vowels rise like ballons."

A momentary stay in the matter-of-fact life—the rough, dumb horsehair, the handful of clear notes, the small, brass candleholder—is a very tenuous distraction for the mother against a winter night that holds death and oblivion. But with her knowledge of the indifference that permeates the world the child will soon enter (the "sky like a pig's backside," the "utter lack of attention"), the mother cherishes this brief respite from disillusionment.

Helen Vendler has reminded us that we are lethargic and slow in appreciating these movingly tender verses that pull toward living the whole of life by means of "the small constructiveness of motherhood."[16] For the filial, passionate bond between mother and child, however thwarted or realized by Aurelia and Sylvia's relationship, opens distinctly new emotional possibilities for all women, as it unravels and demystifies the real subtlety of the mother experience. Yet Sylvia Plath's poems, as well as her relationship with Aurelia, have been obscured by the authority of a suicide's phyrric victory. Scrappy biographical facts, no collected poems, and a largely posthumous *oeuvre* have all bolstered the Plath legend that plays to the cheap seats ("the peanut-crunching crowd") of the suicide sideshow of the last decade. What remains to be recovered and explored in the link between life and the poetic argument is the range of candidly expressed "mother feelings" that mark the finest achievement of Sylvia Plath, mother *and* daughter.

Notes

[1] Sylvia Plath, *Letters Home: Correspondence 1950–1963*, ed. Aurelia Schober Plath (New York: Harper and Row, 1975). References to *Letters Home* in this essay is without direct quotation, since permission to quote was denied by Harper and Row. The reader is referred to the *Letters* for further information.

[2] Adrienne Rich, *Of Woman Born: Motherhood as Experience and Institution* (New York: W. W. Norton and Co., 1976), p. 245. She says: "A woman who has used her anger creatively, will not seek to suppress anger in her daughter in fear that it could become, merely, suicidal" (245). Future references to this book will be cited in the text as *R* with page number.

[3] The letters make it clear that Mrs. Plath, encouraged by her daughter, attempted some creative writing.

[4] "Snowman on the Moor" first appeared in *Poetry* 90 (July 1957): 229 and was also included in the limited edition, *Lyonesse* (London: Rainbow Press, 1971).

[5] Sylvia Plath, *The Colossus and Other Poems* (New York: Vintage Books, 1969). Future references to this edition will be indicated in the text by *Col* with page number.

[6] Sylvia Plath, *Crossing the Water: Transitional Poems* (New York: Harper and Row, 1971). Future references to this edition will be indicated in the text by *CW* with page number.

[7] Helen Vendler, "The Poetry of Sylvia Plath," Ziskind Lecture Series, Part I (13 December 1971), p. 5. This lecture remains unpublished in the Sophia Smith Women's Archives, Smith College.

[8] Vendler, p. 7.

[9] Ingrid Melander, " 'The Disquieting Muses': A Note on a Poem by Sylvia Plath," *Research Studies* 39 (March, 1971): 53–54.

[10] Rich, pp. 247, 248. Rich writes of woman's frequently unresolved choice between two mothers: one the biological mother who represents the culture of domesticity, of "male-centeredness," and the other—usually an artist or a teacher—who represents a world of concretions.

[11] A further proof of the complex vitality which Plath invested in motherhood is her use of the birthing analogy ("Stillborn," "Metaphors") to describe the formation of and significant midcareer changes in her poetry. In *Crossing the Water*, the poet has several poems that deal with this newfound imaginative power with an eye toward exploring the limitations of her poetic art and the particular image of self as artist.

[12] Sylvia Plath, *Ariel* (London: Faber and Faber, 1965, copyright 1965 by Ted Hughes; New York, Harper and Row), p. 44. Future references to this edition will be included in the text as *A* with page numbers.

[13] Five of the six poems in the sequence ("The Bee Meeting," "The Arrival of the Bee Box," "Stings," "Wintering" and "The Swarm") were written in late autumn of 1962 in little more than a week, and are included in *Ariel* (New York: Harper and Row, 1965). "Beekeepers' Daughter," dated much earlier, is included in *The Colossus and Other Poems* (New York: Random Vintage, 1968).

[14] Sylvia Plath, *Winter Trees: Late Poems* (New York: Harper and Row, 1972), pp. 23, 24. Future references will be included in the text as *WT* with page number.

[15] Sylvia Plath, *Three Women: A Monologue for Three Voices* (London: Turret Books, 1968). This radio drama is also included in *Winter Trees*.

[16] Vendler, p. 23.

The Hungry Jewish Mother

> Now they put a baby in her lap. Do not ask me, she would have liked to beg . . . . Unnatural grandmother, not able to make herself embrace a baby . . .
>
> It was not that she had not loved her babies, her children. But when the need was done—oh the power that was lost in the painful damming back and drying up of what still surged, but had nowhere to go . . .
>
> And they put a baby in her lap . . . warm flesh like this had claims and nuzzled away all else and with lovely mouths devoured . . . . the long drunkenness; the drowning into needing and being needed . . .
>
> And all that visit, she could not touch the baby.[1]

Thus Tillie Olsen wrote of the old grandmother in *Tell Me a Riddle*, "Mrs. Unpleasant," typical yenta and nag, who in her dying turns away from all those she was forced to nurture in her life. Her husband calls her every mean, degrading name he can because she refuses to move to "The Haven," a rest home where everything will be done and arranged for her. But she will not cooperate in taking the late-offered comfort he has stolen from her all her life. Throughout the story, the husband's hunger mounts in rhythms with the stomach cancer that is eating his wife alive. His own bitter salt tears are all that stay upon the midnight tray he is forced to fetch himself. Dying in bed, she makes up soliloquies that leave him out.

Too well we know the Jewish mother our male writers have given us, the all-engulfing nurturer who devours the very soul with every spoonful of hot chicken soup she gives, whose every shakerful of salt contains a curse. Too well we know the feeder whose hard-wrung offerings are imbibed as poisons. Yet we do not know enough of the other hungry one who feeds others because it is the only access she

knows to a little bit of love. In Jewish literature by women, mothers
are the "bread givers" who try to make feeding into a replenishing,
ecstatic act. But the mothers are themselves starved in every way,
sucked dry and withered from being asked almost from birth to give a
nurturance they never receive. They are starved not only for the actual
food they are forced to turn over to others, but for the stuff of self and
soul, for love and song. The oldest daughter in *Tell Me a Riddle* cries,
"Pay me back, Mother, pay me back for all you took from me. Those
others you crowded into your heart. The hands I needed to be for you,
the heaviness, the responsibility." But the dying grandmother, her
mother, can only chant:

> "One pound soup meat . . . one soup bone . . . . Bread, day-old . . . .
> Please, in a wooden box . . . for kindling.
>   I ask for stone; she gives me bread—day-old . . . .
>   How can I give it, Clara, how can I give it if I don't have?"[2]

The mother's starvation is, needless to say, scary for the child, who
has no choice but to take. For underlying all the taking is the fear of
being eaten up alive and the guilt of stealing from the empty one. This,
I imagine, is why so many male writers have turned the one who
endlessly spoons out the chicken soup into a mad devourer from whom
they have to flee lest their identities be eaten up. Thus our Portnoys,
knowing on some level that they have been thieves, eliminate their debt
by making their tormented mothers into cardboard demons, distancing
them by robbing them of their pains and hunger and humanity, so some
day they in turn can steal the nurturance they have always counted on
from other women. Thus is the demon Jewish mother shrunk and
manhood reached.

But for our Jewish women writers the journey is far more complicated, for they are both the takers of the food their mothers do not
really have to give, and the future providers. They are at once devourers
and the devoured, and it is this extra layering in their experience which
allows them to enter the pain of their mothers all the men are fleeing
from:

> from the beginning
> she was always dry though
> she'd press me close
> prying open my lips:
> the water warm
> the fruit sour brown
> apples bruised and soft.

hungry for dark i'd sit
and wait devour dreams
of plain sun and sky
large leaves trunks dark
and wet with sweet thick sap.
but mornings
brought back the space
and cement her weakened
body my head against her
breast: my mouth empty.
yet she was all
my comfort.[3]

This is the beginning of Irena Klepfisz's poem from "The Monkey House and Other Cages." Below the title is a heading in parentheses that says, "The voice is that of a female monkey born and raised in a zoo." Irena Klepfisz was born a girl child in Warsaw Poland where "during the war / germans were known / to pick up infants / by their feet / swing them through the air / and smash their heads / against plaster walls. / somehow / i managed to escape that fate."[4] She was born in 1941. But the images of violence and incarceration never leave her work. Her monkey poem continues with the daughter's hunger for a warmth and softness that her mother monkey does not have, to the daughter's first rape before the watching mother's eyes.

Mothers turning over their daughters to the hunger of men while they sit by weakly and watch: this occurs over and over in the literature of our Jewish women writers, from Anzia Yezierska's *Bread Givers*, where each of four daughters in turn is sacrificed so that the Talmud scholar father can be free of toil to focus on the holy light; to E. M. Broner's repeated images of women being sacrificed on altars on men's sexual religious ecstasies in *A Weave of Women*, set in Jerusalem. Though a female baby born in ecstasy can be hammered to death through one man's rage during a ritual Purim rite, the women of "the Land" in *A Weave of Women* are expected to be ever ready and replenishing. Gerda says:

"My body can walk miles. My feet never get bunions, calluses or plantar warts. My thighs do not rub . . . . I climb Masada up and back down and do it again. I have climbed Mount Sinai without losing breath, four hours each way. I came down hungry and ready to cook a meal for a crowd."

Another woman asks, "What can't your body do?" Gerda replies:

"It doesn't know how to say, 'I'm sorry. I apologize. Did I hurt
you?' . . . It doesn't know how to feel what other people are feeling.
Since the camps I have been careful not to know too much about my
surroundings."[5]

The holocaust in all its horror has become the ultimate expression of
the violence done to us; the concentration camp, the black barred cage
which locks us all from our own nurturance and warmth; the hunger.

Yezierska's *Bread Givers* is the story of a woman growing up in a
Lower East Side ghetto. The book deals with the same hungers passed
on from mothers down to daughters, and their helpless rage. The book
begins with the narrrator in the kitchen trying to peel potatoes and
clumsily cutting too much away: "I was about ten years old then. But
from always it was heavy on my heart the worries for the house as if
I was mother."[6] In this book, it is the mother who must pay all the bills
and somehow find the fat to put into her husband's soup so his attention
will be free to concentrate upon the Torah. When the mother enters
and sees her two oldest daughters unable to find work, the third only
wanting to tie ribbons upon her hat and go hear the free music, she lets
her market basket fall from her arm in despair. Her rage at her responsibility, having no better place to go, turns on the youngest and most
helpless daughter, the narrator, the teller of the tale:

> "*Gazlin! Bandit!*" her cry broke through the house. She picked up the
> peelings and shook them free before my eyes. "You'd think potatoes
> grow free in the street. I eat out my heart, running from pushcart to
> pushcart, only to bargain down a penny on five pounds, and you cut
> away my flesh like a murderer."[7]

Out of utter repentance the child goes out to gather bits of unburned
coal from ashcans, even though it makes her "feel like a beggar and a
thief."[8] Far better to rob dregs from strangers than to suck the emptiness
from one's own source of life.

But the narrator's childish efforts cannot sustain the women in her
family. One by one, the narrator watches her mother and sisters weaken
as they feed the father and his work:

> We sat down to the table. With watering mouths and glistening eyes
> we watched Mother skimming off every bit of fat from the top soup
> into Father's big plate, leaving for us only the thin, watery part. We
> watched Father bite into the sour pickle which was special for him only;
> and waited, trembling, with hunger, for our portion.[9]

The father thanks God for the food and tells his assembled family not to worry about feeling starved, for " 'the real food is God's Holy Torah. . . .' At Father's touch, Mother's sad face turned into smiles. His kind look was like the sun shining on her."[10]

Each of the three older daughters as they go out to seek men will try to find that touch of magic radiance that deadens direst need. Bessie, the oldest, finds it in the "cutter" from her sweat shop for whom she makes a spread of snow-white oil cloth to cover the greasy table in the single room where they all eat and sleep and live. But though she has no dowry and is already considered old, her father will not let her go, for she is the best worker, the best wage earner, and the "burden bearer" of the family. Later, after she has lost the man she really loves, her father sells her to an old ugly fishmonger who wants her to raise his five unmanageable grieving children whose mother has just died. She almost rebels, the fishmonger repels her so, but the needs of the bereaved little ones soon draw her in.

Masha, the beautiful one, falls in love with a musician, but her father will not let him in because he is not holy enough. The man her father picks for her, because he makes believe he is a diamond merchant, keeps her half-starved in a hovel.

And the mother, grown old before her time, stands by and watches this, and watches the third daughter, who loved a poet once ("False gods," the father said), sold to a gambler who takes her to empty riches far away on the west coast.

The mother, even as she dies from a gangrenous foot that could have been cut off had anybody cared, had she herself cared, is remembered by the neighbors only by how well she starved herself:

> "Such a good mother, such a virtuous wife," wailed a shawled woman with a nursing baby in her arms and two little tots hanging to her skirts. "Never did she allow herself a bit to eat but left-overs, never a dress but the rags her daughters had thrown away."
> ". . . Only two days ago she told me how they cook the fish in her village sweet and sour—and now, she is dead."
> At this, all the women began rocking and swaying in a wailing chorus.[11]

This is one level of the tale, the hungry mother giving all. But in its very unfolding we find a major turning. For the fourth daughter, who has seen her mother and sisters slain by the age-old patterns, rebels. She leaves her father's house amidst his curses and his blows to find an education and a life that she can call her own. She learns to gather strength from all she suffered through, and will not bend her will under the whips of the husbands who enslave her sisters, her teachers in the college she forces her way into, or the soup server in the corner restaurant who only dishes stew with meat in it to men. Using what she has learned in hunger in the ghetto, she rises in school and in the world. And, interestingly, in her self-made rise, she becomes the only daughter who can take their mother's shyly offered new support. Her mother travels miles to bring her bread and herring when she is starving, studying alone and outcast. The others berate her for going to college, leaving her mother alone to die. But her mother, on her deathbed, greets with a radiant joy this last daughter who has turned into a "teacherin." It is a high moment of the book when, at her mother's funeral, this daughter watches the others let the undertaker slice their clothes to tatters, rending them according to the old Biblical law, and refuses to be a part of it: "I don't believe in this. It's my only suit, and I need it for work. Tearing it wouldn't bring Mother back to life again."

Anzia Yezierska, in her work and in her facing of the hungers that have crippled all women, all mothers in the old tradition, has given us all a chance to carry on the lives our mothers never gave themselves or us.

"Mother, I'm pregnant with a baby girl." This is the ever varying refrain that lilts and sobs and sings through E. M. Broner's book, *Her Mothers*:

> "Mother, I'm giving birth to a baby girl."
> "What does she want to do with her life?"
> "Be a mother."
> "And then what?"
> "A grandmother."
> "No more?"
> "A great-grandmother."
> "And what else?"
> "Nothing else."[12]

This novel interweaves tales of mothers and daughters in modern times to our most ancient foremothers, through the reclamation of literary "mentor-mothers" who, more often than not, gave their life blood away to men. It is the story of a Jewish mother's search for her own biological daughter, conceived at a time in her life when she could not accept or give. The daughter has now grown into her own nerve-wracking adolescence and runs away. It is the tale of how only through finding the strong mothers of the past, the female power figures, and the powers in the self, can any mother truly have her daughter back. It is a long and complicated journey, through sob stories, kitsch, and utmost ecstasies, through petty suburban confusions, and the horrors of the holocaust.

Here is the story of Sarah and Abraham retold in the section entitled "Foremothers" beginning, "Looking for Past Mothers, Way Past Mothers":

Four are the Matriarchs: The First Matriarch

"Mother, I'm pregnant with a baby girl."
"May she be the mother of heroes."

She journeyed to the South for there was a famine in the land. . . .

Avram suffered from thirst, from fear. She like a camel did not seem to have his hunger or his need for water. . . . So he offered her strong body to the passing soldiers to obtain what he could not do without.

They took their pleasure with her while Avram sat outside of the tent, drinking their water, eating their provisions. Then the soldiers brought her to the Great House. They pulled aside her garments from her body. Despite famine, the flesh curved. Despite thirst, the shoulder and buttocks meat was juicy. She was given to Pharaoh, who had her while Avram sat outside of the Great House counting his newly gained sheep, oxen, asses, camels . . . .

The nomadic years passed. Maybe because of the great journey in the desert, or the early famine, or the time she was had by shepherds and soldiers, by princes and pharaoa, Sarai in no way thickened, never bore fruit. All life around her fattened—the camel, the oxen, the she-goat. Trees bore fruit—the date, the fig—but she remained boney.[13]

The great journey in the desert, the early famine, the dryness of the breasts Irena Klepfisz's daughter-monkey first sucked, don't we all know them all? In the larger-than-life Biblical stories the women who were emptied too much became quite literally barren. Later on it was only the feelings of giving and receiving that were sucked dry. But recently our women writers, in retracing those old hungry journeys and those thefts, are teaching us how to take in, to suckle and to grow again.

Beatrix, the mother, starts to cook and feed herself. She reads:

"*Embryein* (gr.) to swell inside. Compare to *sauerkraut*. . . . Each leaf is added, each thick, veined sheet. . . ." If an "unhatched young vertebrate," an "embryo," soaks in that female brine, . . . and all of life is pickled and floating and will be sucked by that originator, that fruitful, happy, lucky originator, no wonder that men, not feminine, must hate us. We are the inception, the water jar, the nourishment, the expelling from the Garden of Eden.

How could they not hate us? . . . They grow too big to slip back in through the slits of nipple, the eye of the navel, the mouth of the womb.

So they punish us at birth and give us pain and punish us in life and give us pain.[14]

It is only through the disconnection with the life-denying forces that women will be able to have back their lives, their long-lost mothers, and give birth to daughters breathing and alive and strong. This is the theme of *A Lament for Three Women*, a play by Karen Malpede in which women of three generations wait in a special cancer research center for their respective father, son, and husband to complete their dying. They have all lived only for these men. Naomi, the oldest, remembers how when her son was young she used to rise with him

"to light the fire and make the breakfast, pack his lunch, and get him off to school. What a flurry we would make in the kitchen. He would pull on his trousers standing by the stove, hopping from one foot to the other. I would stir the oatmeal over his jumping head. Sweeten it with jam or honey, pour in rich milk. And bread, big slices of black bread with cheese between them. . . .

The last weekend they let me take him home I made honey cake for him and lentil soup . . . we drank wine together. . . . I would have lit the candles but I was so busy in the kitchen, I missed the sunset . . . . When I sit with him I pretend he has another fever. I sing to him. A grown man. I sing to him and stroke his forehead. Sitting by his bed I half forget and half expect the fever to break suddenly and his eyes to open clear and out of pain."[15]

Naomi's memories of mothering her son first come out only in a sensual ecstacy. We feel the fullness of each piece of food she handles to pass on to him. But as the younger women tell their stories, Naomi lets her voice rise in fury that the son she fed so well now moans and only feels that he has been betrayed by her:

"I've prayed to God to end my life instead of his. But with every pain he suffers I am stronger. Every time he cries my determination grows. The joke of motherhood. When her child needs her, she endures. Joke again. The child never feels more abandoned, never turns against her with more bitter rage than he does now, watching his own mother watch him die."[16]

Ruth too has always mothered men. She tells of how her father who loved her as he had never loved her mother turned from her in violent rage at having been aroused. But it is Rachel, whose father cried in her arms when he found out that he was dying, kissed her neck, her ear lobes and her lips and made her cry, who felt betrayed when in his pain he turned back to her mother. It is Rachel who asks the other two women for the mothering she never got from men. She says:

"Naomi, as much as your son needed you when he was young, I need you now. Or more than that. When he was a baby sucking at your breast. No. More. When he was a fetus breathing your blood, taking his form from your flesh. I need you that much. I give up my father as I have to. Come with me now. Give up your son since you must . . . . Fear of death keeps him living. Fear of life keeps you clinging to him. It's not unnatural to be frightened, living is a frightening occupation. But remember, you made children from the center of you where eating, feeling, loving are united. Find the healthy breath inside you that allows you to still his heavy breathing. Take life for yourself from the one who is dying."[17]

Lament ends with a mourning, a keening and wailing which is the only way the hurt and hungry women can come close to one another. *Rebeccah*, Karen Malpede's second play, starts with a mother smothering an infant son who cries while they hide during a pogrom. It chronicles the mother's struggle to salvage her life with her surviving daughter, after the men turn her out because of what she's done.

Malpede was very young when she started to write her plays. Her early work goes deep into the roots of human tragedy, the horrors done to women by the world of men. But gradually we see how with the strengthening of feminist philosophy, the themes of love and hope and healing are beginning to supplant the hungers and the pain. Her newest play, *Making Peace*, is about the use of the most primal forms of nurture to undo those barren hungers that have made us hate. It is a play affirming all of human possibility through letting in the wild ecstatic loves the world has not allowed. Upon a heavenly mound three spirits of Utopians who have been hungry in their lives meet and undo the sorrows of their personal pasts, then go back down to earth to help the living ones erase denial. The spirit of Mary Wollstonecraft takes Shaker Mother Ann into her arms and says:

"Mother, take my breast, pretend you gave me birth and that I grew without resentment, without fear, strong enough to share that blessed gift with you. Suck, mother, suck. I suckled both my daughters thus. It was only then I understood the wild release that comes from giving love boundless as the ocean's own throbbing underneath the suckling moon."[18]

Thus, through learning to suckle herself and other women has the

hungry Jewish mother been transformed. From E. M. Broner's rein-
vention of sacred ceremonies of birthing and feeding among a community of women in the old stone house in *A Weave of Women* to Irena
Klepfisz's final poem in *periods of stress*, written to a woman she loves,
women are finding new ways of giving birth to life within each other
and themselves, of being reborn:

> last night i dreamt i was
> a gaunt and lifeless tree
> and you climbed into me to nest . . .
> wherever your human skin
> touched my rough bark i
> sprouted branches till
> lush with leaves i grew
> all green and silver frail
> like tinsel holding you
> asleep in my wooden arms.[19]

Women are beginning to learn their own softness and their songs.
Thus it is a young woman, Jeannie, the granddaughter in *Tell Me a
Riddle*, who puts to words the music the dying woman heard but never
spoke. She looks so beautiful as she tends her grandmother that her
grandfather wonders if she is in love. And, in a way, of course she is,
with all the songs of all the generations of women, long buried, maimed
and trapped. But through the ardor of her listening, we feel that she
might have the strength to set it free.

It is the voice of Tillie Olsen singing hope, through Jeannie, in the
last passage of the book:

> "Grandaddy, Grandaddy, don't cry. She is not there, she promised me.
> On the last day, she said she would go back to when she first heard
> music, a little girl on the road of the village where she was born . . . .
> Leave her there, Grandaddy, it is all right. She promised me. Come
> back, come back and help her poor body to die."[20]

Thus shall we all go back to where the music in us is and find the music
in our mothers that will help us live. As *Her Mothers* ends:

> "Mother, I'm pregnant with a baby girl."
> "What is she doing?"
> "She is singing."
> "Why is she singing?"
> "Because she is unafraid."[21]

Notes

[1] Tillie Olsen, *Tell Me A Riddle* (New York: Dell, 1956), pp. 92–93.

[2] Olsen, p. 123.

[3] Irena Klepfisz, poem from "The Monkey House and Other Cages," *Frontiers*, 3, No. 2 (1978), 12.

[4] Klepfisz, *periods of stress* (Brooklyn: self-published, 1975), p. 7.

[5] E. M. Broner, *A Weave of Women* (New York: Holt, Rinehart, and Winston, 1978), pp. 258–59.

[6] Anzia Yezierska, *Bread Givers* (1925; rpt. New York: Persea Books, 1975), p. 1.

[7] Yezierska, p. 7.

[8] Yezierska, p. 7.

[9] Yezierska, p. 10.

[10] Yezierska, p. 11.

[11] Yezierska, p. 254.

[12] E. M. Broner, *Her Mothers* (New York: Holt, Rinehart, and Winston, 1975), pp. 93–94.

[13] Broner, *Her Mothers*, pp. 149–51.

[14] Broner, *Her Mothers*, p. 217.

[15] Karen Malpede, "A Lament for Three Women," in *A Century of Plays by American Women*, ed. Rachel France (New York: Richard Rosen Press, 1979), p. 206.

[16] Malpede, pp. 204–05.

[17] Malpede, p. 207.

[18] Malpede, "Making Peace: A Fantasy" (unpublished), (New Cycle Theatre, Brooklyn, New York, 21 February 1979), Scene 7.

[19] Klepfisz, *periods of stress*, p. 61.

[20] Olsen, p. 125.

[21] Broner, *Her Mothers*, p. 241.

A Psychological Journey: Mothers and
Daughters in English-Canadian Fiction

The problem, the only problem, is my mother. And she is the one of course that I am trying to get; it is to reach her that this whole journey has been undertaken. With what purpose? To mark her off, to describe, to illumine, to celebrate, to get *rid* of, her: and it did not work, for she looms too close, just as she always did. She is heavy as always, she weighs everything down, and yet she is indistinct, her edges melt and flow. Which means she has stuck as close as ever and refused to fall away, and I could go on and on, applying what skills I have, using what tricks I know, and it would always be the same.

Alice Munro, "The Ottawa Valley"

During the past decade, Margaret Atwood, Margaret Laurence and Alice Munro have acquired an international reputation. Major English-Canadian writers, these women concentrate in their fiction on creating female characters. In fact, a surprisingly large number of Canadian short stories and novels offer female perspectives on Canadian culture. Certainly, the various women's movements of the 1960s and 70s have encouraged women to make their voices heard. This encouragement coincides with the emergence of a distinctive Canadian literature, a phenomenon of the last two decades. Because they are participating in a developing literary tradition, rather than reacting to an already-established one, Canadian women writers are therefore in the enviable position of cooperating in the creation of their country's fictional landscape. With a significant space for themselves, they treat women's psychological struggles with concentrated seriousness and, using a minimum of political rhetoric, attempt to give these struggles a past and a future.

242

Consequently, relationships between mothers and daughters appear not just peripherally but centrally in a proportionally large number of Canadian novels and short stories. Sometimes only isolated and somewhat idiosyncratic aspects of the relationship predominate as, for example, in the fiction of such lesser-known writers as Jane Rule and Margaret Gilboord Gibson. But in that of Atwood, Laurence, Munro and, in a more limited fashion, in one of Sylvia Fraser's novels, the struggle between mothers and daughters emerges dynamically through various stages of its development.[1] Because these latter writers recognize the pervasive influence of the mother—as so many men have recognized for themselves that of the father—they tend to represent it through the daughter's gradually emerging discovery of her own female identity. Interestingly, that discovery repeatedly dramatizes the necessity of coming to terms with the past. What makes Canadian fiction particularly significant for anyone interested in studies of female development is, then, the seriousness with which it treats women's quests and its emphasis on a past that, for women, is bound up with the mother.

The psychological journey that appears in so much of this fiction reveals the ambivalence that characterizes the daughter's feelings about her mother. In her efforts to achieve autonomy, anger and affection vie with each other so that she suffers from her desired separation, often felt to be a desertion of the mother, while, at the same time, she resents her childlike dependence. Indeed, whether the mother appears to be malevolent or benign, her representation exemplifies the anger, guilt, and affection of the daughter as she attempts to accept her own femininity.[2] Such acceptance requires the often painful recognition of the transference of power involved in taking the mother's place. This transference can increase anxiety. As the daughter grows stronger, the mother weakens; the power seems to have been stolen and the victorious daughter can despair of her own victory. On the other hand, where the mother remains all powerful, the daughter agonizes over her own impotence. Difficult though the struggle may be, the longing for freedom can yet propel action. And the resulting journey illustrates an apparently necessary movement that begins with negation (the effort to cut the self off from the past), moves to recognition (the awareness of the conflict between subjection and autonomy) and, where it is successful, concludes with reconciliation (the achieved inclusion of the past in the present). Thus, these English-Canadian novelists suggest that the angry posturing and dreams of radical independence characteristic of much recent feminist writing form a necessary phase in a process that ideally culminates

in reconciliation. Anger does have a crucial function; but more important to these Canadian writers is the transformation of this anger and
hostility into a complex recognition of responsibility. They write of
women's liberation. Yet the liberation they advocate implies a tradition
that includes the positive influences of the ancestral past, disguised as
these may be by the more apparent negative influences.[3]

The adult narrator of Margaret Atwood's novel, *Lady Oracle*, reveals
gradually a past and present dominated by the image of her mother.
We are introduced to Joan Foster just after she has attempted to erad-
icate her past life by a fabricated drowning. Her efforts to establish a
new identity are, however, unsuccessful; she feels constantly watched.
The novel becomes thereafter a series of recollections induced by Joan's
smouldering resentment against a mother whom she variously describes
as a three-headed monster (LO, p. 66), an image in an iron locket (LO,
p. 68), a "rotting albatross" (LO, p. 213). Although her mother is now
dead, Joan cannot forgive the series of betrayals that constitute still the
"war between myself and my mother" (LO, p. 69). Indeed, she objec-
tifies these betrayals in her conviction that she was an unwanted baby,
the "embodiment of her [the mother's] own failure and depression"
(LO, p. 67). She can now confess that in this war even her adolescent
obesity was a weapon to protect herself from being made into an image
of her mother, "thin and beautiful" (LO, p. 88). From this destructive
conflict, her father does not rescue her: "I kept waiting for him to give
me some advice, warn me, instruct me, but he never did any of these
things" (LO, p. 77). Although she betrays sympathy for him, she
imagines that he too was subjected to her overpowering mother.[4]

Such a malevolent maternal image does not usually fade with the
actual mother's death but can continue to haunt the daughter's life.
Towards the end of *Lady Oracle*, the unresolved separation climaxes in
a spectral visitation:

> She'd [the mother] come very close that time, she'd almost done it.
> She'd never let go of me because I had never let her go. It had been she
> standing behind me in the mirror, she was the one who was waiting
> around each turn, her voice whispered the words. She had been the
> lady in the boat, the death barge, the tragic lady with flowing hair and
> stricken eyes, the lady in the tower. She couldn't stand the view from
> the window, life was her curse. How could I renounce her? She needed
> her freedom also; she had been my reflection too long. What was the
> charm, what would set her free? . . . Why did I have to dream about

my mother, sleepwalk out to meet her? My mother was a vortex, a dark
vacuum.

(LO, pp. 329–330)

In this oracular revelation, the past (the narrator's recollections of her
childhood) merges with the present, emphasizing the crucial and ambiguous question, "What would set her free?" The narrator longs for a
charm that will magically expiate the image and allow the albatross to
drop from her neck. And indeed she does experience a partial epiphany
by admitting her own complicity. Although she has overtly rejected her
mother, in fact she has "never let her go." She also finally articulates
the affection that has been buried beneath the hostility: "Could she see
I loved her? I loved her but the glass was between us" (LO, p. 329).
Yet, for Joan Foster, the past that she now admits cannot be eradicated
still whispers threateningly into the present. Although she longs for
reconciliation (and has gone through much to be able to admit this
longing), the novel ends with her journey not quite completed.

Margaret Laurence's *A Jest of God* (republished as *Rachel, Rachel*)
reveals too a disastrously elongated struggle for autonomy in which the
narrator-daughter again and again betrays her ineffectuality. At the age
of thirty-four, the unmarried Rachel still lives at home, tied to her
mother's need, to the "querulous fragility of her face, the over-bright-
ness of her eyes rimmed with the shadows of sickness or disappointment" (JG, p. 114). Although Rachel's descriptions of her mother never
reach grotesque proportions, Mrs. Cameron does emerge as a succubus
living from her daughter's youth and strength. Her apparent gentleness
becomes a disguise for invisible weapons that, similar to Joan Foster's
actual battles with her mother, threaten Rachel's body. Fears of physical
engulfment permeate her thoughts: like the Jonah in the epigraph from
Sandburg's "Losers," she imagines herself "swallowed one time deep in
the dark." Correspondingly, when she speaks, she hears in her own
voice the echo of her mother's words sticking "like burrs to the hair"
(JG, p. 165). Because repetition of her mother's life threatens to stifle
her, the generational cycle becomes confused. Throughout much of the
novel, Rachel therefore betrays a muddled sense of time, "hardly knowing myself whether I am too young or too old" (JG, p. 71) and of her
role: "Surely I love her as much as most parents love their children. I
mean, of course, as much as most children love their parents" (JG, p.
137). Even through her teaching, she fails to compensate for her acute
sense of powerlessness. And, like Joan Foster's, her father too has failed

her; she remembers dreaming of him before his death, "behind the door I cannot open" (JG, p. 24), perhaps advising her to run away but unable to effect her escape. Trapped by the conviction of being "for ever in the wrong" (JG, p. 90)—an expression of the amorphous feeling of guilt experienced by so many daughters—Rachel suffers from a failure to distinguish between love and hate, control and subservience.

Although *A Jest of God* concludes with Rachel's assimilating her mother's power, to do so she must overcome a physical disgust about her own body.[5] Both Joan Foster and Rachel betray in their relationship with their mothers a personal fear of femininity. Alice Munro, in her two collections of frequently anthologized short stories, *Dance of the Happy Shades* and *Something I've Been Meaning To Tell You*, and in her novel, *Lives of Girls and Women*, is also acutely aware of the often negative tension between girls and older women. In a story focused on her poignant memories of a dress made for her by her mother, "Red Dress— 1946," the narrator recalls her disgust as her mother, fitting the dress, "crept around me, her knees creaking, her breath coming heavily . . . her legs were marked with lumps of blue-grey veins. I thought her squatting position shameless, even obscene" (DHS, p. 148). Because she is herself just entering the terrifying yet tempting "sexual competition" (DHS, p. 150) of adolescence, this memory of her mother reflects her own insecurity. Longing to be again a child, she is convinced that she will fail as a woman. So too in *Lives of Girls and Women*, Del Jordan recalls her search for female role models who were both loved and intellectually competent. What she remembers, however, is the "gynecological odor" of the "wrecked survivors of the female life" (LGW, p. 40). Such memories mingle with those about her own body: "Having to be naked myself, the thought of being naked, stabbed me with shame in the pit of my stomach . . . I felt outraged, unbearably, almost exquisitely humiliated" (LGW, p. 42). Thus, although the adult Del can now admit that "I myself was not so different from my mother," she admits to her efforts to conceal that similarity, "knowing what dangers there were" (LGW, p. 80).

What are these dangers? For the narrator of Munro's "Girls and Boys," they coalesce around fears of a repetition believed to be desired by the mother but, in her efforts to be herself, fought against by the daughter: "My mother, I felt was not to be trusted . . . . she was plotting now to get me to stay in the house more . . . it seemed to me she would do this simply out of perversity and to try her power" (DHS, pp. 117–118). And her fears do seem realized when, at the end of the story, her father cuts her off from the world of men with the words "she's only a girl" (DHS, p. 127). Yet the reader sees that her disparagement of her mother has led her to disparage herself.

As each of these short stories and novels reveals, such hostility ends by binding the daughter ever closer to the mother. The seven-year-old heroine of Sylvia Fraser's *Pandora* dramatizes in its nascency the dilemma that for older daughters can become so frightening. In this novel, we follow Pandora through the sometimes traumatic experiences involved in beginning school and making friends. But her gradual separation from her mother pervades her other experiences. She fluctuates between the extremes of hating her "horrible mother" (P, p. 13) and of hiding for protection behind her skirts, of shoving her mother's hand away and of clinging to it, of being "contemptuous of her mother, imitating her father's fury" (P, p. 183) and of siding with her mother against her father. Although she is too young to have accumulated the multitude of experiences that for older daughters constitute the maternal image, Pandora nonetheless clearly illustrates the ambivalence inherent in the struggle for autonomy: "Pandora wants to take her mother's hand, to cling to it possibly, and therein lies her dilemma: She is afraid she will stick to it, glued at the end" (P, p. 253). Fearful of being caught forever in an endless repetition of childhood's dependence (and, eventually, of the mother's life), she fights against her love.

Overt antagonism seems therefore to shield a binding affection that overtly threatens the daughter's freedom. Yet the achieving of autonomy seems to require a recognition of that love; where such recognition is prevented, repetition of the mother's patterns remains uncanny and terrifying. The daughter fears taking her mother's place although events, as if happening behind her back, conspire to remind her of her responsibilities. The threatening reversal of roles increases her anxiety. Time does establish the mother's priority; because she is older, she has power over the daughter. But, as the mother ages, time also takes that priority away. The contradictory questions, "Why should my parents have such power?" and "Why cannot time stand still, holding permanently fixed the elder's preeminence?" trouble all children. In her stories, Munro recognizes the daughter's difficulty in allowing the mother to weaken. The narrator of "The Ottawa Valley" articulates her fears of desertion and her own impotence: " 'So you are not going to get sick at all?' I said, pushing further. I was very much relieved that she had decided against strokes and that I would not have to be the mother" (*Something*, p. 244). As the quotation from "The Ottawa Valley" used to introduce this paper reveals, even when she is an adult and her mother is dead, this narrator continues to be perplexed. The mother's image, although by no means hostile, still "looms too close . . . is heavy as always . . . weighs everything down" (*Something*, p. 246).

The centrality of the reversal of roles suggests that these writers recognize the complexity and the significance of the daughter's relationship with her mother. Think for a moment of the quantity of literature devoted to female characters who are praised for remaining childlike or who are punished for striving for independence. These Canadian writers, on the contrary, expect women to aim towards autonomy. Their stressing of the struggle implies its importance beyond the individual woman and even beyond the family structure itself. We are being shown, rather, the stages of the development of strong and autonomous women. Reconciliation, or at least the possibility of it, dignifies the journey and allows women a success that precludes their victimization. Even in *A Jest of God*, where throughout much of the novel Rachel has seemed the archetypal victim, satisfactory reversal of roles occurs. Her affair with Steve and, more important, her imagined pregnancy encourage a continuation of the journey that curtails her extended childhood. Under the influence of anasthetic, Rachel forms the words that rid her of her mother's negative domination: "*I am the mother now*" (JG, p. 219). Significantly, she can now accept without guilt the necessary exchange of power: "I really wonder now why I have been so ruthlessly careful of her, as though to preserve her through eternity, a dried flower under glass. It isn't up to me. It never was. I can take care, but only some" (JG, pp. 231–232). The breaking of the glass so that the withered flower can blossom symbolizes Rachel's vital assimilation of her mother's power.[6]

The exchange of roles experienced by Rachel is figurative; when the daughter does in fact become a mother, she experiences an actual exchange. Although motherhood does not guarantee a cessation of conflict (and may even exacerbate it), in this fiction it usually encourages a reconciliation of the past with the present. Thus it symbolizes the successful outcome of the journey. In *The Fire-Dwellers*, Laurence complements her portrait of Rachel with that of her sister, Stacey MacAindra. Married and a mother, Stacey seems a Janus-like symbol, "able to look both ways," (FD, p. 47) and thus able, as it were, to hold together the past and the future. Unlike Rachel, she has physically escaped from her mother through an early marriage. But psychically, she too must free herself. Thus, she evinces a growing need to understand her mother's attitude towards her own womanhood. "Please," she imagines writing, "write immediately and let me know what was actually in your mind all those years because I haven't a clue and it's only now that this bothers me" (FD, p. 150). Throughout the novel, mirrors suggest the absorption of the past in the present and the acceptance of difference in sameness. Because her own daughter, Katie, reminds her of herself, her memories are given concrete form. As the cycle revolves, the negative maternal image, constructed partially to facilitate separation, largely disappears: "I never got on well with her as a kid but after my own kids I felt different. I guess I could see why she used to fuss—it was because she was scared about us" (FD, p. 194). By experiencing herself the complexities of parenthood, Stacey breaks through the separating glass that so troubles Joan Foster. And, because she can now forgive herself for what had earlier seemed a desertion of her mother, she can tolerate the mother's weight. Simultaneously, she recognizes her own capacity to endure.

Through such affirmation of strength, the daughter honors her female heritage. From an enlightened perspective, the heroine of Laurence's *A Bird in the House* thus reviews her relationship with her mother. Recalling her mother's "look of distracted exhaustion at being presented with something else she was expected to solve and did not know how any more than I" (BH, p. 163), and her own incapacity to "touch her because of the freezing burden of my inexperience" (BH, p. 70), Vanessa now allows the impotence of childhood its proper place. She knows that she has, in a sense, completed her mother by fulfilling many of her mother's ambitions. Such completion implies predestination: "I did not feel nearly as free as I had expected to feel" (BH, p. 203). But it offers too a different and novel life. Vanessa can therefore admit without resentment that "of all the deaths in the family, hers [the mother's] remained unhealed in my mind the longest" (BH, p. 206). The maternal image no longer threatens to weigh her down and the female legacy is passed on to her own children with love: "I remembered saying things that my mother had said to me, the clichés of affection, perhaps inherited from her mother" (BH, pp. 206–207). Although the past cannot be annihilated, the hostility can be transformed. Sympathy replaces anger; understanding replaces guilt.

The struggle with the mother thus evolves. In a recent novel by Carol Shields, *Small Ceremonies*, the narrator-mother looks at her daughter: "Always at such moments she reminds me of someone, someone half recalled but never quite brought into focus. I can never think who it is. But today I see for the first time who it is she reminds me of: it's me" (SC, p. 168). So it is that the daughter inevitably carries her mother with her. But so also anxiety dominates her efforts to achieve autonomy. On the one hand, she longs to purge herself of a past that threatens her; on the other, she can give substance to herself only by celebrating her roots. Caught between a desired independence that belittles her mother's influence and a profound attachment that increases it, she longs to reorder time. The traumas of separation therefore reach their peak in the exchange of roles. If no exchange occurs, reconciliation becomes difficult. Anger and guilt blind the daughter to the positive effects of influence and prevent her from assuming joyfully her own role in the generational cycle. In Atwood's *Surfacing*, the dead mother's leather jacket bears part of the weight of a past that stultifies her daughter throughout much of the novel: "My mother's jacket is hanging on a nail beside the window, there's nobody in it: I press my forehead against it. Leather smell, the smell of loss; irrecoverable" (S, p. 201). Yet in this fiction, the greater the attempt to shear away the past—to make it indeed irrecoverable—the more hopelessly entrapped the daughter becomes. Her salvation lies rather in discovering in the depths of her anger an unarticulated love; to value her own femininity, she must acknowledge her debt to her mother.

As I have suggested, this concentration on the ambivalent relationship with the mother results in fictional worlds that allow women a representative place in the struggle for survival. Moral and spiritual rites of passage, the daughter's efforts to come to terms with her femininity underline the general human perplexity in the face of life's transitions. Margaret Laurence writes in her collection of essays, *Heart of a Stranger*: "This is where my world began. A world which includes the ancestors. . . . A world which formed me, and continues to do so, even while I fought it in some of its aspects, and continue to do so. A world which gave me my own lifework to do, and because it was here that I learned the sight of my own particular eyes."[7] Yes, the Canadian prairie has influenced Laurence. But so too has her maternal past. From a woman's perspective, the ancestral past is recreated and the shape of her fiction formed.

Let me finally, without unduly restricting its relevance only to Canada, propose an analogy between the fictional journey I have described and the patterns of Canadian history. Apart from the influence of the contemporary women's movement, perhaps the fact that so many major Canadian writers are women (and so much of their work devoted to studies of female characters) implies a cultural tolerance for women's perspectives. That this tolerance should be marked in Canada may, then, parallel her characteristic role in world politics. William Kilbourn reminds us that Canada, "in contrast to the United States, is founded on the organic growth of tradition rather than an explicit act of the revolutionary will."[8] More chauvinistically, he further suggests that "in a masculine world of the assertive will and the cutting edge of the intellect, a certain Canadian tendency to the amorphous permissive feminine principle of openness and toleration and acceptance offers the possibility of healing."[9] The sexual stereotyping in this latter statement is certainly questionable; yet the qualities of openness, tolerance, and acceptance, isolated by Kilbourn, are highly evident in the fiction here discussed. Traditionally, women have chosen assimilation over aggression, incorporation over isolation. As Laurence's persuasive matriarch, Hagar Shipley, realizes, the radical breaking with tradition can result, not in freedom, but in a shackling loneliness (SA, p. 292). Thus, I suggest that the struggle with the mother—a psychological journey that reveals the daughter's efforts to incorporate the past—illustrates also a profoundly Canadian quest for a kingdom where hostility can be transformed peacefully to a unifying reconciliation.

Notes

[1] In this paper, I concentrate on the following novels and short stories. The page references and abbreviated titles are given in the text: Margaret Atwood, *Lady Oracle* (Toronto: McClelland and Stewart, 1976), LO; Sylvia Fraser, *Pandora* (Boston: Little, Brown and Company, 1972), P; Margaret Laurence, *A Bird in the House* (New York: Alfred A. Knopf, 1970), BH; *A Jest of God* (New York: Alfred A. Knopf, 1966), JG; *The Fire-Dwellers* (New York: Alfred A. Knopf, 1969), FD; Alice Munro, *Dance of the Happy Shades* (Toronto: Ryerson Press, 1968), DHS; *Lives of Girls and Women* (New York: McGraw-Hill Ryerson, 1971), LGW; *Something I've Been Meaning To Tell You* (Toronto: McGraw-Hill Ryerson, 1974), *Something*. I mention briefly several other novels: Margaret Atwood, *Surfacing* (New York: Simon and Schuster, 1972) S; Marian Engel, *No Clouds of Glory*, also published as *Sarah Bastard's Notebook* (New York: Harcourt, Brace and World, 1968), NCG; Margaret Laurence, *The Stone Angel* (New York: Alfred A. Knopf, 1964), SA; Carol Shields, *Small Ceremonies* (Toronto: McGraw-Hill Ryerson, 1976), SC.

[2] In her paper, "Feminine Guilt and the Oedipus Complex," Janine Chasseguet-Smirgel writes: "The relation between mother and daughter is handicapped from the start. . . . This state is due to the sexual identity between mother and daughter." Unlike the boy whose penis allows him to differentiate himself from his mother and to replace feelings of impotence with convictions of power, "the girl cannot free herself from this [maternal] omnipotence as she has nothing with which to oppose her mother, no narcissitic virtue the mother does not also possess." *Female Sexuality*, ed. Janine Chasseguet-Smirgel (Ann Arbor: University of Michigan Press, 1970), pp. 98–115.

[3] In an interview with Graeme Gibson, Margaret Laurence claimed: "I don't think that real liberation comes from turning your back on the whole past or your ancestral past. Rather, it comes from coming to some kind of terms with it, knowing there is a certain amount of mental baggage which you would just as soon not carry but, nevertheless, you're stuck with it." *Eleven Canadian Novelists,* interviewed by Graeme Gibson (Toronto: Anansi, 1973), p. 203.

[4] Juliet Mitchell, in *Psychoanalysis and Feminism* (New York: Random House, 1974), writes: "In psychosis the mother and child remain a dyad, only the triadic structure of the Oedipus complex can break up this 'symbiotic' predicament" (p. 291). More specifically, "the father, in the context of the Oedipus complex, is not a part of the dyadic relationship of mother and child, but a third term. The self and other of the mother-and-child has its duality broken by the intervention of this third term" (p. 392).

[5] See Karen Horney's chapter, "Inhibited Femininity," and the later chapter, "Psychogenic Factors in Functional Female Disorders," *Feminine Psychology* (New York: W. W. Norton, 1967).

[6] Another writer sensitive to the transference of power from mother to daughter is Marian Engel, In *No Clouds of Glory,* the heroine, Sarah, reviews her relationship with her mother: "For a time we had hated each other; later and before, there was an element of fear. I had been too long dependent on her good opinion, had stayed too long adolescent, clinging to her affection; then disliked her because of this. Now, feelings had fallen into place: detachment had set in. She was preparing to be old, and I was preparing to be free" (NCG, p. 148).

[7] *Heart of a Stranger* (Toronto: McClelland Stewart, 1976), p. 219.

[8] Kilbourn is here paraphrasing the historian William Morton. See William Kilbourn's essay, "The Quest for the Peaceable Kingdom," *Canadian Writing Today,* ed. Mordecai Richler (Middlesex: Penguin Books, 1970), p. 49.

[9] Kilbourn, p. 53.

Part Six
THE NEW MATRILINEAGE

Introduction

We who have been trained in academe have not been accustomed to looking in the private literature by women—"oral history, letters, diaries, songs, tales, quips, reminscences." But as Professor Nan Bauer Maglin reminds us, it is in this "hidden" literature that we can discover the themes of matrilineage, the record of our mothers' lives. It is women versed in the oral tradition, frequently minority women, who have shown us the way back to our mothers. We hear the voices of lost mothers as we read literature by Black writers such as Alice Walker, Margaret Walker, Gayle Jones, Nikki Giovanni, Lucille Clifton, and Carolyn Rodgers—all minority daughter-writers whom Maglin discusses in her essay.

One important theme running throughout all these writings is the sense that the daughter is no longer alone. The lost mother is found. One consequence of the woman's movement is a new emphasis on sisterhood, on shared daughterhood. As Maglin states, there is a "need to recite one's matrilineage, to find a ritual to both get back there and preserve it." "The sudden new sense the daughter has of the mother; the realization that she, her mother, is a strong woman; and that her voice reverberates with her mother's"—all this is part of the new matrilineage.

Other minority women, too, look back to their mothers. As Professor Helen Bannan shows, in the recent generation of southwestern Native Americans, the matrilineage of the ancestral past is being restored. Spider Woman, "the grandmother of earth and of all living things" once again spins the web of life that connects one generation of women to another. Bannan first surveys the social structure of the

Native Americans of the southwest, emphasizing that the mother-daughter relationship, before the advent of the white man and the white man's ways, was a "lifelong tie, often economic as well as emotional, and intimately involving grandmothers in the rearing of the next generation." Again, the *unwritten* and unpublished record tells the tale of mother-daughter, in story, myth, song, ceremony, legend, and sacred ritual.

After the nineteenth century—a time of rape and raid, forced separation and Europeanization of the Native American—there was a brief period of uncertainty, a time when the daughters, newly educated in "Indian schools," forgot their mothers. But the daughters of these women long for their grandmother's fireside teachings and search again for Spider Woman. It is in the autobiography and poetry of this third generation that we once more hear the voice of Spider Woman:

> The earth is your mother
> she holds you.
>
> There never was a time
> when this
> was not so.

In her essay on immigrant and minority women, Ms. Natalie M. Rosinsky makes essentially the same point. She shows how in the fiction by these oppressed women, "each protagonist comes to recognize her mother as fellow victim rather than total villain." The protagonists "discover the deeper rapport that—along with suffering—unites them to their mothers."

It is in the final essay, by Professor Lynn Z. Bloom, that the many strands of this section are interwoven. With autobiography, the private writing becomes public. The minority woman, as well as the daughter-writers who are not members of an oppressed "class," join together in their search for mothers. Finally, all of the famous daughters, by the very process of writing about their lives, pay a debt of gratitude and acknowledge publicly their "appreciation of this maternal love."

When the daughter assumes the role of autobiographer, she becomes the mother, Demeter, searching out the lost Persephone: "The daughter-as-autobiographer becomes her own mother, she also becomes the re-creator of her maternal parent and the controlling adult in their literary relationship." Bloom continues, "As daughters grow, so do their mothers." Not surprisingly then, we find fully realized mothers in the autobiographies of women whose own lives have become rich. Their autobiographies provide, for the reader, another kind of legacy: "Through the examples of these daughter-autobiographers, we, too, can come to terms with our own inheritance, and even translate it into autobiography, pride of generation."

Few of the women writers of the past were mothers. Perhaps in other times motherhood was—or was meant to be—a full-time occupation. Motherhood excluded authorhood. No wonder the daughter-author so often excluded mention of a mother, so often created motherless daughters who faced the world alone.

At last we have a new generation of mother-writers. In autobiographies, short stories, novels, plays, poems, movies, personal statements, writers are acknowledging their mothers, looking back to their mothers' mothers, and the mothers before them that extend back through time. The rebellious daughter has reclaimed her mother.

The essays which follow present the inheritance these daughters are accepting from their mothers and indicate the new literature to explore: minority women, unsung women, immigrant women, lesbian women, poor women, white middle-class heterosexual women, all celebrated in verse, prose, in various forms, with varied meters.

More than four thousand years ago the temple priestess Enheduanna sang hymns of praise to her mother-goddess, Inanna. Again, we hear her refrain.

E. M. B.
C. N. D.

"Don't never forget the bridge that you crossed over on": The Literature of Matrilineage

Women are now consciously exploring the previously unconscious bonds that have tied them to both their real as well as their historical mothers and grandmothers. In relation to this there is a growing body of literature of matrilineage; women are writing about their female heritage and their female future.[1] While this is not a totally new subject for literature, it is a new passion for the women of this generation, a passion based on the feminist movement and new theory about women, history, and literature.

In the academic fields of history and literature the "private" sphere is being examined and revealed—the household, the family, the bed, the nursery, and the kinship system. Carroll Smith-Rosenberg describes the effect of this approach on history:

> Our concern with the private, the domestic, and the intrapsychic has altered our methodology and our hierarchy of historical significance. On the most elementary level it has demonstrated the need to expand the nature of our sources and to turn to the behavioral sciences for frameworks of interpretive conceptualization . . . We begin to question whether women's peculiar experiences and needs may have causally affected developments in the public sphere. We have, in short, redefined what is significant about our past.[2]

A parallel process is occurring in the study of literature. The idea of what is great literature, what is art, the notion or definition of universal and regional literature, the traditional literary canon and traditional literary history is being seen as ideologically antiwoman. As Florence Howe explains:

> The very idea of a canon of literature may emerge as one tactic, a kind

of literary credentialing process, for limiting the potential strength of the female sub-culture. Similarly, it may become evident that the division between what is generally considered "art" and what is generally considered "handicraft" are themselves ideologies, serving key roles in the sexual politics of culture.[3]

Many women writers are consciously working to overcome the artificial preferences given to art over life, the "world" over the home, the man over the woman. Ntozake Shange, for example, writes of her work:

> My work attempts to ferret out what i know & touch in a woman's body. if i really am commited to pulling the so-called personal outta the realm of non-art. that's why i have dreams and recipes, great descriptions of kitchens & handiwork in *sassafrass, cypress* & *indigo*. that's why in *for colored girls* . . . i discuss the simple reality of going home at nite, of washing one's body, looking out the window with a woman's eyes. we must learn our common symbols, preen them and share them with the world.[4]

Thus, the new literature includes oral history, letters, diaries, songs, tales, quips, reminiscences because it recognizes the meaningfulness of women's daily lives and validates the forms in which it has been transmitted.

In the literature of matrilineage, five interconnecting themes appear and reappear:

1. the recognition by the daughter that her voice is not entirely her own;

2. the importance of trying to really see one's mother in spite of or beyond the blindness and skewed vision that growing up together causes;

3. the amazement and humility about the strength of our mothers;

4. the need to recite one's matrilineage, to find a ritual to both get back there and preserve it;

5. and still, the anger and despair about the pain and the silence borne and handed on from mother and daughter.

Because of my own personal-political concerns as well as the fact that I live and teach in New York City, the literature I look at reflects the cosmopolitan variety of the city's ethnic roots; however, the tracing of anyone's matrilineage by its process brings up a rich rainbow of heritage.

Argentinian poet Alfonsina Storni's description of the sources of her own words in "It May Be" is a description that we owe to our mothers not only our craziness but our creativity:

> Maybe all that my verses have expressed
> is simply what was never allowed to be;
> only what was hidden and suppressed
> from woman to woman, from family to family.[5]

Virginia Woolf and then Tillie Olsen pointed out this indebtedness we share to not only our mothers' voices but their silences also, as has Alice Walker in her article "In Search of Our Mothers' Gardens." She connects her art to her (biological and symbolic) mothers' spirituality; to her songs, gardens, and quilts; to her ability to hold on:

> . . . it is to my mother—and all our mothers who were not famous—
> that I went in search of the secret of what has fed that muzzled and
> often mutilated, but vibrant, creative spirit that the Black woman has
> inherited, and that pops out in wild and unlikely places to this day.
> . . . Therefore we must fearlessly pull out of ourselves and look at and
> identify with our lives the living creativity some of our great-grand-
> mothers were not allowed to know.[6]

For many women writers, their stories came from listening to people talk in their families. Gayle Jones, author of *Corregidor* and *Eva's Ma*, recalls:

> My first stories were heard stories—from grown-up people talking. I
> think it's important that we—my brother and I—were never sent out of
> the room when grown-up people were talking. So we heard stories. So
> I've always heard stories of people generations older than me. I think
> that's important. I think that's the important thing.
>   Also, my mother would write stories for us and read them to us.
> She would read other stories too, but my favorite ones were the ones
> she wrote herself and read to us. My favorite one of those was a story
> called, "Esapher and the Wizard." So I first knew stories as things that
> were heard. That you listened to. That someone spoke. The stories we
> heard in school—I didn't really make connections with them as stories.
> I just remember sitting around in the circle and different people being
> called on to read a sentence. But my mother's reading the stories—I
> connected with that. And I connected with the stories people were
> telling about things that happened back before I was born.[7]

Margaret Walker promised her grandmother that when she grew up she would write the story of her great-grandmother (who died in 1915):

> Since my grandmother lived with us until I was an adult, it was natural
> throughout my formative years for me to hear stories of slave life in
> Georgia . . . My mother recalls how often she and my father came in
> from night school well past bedtime and found me enthralled with my

grandmother's stories. Annoyed, she would ask, "Mama, why won't you let this child go to bed? Why will you keep her up until this time of night?" And grandmother usually answered guiltily, "Go to bed, Margaret. Go to bed right now." My father would add, "Telling her all those harrowing tales, just nothing but tall tales." Grandmother grew indignant then, saying, "I'm not telling her tales; I'm telling her the naked truth."

As I grew older I realized the importance of the story my grandmother was telling . . .[8]

Jubilee kept Margaret Walker's promise. The debt to tell the stories of our matrilineage is to ourselves as Grace Paley depicts it in the story "Debts." A writer called upon by a lady to help her write the story of her grandfather from the family archives says:

Actually, I owed nothing to the lady who'd called. It was possible that I did owe something to my own family and the families of my friends. That is to tell their stories as simply as possible, in order, you might say, to save a few lives.[9]

Sometimes our mothers' voices seem to drench us with their absorption in daily life or their demands for our conformity as Frances Chung remembers:

mother talking to me in songs
of shopping bags and movie star calendars
given for free at the grocery store
(she wants a grandson)[10]

Sometimes our mothers do not allow us our silences:

My pumpkin mother
raging, used to make words
like weeds, sprout
in my artichoke ears
until I left her[11]

And yet, looking back at our mothers and listening harder to the silences beneath their voices, we should understand their "hopes of mooncakes dragon bracelets/and ginger soup."[12]

Listening to, and seeing, really seeing, our mothers, grandmothers, and foremothers then is not such an easy task, although we matrilineage explorers try. For example, Nikki Giovanni's poem "Mothers" alerts us to the notion that we do not often or usually really see the people with whom we live, especially the woman who nurtured us. She recalls a moment when she first "consciously saw" her mother:

we were living in a three room
apartment on burns avenue

mommy always sat in the dark
I don't know how i knew that but she did . . .

she was sitting on a chair
the room was bathed in moodlight diffused through
thousands of panes landlords who rented
to people with children were prone to put in windows

she may have been smoking but maybe not
her hair was three-quarters her height
which made me a strong believer in the samson myth
and very black

i'm sure I just hung by the door
i remember thinking: what a beautiful lady . . .[13]

This scene occurred when she was a little girl getting up "perhaps because i had wet/the bed," but she only comprehended this remembered vision visting her mother now that she, herself, is a mother.

"The Magic Mama" by Lucille Clifton is an autobiographical story of a daughter, now grown, finally seeing her mother, now dead. She is no longer the mother of spells and fits, waiting and sitting in her chair, who later hid in the attic "flitting through our rooms like a shadowy maid"; she is no longer the mother to be ashamed of, rather she is now understood to be the person whose creative spirit was suppressed. "A book of verse she wrote was accepted by a publisher but the family didn't approve; we don't want everybody reading about our Mama, you ain't no poetry writer, you a mother; and so she burned it." The daughter is now seeing, grieves realizing that she is not a self-created orphan but that she is her mother's daughter, writing out of this heritage:

"Everything for her, everything, all
poems, all movings up, all goodnesses,
everything begging, begging, Mama, Mama
of Magic, forgive. Forgive. Forgive.[14]

Often it is difficult for a daughter to identify with her mother, having been excluded from an intimacy that would help her to know her mother. In Helen Wong Huie's poem, "My Mother's Arms," the daughter never sensed that her mother had deep feelings:

When my mother was young

> she must have been in pain
> I don't remember her holding me.[15]

However, looking backwards daughters do uncover their mothers' and grandmothers' strengths. Margaret Walker's 1942 poem "Lineage" describes the physical and spiritual strength of our grandmothers to survive and asks the question: "My grandmothers were strong./Why am I not as they?"[16] Alice Walker's early 1970s poem "Women" acknowledges a similar strength in the daughters of Margaret Walker's grandmothers. These women fought to win for their children the rights and privileges supposedly inherent in American life:

> They were women then
> My mama's generation
> Husky of voice—Stout of
> Step
> With fists as well as
> Hands
> How they battered down
> Doors . . .[17]

In Carole Bovoso's article "Discovering my Foremothers,"[18] Cynthia Ozick's article "Passage to the New World,"[19] and Cara DeVito's videotape "Ama L'Uomo Tuo" (Always Love Your Man),[20] we were told stories of female "spunk."[21] For instance, Carole Bovoso's great-grandmother, Frances Anne Rollin, was born in 1847 in Charleston, S.C. Having been denied first class passage on a steamer boat because she was Black, she filed a complaint which led to the end of discrimination on that boat. She wrote a book about Martin R. Delany "who has been called the Father of Black Nationalism," but could only get it published under the name "Frank A. Rollin." During her research and writing she was forced to support herself by taking a job sewing for a woman. She writes in her diary on July 1, 1868:

> Went out to sew today. I thought when I began literature that that ended, but I find it otherwise.[22]

Rollin's daughter Iona, born in 1872, was one of four women to graduate from Howard Medical School in 1903. It appears that she had to restrict her practice to women and so she worked for women by travelling in the South instructing midwives and by opening a home in Washington, D.C., for Black unwed mothers.

Whereas Bovoso's foremothers recorded their experiences in diaries, Ozick found her mother's story in the "heaps of manuscripts that litter her tables and bureaus." Her mother Shipra, now called Celia, wrote about her 1906 escape from Czarist Russia at age nine with her mother and four siblings. Cynthia

> used to hear it often in early childhood; my mother's mother first told me the story. It had almost become a fable, that tale of what we used to call *dimayse fun dem grenets*, the "Story of the Border." What makes it even more of a fable is its mythlike universality—many thousands of Jews had to flee Russia by escaping over those same bristling borders.[23]

Cara Devito spent a week videotaping her seventy-five-year-old Sicilian-born grandmother who, while still cleaning and cooking, talked of her past life, and especially of her fifty year marriage to Benny, who had recently died. She told Cara of some brutal times. Benny beat her up because she danced with another man (a friend of the family) or because she refused to pick up the toilet paper he deliberately dropped on the floor. About the abortion she was forced to have when she was six months pregnant, she says "only God knows the pain" she suffered. Over and over she cried out for her mother. When Cara asked why she had married him, she explained that she had been living in New York City with a mean sister-in-law and she just had to get out of the house. She figured that Benny, who was a businessman, would always provide bread for her and her planned-for children. And that he did, although he called her "lost bread" for the money she never earned (although it appears that she did earn some money embroidering). The title words are the words she leaves Cara with: "Always Love Your Man—with all his faults."

In the literature of matrilineage often the strength of the women in our past is sentimentalized or is magnified so that our own strength appears to be negligible—especially in terms of the hard physical and social conditions of the past. Sometimes our geneological and historical mothers become not persons but symbols (which we need) and lose their multidimensionality. Lucille Clifton's poem "My Mama moved among the days" is not simplistic; we see her mother's strength and her mother's fear. She praises her mother who

> seemed like what she touched was hers
> seemed like what touched her couldn't hold
>
> although
>
> she got us almost through the high grass
>
> it
>
> then seemed like she turned around and ran
> right back in
> right back on in[24]

But to find this heritage, to connect oneself in a positive way does give us strength for we so often feel like motherless daughters, orphans with no past. Lucille Clifton's book *Generations: A Memoir* is a moving literary rendering of the piecing together of one's matrilineage:

> And I could tell you about things we been through, some awful ones, some wonderful, but I know that the things that make us are more than that, our lives are more than the days in them, our lives are our line and we go on. I type that and I swear I can see Ca'line standing in the green of Virginia, in the green of Afrika, and I swear she makes no sound but she nods her head and smiles.
>
> > The generations of Caroline Donald born in Afrika in
> > 1823 and Sam Louis Sale born in America in 1777 are
> > Lucille
> > who had a son named
> > Genie
> > who had a son named
> > Samuel
> > who married
> > Thelma Moore and the blood became Magic and their
> > daughter is
> > Thelma Lucille
> > who married Fred Clifton and the blood became whole and
> > their children are
> > Sidney
> > Fredrica
> > Gillian
> > Alexia four daughters and
> > Channing
> > Graham two sons
> > and the line goes on.
> > "Don't you worry, mister, don't you worry."[25]

Similarly, E. M. Broner's novel *Her Mothers* is a fictional journey into personal and historical matrilineage. Beatrix Palmer, archivist, oral historian, and writer of such books on women as *The Pioneers, Unafraid Women, Remnants,* and the proposed anthology *Mothers and Daughters,* finds herself and her runaway daughter as she merges and submerges in the women in her family, her life, and the past. In many variations she recites her lineage beginning with herself and ending with her daughter Lena:

> The mother is Western; in fact, Midwestern. Beatrix's mother is European. Beatrix's mother's mother, Lena Gurnev, is Sephardic. Lena is Eastern.[26]

While giving us a kind of strength of understanding, the discovery of our mothers' lives and the voicing of our mothers' silences do not always yield warm insights and female solidarity. Poet Joan Larkin in "Rhyme of My Inheritance" lists some of those painful gifts of family history:

> My mother gave me a bitter tongue.
> My father gave me a turned back.
> My grandmother showed me her burned hands.
> My brother showed me a difficult book.
> These were their gifts; the rest was talk.[27]

And yet, and still, recognizing one's matrilineage in the personal and historical sense and sharing that process of discovery through the written word can have an emotionally powerful and profoundly inspiring impact. Carolyn Rodger's poem "It Is Deep (don't never forget the bridge that you crossed over on)" articulates some of the themes of the literature of matrilineage: the distance between mother and daughter; the sudden new sense the daughter has of the mother; the realization that she, her mother, is a strong woman; and that her voice reverberates with her mother's. She, the "I" of the poem, is far from her mother: her mother has never read her poetry; her mother thinks she is a communist and will not listen to her talk of Blackness. In need, however, her mother comes with money for the rent, the phone, and food. She, the poet, like Giovanni, like Clifton, really sees her mother in the present, in the past, and in history as the line of women ("the bridge") that brought her as far as she has come:

> there she was, standing in my room
> not loudly condemning that day and
> not remembering that I grew hearing her
> curse the factory where she "cut uh slave"
> and the cheap j-boss wouldn't allow a union,
> not remembering that I heard the tears when
> they told her a high school diploma was not enough,
> and here now, not able to understand, what she had
> been forced to deny, still . . .
>
> My mother, religious-negro, proud of
> having waded through a storm, is very obviously
> a sturdy Black bridge that I crossed over, on.[28]

Notes

1 There is a growing interdisciplinary field of research and writing concerned with matrilineage, as is indicated in the bibliography included in this collection of essays.

2 Carroll Smith-Rosenberg, "The New Woman and the New History," *Feminist Studies*, 3 (Fall 1975), 185. See also, Gerda Lerner, "New Approaches to the Study of Women in American History," *Journal of Social History*, 3 (1969), 53–62; Lois Banner, "On Writing Women's History," in *The Family in History: Interdisciplinary Essays*, ed. Theodore K. Rabb and Robert I. Rothberg (New York: Harper and Row, 1973), pp. 159–70; and the review essay on American history by Barbara Sicherman in *Signs*, 1 (1975), 461–85.

3 Florence Howe, "Feminism and the Study of Literature," *Radical Teacher*, 3 (Nov. 1976), p. 10. See also, for example, the review essay on literary criticism by Elaine Showalter in *Signs*, 1 (1975), 435–60, and Emily Toth, "Some Introductory Notes on Women Regionalists," *The Kate Chopin Newsletter*, 2, No. 2 (Fall 1976), 1–3.

4 Ntozake Shange, "Ntozake Shange Interviews Herself," *Ms.*, December, 1977, pp. 70 and 72.

5 Alfonsina Storni, *"It May Be,"* in *The Other Voice: Twentieth Century Women's Poetry in Translation*, ed. Joanna Bankier, et. al. (New York: Norton, 1976), p. 20.

6 Alice Walker, "In Search of Our Mothers' Gardens," *Generation: Women in the South, Southern Exposure*, 4, No. 4, p. 63.

7 Gayle Jones, "An Interview," *Massachusetts Review*, 18 (Winter 1977), 692.

8 Margaret Walker, *How I Wrote Jubilee* (Chicago: Third World Press, 1977), pp. 11–12. See also Shebar Windston, *"Lilith* Interview: Esther Broner," *Lilith*, Fall–Winter 1978, p. 32, where Broner talks about the legends her grandmother told her.

9 Grace Paley, "Debts," in *Enormous Changes at the Last Minute* (New York: Dell, 1975), pp. 17–18.

10 Frances Chung, "they want me to settle down. . .," in *Ordinary Women/Mujeres Comunes* (New York: Ordinary Women, 1978), p. 36

11 Teru Kanazawa, "Song to My Nisei Mother," *Ordinary Women*, p. 108.

12 Kanazawa, p. 108. As Alice Walker puts it: "They dreamed dreams that no one knew—not even themselves, in any coherent fashion—and saw visions no one could understand." "In Search," p. 60.

13 Nikki Giovanni, "Mothers," *My House* (New York: William Morrow, 1972), pp. 6–7.

14 "The Magic Mama" from *Good Times* by Lucille Clifton. This story reminds me of Adrienne Rich's "A Woman Mourned by Daughters," if only because of the sense of the mother in her death and in her life. Adrienne Rich, *Poems: Selected and New, 1950–1974* (New York: Norton, 1966), p. 57.

15 Helen Wong Huie, "My Mother's Arms," *Ordinary Women*, p. 92.

16 Margaret Walker, "Lineage," in *For My People* (New Haven: Yale Univ. Press, 1945), p. 25.

17 Alice Walker, "Women," in *Revolutionary Petunias and Other Poems* (New York: Harcourt, Brace, Jovanovich, 1973), p. 5. The poem is also in her article, "In Search of Our Mothers' Gardens." See also, Nikki Giovanni's poem "Legacies" and Alice Walker's poem "Burial," both about their grandmothers' spirits.

18 Carole Bovoso, "Discovering My Foremothers," *Ms.*, September, 1977, p. 56.

19 Cynthia Ozick, "Passage to the New World," *Ms.*, August, 1977, pp. 70–72, and Shiphra Regeson Ozick, "Escape From Czarist Russia," *Ms.*, same issue, pp. 72, 74, and 87.

20 Cara Devito, "Ama L'Uomo Tuo," available from Electronic Arts Intermix, Inc., 84 Fifth Avenue, New York, New York 10011.

21 Ozick, p. 70.

22 Bovoso, p. 56.

23 Ozick, p. 72.

266

[24] Lucille Clifton, "My Mama moved among the days," *Good Times* (New York: Random House, 1969), p. 2.

[25] Clifton's book is *Generations: A Memoir* (New York: Random House, 1976).

[26] E. M. Broner, *Her Mothers* (New York: Berkley Publishing, 1976), p. 19.

[27] Joan Larkin, "Inheritance," in *Housework* (New York: Out and Out Books, 1975), p. 6.

[28] Carolyn M. Rodgers, "It is Deep (don't never forget the bridge that you crossed over on)" (Chicago: Third World Press, 1969).

Spider Woman's Web: Mothers and Daughters in Southwestern Native American Literature

> Then the Spider Woman, being [a] very intelligent person, again cau-
> tioned us to be on guard, to never let go of the Life Pattern given to us
> by the Great Spirit.
>
> Andrew Hermequaftewa, Hopi[1]

Spider Woman, "the grandmother of earth and of all living things,"[2]
weaves the thread of a common theme throughout the traditional oral
literatures of several Southwestern Native American peoples. In many
tales, she appears as a tiny figure who welcomes poor wanderers into
her underground home, giving them advice and power enabling them
to survive their journeys through alien lands populated by vengeful
supernaturals.[3] The exploits of these sojourners, and Spider Woman's
grandmotherly kindness, are remembered in mythology, which forms
the living heart of each Indian culture, the center of the Life Pattern.

Spider Woman's concern for the preservation of the Life Pattern
allows us to picture it as her web, spun of tribal experience and memory,
with strands as strong as steel. The image of the web reflects the
intricacy and organic wholeness of each Native American culture, its
ties to the earth, and its capacity for growth, as additional concentric
circles expand the structure without altering its basic design.

This paper will survey the vast body of Southwestern Native American literature—traditional oral materials, collected autobiographies, and
contemporary writings—to trace the filaments that form the radial arms
of the web, the kinship bonds between mothers and daughters that tie
individuals in succeeding generations to each other, and to the central
core of ancient cultural traditions. Since many Southwestern peoples

trace descent through the female line, relationships between mothers and daughters bear much of the responsibility for holding the web of life together by reciprocal rights and obligations that provide solidarity and continuity to the culture as a circular whole. For instance, the most important Navajo social entity is the matrilineal clan; clan members, who call each other "mother," "can expect to receive food, shelter, economic support, ceremonial cooperation, and an inheritance" from each other.[4] In addition, customs of most matrilineal societies require a newly married couple to establish a home near that of the wife's mother, making the mother-daughter relationship a lifelong tie, often economic as well as emotional, and intimately involving grandmothers in the rearing of the next generation.

One of the principal traditional methods of educating children is storytelling: Native American societies value literature as an integral part of life. The purpose of Indian oral literature is not mere self-expression, although gifted storytellers are recognized as specialists and artists among their people. Rather, "the tribes seek, through song, ceremony, legend, sacred stories (myths), and tales to embody, articulate, and share reality, to bring the isolated private self into harmony and balance with this reality, to verbalize the sense of the majesty and reverent mystery of all things, and to actualize, in language, those truths of being and experience that give to humanity its greatest significance and dignity."[5] Oral literatures express such truths by describing the activities of deities, animals, and people, all of whom share typically human weaknesses, emotions, and motivations, and all of whom are actively involved in creating, upsetting, and restoring the harmony of the universe.

Since this harmony requires strong bonds between female kin, oral literatures illustrate the expected behavior of mothers and daughters, by some positive and much negative example. The first responsibility of mothers to their children is care, including complete faithfulness to prenatal and neonatal ritual prescriptions,[6] as well as provision for physical well-being. The White Mountain Apache teach this duty by relating the experience of Porcupine, a widowed mother without other kin, who, preferring gambling to child care, abandons her son and daughter. An old woman adopts the waifs, teaches the maturing daughter food-gathering techniques, and later makes the young woman marry her son. When this industrious couple acquires a widespread reputation for generously distributing their surplus food, the runaway mother decides to visit her daughter and share in the bounty. The daughter, however, refuses to feed Porcupine or allow her to see her grandchild. Finally, Porcupine begs for the scrotum of a deer; her daughter puts a rock in it, and throws it at her mother, knocking her over. Porcupine's hunger overcomes her pride: she picks up the scrotum, cooks, and eats it.[7] By abandoning her daughter, Porcupine effectively severs herself from the web of kinship, losing her maternal rights to the sustenance, love, and honor of her daughter and the next generation, a very heavy penalty.

If mothers, then, must care for their daughters, reciprocity demands that daughters care for mothers, respect, obey, and help them. In a Pima legend, the adolescent Yellow Bird is anxious to do her share of domestic work, but insists on gathering palo verde pods herself, rather than waiting to accompany her mother. Her intransigent independence places Yellow Bird in the danger her mother foresaw: the girl is captured by Whirlwind and taken to the top of a mountain. Her parents invoke supernatural aid, and Yellow Bird climbs down a magical vine, thereafter to respect her mother's wishes.[8] Tewa pueblo tales show that a disobedient or careless daughter may be scolded or whipped by her mother, as Cactus clan girl is when she comes home with a broken water jar. Discipline does not mean lack of maternal love; when the daughter protests this treatment by running away from home, her mother is so grief-stricken and lonesome that she becomes physically ill. After Spider Woman befriends the girl, gives her a never-empty water jar, and sends her home, the mother's health is restored.[9] This tale includes morals for three generations: daughters must be careful and obedient, mother must avoid punishing daughters too harshly, and grandmothers must listen and counsel wisely to restore family harmony.

Many Southwestern Native American peoples mark the onset of a daughter's menses in ceremonies that teach the adolescent the serious responsibilities of womanhood, and joyfully incorporate her as an adult member of the society, capable of weaving new strands into the kinship web. Mothers are intimately involved in preparing their daughters for this event, through which specially chosen female sponsors guide the girls. Navajo ceremonial mothers follow the example of First Woman, who performed the first Kinaaldá (Walked Into Beauty) Ceremony for Changing Woman, the beneficient Holy Person "born of darkness and the dawn," whom First Woman found and raised.[10] In the Apache girl's puberty ceremony, the adolescent daughter represents the supernatural White Painted Woman, and receives her gifts, which this Chiricahua song enumerates:

> White Painted Woman carries this girl;
> She carries her through long life,
> She carries her to good fortune,
> She carries her to old age,
> She bears her to peaceful sleep.[11]

Soon after achieving womanhood status, Southwestern daughters are expected to assume the responsibilities of that rank; as the Navajo say, "a girl's first bleeding is an order from the Holy People to marry.[12] Girls who hesitate may be considered unfeminine and given different orders, as are the Blue Corn Girls in a Tewa story. Their pueblo's Outside Chief responds to their refusal to marry by saying, "I think you are men, and you have to go to the war." The frightened, untrained girls appeal to Spider Woman, who gives them songs and charms that make them successful warriors.[13]

Most girls, however, marry; in many Apache tales, a daughter's early marriage or prolonged maidenhood is her mother's decision. After rejecting her daughters' suitors for 28 years, one legendary Jicarilla Apache mother vows to wed them to anyone bringing her cold water from melted snow to relieve the summer heat. When a poor boy fulfills her condition, she keeps her promise. Although one of the daughters is silently ashamed of his appearance, "The girls didn't say anything. Their mother told them what they had to do," and they marry him.[14] In pueblo tales, mothers encourage their daughters to marry, but allow them to make their own choices. Maternal patience with reluctant daughters is sometimes rewarded by the eventual but temporary addition of a Kachina or other supernatural son-in-law to the household.[15] However, other long-single girls are bewitched into marrying the trickster Coyote, shaming their families.[16] The message to daughters is clear: marry early, choose your own kind, and start your family in your mother's village. Thus, the web of kinship and cultural continuity remains intact and grows.

Oral literature thus sketches the basic outline of the traditional Life Pattern that Spider Woman urged Native Americans to keep. Countless generations of mothers and daughters have followed the behavioral lessons of the tales, although this became increasingly difficult after new peoples, intent on conquest, entered their homelands. If we can again imagine the Life Pattern as a spider's web anchored between a cholla cactus and a pinyon tree firmly rooted in the Southwestern earth, the Spanish and American invasions were like violent gusts of wind, straining the web and threatening to loosen its moorings. The web was strong and so were the women who helped to weave it, but the winds of change tested Indian endurance to the limit.

While the Spanish empire (1540–1821) and Mexican republic (1821–1848) ruled the Southwest, governmental control of this remote frontier was generally lax. However, Native American societies deeply felt the side effects of Spanish conquest: Spanish sheep and horses totally altered the economic basis of Navajo and Apache societies, Spanish missionaries drove pueblo religions underground, and Spanish presence and example greatly increased raiding, both among different Indian groups and between Indians and Hispanic settlers.[17] Women were most prized as captives; thus, mothers and daughters were often forcibly separated, sometimes for life. Some Native American captives escaped, walking incredible distances or stealing horses to enable them to rejoin their families.[18]

In spite of this constant danger of enslavement, Native American mothers and daughters continued to live out the Life Pattern handed down to them. The recorded memories of the oldest Native American women of the twentieth century reach back to the time before their homelands were called "reservations," when they were young girls whose mothers strictly adhered to the ideals, roles, and rituals prescribed in traditional oral literatures. Thus, when Helen Sekaquaptewa was an infant, her mother and paternal grandmother carried her to the edge of the mesa at dawn, and asked the sun to "take notice of this little Hopi baby girl and bless her with life, health, and a family."[19] Helen remembers her next formal step into Hopi society, the initiation ceremony that shows young Hopi children that Kachina dancers are not gods, but men wearing masks. Helen's mother lovingly protected her by wrapping a belt under her clothes to absorb the sting of the whipping the ritual requires.[20]

Mothers also demonstrated their concern by carefully teaching their daughters the skills expected of women in their societies. As Navajo Myrtle Begay recalls, "Mother used to tell us she wouldn't be around all our lives; so we would have to learn to do the things that had to be done."[21] Girls had many such things to learn; before Navajo Kay Bennett was ten, she herded the family's sheep, carded wool, swept yard and hogan, cared for her infant niece, "ground corn, chopped wood, hauled water, and could handle horses as well as a man."[22] "All traditional education came to us through actions and lectures,"[23] as mothers kept daughters at their sides, patiently encouraging them to imitate their actions. While very young, Maria Chona, a Papago, began helping her mother grind wild grass seed for gruel; by the time she reached ten, Maria "did it all, for then a daughter should be able to take over the work and let her mother sit down to baskets."[24] Anna Moore Shaw, a Pima, explains this widely shared traditional attitude: "As a mother grows old, her legs become tired, and the daughter must help with the cooking . . . [and] perform the many heavy chores required of a Pima woman."[25] The process of traditional vocational education thus was circular, reflecting again the emphasis on generational continuity in Native American life.

Mothers also taught their daughters the more abstract requirements of womanhood in their cultures: the values, behaviors, and rituals that must be observed to win respectable status, and preserve family harmony. Discipline was essential to this training; both Lina Zuni and Anna Moore Shaw, a Zuni and a Pima, remember with shame their mothers' scoldings and saddened looks caused by their willful breaking of water jars, the same offense Cactus clan girl was punished for in the Tewa pueblo story.[26] Mothers and grandmothers lectured their descendants, and told stories illustrating the consequences of ignoring their advice. In her old age, Lina Zuni lived with her daughter and grandchildren, and took her role as a teacher seriously: "Every day I tell my children something. Perhaps they listen to me. Perhaps that is why we live together nicely."[27] Navajo Kay Bennett's mother gave her "her undivided attention, . . . and she talked on and on, as if she felt that this was her last chance to pass on all the knowledge acquired . . . during her full life, and to make sure it would not be lost to her family when she died."[28]

The lessons of mothers and grandmothers became more intensive as daughters approached puberty. When Maria Chona had her first period, she was isolated in the menstrual hut required by her Papago culture, and taught her womanly responsibilities as she prepared for the joyful ceremony which would follow her seclusion. Maria paid careful attention to the ceremonial mother chosen to instruct her: "I listened to her. . . . I wanted to be a good woman! And I have been."[29] Other daughters similarly valued their mothers' advice; as Navajo Myrtle Begay states, "How true her words were. . . . Today, I do exactly what she taught me. With a mother like that, it is hard to forget her teachings."[30] When such lessons are remembered, the Life Pattern remains intact.

However, the winds of change increased in velocity towards the end of the nineteenth century, when American conquerors threatened the

Native American web of life by attempting to force forgetfulness of traditional teachings. At first, many Indian mothers feared an American escalation of conventional raiding. When eastern emigrants approached the Paiutes' Nevada homeland, Sarah Winnemucca's mother buried her in sand to prevent her capture.[31] Paiute mothers soon became accustomed to Americans rushing across their lands towards the California goldfields, but they never trusted the newcomers, who earned a reputation for rape. "The mothers are afraid to have children, for fear they shall have daughters, who are not safe even in their mother's presence."[32]

However, the greatest American threat to Native American generational continuity was the governmental policy of capturing Indian children for boarding schools, where, in the name of vocational education, Indian children were taught to reject their heritage and adopt American cultural patterns. The word "capture" should be taken literally; in the early 1900s, mothers and grandmothers hid their daughters from officials combing the reservations for children to fill their classrooms. As Polingaysi Qoyawayma's mother said, "It is not the Hopi way of caring for children, this tearing them from their homes and their mothers."[33] Some Navajo mothers managed to delay or prevent the schooling of their daughters, training them instead in traditional skills crucial to family survival; as Molly Richardson's mother stated, "the only child in the family . . . was needed to herd the sheep."[34]

Eventually, however, most daughters were caught, perhaps due to battle fatigue, as Hopi Helen Sekaquaptewa suggests. "Maybe both my mother and myself got a little tired of getting up early every morning and running off to hide all day."[35] After their initial culture shock and homesickness, many Native American daughters became adjusted to the school environment in which they were totally immersed, winter and summer, for years at a time. As Helen recalls, "I had lived at the school so long it seemed like my home."[36]

When the daughters returned to their reservations, they had difficulties readjusting to homes and traditions they had been taught to regard as unclean, primitive, and pagan. Helen Sekaquaptewa remembers that she "didn't feel at ease in the home of my parents" when she rejoined her Hopi family after thirteen years in school. Her mother welcomed her, saying "she was glad I was home. If I would stay there, she would not urge me to change my ways."[37] Some daughters did not reciprocate this maternal example of restraint; Polingaysi Qoyawayma tried to teach her Hopi parents her newly acquired American values, arousing her mother's protest: "What shall I do with my daughter, who is now my mother?"[38]

Thus, American schooling disrupted the traditional pattern of Native American education, by interrupting mothers' training of their daughters, and by encouraging daughters to scorn the lessons their mothers could teach. Consequently, some traditional knowledge was lost by this generation; as Navajo Ada Damon states with some sadness, "I really don't know too much. I was small, you see, when I went to school."[39] Nevertheless, Damon's oral history records her close ties to her aged mother. Education is a powerful force, but not strong enough to obliterate centuries of tradition. As Polingaysi's mother told her Americanized daughter, "You are still a Hopi. . . . You will not forget the pattern life of the Hopi."[40]

Her mother was right; after Polingaysi's initial rebellion against all things Hopi, she began to work out a lifestyle that would reconcile the two cultures. As an unmarried woman who built her own home, Polingaysi broke Hopi tradition; as a teacher in government day school, she adapted the assimilative curriculum to fit her Hopi students by using traditional stories to introduce reading and counting. Living with contradiction is never easy; Polingaysi recalls feeling "forever on the defensive, both with her own people and the white people."[41] Despite the difficulties inherent in what Pima Anna Moore Shaw calls "a lifetime of treading the bridge between two cultures,"[42] many daughters of this generation chose that path. Hopi Helen Sekaquaptewa summarizes the trend, "Our lives were a combination of what we thought was the good of both cultures."[43]

When these daughters became mothers, they tried to pass on to their daughters this new tradition of combination. Anna Moore Shaw encouraged her daughter Adeline to attend school, but also tried to teach her Pima language and literature, which as a child, Adeline refused to learn. Her mother writes that "in the midst of the bustle of Phoenix, this must have all seemed so irrelevant," and worries that "perhaps in [her children's] involvement with the white man's schooling they missed the opportunity to absorb the ways of the Indian."[44]

Have the winds of change, then, finally broken the web of tradition? Contemporary Native American literature suggests otherwise. The granddaughters of the first educated generation appreciate the traditions that their grandmothers still remember and teach, and reaffirm the ancient continuity of maternal strength in their writings. Some express anger at their mother's lack of loyalty to older ways, but more seek to recreate and understand the experiences of that generation, and tie the past to present and future. In "Lullaby," Leslie Silko from Laguna pueblo tells the story of Ayah, a Navajo mother who still feels the pain of her children being taken from her to recover in a sanatorium, and to die in the Viet Nam war. Ayah comforts her dying husband by singing a lullaby she doesn't remember singing to her daughter, but one she knows her mother and grandmother sang for her:

> The earth is your mother,
> she holds you.
> . . . .
> There never was a time
> when this
> was not so.[45]

Thus, the tradition was not forgotten by the mothers, in spite of their education in assimilation that poet Soge Track recalls in her "Indian Love Letter" from Taos pueblo:

> If you were taken to
> the mission school,
> not because you wanted,
> but someone thought it best for you
> you too would change.[46]

Later in the poem, Track pledges herself to "live by the old ways," but she urges others to "be not too hard" on those mothers who, forced to change in their youth, find a return to tradition hard to understand.[47]

Native American granddaughters are following Spider Woman's advice to hold fast the web of tradition, and, like their maternal ancestors, they use their powers to increase that web, preserving its basic design while incorporating new materials and experiences into its structure. These lines from "Grandmother," by part-Luguna poet Paula Gunn Allen, celebrate Spider Woman's legacy of continuity:

> she was given the work of weaving the strands
> of her body, her pain, her vision
> into creation, and the gift of having made it,
> to disappear.
> After her,
> the women and the men weave blankets into tales of life,
> memories of light and ladders,
> infinity-eyes, and rain.

> After her I sit on my laddered rain-bearing rug
> and mend the tear with string.[48]

Thus repaired, the web of life and of female kinship remains, despite the winds of change, still tied to cholla and pinyon, and to the living Southwestern earth.

Notes

[1] Quoted in Hamilton A. Tyler, *Pueblo Gods and Myths* (Norman: University of Oklahoma Press, 1964), p. 97.

[2] "How the People Came to the Middle Place," Tewa, in Alice Marriott and Carol K. Rachlin, *American Indian Mythology* (New York: Thomas Y. Crowell, 1968), p. 67.

[3] For example, see "Handmark Boy," in Elsie Clews Parsons, *Tewa Tales*, Memoirs of the American Folk-Lore Society, Vol. 19 (New York: G. E. Stechert, 1926), pp. 195–210; "He Goes to His Father," in Grenville Goodwin, *Myths and Tales of the White Mountain Apache*, Memoirs of the American Folklore Society, Vol. 33 (New York: J. J. Augustin, 1939), pp. 3–12; "Changing Woman," in *Navajo History, Volume 1*, ed. by Ethelou Yazzie (Many Farms, Arizona: Navajo Community College Press, 1971), pp. 31–57; "How the Crow Clan Became Also the Kachina Clan," in Edmund Nequatewa, *Truth of a Hopi* (1936; rpt. [Flagstaff, Arizona]: Northland Press, 1967), pp. 79–83.

[4] Peggy Schneider, *Children of Changing Woman: Myth, Symbol and Navajo Women* (Santa Fe: Wheelwright Museum, 1977), p. 2.

[5] Paula Gunn Allen, "The Sacred Hoop: A Contemporary Indian Perspective on American Indian Literature," in *The Literature of the American Indians: Views and Interpretations*, ed. Abraham Chapman (New York: New American Library, 1975), p. 113.

[6] For all that this involves for pueblo mothers, see a series of articles by Elsie Clews Parsons in *Man: A Monthly Record of Anthropological Science*: "Mothers and Children at Zuni, New Mexico," 19 (Nov. 1919), pp. 168–73; "Hopi Mothers and Children," 21 (July 1921), pp. 98–104; and "Tewa Mothers and Children," 24 (Oct. 1924), pp. 148–151.

[7] "The Abandoned Children," told by Bane Tithla, in Goodwin, *Myths of White Mountain Apache*, pp. 141–42. Another story of similar theme is "The Two Orphans and Their Grandmother," in *The Zunis: Self-Portrayals* (Albuquerque: University of New Mexico Press, 1972), pp. 27–36.

[8] "Little Yellow Bird," in Anna Moore Shaw, *Pima Indian Legends* (Tucson: University of Arizona Press, 1968), pp. 195–210.

[9] "The Broken Water Jar," in Parsons, *Tewa Tales*, pp. 210–17.

[10] "Changing Woman," in *Navajo History*, pp. 31–34; for a complete description of the four-day ceremony, see Charlotte Johnson Frisbee, *Kinaaldá: A Study of the Navaho Girl's Puberty Ceremony* (Middletown, Connecticut: Wesleyan University Press, 1967).

[11] Quoted in Morris Opler, *An Apache Lifeway: The Economic, Social, and Religious Institutions of the Chiricahua Indians* (1941; rpt. New York: Cooper Square Publishers, 1965), p. 128.

[12] Frisbee, *Kinaaldá*, p. 7.

[13] "Blue Corn Girls Are Sent to War," in Parsons, *Tewa Tales*, pp. 59–61. Another similarly drafted Tewa girl was glad to fight; her face turned into a mask during

battle, and she was chosen war chief of her clan, in "Warrior Girl," ibid., pp. 191–92.

14 "How a Poor Boy Won His Wives," in Morris Edward Opler, *Myths and Tales of the Jicarilla Apache Indians*, Memoirs of the American Folklore Society, vol. 38 (New York: G. E. Stechert, 1938), pp. 387–89.

15 "Handmark Boy," in Parsons, *Tewa Tales*, pp. 195–210; "The Kana-a Kachinas of Sunset Crater," in Nequatewa, *Truth*, pp. 105–10.

16 "Dove Boy and Coyote," pp. 233–42, and "Cloud Boys and Coyote," pp. 242–46, in Parsons, *Tewa Tales*.

17 See Jack D. Forbes, *Apache, Navaho and Spaniard* (Norman: University of Oklahoma Press, 1960); Edward H. Spicer, *Cycles of Conquest: The Impact of Spain, Mexico, and the United States on the Indians of the Southwest, 1533–1960* (Tucson: University of Arizona Press, 1962).

18 See the stories told by Frank Johnson and Chahadineli Benally in *Navajo Stories of the Long Walk Period*, ed. by Broderick H. Johnson (Tsaile, Arizona: Navajo Community College Press, 1973), pp. 86–91 and 57–74; and by Anna Price in *Western Apache Raiding and Warfare: from the Notes of Grenville Goodwin* (Tucson: University of Arizona Press, 1971), p. 31.

19 Helen Sekaquaptewa as told to Louise Udall, *Me and Mine: The Life Story of Helen Sekaquaptewa* (Tucson: University of Arizona Press, 1969), p. 7.

20 Ibid., pp. 24, 28.

21 Myrtle Begay, in *Stories of Traditional Navajo Life and Culture*, ed. by Broderick H. Johnson (Tsaile, Arizona: Navajo Community College Press, 1977), p. 58.

22 Kay Bennett, *Kaibah: Recollections of a Navajo Girlhood* (1964; rpt. n.p.: the author, 1975), p. 188.

23 Begay, in *Stories of Traditional Navajo*, p. 60.

24 Ruth Underhill, *The Autobiography of a Papago Woman*, Memoirs of the American Anthropological Association, No. 46 (Menasha, Wisconsin: American Anthropological Association, 1936), p. 8.

25 Anna Moore Shaw, *A Pima Past* (Tucson: University of Arizona Press, 1974), p. 47.

26 Lina Zuni, "An Autobiography," in Ruth L. Bunzel, *Zuni Texts*, Publications of the American Ethnological Society, vol. 15 (New York: G. E. Stechert, 1933), pp. 78–79; Shaw, *Pima Past*, pp. 108–09; "The Broken Water Jar," in Parsons, *Tewa Tales*, pp. 210–17.

27 Lina Zuni, "Landslide," in *Zuni Texts*, p. 58.

28 Bennett, *Kaibah*, p. 183.

29 Underhill, *Autobiography of Papago*, p. 32; see also Shaw, *Pima Past*, pp. 53–55; and Sarah Winnemucca Hopkins, *Life Among the Piutes: Their Wrongs and Claims* (1883; rpt. Bishop, California: Chalfant Press, 1969), p. 48.

30 Begay, in *Stories of Traditional Navajo*, p. 60.

31 Winnemucca Hopkins, *Life*, p. 11.

32 Ibid., p. 48.

33 Polingaysi Qoyawayma (Elizabeth Q. White) as told to Vada F. Carlson, *No Turning Back: A Hopi Indian Woman's Struggle to Live in Two Worlds* (Albuquerque: University of New Mexico Press, 1964), p. 18.

34 Molly Richardson, in *Stories of Traditional Navajo*, p. 271; see also Bennett, *Kaibah*, pp. 21–22, 204.

35 Sekaquaptewa, *Me and Mine*, p. 11.

36 Ibid., p. 133.

37 Ibid., pp. 144–45.

38 Qoyawayma, *No Turning Back*, p. 83.

39 Ada Damon, in Yvonne Ashley, " 'That's the Way We Were Raised': An Oral Interview with Ada Damon," *Frontiers: A Journal of Women Studies*, 2 (Summer 1977), 83.

[40] Qoyawayma, *No Turning Back*, p. 72.

[41] Ibid., 134.

[42] Shaw, *Pima Past*, p. 230.

[43] Sekaquaptewa, *Me and Mine*, p. 43.

[44] Shaw, *Pima Past*, p. 232.

[45] Leslie Silko, "Lullaby," in *Southwest: A Contemporary Anthology*, ed. by Karl and Jane Kopp (Albuquerque: Red Earth Press, 1977), p. 249.

[46] Soge Track, "Indian Love Letter," in *Voices from Wah'kon-Tah: Contemporary Poetry of Native Americans*, ed. by Robert K. Dodge and Joseph B. McCullough (New York: International Publishers, 1974), p. 104.

[47] Ibid., p. 104.

[48] Paula Gunn Allen, "Grandmother," in *Southwest*, p. 184.

Mothers and Daughters: Another Minority Group

In *Of Woman Born: Motherhood as Experience and Institution*, Adrienne Rich concludes that "The loss of the daughter to the mother, the mother to the daughter, is the essential female tragedy."[1] This loss is one of psychological nurturence. Instead of recognizing "a knowledge that is subliminal, subversive, preverbal: the knowledge flowing between two alike bodies, one of which has spent nine months inside the other . . . " (Rich, p. 220), mother and daughter are estranged by patriarchal norms for female behavior and self-identity. Being a "good" woman in a sexist society requires conformity to feminine stereotypes such as passivity, spirituality, or irrationality;[2] being a "good" mother entails indoctrinating one's daughter with these false ideals. As Mary Daly has noted, "mothers in our culture are cajoled into killing off the self-actualization of their daughters, and daughters learn to hate them for it, instead of seeing the real enemy."[3] This "real enemy" is a culture which denigrates female potential and achievement.

Rich maintains that "This cathexis between mother and daughter—essential, distorted, misused—is the great unwritten story" (Rich, p. 225). However, women have begun to write about this crucial relationship. Members of racial, ethnic, sexual, and economic minority groups, in particular, have delineated their apprehension of the social forces which intervene between mother and daughter. Perhaps because the added oppression of minority group membership exacerbates this often painful relationship, these writers seem particularly aware of its tragic destructiveness. And, as will be indicated later, their unusual understanding very often leads to—at least metaphorically—a healing acceptance on the daughter's part of her mother's victimization. The "real enemy" appears easier to see when more than one oppression unites the two women. This essay examines literature written by Chicana, Black, and Jewish women who have perceived the many connections between ethnicity and the mother-daughter bond. Since poverty and sexual orientation "ghettoize" women in ways similar to ethnic minority group membership, literature by and about poor and lesbian women is also discussed.

Guadalupe Valdés-Fallis' short story, "Recuerdo," is a moving statement of the dilemma that confronts a poor, Chicana mother. Although Rosa knows that her daughter Maruca will undoubtedly hate her duties as Don Lorenzo's mistress, she lies to her child and tells her that the liaison will make her happy. Happiness, for the older woman, is the economic security she has never known, and her social milieu and conditioning cannot generate any other kind of advice. Rosa can envision no alternative to the mandatory "man to protect them. . . . "[4] Consequently, despite the intimation that Rosa has herself been seduced by Don Lorenzo, she isolates herself from her own visceral reaction to the predicament she and Maruca share and compromises her daughter's hopes. For several moments, she even experiences elation because a man of such wealth is attracted to Maruca. After this betrayal of trust, Rosa feels "alone" (*R*, p. 3) although she remains surrounded by her other children. This isolation is psychic: it stems most probably from Rosa's subconscious realization that, in Phyllis Chesler's words, her "legacy" to her daughter "is one of capitulation."[5]

Although Chesler's analysis of the maddening effects such capitulation may have on conventional mothers and daughters does not focus upon minority groups, its applicability to Rosa and Maruca's situation is undeniable: their culture, with its macho validation of women's subservient domestic role and attendant inferior education, is not alien to mainstream American society but is rather an intensification of it. The women's poverty, which leads Rosa to prostitute her daughter as well as herself, is a stark, grim version of the economic dependency that prompts anxious middle- and upper-class women to see their daughters "well-married." A headstrong young woman seems no match for this pervasive convention of female dependence; thus, Valdés-Fallis' story— told from the resigned and unquestioning mother's point of view— implies that Maruca herself may one day pass this legacy on to *her* daughter.

Toni Morrison's "SEEMOTHERMOTHERISVERYNICE" differs from "Recuerdo" in that Morrison depicts her Black protagonist's life before such capitulation occurs. Pauline's illusory expectations about life and romance are both fostered and destroyed by a racist, socially and economically stratified culture; this destruction is metaphorically comparable to the loss of her tooth. Even before the decay is apparent, "there must have been the conditions, the setting that would allow it to exist in the first place."[6] The "conditions" which transform visually imaginative, loving, and dreamy young Pauline into a woman who beats into her daughter "a fear of growing up, fear of other people, fear of life" (*SEE*, p. 110) are numerous. They include White norms of beauty which exclude her, social ostracism by Black and White neighbors alike because of her "country ways," and the strain that economic discrimination against Black men places upon her marriage. It is not surprising that Pauline's tooth crumbles as she eats candy in a movie house; she is voraciously seeking spiritual satisfaction from a decadent White art form which offers little nourishment to women as Black or as poor as she. Pauline hardens herself until "[a]ll the meaningfulness of her life" is "in her work" (*SEE*, p. 110).

Ironically, this work involves not only tending a White family's home but pampering its children; the indulgence a Black "mammy" may show to White charges contrasts markedly with the firm authority she is expected to wield with her own children. And, as Morrison notes, it is easier for Pauline to savor such maternal chores as bathing a small child when there is "[n]o zinc tub, no buckets of stove heated water, no flaky, stiff, grayish towels washed in a kitchen sink, dried in a dusty backyard, no tangled black puffs of rough wool to comb" (*SEE*, p. 108). Because class and color separate Pauline's reality from the illusory one that the cinema projects and her employers seem to embody, her own destructive separation of maternal duty from affection is validated. Her emotional cruelty to her children is justified because "she is fulfilling a mother's role conscientiously" (*SEE*, p. 110); "SEEMOTHERMOTH-ERISVERYNICE" is the accolade that Pauline ironically earns from her society for her self-destructive and daughter-destructive behavior. She has conformed to an acceptable stereotype of motherhood.

Beyond conformity to sterotype, Pauline's transformation is a literary manifestation of Rich's observation that "power relations between mother and child are often simply a reflection of power relations in patriarchal society. . . . Powerless women have always used mothering as a channel . . . for their own human will to power" (Rich, p. 38). Thus, Pauline—unable to individually alter the norms that circumscribe and fragment her existence—*is* capable of molding her children to fit these norms, and she seizes this opportunity to affirm, through the exercise of such power, her own self-worth and identity. However, even mothers who transcend this temptation to exercise authority cannot escape the rigid social delimitations of their role. Motherhood and its attributes are precisely, narrowly, and unrealistically defined. According to patriarchal norms. "[M]other Love is supposed to be continuous, unconditional. Love and anger cannot coexist. Female anger threatens the institution of motherhood" (Rich, p. 46). Thus, in Morrison's novel, *Sula*,[7] Eva Peace's anger at her grown daughter Hannah's query, "Mamma, did you ever love us?" is by definition a nonmaternal reaction. Hannah's question arises because Eva has failed to exhibit "continual, unconditional" love in other socially acceptable ways, such as playing with her children. Eva's reply, that she "stayed alive" (*Sula*, p. 60) for her children, indicates the inapplicability of society's maternal stereotypes to women in general and minority women in particular. Overcoming racial and economic oppression to support her children, Eva has not had time to channel her energies into the genteel pastimes prescribed by mainstream culture. She later exhibits the intensity of her devotion by sacrificing her life in an effort to save Hannah's.

Because society's definition of motherhood is unrealistically limited, rigid, and unsuited to the social and economic demands actually made upon women, Hannah perceives her mother's unconventional strength as weakness or failure. As a result, the emotional support both women might have found in their relationship never materializes. The mothers in Toni Cade Bambara's "My Man Bovanne" and Alice Walker's "Everyday Use" are similarly condemned by their daughters. Ironically, in both these short stories the social norms which mothers fail to fulfill are the theoretically liberating ones of Black Nationalism.

Elo, in Bambara's story, ignores her mother's goodness and warmth because the older woman's appearance and behavior are unacceptably old-fashioned. Because events are narrated from Hazel's viewpoint, the extent of Elo's self-deception is apparent: we are privileged to know what she and her brothers fail or refuse to see—that their mother is not dancing licentiously with blind Bovanne but is rather "[t]ouch talkin like the heel of the hand on the tambourine or on a drum."[8] Hazel's direct warmth and compassion conflict with the social proprieties which now concern her politically active children in their efforts to gain community support. It is Elo, though, with whom Hazel has been closest, who speaks most sharply to the older woman and is most estranged from her. Hazel painfully notes the ambivalence with which her daughter touches her shoulder, "the hand landin light and not sure it supposed to be there" (*My Man*, p. 73). Bambara's narrative suggests that the mother-daughter bond, rather than mother-son ties, is most affected by socialization pressures. This effect corresponds with the proportionately greater pressure women individually experience to accede to social norms.

In Walker's short story, Dee speaks glowingly about her "heritage"[9] but can only see its artifacts and insults her mother, who embodies many of its best values. As the older woman realizes, Dee scorns her mother's unconventional strength, her "rough, man-working hands" and would prefer her to be "a hundred pounds lighter . . . " with a "quick and witty tongue" (*Use*, p. 79). The devastating effects of this scorn are implied in Walker's vivid imagery. Mrs. Johnson recalls that Dee's social ambition had "burned" her and her other daughter "with a lot of knowledge we didn't necessarily need to know . . . " (*Use*, p. 80), that her "scalding humor" had "erupted like bubbles in lye" (*Use*, p. 81). Although Mrs. Johnson, who narrates "Everyday Use," never consciously associates Dee's rage with the fire that had destroyed their embarassingly ramshackle house and scarred Maggie, her recollection of Dee's "look of concentration" as the house fell, her memory of almost asking the girl, "Why don't you do a dance around the ashes?" (*Use*, p. 80), combines tellingly with the language Walker provides her. The reader concludes that Dee was at least *capable* of such destruction; her emotional callousness, cloaked in fashionable Black Nationalism, is nearly as heartless. Ironically, as her mother observes, Dee—or Wangero, as she now terms herself—consistently includes the Johnson's newer, tin-roofed house in her purported family snapshots in order to document her now-fashionable rural heritage. This documentation is more significant to her than the actuality. Similarly, Dee wants her grandmother's quilts—part of Maggie's promised dowery—not because she feels a sense of identity with the Black woman who lovingly made them but because they are fashionable and valuable. Horrified at the prospect of her sister's putting the quilts to "everyday use" (*Use*, p. 87), Dee indicates how far removed her professed loyalties actually are from her everyday life. For this daughter, estranged from mother and sister by her internalization of shifting social norms, a sense of female community, of female self-worth and identity which transcends superimposed convention, is merely a ploy to acquire greater social prestige. Thus, sentimental Maggie, scarred in spirit as well as body, actually seems—to both Hazel Johnson and the reader—the more attractive of the two daughters.

Pat Parker, a Black, lesbian poet, recognizes the pitfall that Bambara's and Walker's protagonists have fallen into when she writes that she is "a product" of her parents' struggles and "not a political consciousness."[10] This line voices an awareness that it is as treacherously easy for daughters as it is for mothers to internalize misleading norms. Although, as a militant lesbian, she might denounce her mother's lifestyle and rejection of homosexuality, Parker instead chooses to detail the various forces that have shaped the older woman's life. The poet recognizes and separates the different kinds of oppression experienced by her parents because of their genders in the different images she uses to describe them. Permitted a modicum of self-actualization by society because he is male, her father speaks of "bellowing my needs" while her mother, who is doubly oppressed, is left passively "choking on my needs" (Parker, "My hands are big"). The helplessness that "choking" conveys suggests that Parker indeed believes that her mother is more society's victim than her father is. However, although Parker empathizes with her mother's predicament, she also realizes that the older woman would be dismayed by her daughter's unconventional life-style. The codification of the institution of motherhood, as opposed to the relative fluidity of fatherhood, leads Parker to have her mother voice the despairing refrain in her poem of lesbian identity, "Lord, what kind of child is this?" (Parker, "My lover is a woman"). Because it is Parker's mother who, in society's eyes, would be held culpable for the poet's "perversion," it is appropriate that the older woman guiltily experience the anguish this lament conveys.

In the literary works discussed so far, the strain placed upon mother-daughter relationships by social definitions of motherhood and "proper" female behavior is exacerbated by the women's being members of other oppressed groups. Social conventions appear to be more rigid, acceptable options more limited, for women who are poor, Black or Brown, lesbian, or from cultures which are explicitly as well as implicitly male-oriented. However, other works by minority group authors suggest that this double or triple oppression may ultimately provide its victims with enough insight into their shared burdens to successfully dislodge at least some of them. In Anzia Yezierska's *Bread Givers*, Agnes Smedley's *Daughter of Earth*, Natalie L. M. Petesch's *The Odyssey of Katinou Kalokovich*, and Rita Mae Brown's *Rubyfruit Jungle*, the central character is a minority group daughter who, in addition to her other problems, is alienated from a conventional mother. Maturing by suffering discrimination comparable to that experienced by her mother, each protagonist

Natalie M. Rosinsky

comes to recognize her mother as fellow victim rather than total villain. Once this awareness is reached, the heroines of these novels effect a reconciliation with their mothers which enables them to achieve some productive action. For Yezierska, Smedley, Petesch, and Brown, such a reconciliation appears not only possible but necessary. Ironically, it is the blatancy of double or triple oppression which enables each daughter to comprehend her mother's plight.

In *The Odyssey of Katinou Kalokovich* and *Rubyfruit Jungle*, the protagonists' reconciliations with their mothers involve a literal confrontation. Katinou flees her home because her father's selfishness and callousness, validated by misogynistic Jewish tradition, make life intolerable. However, she comes to recognize the fact that it is not her father she must escape but rather "the rules which guided and restricted the women in Channa's [her mother's] world."[11] Kate originally fears that Channa's miserable lot is the result "of some genetic fault against which she, Kate, must be eternally vigilant. . . . " (*Odyssey*, pp. 59–60). This mistaken belief that Channa alone is responsible for her predicament is eradicated by the women's meeting after Kate's youngest brother is born.

Witnessing the terrific struggle tubercular Channa engages in to care for the infant and her disproportionate feelings of total failure when she cannot nurse him, Kate comes to understand the internalization of values that her mother has undergone. Successful motherhood for Channa is fulfillment of her biological function: this success is the only means available to her to validate her existence. Until this time, Kate has wondered whether Channa's obvious lies about the benefits of married life are "[t]o convince herself, or to convince Kate" (*Odyssey*, p. 108). Now, her mother's struggle does convince Katinou of Channa's need for, and self-destructive belief in, the only ideals she has, those obvious lies. Recognizing and accepting her mother's self-deception for what it is, a socially induced malaise rather than a genetic flaw, Kate need no longer be estranged from her as Joseph K's, her father's, passive accomplice. As Rich writes, "Matrophobia . . . is the fear not of one's mother or of motherhood but of *becoming* one's mother" (Rich, p. 235). Petesch's protagonist has learned that this metamorphosis need not occur. With this knowledge, she can affirm her own identity, openly continuing to paint despite her father's opposition, while she fulfills her heartfelt obligation to Channa and the infant.

Molly, the lesbian heroine of *Rubyfruit Jungle*, is raised by a foster mother who, like Channa in Petesch's novel, believes the stereotype that true motherhood must involve bearing a child. Lamentingly, Carrie exclaims "I'll never know what it's like to be a real mother."[12] Although this belief saddens Carrie, it is also a convenient excuse for her failure to domesticate Molly. Not being bound to the unconventional girl by blood, she cannot be held accountable for her behavior; Molly's lesbianism, like Parker's, might be construed as the result of maternal failure. Still, Molly's sexual preferences seem so tainted to Carrie, whose self-identity rests exclusively on her socially defined roles as wife and mother, that the older woman rejects her when these become known.

It is not until Molly has experienced further social discrimination as a lesbian and time has reminded Carrie of her loneliness and mortality that the two women meet again. There is genuine feeling in Carrie's final declaration, "I love you. You're the only thing I keep living for" (*RJ*, p. 212); however, as Molly undoubtedly realizes at this point, the scantiness of her foster mother's emotional sustenance results from her internalization of social norms. According to patriarchal definitions of motherhood, a woman should not have anything to live for beyond her children. Carrie's plight in old age is a direct result of her adherance to convention. Rather than seek companionship outside her family sphere, she turns to the once-rejected Molly because this reunion is sanctioned by social norms in a way that nonfamily attachments—for women—are not. Molly accepts and returns Carrie's affection, validates her denial of ever having disowned her, and commemorates Carrie's genuine strength in the face of economic oppression by making her the subject of a film documentary. This film is the senior project which enables Molly to earn her college degree. Thus, the women's reconciliation is not only emotionally rewarding for them but—in a parallel to Katinou Kalokov-ich's experience—is also vital to the daughter's individual development.

In *Bread Givers* and *Daughter of Earth*, the protagonists' productive reconciliations with their mothers involve a psychic, rather than a physical reunion. Sara, Yezierska's heroine, has witnessed and suffered her mother's acquiescence to Reb Smolinsky's belief in man's God-given superiority. Although Shenah manifests her love by carrying a feather bed to Sara one bitter winter night, this maternal affection is secondary to her internalized belief that men, and women's relationships with them, are of more importance than female bonds. Shenah gives her husband the choicest bits of food, tolerates his foolish mismanagement of their money, and permits him to arrange disastrous marriages for her three oldest daughters. This passivity, accompanied by only the subtlest verbalizations of her dismay in mutterings about her "bitter heart,"[13] ultimately affects her relationship with Sara. When the emancipated girl regretfully concludes that she hasn't the "time to go to see her" mother (*BG*, p. 172), she literally refers to the travelling time, needed study periods, and long work hours which separate the two women. However, on the metaphorical level, her decision indicates an awareness of the lack of emotional support her mother has—or can—give her: the metaphorical "time" which separates them is rooted in the thousands of years and generations of Jewish women who have accepted a subservient role in their culture.

After achieving her goal of a college degree, Sara returns home to find Shenah dying. The emotional intensity of this situation, combined with the fact that Shenah's passivity can no longer hinder her daughter's quest for self-identity, enables Sara to accept the female pain which is inescapably part of her heritage. She sees "worlds of pain . . . dumb in that helpless gaze" (*BG*, p. 251) and can accept without bitterness her mother's failure to help her daughters. As she narrates, "the love light of Mother's eyes flowed into mine. I felt literally Mother's soul enter my soul like a miracle" (*BG*, p. 252). This reconciliation precedes and makes possible Sara's subsequent reconciliation with her father. It is also, despite Sara's apparent male-orientation, a more significant phase of her emotional development; all Sara and her father can ultimately share is a home and a one-sided understanding, but Sara and her mother have experienced a common pain and love which transcend temporal situations. For one, tragically brief moment, they have recognized the bonds of experience and nature that unite them.

Commenting on the destructive institution of motherhood in patriarchal, oppressive societies, Rich notes that "It is not simply that such mothers feel both responsible and powerless. It is that they carry their own guilt and self-hatred over into their daughters' experiences" (Rich, p. 244). This remark is applicable to the experiences of Marie Rogers, Agnes Smedley's protagonist in *Daughter of Earth*. In her unhappiness, Marie's mother, who is oppressed by great poverty as well as by her gender, beats her daughter until Marie's "need of her love"[14] is destroyed. Mrs. Rogers is male-oriented because she needs her husband's income to survive and maintain her family; she talks to Marie "as if we were friends" only when Mr. Rogers is "not there" (*DoE*, p. 41). However, Mrs. Rogers' abused condition is so obvious that Marie finds that "a bond of misery" (*DoE*, p. 114) unites the two women even when affection does not. Marie stands up to her father when, maddened by the frustrations of his economic situation, he attempts to beat his wife.

Mrs. Rogers, on the other hand, has internalized her lack of self-worth to such an extent that she cannot voice an affinity with the plucky Marie until, dying, she calls Marie "daughter" for the first time (*DoE*, p. 135). Marie embraces her mother for the first time in death.

It takes time for Marie's deathbed reconciliation with her mother, so similar to Sara Smolinsky's reunion in *Bread Givers*, to penetrate her psyche. The bitterness between the two women has been too great, the struggle to make her way in the world too energy-consuming to permit Marie to reflect on this meeting's significance. However, in her moments of deepest pain—during the dissolution of her marriage to Anand be- cause of his internalized bias against her past sexual activities—Smed- ley's protagonist seems to apprehend the importance of this relationship and final meeting. She dreams of confronting death, which appears as a woman with her mother's face (*DoE*, pp. 399–400). It is after she has the courage to approach and kiss this terrifying dream-image that she is able to acknowledge her marriage's failure. This acceptance of pain and loss, both in her past maternal relationship and with Anand, enables Marie to act productively: to leave Anand before his jealousy destroys her. Smedley's organization of dream sequences—several nightmares occur before this final apocalyptic image—suggests that Marie's re- membrance of the horror of her mother's life and of their painful interaction is a necessary prelude to this final, defensive assertion of female independence. She will not permit herself to be psychologically abused as Mrs. Rogers was. Thus, Marie's reconciliation with her mother, her acceptance of their painful relationship and recognition of the social pressures which had caused Mrs. Rogers' apparent cruelty and indifference, enables her to perceive the comparable forces affecting her own life; as a result, Marie can combat male prejudice and female passivity before they irrevocably damage her.

The theme of mother-daughter relationships distorted by such ex- ternal and internal biases cuts across time, place, and genre within minority women's writing. Their fiction indicates that this distortion is intensified by the further constraints our society imposes upon people who are poor, Black, lesbian, or members of explicitly patriarchal reli- gions or cultures. However, the very intensity of his doubled oppression may provide a means to deflect it. In four of these novels, daughter and mother come to some kind of reconciliation, a recognition of the fact that they are not natural enemies but rather fellow victims. With such knowledge, the potential for change, for fostering positive female rela- tionships, grows.

An analysis of mother-daughter relationships in woman's minority group literature is thus both disheartening and encouraging. It is disheartening to see the pain inflicted upon so many women; it is encouraging to realize that individual women can transcend this mutilation to discover the deeper rapport that—along with suffering—unites them to their mothers. Dramatizing the shock of self-recognition, these works are political as well as aesthetic statements.

Notes

[1] Adrienne Rich, *Of Woman Born: Motherhood as Experience and Institution* (New York: Norton, 1976), p. 237. Sources of subsequent quotations are included parenthetically in the body of the paper.

[2] See Mary Ellmann, *Thinking About Women* (New York: Harcourt, Brace, Jovanovich, 1968), pp. 55–145, for a detailed discussion of these and similarly misconceived stereotypes.

[3] Mary Daly, *Beyond God the Father: Toward a Philosophy of Women's Liberation* (Boston: Beacon Press, 1973), p. 149.

[4] Guadalupe Valdés-Fallis, "Recuerdo," unpublished ditto, p. 2. Sources of subsequent quotations are included parenthetically in the body of the paper.

[5] Phyllis Chesler, *Women and Madness* (New York: Avon Books, 1972), p. 18.

[6] Toni Morrison, "SEEMOTHERMOTHERISVERYNICE," in *Black-Eyed Susans*, ed. Mary Helen Washington (New York: Anchor Press, 1975), p. 99. Sources of subsequent quotations are included parenthetically in the body of the paper.

[7] Toni Morrison, *Sula* (New York: Alfred A. Knopf, 1973), p. 58. Sources of all subsequent quotations are included parenthetically in the body of the paper.

[8] Toni Cade Bambara, "My Man Bovanne," in *Black-Eyed Susans*. p. 70. Sources of subsequent quotations are included parenthetically in the body of the paper.

[9] Alice Walker, "Everyday Use," in *Black-Eyed Susans*, p. 88. Sources of subsequent quotations are included parenthetically in the body of the paper.

[10] Pat Parker, "My hands are big" and "My lover is a woman," in *Pit Stop* (Oakland, Cal.: The Women's Press Collective, 1973), unpaginated. Sources of subsequent quotations from this volume of poetry are included parenthetically in the body of the paper.

[11] Natalie L. M. Petesch, *The Odyssey of Katinou Kalokovich*, (Tampa, Fla.: United Sisters, 1974), p. 110. Sources of subsequent quotations are included parenthetically in the body of the paper.

[12] Rita Mae Brown, *Rubyfruit Jungle* (Plainfield, Vt.: Daughters, Inc., 1973), p. 36. Sources of subsequent quotations are included parenthetically in the body of the paper.

[13] Anzia Yezierska, *Bread Givers* (New York: George Braziller, 1925), p. 55. Sources of subsequent quotations are included parenthetically in the body of the paper.

[14] Agnes Smedley, *Daughter of Earth* (New York: The Feminist Press, 1973), p. 12. Sources of subsequent quotations are included parenthetically in the body of the paper.

24

Heritages: Dimensions of Mother-Daughter Relationships in Women's Autobiographies

A heritage is a gift from the past and a hope for the continuity of the future; as such, mother-daughter relationships are vital, important linkings of the generations, as varied as the women who comprise them. In women's autobiography, the attempt to cope with one's maternal heritage is both challenging and problematic as the daughters, the autobiographers studied here, try to present and interpret the relationships with their mothers or mother-surrogates.

Two fundamental issues of this topic, which this essay will explore, are: What have the mothers in women's autobiographies provided as heritages? And how have the daughters responded to their legacies? The most significant dimensions of maternal heritages that offer some answers to these questions are: the nurturing and conveyance of a sense of self; the transmission of human values through mothers who serve, directly or indirectly, as positive or negative role models; and the fostering of a group identity—national, racial, or cultural. Evidence for the ensuing discussion will be obtained from characteristic autobiographies of literary quality by twentieth century women: Maya Angelou, Simone de Beauvoir, Sally Carrighar, Nikki Giovanni, Jane Howard, Maxine Hong Kingston, and Margaret Mead.[1]

It is useful to interpret this evidence with an awareness of the dynamics of the autobiographical process of writing about one's mother. Autobiography may be defined as a drama in which the autobiographer functions as both the playwright and the principal character. This definition has several significant implications. Playwright and heroine are distinctly different roles, despite the fact that one person (whose continuity and integrity of personality are assumed—by the audience, at least) performs both—and controls both. Thus in women's autobiog raphies the author, in recreating and interpreting her childhood and maturing self, assumes a number of the functions that her own mother fulfilled in the actual family history.

So not only, in this sense, does the daughter-as-autobiographer become her own mother, she also becomes the recreator of her maternal parent and the controlling adult in their literary relationship. Thus the autobiographical act has added another major dimension to the ways in which mothers and their daughters get along, in addition to those that constituted their actual lives together. This may be an unfamiliar po sition for the daughter; it is certainly a reversal of the power and dominance that prevailed during the first twenty years of her life, a span of time that receives considerable attention in these autobiogra phies.

In the autobiographies studied here lies the locus of belief; the readers accept the daughters' interpretive power and authority without question. As credible autobiographers, these daughters encourage the readers' primary allegiance to themselves, rather than to any other characters in the autobiography, however sympathetic they may be. As a consequence, the answers to the fundamental questions of this essay are essentially the psychological truth, an exploration of their meaning to the daughters who are presenting the mother-daughter relationships to their readers. Whether the mothers, other family members, or even documentary evidence would support these interpretations is immaterial. The interpretation is the reality of concern to readers and critics alike.

The sense of self that each of these women autobiographers dem onstrates both verifies this theory of autobiography and illustrates its practice. Each has exhibited extraordinary accomplishment through her excellence in her chosen profession, whether as an anthropologist (Mead), dancer (Angelou), naturalist (Carrighar), journalist (Howard), philosopher (de Beauvoir), or writer (everyone). Each has excelled in highly competitive professions and activities requiring individual talent, creativity, self-discipline, and hard work. Each has succeeded on her own terms and in her own independent way. These successes could furnish considerable grounds for a realistic sense of pride, yet these women do not appear to be writing their autobiographies to tout their professional achievements but rather to identify the human dimensions of who they are and how they got that way.

Likewise, each of these autobiographers has succeeded in recreating her life story on her own terms, according to the dimensions she wishes to impose on it. Only rarely does she seek information from others about her past, consult documents, or return to familiar places. Her sources are largely her memory, psyche, and imagination, sometimes supplemented by her diaries and correspondence. The autobiography thus becomes its author's synthesis of existence and essence.[2]

What egotism to rely on memory, frail and fallible at best, for an understanding of events and relationships that occurred two to seven decades earlier. What egotism, at a much later date, to impose significance on people and phenomena that may have been but dimly (if at all) understood at the time they occurred. What egotism, what a strong sense of self, to believe in the truth of these mental constructs, in the validity of one's selection process, so necessary to autobiography. In these respects each of the autobiographers studied here is appropriately egotistical, assertive of her selfhood.

This sense of self, of self-worth and self-confidence as an adult, has been derived partly from a heritage of love and admiration from others. From all these autobiographers but Carrighar this heritage of love came from a mother or mother surrogate. Each of these autobiographers (including Carrighar) was as a child and/or adult a cherished person in someone else's imagination. As Mead acknowledges: "I was first child, wanted and loved" (p. 45); and was always told by parents or grand-mother, " 'There's no one like Margaret' " (p. 29). Jane Howard grew up to the litany of her mother's unwavering love, expressed in the bedtime goodnight ritual, "I love you up to the sky and down again . . . " (p. 14) and in the crayoned posters, "WELCOME HOME! YEA, JANIE!" (p. 14). After being silenced out of childhood at eight when she was raped by her mother's lover, Maya Angelou was restored to human communication by Mrs. Flowers, a perceptive mother-sub-stitute who singled her out for attention: "She had made tea cookies for *me* and read to *me* from her favorite book. It was enough to prove that she liked me for just being myself" (p. 85).

There is no calculus of love. Except for Mrs. Carrighar, the auto-biographers' mothers or their equivalents loved their daughters freely, naturally, abundantly, without conscious discussion or analysis. As children and adolescents the daughters flourished under this nurturing, and reciprocated the love. Yet they, like their mothers, took it for granted—a solid, inviolable buttress against the less caring outer world. As the daughters became teenagers some (Kingston and de Beauvoir) rebelled against what they saw as the excess of maternal control that sometimes accompanies motherly devotion. The self-confidence that this love gave them also provided the strength to distance themselves from its smothering effects. Having grown secure with maturity and the passage of time, the daughters then write their autobiographies which include public acknowledgement of their appreciation of this maternal love, as well as an anatomization of their rebellion against it.

In some cases the mother's or grandmother's positive sense of her own significance and abilities, and her expectation of making some impact on the world, are conveyed intact to the daughter or grand-daughter, who adopts them for herself. These values are communicated more by living example than by preaching; these role models did not consciously think of themselves as such. For instance, Mead's paternal grandmother, "the most decisive influence in my life" (p. 45), "simply commanded respect and obedience by her complete expectation that she would be obeyed [and later] . . . became my model . . . for the modern parent" (p. 45). Angelou, too, gained enormous strength from her Grandmomma Henderson's strength, integrity, and business acumen: "I saw only her power and strength. She was taller than any woman in my personal world" (p. 38)—literally and symbolically.

These powerful women, and Kingston's and Mead's mothers as well, had lives of their own to lead. Mrs. Hong and Momma Henderson ran a laundry and a general store, respectively, to help support their families. Grandmother Mead and her daughter-in-law combined domestic duties with intellectual and community pursuits. Their endeavors, which gave these women self-esteem and widespread community respect, required considerable thought and effort. These women were active in responding to external circumstances, and not reactive as the homebound mothers (Mme. de Beauvoir and Mrs. Howard) tended to be. So it is not surprising that their daughters, too, adopted an active, assertive approach to their world and their expectations of it.

Another significant aspect of the heritage from mothers to daughters is the direct or indirect transmission of human values through mothers who serve as positive or negative role models. The mother-daughter relationships of Howard and Mead illustrate the inculcation of positive values by positive example. These mothers and daughters are integral in each others' lives; they communicate continually and intimately, even when they disagree. They respect and love one another. Though Howard laments that she and her mother "never developed enough rapport" (p. 15), her autobiography is in part a tribute to the significance of their relationship, and is a loving endeavor to analyze its implications.

Howard's mother approached her family, friends, and activities with unwavering optimism and good will: "Friendship was her vocation," explains her daughter (p. 16). "She felt most herself . . . in a roomful of approving others" (p. 14). Howard's own values reflect her mother's: "We who are unmarried . . . must deepen and cultivate our friendships until water acquires the consistency of blood, until we develop new networks as sustaining as orthodox families" (p. 17). Thus Howard's numerous vignettes of representative American women explore the patterns, dimensions, and significance of friendships and family relationships in contemporary society. And she continually measures her own life, as an independent, ambivalently single career woman of forty, against the comfortable marriages of her mother and sister, and the comforting presence of their children, automatic friends-in-residence.

Throughout *Blackberry Winter* Mead regards her family fondly, but with an anthropologist's analytical eye. She emphasizes that her mother, even with four young children to care for, maintained an independent and active intellectual life and tried, through constant activity, to right the world's "wrongs to the poor and the downtrodden, to foreigners, to Negroes, to women" (p. 22). Mead's life and writings illustrate her adoption of her mother's values, and her personal modification of her mother's roles as scholar, household manager, and loving parent. Mead acknowledges that "In my life I realized every one of her unrealized ambitions" (p. 29)—and duplicated those that her mother accomplished, as well. Mead, like her mother, earned a doctorate; became a crusader and spokeswoman for the rights of women, minorities, immigrants; managed (but did not often tend) her household, which, like her mother's, was a gathering place for personal and professional meetings with innumerable peoples of the world.[3]

Mead's and Howard's mothers are in the estimation of themselves, their daughters, and society, good mothers. They are continually present in the home (despite extensive community involvements), and are the stabilizing influence in households from which the fathers are often absent, physically or psychologically. They provide their daughters with a morally wholesome environment, ample opportunities for cultural stimulation, and the best education they can afford. Mrs. Mead and Mrs. Howard are neither dogmatic nor intolerant on most issues; they do not try to force their daughters to accept uncongenial beliefs or attitudes, no matter now divergent their respective views may be. (Thus Howard could grow up to be an active Democrat, despite her mother's complacent Republicanism that led her to refer to "that *darling* Nixon" [p. 39].) As a consequence, these mothers have maintained rapport, continual communication; they have imparted to their daughters much that they value, in part because they have been flexible enough to accommodate differences without causing rupture.

The Meads and the Howards represent, in many ways, the American cultural ideal of mother-daughter relationships, from the daughter's infancy through creative, productive, self-assertive adulthood. These daughters as independent adults freely choose life work, life-styles, and values compatible—though not identical—with those of their mothers. They remain on good terms with their mothers in adulthood, as they did throughout childhood; both mothers and daughters value their intimate association enormously. The attainment of a flexible balance between control and casualness, self-interest and solicitude, on the parts of both mothers and daughters fulfills the ideals of these women and their society.

However, even among the autobiographies of outstanding, strong women studied here, this relationship is not the norm. Nor do all the autobiographers judge their mothers by these normative criteria. Some of the other mothers are much more remote from their daughters, physically and psychologically. Yet these mothers, or their idealized essences, have nevertheless been profoundly influential as positive role models and possessors of characteristics or values their daughters wished to acquire. The impact of these more distant mothers has not been intentional, nor has it emanated from them; rather, it has been willed into existence by the daughters at an early age.

In this fashion, Maya Angelou's intermittently absent mother exercised an enormous influence over her daughter. In early childhood Maya learned from the example of her stern, devotedly nurturing Grandmomma what a loving mother should be like, and transposed this ideal to the vague image of her absent biological mother. Because Maya "couldn't believe that our mother would laugh and eat oranges in the sunshine without her children" (p. 42), she imagined her mother safely dead, and "could cry anytime I wanted by picturing my mother (I didn't quite know what she looked like) lying in her coffin" (p. 43).

Later Maya met her mother. Maya "had never seen a woman as pretty as she who was called 'Mother'" (p. 50). Consequently, she was "too beautiful to have children" (p. 50)—especially, thought Maya, a daughter as unattractive as herself, so different from the ideal of feminine beauty which both mother and daughter shared. Her acceptance of this value helped to alienate her from the mother with whom she had longed to be so close (see p. 56). The estrangement from her now-real mother was as painful as was her physical separation from her imagined and unreal parent. So Maya felt that she had to earn her mother's love, by making accommodations to her mother's big city pastimes, lovers, and carefree manner of living. When her mother repaid Maya's intense longing with casual carelessness, Maya attributed this detachment to her own imagined deficiencies, rather than to her mother's departure from the ideal.

Even though Maya remains the heroine of her own autobiography and the readers ally with her, they are not likely to share the attitudes toward careless motherhood and accepting daughterhood that she so uncritically presents. Indeed, the readers' independent judgment may consider as negative some of the values that the autobiographer and her mother accept as positive.

In other instances, however, the readers clearly ally with the auto-biographers against mothers who transmit values which their daughters reject. These women may be interpreted as negative role models, even in the instances in which conventional society would consider them "good" mothers. Their negative influence can be either constructive or destructive, as the extremes of de Beauvoir's and Carrighar's mothers indicate.

De Beauvoir's mother was the very model of a proper petit bourgeois turn-of-the-century housewife, duty-bound to the cultural norms of subservient wifehood, vigilant motherhood, and fervent piety (p. 38). As a young child Simone regards her mother's example as "unassailable" (p. 38), and recognizes that her "mother's whole education and upbring-ing had convinced her that for a woman the greatest thing was to become the mother of a family" (p. 104). Her mother's fulfillment of this role requires that Simone play "the dutiful daughter" (p. 104), which she does until she is eight (see p. 40). But as Simone gets older she resents this imposed dependency (p. 104) and gradually comes to regard motherhood not with the joy and obligation of her mother's perspective, but as burdensome and boring. To escape this "servitude," she determines not to have any children (p. 56).

So she begins to distance herself, a form of rebellion so subtle that for a while she is scarcely cognizant of her implicit deviation from her mother's rigid, pious standards. Her behavior and speech becomes guarded (p. 40). In her increasing sophistication she realizes that adults "had no access to secret worlds" more splendid than the mundane existence of children (p. 87).

With this disillusionment comes de Beauvoir's recognition of herself "as the basis of my own apotheosis" (p. 57). By the time she has reached secondary school, "My education, my culture, and the present state of society all conspired to convince me that women belong to an inferior caste" (p. 143). In rejecting her mother's values and behavior as a role model, she is rejecting her sex as well; she accepts with pride her father's accolade: "Simone has a man's brain; she thinks like a man; she *is* a man" (p. 119). "I valued my independence," she declares. "I would write and have a life of my own; I never thought of myself as a man's female companion: we would be two comrades" (p. 142).

To a large extent, as de Beauvoir's life-style and philosophical, fictional, and autobiographical works show, she has consistently fulfilled her adolescent ideal. Thereby she has rejected the roles and values which Mme. de Beauvoir represented and held sacred. De Beauvoir substituted her own philosophical values for the traditional, pragmatic, emotion-laden values of her time and her culture. Consequently, even those readers whose own lives are unashamedly bourgeois can understand and accept her rationale, and ally with the autobiographer against her mother as they read.

In contrast to Mme. de Beauvoir, whose culture upheld her as a role model even if her daughter didn't, Sally Carrighar's mother would have been considered a devastatingly negative role model by any standard. She was a paranoid psychotic (p. 12). She regarded her daughter as a threat and rival from the moment of Sally's birth (p. 15), and continually tried to psychologically devastate and physically destroy her firstborn. This mother completely rejected her daughter. Throughout Mrs. Carrighar's long life (until over 90), she avoided any form of closeness with Sally, whether intimate or superficial (p. 5)—even conversation. At Sally's approach, "with a shudder, as if she had been touched by a snake or a lizard, she would start up from her chair" (p. 8). Once, for a trivial offense, this mother strangled her six-year-old daughter almost to unconsciousness and beat her so severely that she was ill for several months (p. 33).

But it was not until Sally went to school and realized how other mothers loved and nurtured their children that she recognized her own mother's true hatred. A cyclone struck without warning while most of the schoolchildren were outdoors; they were battered by wind, rain, and falling limbs. Soon their mothers came, bringing dry clothes and loving solace (p. 44). Mrs. Carrighar's conspicuous absence caused Sally to recognize that her mother "wished I was dead" (p. 44), a conclusion confirmed throughout her childhood by repeated incidents of deliberate cruelty (p. 84), starvation,[4] and her mother's sinister refrain that became thematic of their relationship: "It is likely that many people who seem to die natural deaths have in fact been poisoned by their families" (p. 88).

Reacting to her mother's behavior, Sally withdrew in self-defense. This led, at seven, to learning "to fix my own hair so I would not have to be touched" (p. 45) and to doing her homework in independent isolation (p. 45). At twelve Sally rebelled covertly, resisting her mother's "every wish and suggestion" (p. 88). Her insecurity, however, stimulated a desire to earn perfect grades and concomitant parental approval, and to "avoid even the smallest offense because that could mean [my death]" (p. 45).

Both behaviors persisted throughout adulthood, even though after Sally fled to college she never psychologically came back to "that family where . . . in my own eyes I was a kind of non-person" (p. 132). She resolved never to "risk being trapped in a family again" (p. 79) and so never to marry. But it was only with the aid of intensive psychotherapy as an adult that Carrighar was able to break free of her mother's malevolent influence and become an adult fully functioning on her own terms. After considerable struggle, she became a nature writer psychologically secure in her physical isolation and economically independent through her writings. Nevertheless, her autobiography reveals an intermittent emotional yearning for a closeness with her mother that she intellectually recognizes will never come.

As these autobiographies show, a daughter's rebellion against the values of a thoroughly conventional, well-meaning mother such as Mme. de Beauvoir is a common adjunct to the process of adolescent maturity. Although the daughter may eventually adopt different values, inspired by other role models or her own independent thinking as de Beauvoir did, in many instances the tension accompanying the process of change is reduced, if not resolved, upon the daughter's maturity. Either the mother becomes resigned to the daughter's new values, or both sides modify somewhat and accommodate each other in an essentially constructive relationship. However, with a destructively negative role model such as Carrighar's mother there can be no healthy compromise. Unless the sick mother can be cured, the daughter has to leave in order to survive. To sustain her mother's image of her as horrible and worthless is to die spiritually and creatively, if not physically; a healthy daughter, in self-defense, must not play out a sick role.

Mothers also transmit to their daughters a sense of identification with a particular national, racial, or culture group. Whether minority or majority, native-born or immigrant, poor or middle income, unschooled or highly educated, all the mothers in these autobiographies do this deliberately, even Carrighar's. They regard this contribution to their daughter's heritage, this extension of themselves, as highly significant—though the daughters' reactions vary.

At the one extreme is Nikki Giovanni's affirmation of the strong positive Black identity bequeathed by her family—particularly by her grandmother, mother, and older sister. For both personal and political reasons she exults: "I've always known I was colored. When I was a Negro I knew I was colored; now that I'm Black I know which color it is. Any identity crisis I may have had never centered on race. . . . I came to grips with Blackdom when I [first] grabbed my mamma" (p. 24).

Underlying the ambiguous humor here and throughout the book is Giovanni's intense pride in her immediate family: in her grandmother, "the height of 'We ain't taking no shit, John Brown, off nobody ' " (p. 26); her father, "a real hip down-home big-time dude" (p. 25); her mother, "the woman of the world, the prize of all times" (p. 27); and her older sister, "a smart Nigger" (p. 29). Giovanni summarizes, "My family on my grandmother's side are fighters. My family on my father's side are survivors. I'm a revolutionist" (p. 33). Throughout her childhood, adolescence, and adulthood, Giovanni's family has conspired by means of personal examples as well as exhortation to make her proud of her heritage and of herself. Much of her strength derives from the power that such pride makes possible.

A more ambivalent but ultimately positive reaction to her Chinese heritage is Maxine Hong Kingston's *Woman Warrior*. From early childhood on, Kingston has always had to deal with a duality of viewpoints—her own, as a first generation American, and her mother's. Brave Orchid looks forever back to China. For thirty-six years, ever since immigrating to San Francisco, Brave Orchid has saved money for the family's eventual return to China (p. 115). Although she herself was an independent, respected doctor in China, in America she maintains the traditional Chinese sexism, favoring her sons and quoting such adages as "When fishing for treasures in the flood, be careful not to pull in girls" (p. 62)—who have been drowned by their parents. She sends her six children to Chinese school (after American school) (p. 194), celebrates a myriad of mysteriously undefined Chinese holidays (p. 215), cooks Chinese food, including skunks, hawks, snakes, and squid eyes (pp. 106, 108). She distances the Americans whose roles she can't cope with by regarding them as ghosts: "Bus Ghosts, Police Ghosts, Fire Ghosts, Meter Reader Ghosts" (p. 113).

As a child and adolescent, Kingston embraces American culture and looks forward to an American future. She vehemently rejects both a return to China and the Chinese stereotype which her mother embodies on American soil. She loathes the Chinese "word for the female *I*—which is 'slave' " (p. 56). She refuses to cook, and cracks dishes when she has to wash them: " 'Bad girl,' my mother yelled, and sometimes that made me gloat rather than cry. Isn't a bad girl almost a boy?" (p. 56). In rejecting the conventional Chinese view of girls as worthless and inept, Kingston has implicitly accepted the Chinese concept of boys as rebellious and valuable. So she resolves, through rebelling against her mother, to reject the Chinese stereotype of girls and to be instead like a Chinese boy. In the process she makes herself unfeminine—silent, surly, clumsy, and ugly. Thereby she refuses to accomodate the American ideal of girlish beauty and demeanor—as well as the Chinese, with which it is congruent. She spurns the prospect of a Chinese immigrant husband: "I put on my shoes with open flaps and flapped about like a Wino Ghost. From then on, I wore those shoes to parties, whenever the mothers gathered to talk about marriages" (p. 226).

As an adult, Kingston writes *Woman Warrior*, partly to exorcise the hordes of ghosts, partly to come to terms with both her mother and her Chinese-American heritage. In the process she realizes that she and her mother are much alike as mature women—intelligent, energetic, determined, courageous, analysts and conveyers of a complex culture in an alien land. Brave Orchid has been a powerful role model all along, though Kingston herself has had to mature in order to acknowledge and accept the influence: "I am practically the first daughter of a first daughter" (p. 127).

The act of exorcism has also become an act of acknowledgement: "Even now China wraps double binds around my feet" (p. 57). But the ghosts are gone: "I've found some places in this country that are ghost-free. And I think I belong there . . . " (p. 127). But the dual culture remains in a way that Kingston, now an adult American woman but still and always a Chinese daughter, can understand and love—on her own terms. As an adult, Kingston transposes the independence of her adolescent rebellion into a life in Hawaii, remote from San Francisco's Chinese ghetto and free of her mother's domination. Through her profession as a writer, Kingston interprets and thus controls the influence of both her mother and her Chinese culture. She accepts her daughterhood, her womanhood, and her Chinese background in ways that do not compromise this independence. She becomes attractive and marries—an American—without the sevility that one aspect of the Chinese culture would encourage. Instead, she selects for her Chinese image that of the Woman Warrior, a strong, independent, female defender of Chinese people and their territory—a role, in fact, taught her by her Chinese mother (p. 127). Thus Kingston's autobiography becomes a meaningful tribute to her cultural duality.

As the example of Giovanni's autobiography shows, a group identity is sometimes imbibed in the cradle and reinforced without apparent stress as the daughter matures. Or, as Kingston demonstrates, the group identity can be imposed, resisted, debated—but not wholly rejected. Its racial aspects are permanent. Its cultural aspects may be modified, but they do not disappear if the daughter values them and can control and integrate them into her bi-cultural adult life.

The autobiographies studied here provide ample substance for discussing significant dimensions of the legacies of mothers, and their daughters' responses to their heritages. Many of these autobiographers candidly and copiously illustrate, as well, the truth of Mead's dictum, "Watching a parent grow is one of the most reassuring experiences anyone can have, a privilege that comes only to those whose parents live beyond their children's early adulthood" (p. 44). As daughters grow, so do their mothers. Perhaps through the examples of these daughter autobiographers, we, too, can come to terms with our own inheritance, and even translate it into autobiography, pride of generation.

Notes

[1] Maya Angelou, *I Know Why the Caged Bird Sings* (1970; rpt. New York: Bantam, 1971); Simone de Beauvoir, *Memoirs of a Dutiful Daughter*, tr. James Kirup (1959; rpt. New York: Popular Library, 1963); Sally Carrighar, *Home to the Wilderness* (1973; rpt. Baltimore: Penguin, 1974); Nikki Giovanni, *Gemini: An Extended Autobiographical Statement on My First Twenty-Five Years of Being a Black Poet* (1971; rpt. New York: Viking, 1973); Jane Howard, *A Different Woman* (1973; rpt. New York: Avon, 1974); Maxine Hong Kingston, *The Woman Warrior: Memoirs of a Girlhood Among Ghosts* (1976; rpt. New York: Vintage, 1977); Margaret Mead, *Blackberry Winter: My Earlier Years* (New York: Simon and Schuster, 1972). All page references cited throughout this essay are to these editions.

[2] In *Memories of a Catholic Girlhood* (New York: Harcourt Brace, 1957), Mary McCarthy's introduction and authorial commentary on each chapter offer a much more explicit account of the autobiographical process than do any of the volumes examined here.

As a writer, she tried hard to compensate for the absence of family information that her orphanhood was a consequence of, yet throughout the volume her emphasis is on the "memories" of the title, and she acknowledges that "I have wished that I were writing fiction. The temptation to invent has been very strong, particularly where recollection is hazy and I remember the substance of an event but not the details . . . " (p. 4).

[3] See Mead's *Letters from the Field*, 1925–1975, World Perspectives Series, ed. Ruth N. Anshen (New York: Harper & Row, 1978), passim.

[4] Sally's loving and protective father was out of town on extended business trips and often unaware of these cruelties and unable to intervene.

Part Seven
BIBLIOGRAPHY

GAIL M. RUDENSTEIN
CAROL FARLEY KESSLER
ANN M. MOORE

Introduction

In this preliminary bibliography, we have begun the task of cataloguing literature about mothers and daughters. Although this is not an exhaustive or comprehensive survey, we hope it will provide a starting place for those interested in reading or teaching literary mothers and daughters. We present a number of works of literature by women writers, mainly of the nineteenth and twentieth centuries, that treat the mother-daughter relationship (and, in a few cases, the grandmother-granddaughter relationship) at least more than tangentially. The works are listed generically—as autobiography, drama, fiction, and poetry. The autobiography section includes daughters' biographies of their mothers.

Our criterion for selecting primary works was quite simple. We asked ourselves whether a scholar would find a given work useful for studying the mother-daughter relationship. If this relationship is a major part of a given work, the title is asterisked. If the relationship is present but not central, the title is not asterisked. In order to free space to permit the largest possible sampling of mother-daughter works, we provide only minimal bibliographical citations for primary materials. Wherever possible, we give dates of birth and death for the authors of the primary sources, as well as the publication dates of their writings. Occasional juvenile works appear with a J following the publication date. In the case of anthologies, we place the title first, followed as needed by the pertinent selections.

To aid readers in identifying the national origin of authors not writing in English, we use the following symbol system:

F	- French	It	- Italian
FA	- French Algerian	Ne	- Netherlands
FB	- Belgian	No	- Norway
FC	- French Canadian	PA	- Portuguese American
Ge	- German	Sp	- Spanish
Gr	- Greek	SpA	- Spanish American
In	- Indian	Sw	- Swedish

When possible, we provide the original language title for translated works.

In addition, we provide a section entitled "Interdisciplinary Background," in which we list works primarily by anthropologists, historians, psychologists, and sociologists. A few biographies having particular emphasis upon a mother-daughter relationship appear here, too. We have deliberately limited our coverage of literary criticism in this section to those articles which *specifically* analyze the mother-daughter relationship or contain a minimum of 25 pages devoted to the relationship. We use the MLA format for citations of "Interdisciplinary Background."

In compiling this bibliography, we have become aware that certain writers, genres, and ethnic/national groups require further investigation. The interpretation of mother-daughter relationships in non-American major writers still needs attention. In addition, our consideration of drama and poetry emphasizes twentieth-century American women; literature of Continental Europe and the Third World should be more extensively examined as well. And we have not covered myths, folklore, or fairytales. Our listings of works should be considered an introduction to a given author's treatment of the mother-daughter relationship. It is our hope that we can continue to expand and revise this bibliography to reflect the outpouring of literature and scholarship concerning the mother-daughter relationship.

So broadly based an undertaking as this bibliography naturally incurs debts both to individual contributors and to reference guides. The following scholars provided support and suggestions for the project: Karen Achberger; Jane Bakerman; Helen M. Bannan; Françoise Calin; Jan Fergus; Juliann Fleenor; Judith Kegan Gardiner; Susan Graham; Dorothy O. Helly; Katherine Henderson; Lorna Irvine; Robert Jackson; Louise Knauer; Rachel Major; Barbara May; Naomi Pasachoff; Margaret Perry; Steven F. Rendall; Barbara Rigney; Vivian Rosenberg; Adeline Tintner; Betty Travitsky; Suzanne Uphaus; Jacqueline Zeff; and Bonnie Zimmerman. We also wish to thank the reference librarians at the

Canadey Library, Bryn Mawr College; Ludington Library, Bryn Mawr, PA; and Van Pelt Library, University of Pennsylvania.

Among those references that were particularly helpful, we would like to cite *Women and Literature: An Annotated Bibliography of Women Writers* (1976; Women and Literature Collective, Box 441, Cambridge, MA 02138). Also helpful was the "Selected Bibliography" compiled for the conference "The Future of Motherhood: Challenge and Option," June 2–4, 1978, Ohio State University, Columbus.

We hope that readers find this preliminary compilation useful and we welcome suggestions and additions as follows:

Continental European to:
Ann M. Moore
University of Oregon
Eugene, Oregon

Twentieth-century American and British to:
Gail M. Rudenstein
University of Pennsylvania
Philadelphia, Pennsylvania

All others to:
Carol Farley Kessler
University of Pennsylvania
Philadelphia, Pennsylvania

25

Mothers and Daughters in Literature: A Preliminary Bibliography

---

I. AUTOBIOGRAPHY / BIOGRAPHY

Alta, b. 1942. *Momma: A Start on All the Untold Stories,* 1974.
Angelou, Maya, b. 1928. **Gather Together in My Name,* 1975. **I Know Why the Caged Bird Sings,* 1969.
Antin, Mary, 1881–1949. *The Promised Land,* 1912.
(F) Beauvoir, Simone de, b. 1908. **A Very Easy Death (Une Morte très Douce,* 1964), 1965. **Memoirs of a Dutiful Daughter (Memoires d'une jeune fille rangée),* 1958.
Bernard, Jessie, b. 1903. *Self Portrait of a Family,* 1978.
Bennett, Kay. *Kaibah: Recollections of a Navajo Girlhood,* 1964.
Bentley, Phyllis, b. 1894. **O Dreams, O Destinations,* 1962.
Bjorn, Thyra Ferre, 1905–1975. **Dear Papa,* 1963. **Mama's Way,* 1959. **Papa's Daughter,* 1958. **Papa's Wife,* 1955.
Bowen, Catherine Drinker, 1897–1973. *Family Portrait,* 1970.
Calisher, Hortense, b. 1911. *Herself,* 1972.
Campbell, Maria. *Halfbreed,* 1973.
Carrighar, Sally. *Home to the Wilderness,* 1973.
Chicago, Judy, b. 1939. *Through the Flower: My Struggle As A Woman Artist,* 1975.
Clifton, Lucille, b. 1936. *Generations,* 1976.
(F) Colette, Sidonie Gabrielle, 1873–1954. *Earthly Paradise,* 1966. **My Mother's House,* 1953. *Sido,* 1953.
Crawford [Medlinsky Koontz], Christina, b. 1940. **Mommie Dearest,* 1978.
Curie, Eve, b. 1904. *Madame Curie, A Biography,* 1937.
Eastman, Elaine Goodale, 1863–1953. *Hundred Maples,* 1935.
Elliott, Maud Howe, 1854–1948. **Three Generations,* 1923.
Ellis, Anne, 1875–1938. *The Life of an Ordinary Woman,* 1929.
Fawcett, Millicent Garrett, 1847–1929. *What I Remember,* 1925.
Ferber, Edna, 1887–1968. *A Peculiar Treasure,* 1939.
Fisher, Dorothy Canfield, 1879–1957. *A Harvest of Stories From A Half Century of Writing,* 1956:* "What My Mother Taught Me."
Flynn, Elizabeth Gurley. *The Rebel Girl: An Autobiography, My First Life (1906–1926),* 1973.
Forbes, Kathryn/Kathryn Anderson McLean, 1909–1966. **Mama's Bank Account,* 1943.
Frank, Anne, 1929–1945. *The Diary of a Young Girl,* 1952.

309

Giovanni, Nikki, b. 1943. *Gemini*, 1971.

Glasgow, Ellen, 1873–1945. *The Woman Within*, 1954.

Goldman, Emma, 1869–1940. *Living My Life*, 1931.

Han, Suyin, b. 1917. *The Crippled Tree*, 1965.

Haywood, Brooke, b. 1937. *Haywire*, 1972.

Hellman, Lillian, b. 1905. *Pentimento*, 1973. *An Unfinished Woman*, 1969.

Howard, Jane, b. 1935. *A Different Woman*, 1973.

Killilea, Marie, b. 1913. *Karen*, 1952.

Kingston, Maxine Hong, b. 1940. **The Woman Warrior: Memoir of a Girlhood among Ghosts*, 1976.

Lazarre, Jane. **The Mother Knot*, 1976.

Lisle, Honor, fl. 1528–1540. *Letters* . . . (ed. Green), 1846: "Letters to her daughters (1532–1540)."

(F) Martin, Claire, b. 1914. *In an Iron Glove (Dans un gant de far*, 1965, and *La Joue droite*, 1966), tr. P. Stratford, 1968.

Martineau, Harriet, 1802–1876. *Autobiography* (ed. M. W. Chapman), 1877.

McCarthy, Mary, b. 1912. *Memories of a Catholic Girlhood*, 1957.

Mead, Margaret, 1901-1978. *Blackberry Winter: My Earlier Years*, 1972.

(Ge) Meysenbug, Malwida von, 1816–1903. *Rebel in Bombazine* (ed. M. Adams), tr. E. von Meysenbug Lyons, 1936.

Moody, Anne, b. 1940. *Coming of Age in Mississippi*, 1968.

Nin, Anaïs, 1903–1977. *The Diary of Anaïs Nin, Volume 5, 1948–1955*, 1975.

Pankhurst, Emmeline, 1858–1928. *My Own Story*, 1914.

Pinzer [Jones Benjamin], Maimie, b. 1885. *The Maimie Papers* (ed. R. Rosen and S. Davidson), 1977.

Plath, Sylvia, 1932–1963. **Letters Home: Correspondence 1950–1963*, 1975.

Qoyawayma, Polingaysi/Elizabeth Q. White, b. 1892. *No Turning Back: A Hopi Woman's Struggle to Live in Two Worlds*, 1964.

Rama Rau, Santha, b. 1923. *Remember the House*, 1956.

Richards, Laura Howe, 1850–1943, and Maude Howe Elliott, 1854–1948. *Julia Ward Howe*, 1915.

Roosevelt, Eleanor, 1884–1962. *The Autobiography of Eleanor Roosevelt*, 1961. *This is My Story*, 1937.

(F) Sand, George/Amandine Aurore Dupin Dudevant, 1804–1876. *Story of My Life (Histoire de ma vie)*, 1854.

Sanford [Williams], Mollie Dorsey, b. 1839. *Mollie: The Journal of Mollie Dorsey Sanford in Nebraska and Colorado Territories, 1857–1866*, 1959.

Sarton, May, b. 1912. *I Knew a Phoenix*, 1959.

Schreiber, Flora Rheta, b. 1918. *Sybil*, 1973.

Sekaquaptewa, Helen, b. 1898. *Me and Mine: The Life Story of Helen Sekaquaptewa*, 1969.

(F) Sévigné, Marie de Rabutin Chantal, 1626–1696. **Lettres*, 1726. **Letters of Madame de Sévigné to Her Daughter and Her Friends* (ed. R. Aldington), 1937.

Sexton, Anne, 1928–1974. **Anne Sexton: A Self-Portrait in Letters*, 1977.

Shaw, Anna Howard, 1847–1919. *The Story of a Pioneer*, 1915.

(F) Staël, Anne-Louise-Germaine Necker de, 1766–1817. *Choix de lettres* (ed. G. Solovieff), 1970.

Stein, Gertrude, 1874–1946. *The Autobiography of Alice B. Toklas*, 1933.

Stern, Elizabeth G./Leah Morton, 1890–1954. **Gambler's Wife*, 1931. *I Am a Woman and a Jew*, 1926. **A Marriage Was Made*, 1928. **My Mother and I*, 1917. **This Ecstasy*, 1927.

Suckow, Ruth, 1892–1960. *Some Others and Myself*, 1952: "A Memoir."

Sullivan, Judy. *Mama Doesn't Live Here Anymore*, 1974.

(Sp) Teresa de Jesús, 1515–1582. *Obras completas*, 1951: "Libro de la vida."

Ullmann, Liv, b. 1939. *Changing*, 1976.

Victoria, Queen of Great Britain, 1819–1901. *Dearest Child: Letters Between Queen Victoria and the Princess Royal, 1858–1861*, 1965. *Dearest Mama: Letters Between Queen Victoria and the Crown Princess of Prussia, 1861–1864*, 1969. *Queen Victoria at Windsor and Balmoral: Letters from Her Grand-daughter Princess Victoria, June 1889*, 1959. *Your Dear Letter: Private Correspondence of Queen Victoria and the Crown Princess of Prussia, 1865–1871*, 1972.
Vorse, Mary Marvin Heaton, 1881–1966. *The Autobiography of an Elderly Woman*, 1911.
West, Jessamyn, b. 1907. *The Woman Said Yes: Encounters with Life and Death*, 1976.
Wong, Jade Snow, b. 1922. *Fifth Chinese Daughter*, 1950.
Yezierska, Anzia, 1885–1970. *Bread Givers*, 1925.

II. DRAMA

(SpA) Aguirre, Isidora, b. 1919. *Spanish Literature in Translation* (ed. W. K. Jones), 1966. *Las Tres Pascualas*, 1957.
Boothe [Luce], Claire, b. 1903. *The Women*, 1936.
Bowles, Jane, 1917–1973. *In the Summer House*, 1953.
Ferber, Edna, 1887–1968. *The Royal Family* (with S. S. Kaufman), 1923.
(SpA) Garro, Elena, b. 1920. *Selected Latin American One-Act Plays* (ed. F. Colecchia and J. Matas): "A Solid Home" ("Un Logar Sólido"), 1957.
Glaspell, Susan Keating, 1876?–1948. *The Verge*, 1921.
Griffin, Susan, b. 1942. *Voices*, 1975.
Hansberry, Lorraine, 1930–1965. *A Raisin in the Sun*, 1958.
(FC) Hébert, Anne, b. 1916. *Le Temps Sauvage*, 1963.
Hellman, Lillian, b. 1905. *Another Part of the Forest*, 1946. *The Little Foxes*, 1939.
Lamb, Myrna, b. 1930. *Apple Pie*, 1974.
Moore, Honor, "Mourning Pictures," *The New Women's Theatre*, (ed. H. Moore), 1977. Ursula Molinaro, *Breakfast Past Noon*.
Shange, Ntozake. *For Colored Girls Who Have Considered Suicide When The Rainbow is Enuf*, 1977.
Terry, Megan, b. 1932. *Calm Down Mother: A Transformation for Three Women*, 1966.

III. FICTION

A. American

Alcott, Louisa May, 1832–1888. *Behind a Mask* (ed. M. Stern, 1975): "Behind a Mask," 1866; The Mysterious Key," 1867. *Jo's Boys, and How They Turned Out*, 1886J. *Little Men: Life at Plumfield with Jo's Boys*, 1871J. *Little Women: or Meg, Jo, Beth and Amy*, 1868J. *An Old-Fashioned Girl*, 1870J. *Plots and Counterplots* (ed. M. Stern, 1976): "A Marble Woman," 1865. *Under the Lilacs*, 1878J. *Work: A Story of Experience*, 1873.
Adams, Alice, b. 1926. *Families and Survivors*, 1974.
Alther, Lisa, b. 1944. *Kinflicks*, 1976.
Anderson, Barbara, b. 1891. *Southbound*, 1949.
Arnow, Harriette, b. 1908. *The Dollmaker*, 1954. *Hunter's Horn*, 1949. *Mountain Path*, 1939. "Washer Woman's Day," *Southern Review* I, 1936. *The Weedkiller's Daughter*, 1970.
Atherton, Gertrude, 1857–1948. *Patience Sparhawk and Her Times*, 1897. *Splendid Idle Fortunes: Stories of Old California*, 1902: "Head of a Priest."

Austin, Mary Hunter, 1868–1934. *A Woman of Genius*, 1912.

Bambera, Toni Cade. *Gorilla, My Love*, 1972: "My Man Bovanne."

Barnes, Djuna, b. 1892. *A Book*, 1923: "Cassation." *Night Among the Horses*, 1929: "Aller et Retour." *Spillway*, 1962.

Barnes, Margaret Ayer, 1886–1967. *Prevailing Winds*, 1928: "Perpetual Care." *Years of Grace*, 1930. *Westward Passage*, 1931. *Within This Present*, 1933. *Wisdom's Gate*, 1938.

Benson, Sally, b. 1900. *Women and Children First*, 1943: "Birds In Their Nest Agree."

Bernays [Kaplan], Anne, b. 1930. *Growing Up Rich*, 1975.

Betts, Doris, b. 1932. *Beasts of the Southern Wild and Other Stories*, 1973.

Bitches and Sad Ladies (ed. P. Rotter), 1975.

Black-Eyed Susans: Classic Stories by and About Black Women (ed. M. H. Washington), 1975.

Blume, Judy Sussman Kitchens, b. 1938. *Are You There God? It's Me, Margaret*, 1970J. **Starring Sally J. Freedman as Herself*, 1977J. *Deenie*, 1973J.

Boyd, Blanche M., b. 1945. *Nerves*, 1973.

Boyle, Kay, b. 1903. **The Underground Woman*, 1975. *The White Horses of Vienna*, 1936: "Convalescence."

Brewster, Elizabeth Winifred, b. 1922. *The Sisters*, 1974.

Brooks, Gwendolyn, b. 1917. *Maud Martha*, 1953.

Broner, E. M. **Her Mothers*, 1975. **Journal/Nocturnal*, 1968. *A Weave of Women*, 1978.

Brown, Alice, 1857–1948. *Country Neighbors*, 1910: "A Flower in April." *The Country Road*, 1906: "A Day Off," "A Winter's Courting." *John Winterbourne's Family*, 1910. *Meadow-Grass*, 1895: "A Righteous Bargain."

Brown, Rita Mae, b. 1944. **Rubyfruit Jungle*, 1973.

Brown, Rosellen, b. 1939. **The Autobiography of My Mother*, 1976.

Buck, Pearl Sydenstricker/John Sedges, 1892–1973. *The Exile*, 1936. **The Mother*, 1934. *Secrets of the Heart*, 1976: "Here and Now." **The Three Daughters of Madame Liang*, 1969.

Burch, Pat, b. 1944. *Early Losses*, 1973.

Burnett, Frances Hodgson, 1849–1924. *The Head of the House of Coombe*, 1922J.

By and About Women: An Anthology of Short Fiction (ed. B. K. Schneiderman), 1973.

Calisher, Hortense, b. 1911. *The Collected Stories of Hortense Calisher*, 1975: "Old Stock." "Gargantua," *Harper's Bazaar*, 3039, Feb. 1965. *In the Absence of Angels*, 1951: "The Middle Drawer."

Cather, Willa, 1873–1947. **Obscure Destinies*, 1932: "Old Mrs. Harris." *Sapphira and the Slave Girl*, 1940. **Song of the Lark*, 1915.

Cavanna, Betty, b. 1909. **Almost Like Sisters*, 1963J. *Betty Cavanna Presents*, 1964J: "Oh, Mother!"

Chase, Mary Ellen, 1887–1973. *Mary Peters*, 1934.

Chopin, Kate, 1851–1904. "Mrs. Mobry's Reason," 1891.

Didion, Joan, b. 1934. **A Book of Common Prayer*, 1977.

Embry, Margaret Jacob, b. 1919. *Shadi*, 1971.

Enright, Elizabeth, b. 1909. *The Melendy Family*, 1947J. *Moment Before the Rain*, 1955J: "The Playground," "When the Bough Breaks."

Fauset, Jessie Redmon, 1885–1961. *Chinaberry Tree*, 1931. *Comedy: American Style*, 1934. *There Is Confusion*, 1924. **Plum Bun*, 1929.

Ferber, Edna, 1887–1968. *Fanny Herself*, 1917. **The Girls*, 1921. **Mother Knows Best*, 1928.

Fisher, Dorothy F. Canfield, 1879–1957. *A Harvest of Stories from a Half Century of Writing*, 1956: *"Married Children." **Her Son's Wife*, 1926. **The Bent Twig*, 1915.

Fitzgerald, Zelda, 1900–1948. *Save Me the Waltz*, 1932.

French, Marilyn, b. 1929. **The Women's Room*, 1977.

Freeman, Mary E. Wilkins, 1852–1930. *A Humble Romance and Other Stories*, 1887: "A Lover of Flowers," *"A Modern Dragon," "An Independent Thinker," "A Souvenir,"

*"A Taste of Honey," "In Butterfly Time." *A New England Nun and Other Stories,* 1891: "A Gentle Ghost," *"Louisa," "Up Primrose Hill." *The Jamesons,* 1899. *Jane Field,* 1893. *Pembroke,* 1894. *The Portion of Labor,* 1901. *The Winning Lady and Others,* 1909: *"Old Woman Magoun."

Fuller, Anna, 1853–1916. *Pratt Portraits: Sketched in a New England Suburb,* 1897: "Harriet," "Old Lady Pratt."

Gale, Zona, 1874–1938. *A Daughter of the Morning,* 1915. *Miss Lulu Bett,* 1920. *When I Was a Little Girl,* 1913.

Gerber, Merrill Joan, b. 1938. *Stop Here, My Friend,* 1965: "The Cost Depends on What You Reckon It In," "Forty Watts," "How Love Came to Grandmother," "Stop Here, My Friend."

Gerould, Geraldine Fullerton, 1879–1944. *Great Tradition and Other Stories,* 1915: title story.

Gilman, Charlotte Perkins, 1860–1935. *The Crux,* 1911.

Glasgow, Ellen, 1873–1945. *Barren Ground,* 1925. *Deliverance,* 1904. *In This Our Life,* 1941. *Life and Gabriella: The Story of a Woman's Courage,* 1916. *The Romantic Comedians,* 1926. *The Sheltered Life,* 1932. *They Stooped to Folly,* 1929. *Vein of Iron,* 1935. *Virginia,* 1913.

Glaspell, Susan, 1882–1948. *Brook Evans,* 1928. *Fidelity,* 1915. *Fugitive's Return,* 1929. *Judd Rankin's Daughter,* 1945. *The Morning Is Near Us,* 1939. *Norma Ashe,* 1942.

Godwin, Gail, b. 1937. *The Odd Woman,* 1974. *Dream Children,* 1976: "The Woman Who Kept Her Poet."

Gollier, Celia Fremlin, b. 1914. *Ms. Mysteries* (ed. A. Liebman, 1976): "Don't Be Frightened." *Possession,* 1969.

Gordon, Caroline, b. 1895. *None Shall Look Back,* 1937. *Strange Children,* 1951.

Grau, Shirley, b. 1929. *The House on Coliseum Street,* 1961. *The Wind Shifting West,* 1973: "Homecoming," "The Other Way."

Gray, Francine du Plessix, b. 1930. *Lovers and Tyrants,* 1976.

Green, Hannah/Joanne Greenberg, b. 1932. *I Never Promised You A Rose Garden,* 1964.

Hale, Nancy, b. 1908. *Empress' Ring,* 1955: "Snows of Childhood." *The Pattern of Perfection,* 1960: "Rich People." *Prize Stories of 1968:* "The Most Elegant Drawing Room in Europe."

Hearon, Shelby, b. 1931. *Hannah's House,* 1975.

Herbst, Josephine, 1897–1969. *Nothing Is Sacred,* 1928. *Pity Is Not Enough,* 1933.

Howard, Maureen, b. 1930. *Bridgeport Bus,* 1965.

Hurst, Fannie, 1889–1968. *Stardust: The Story of an American Girl,* 1921: "She Walks in Beauty."

Hurston, Zora Neale, 1902–1960. *Dust Tracks on a Road,* 1942.

Jackson, Helen Maria Fiske Hunt, 1831–1885. *Mercy Philbrick's Choice,* 1876.

Jackson, Shirley Hardie, 1919–1965. *Life Among the Savages,* 1953. *Raising Demons,* 1957. *The Road Through the Wall,* 1948.

Jewett, Sarah Orne, 1849–1909. *The Country of the Pointed Firs,* 1896. *King of Folly Island,* 1886: title story. *Life of Nancy,* 1895: "The Hilton's Holiday." *The Marsh Island,* 1885. *The White Heron,* 1886: "The Dulham Ladies," "Farmer Finch."

Jong, Erica, b. 1942. *Fear of Flying,* 1973.

Katzenbach, Maria, b. 1953. *The Grab,* 1978.

Kaufman, Sue, 1926–1977. *The Master and Other Stories,* 1976: "Summer Librarian," "Why Do You Look So Beautiful?"

Kelley, Edith Summers, 1884–1956. *Weeds,* 1923.

Klein, Norma, b. 1938. *Mom, the Wolf Man, and Me,* 1972J.

Lane, Rose Wilder, b. 1887. *Old Home Town,* 1935: "Long Skirts," "Thankless Child."

Leffland, Ella, b. 1931. *Mrs. Munck,* 1970.

L'Engle, Madeleine, b. 1918. *Meet the Austins,* 1960J. *Summer of the Great Grandmother,* 1974.

Loeser, Katinka, b. 1913. *Tomorrow Will Be Monday: Stories About Parents and Children*, 1964: "Baby," "Whose Little Girl Are You?"

McCord, Jean, b. 1924. *Deep Where the Octopi Lie*, 1968: "I Left It All Behind When I Ran." *Bitter Is the Hawk's Path*, 1971: "Trial By Summer."

McCullers, Carson Smith, 1917–1967. *The Mortgaged Heart*, 1971: "Breath from the Sky," "Like That."

Marshall, Paule, b. 1929. *Brown Girl, Brownstones*, 1959.

Martin, Helen Reimensnyder, 1868–1939. *Maggie of Virginsburg: A Story of the Pennsylvania Dutch*, 1918. *Martha of the Mennonite Country*, 1915.

Mathis, Sharon Bell, b. 1937. *Listen for the Fig Tree*, 1974.

Merril, Judith, b. 1923. *The Best of Judith Merril*, 1976: "Daughters of Earth."

Meriwether, Louise. *Daddy Was a Number Runner*, 1970.

Metalious, Grace, 1924–1964. *Peyton Place*, 1956.

Moody, Anne, b. 1940. *Mr. Death*, 1975: "The Cow."

Morrison, Toni, b. 1931. *The Bluest Eye*, 1970. *Sula*, 1974.

Motherlove (ed. S. Spinner), 1978.

Norris, Kathleen, 1880–1966. *Mother*, 1911.

Oates, Joyce Carol, b. 1938. *By the North Gate*, 1963: "Images." *Do With Me What You Will*, 1973. *The Goddess and Other Women*, 1974: *". . . and Answers," *"The Daughter." *The Seduction and Other Stories*, 1975: "The Madwoman." *them*, 1969. *The Wheel of Love and Other Stories*, 1970: "Matter and Energy," "You." *Where Are You Going, Where Have You Been? Stories of Young America*, 1974: "Back There."

O'Connor, Flannery, 1925–1964. *The Complete Stories*, 1972: "A Circle in the Fire," "Good Country People," "The Life You Save May Be Your Own," "A Temple of the Holy Ghost," "Why Do the Heathen Rage?"

Olsen, Tillie, b. 1913. *Tell Me a Riddle*, 1961. *Yonnondio: From the Thirties*, 1974.

Paley, Grace, b. 1922. *The Little Disturbances of Man*, 1959: "A Woman Young and Old."

Parker, Dorothy, 1893–1967. *The Viking Portable Dorothy Parker*, 1973: "Clothe the Naked," "Horsie," "Lolita."

Patton, Frances Gray, b. 1906. *Piece of Luck*, 1955: "Mothers and Daughters." *Twenty-Eight Stories*, 1969: "Grade 5B and the Well-Fed Rat."

Peterkin, Julia Mood, 1880–1961. *Green Thursday*, 1924. *Scarlet Sister Mary*, 1928.

Petesch, Natalie L. M. *After the First Death There Is No Other*, 1974: "Nails." *The Odyssey of Katinou Kalokovich*, 1974.

Phelps, Elizabeth Stuart, 1815–1852. *The Angel over the Right Shoulder*, 1852. *Kitty Brown* series, 1851–1853J. *The Last Leaf from Sunny Side*, 1853: "The Cloudy Morning," "The Night After Christmas." *Little Mary*, 1854J. *The Sunny Side*, 1851.

Phelps [Ward], Elizabeth Stuart, 1844–1911. *Beyond the Gates*, 1883. *Confessions of a Wife*, 1902. *Gypsy* series, 1866–1867J. *Hedged In*, 1871. *The Madonna of the Tubs*, 1886. *Men, Women, and Ghosts*, 1869: "Calico," *"One of the Elect." *Mercy Gliddon's Work*, 1865J. *My Cousin and I*, 1879J. *Sealed Orders*, 1880: "Cloth of Gold," "Long, Long Ago," *"Miss Mildred's Friends," *"Old Mother Goose," *The Story of Avis*, 1877. *Wide Awake* V.18–19, 1883–1884J: "A Brave Girl."

Piercy, Marge, b. 1936. *Small Changes*, 1972.

Plath, Sylvia, 1932–1963. *The Bell Jar*, 1962.

Popkin, Zelda, b. 1898. *A Death of Innocence*, 1971.

Porte, Eleanor H., 1868–1920. *Pollyanna*, 1913J.

Porter, Katherine Anne, b. 1894. *The Leaning Tower*: "The Old Order" series, 1937. *Pale Horse, Pale Rider*: "Old Mortality," 1936.

Rascoe, Judith. *Yours, and Mine: Novella and Stories*, 1973: "The Mother of Good Fortune."

Roberts, Elizabeth Madox, 1886–1941. *The Great Meadow*, 1930. *The Time of Man*, 1926.

Rodgers, Mary, b. 1931. *Freaky Friday*, 1972J.

Roiphe, Anne Richardson, b. 1935. *Long Division*, 1972.

Russ, Joanna, b. 1937. *Woman as Writer* (ed. J. L. Webber and J. Grummen), 1978: "When It Changed," 1972.

Rees, Barbara, b. 1934. *Try Another Country: Three Short Novels*, 1969: "Mrs. Wall, Mrs. Wall."

Schaeffer, Susan Fromberg, b. 1941. *Falling*, 1973.

See, Carolyn, b. 1934. *Mothers, Daughters*, 1977.

Sharp, Margery, b. 1915. *The Nutmeg Tree*, 1938.

Shelnutt, Eve, b. 1942. *Shenandoah*, 1974: "Angel."

Shreve, Susan Richards, b. 1939. *A Woman Like That*, 1977.

Smedley, Agnes, 1890–1950. *Daughter of Earth*, 1929.

Shulman, Alix Kates, b. 1932. *Memoirs of an Ex-Prom Queen*, 1972.

Singmaster [Lewars], Elsie, 1879–1958. *Love Will Come* (ed. A. Stowe), 1959: "What Amelia Wanted."

Smith, Betty, 1904–1972. *A Tree Grows in Brooklyn*, 1943.

Sorensen, Virginia, b. 1912.*The Evening and the Morning*, 1949.

Spencer, Cornelia/Grace S. Yaukey. *Three Sisters: The Story of the Soong Family of China*, 1939.

Spencer, Elizabeth, b. 1921. *The Light in the Piazza*, 1960.

Stafford, Jean, b. 1915. *Boston Adventure*, 1944.

Stowe, Harriet Beecher, 1811–1896. *A Minister's Wooing*, 1859. *Poganuc People*, 1878. *Uncle Tom's Cabin*, 1852. *We and Our Neighbors*, 1875.

Stratton-Porter, Gene, 1863–1924. *A Girl of the Limberlost*, 1909.

Suckow, Ruth, 1892–1960. *The Best of the Lot*, 1922. *The Bonney Family*, 1926. *Children and Older People*, 1931: "Midwestern Primitive," "The Valentine Box." *Cora*, 1929. *Country People*, 1924. *The Folks*, 1934. *Iowa Interiors*, 1926: "Four Generations," "A Home-Coming," *"A Start in Life," "Up-rooted." The Kramer Girls*, 1931. *The Odyssey of a Nice Girl*, 1925. *Some Others and Myself*, 1952: "Mrs. Vogel and Ollie."

Time of Understanding: Stories of Girls Learning to Get Along with Their Parents (ed. H. Ferris), 1963: Hila Colman, "Suddenly You're in Love." Gertrude Crampton, "Medal for Mums." Rita C. Foster, "Easter Present."

Tyler, Anne, b. 1941. *Earthly Possessions*, 1977.

Vreuls, Diane. *Are We There Yet?*, 1975.

Walker, Alice, b. 1944. *In Love and Trouble*, 1973: "Everyday Use." *The Third Life of Grange Copeland*, 1970.

Walker, Margaret, b. 1915. *Jubilee*, 1966.

Walker, Mildred, b. 1905. *Winter Wheat*, 1944.

Weldon, Fay, b. 1933. *Female Friends*, 1975. *Remember Me*, 1976.

Welty, Eudora, b. 1909. *Bride of the Innisfallen and Other Stories*, 1955: "Going to Naples." *Delta Wedding*, 1946. *The Golden Apples*, 1949: "The Humming Birds." *The Optimist's Daughter*, 1973.

West, Jessamyn, b. 1907. *Cress Delahanty*, 1953. *Crimson Ramblers of the World, Farewell*, 1970: "Mother's Day," "Up a Tree." *Love, Death, and the Ladies' Drill Team*, 1955: "Little Collar for the Monkey." *A Matter of Time*, 1966. *South of the Angels*, 1960. *The Witch Diggers*, 1951.

Weston, Christine Goutiere, b. 1904. *The Wise Children*, 1957.

Wharton, Edith, 1862–1937. *The Children*, 1928. *The Custom of the Country*, 1913. *The Mother's Recompense*, 1925. *Old New York*, 1924: "The Old Maid." *The World Over*, 1934: "Roman Fever." *Xingu and Other Stories*, 1916: "Autres Temps . . ."

Whitney, Phyllis Ayame, b. 1903. *The Trembling Hills*, 1956. *The Turquoise Mask*, 1974.

Wilder, Laura Ingalls, 1867–1957. *Little House* series, 1932–1943J.

Wilkinson, Sylvia, b. 1940. *Moss on the North Side*, 1966.

Wolff, Maritta M., b. 1918. *Whistle Stop*, 1941.
Yglesias, Helen, b. 1915. *Family Feeling*, 1976.
Young, Marguerite, b. 1909, **Miss MacIntosh, My Darling*, 1965.

B. British and Commonwealth Fiction

Atwood, Margaret, b. 1939. *Dancing Girls*, 1977: "Giving Birth." **Lady Oracle*, 1976. *Surfacing*, 1972.
Austen, Jane, 1775–1817. *Mansfield Park*, 1814. **Pride and Prejudice*, 1813. **Sense and Sensibility*, 1811.
Bower, Elizabeth, 1899–1973. *Early Stones*, 1951: "Coming Home."
Brontë, Charlotte, 1816–1855. *Five Novellettes* (ed. W. Gérin, 1971): "Charlotte Vernon," 1839.
Brontë, Emily, 1818–1848. *Wuthering Heights*, 1848.
Burney, Fanny, 1752–1840. *Camilla*, 1776. *Evelina*, 1778.
Compton-Burnett, Ivy, 1892–1969. *A Family and a Fortune*, 1964.
Crawford, Isabella Valancy, 1850–1887. *Selected Stories of Isabella Valancy Crawford* (ed. P. Petrone), 1975: "*La Tricoteuse*."
Drabble, Margaret, b. 1939. **Jerusalem the Golden*, 1967. *The Realms of Gold*, 1976. **A Summer Bird Cage*, 1962.
Duffy, Maureen, b. 1933. *That's How It Was*, 1962.
Eliot, George/Mary Ann Evans, 1819–1880. **Daniel Deronda*, 1876. *Middlemarch*, 1872. **The Mill on the Floss*, 1860.
Engel, Marian, b. 1933. *The Honeyman Festival*, 1970. *Inside the Easter Egg*, 1975: ***"Bicycle Story," "Inside the Easter Egg," ***"Meredith and the Lousy Latin Lover," ***"Ruth." *Joanne*, 1973. *No Clouds of Glory (Sarah Bastard's Notebook)*, 1968.
Ferrier, Susan Edmonstone, 1782–1854. *The Inheritance*, 1824. *Marriage, A Novel*, 1818.
Gallant, Mavis, b. 1922. *My Heart Is Broken*, 1974: ***"Its Image on the Mirror." *The Other Paris*, 1956: "Day Like Any Other," "Going Ashore."
Gaskell, Elizabeth Cleghorn Stevenson, 1810–1865. *Lizzie Leigh and Other Tales*, 1865: title story. **Wives and Daughters*, 1866.
Gaskin, Catherine, b. 1929. **The Lynmara Legacy*, 1976.
Gilboord, Margaret. *The Butterfly Ward*, 1976: "Ada," title story, "The Phase."
Godden, [Margaret] Rumer, b. 1907. *The Battle of Villa Fiorita*, 1963.
Gardiner, Nadine, b. 1923. *Selected Stories*, 1975–76: "A Company of Laughing Faces."
Grand, Sarah/Frances Elizabeth Clarke MacFall, 1854–1945. *The Beth Book*, 1897.
Hardwick, Mollie. **Beauty's Daughter*, 1977.
Harvor, Beth. **Women and Children: Eleven Stories*, 1973.
Howard, Elizabeth Jane, b. 1923. *Mr. Wrong*, 1975: "Child's Play," "Whip Hand."
Jewsbury, Geraldine, 1812–1880. *The Half-Sisters*, 1848.
Johnson, Pamela Hansford, b. 1912. **An Avenue of Stone*, 1948.
Laurence, Margaret, b. 1926. **A Bird in the House*, 1970. **The Diviners*, 1974. *The Fire-Dwellers*, 1969. **A Jest of God*, 1966. *The Stone Angel*, 1964.
Lavin, Mary, b. 1912. *Modern Irish Short Stories*, (ed. M. O'Donovan), 1957: "The Will." *Happiness, and Other Stories*, 1970: "Happiness." *A Memory, and Other Stories*, 1973: "Villa Violetta."
Lehmann, Rosamund, b. 1903. *The Ballad and The Source*, 1945.
Lessing, Doris, b. 1919. *A Proper Marriage*, 1954. *The Four-Gated City*, 1969. *The Golden Notebook*, 1962. **Martha Quest*, 1952.
Lofts, Norah Robinson, b. 1904. *Heaven In Your Hand*, 1958: "Rapunzel, Rapunzel, Bind Up Your Hair!" **Nethergate*, 1973.
McCullough, Colleen, b. 1937? *The Thorn Birds*, 1977.
Macauley, Rose, 1881–1958. *Dangerous Ages*, 1921.
Mansfield, Katherine, 1888–1923. *Stories:* "Bliss," "The Garden Party," "Prelude."

Marshall Joyce, b. 1931. *A Private Place*, 1975: "The Little White Girl," "Salvage."

Maynard, Fredelle Bruser. *Raisin and Almonds*, 1972.

Montgomery, Lucy Maud, 1874–1942. *Anne of Green Gables*, 1908J.

Mortimer, Penelope Ruth, b. 1918. *The Home*, 1971.

Munro, Alice, b. 1931. *Dance of the Happy Shades*, 1968: "Boys and Girls," "Dance of the Happy Shades," "Images," *"The Peace of Utrecht," *"Red Dress—1946," "The Time of Death." *Lives of Girls and Women*, 1971. *Something I've Been Meaning to Tell You*, 1974: "Executioners," "Forgiveness in Families," "Memorial," *"The Ottawa Valley," "Winter Wind."

Norton, Caroline, 1808–1877. *Stuart of Dunleath*, 1851.

Ostenso, Martha, 1900–1913. *Wild Geese*, 1925.

Rhys, Jean, b. 1894. *After Leaving Mr. MacKenzie*, 1931. *Wide Sargasso Sea*, 1966.

Ritchie, Anna Isabella Thackeray, 1837–1919. *The Story of Elizabeth*, 1863.

Sinclair, May, 1867–1946. *Mary Olivier: A Life*, 1919.

Spark, Muriel, b. 1918. *Collected Stories*, 1968: "The Pawnbroker's Wife," *The Mandelbaum Gate*, 1965.

Stead, Christina, 1902. *The Man Who Loved Children*, 1940.

Stern, Gladys Bronwyn, 1890–1973. *Donkey Shoe*, 1952. *The Matriarch*, 1925. *Pelican Walking*, 1934: "Nectarine Life." *Shining and Free*, 1930. *Women in the Hall*, 1939.

Taylor, Elizabeth, b. 1912. *A Dedicated Man and Other Stories*, 1965: "Girl Reading," "Mr. Wharton."

Tellers of Tales (ed. S. Maugham), 1939.

Thomas, Audrey, b. 1935. *Mrs. Blood*, 1970. *Songs My Mother Taught Me*, 1973. *Ten Green Bottles*, 1967: "If One Green Bottle," "One Is One and All Alone."

Ward, Mrs. Humphrey/Mary Augusta Arnold Ward, 1851–1920. *Rose's Daughter*, 1903.

Watson, Sheila, b. 1919. *The Double Hook*, 1959.

West, Rebecca, b. 1892. *The Birds Fall Down*, 1966. *The Fountain Overflows*, 1956.

Wiseman, Adele, b. 1928. *Crackpot*, 1974.

Wollstonecraft, Mary, 1759–1797. *Mary: A Fiction*, 1793.

Woolf, Virginia, 1882–1941. *Mrs. Dalloway*, 1925. *Night and Day*, 1919. *To the Lighthouse*, 1927. *The Years*, 1937.

C. Translated, Continental, and Other Fiction

(F) Anon. (attrib. Mme. de Lafayette). *Isabelle ou le journal amoureux d'Espagne*, 1675.

(F) Beauvoir, Simone de, b. 1908. *Les Mandarins*, 1954. *The Woman Destroyed*, 1967: "Monologue."

(Ge) Bedford, Sybille, b. 1911. *A Compass Error*, 1968. *A Favorite of the Gods*, 1963.

(FC) Blais, Marie-Claire, b. 1939. *Mad Shadows*, 1959. *The Manuscripts of Pauline Archange*, 1969. *Une Saison dans la vie d'Emmannuel*, 1966.

(SpA) Brunet, Marta, b. 1901. *Reloj del sol*, 1930: "Francina."

(F) Charrière, Isabella Agretu van Tyyl de, d. 1805. *Four Tales by Zelide*, 1926: "Letters from Lausanne."

(F) Colette, Sidonie Gabrielle, 1873–1954. *Break of Day*, 1961. *Gigi*, 1942. *The Other Woman*, 1972: "Secrets."

(FB) Dubrau, Louis, b. 1904. *La Belle et la bête*, 1961.

(F) Etcherelli, Claire, b. 1934. "A propos de Clémence," 1971. *Elise ou la vraie vie*, 1967.

(Ge) Frischmuth, Barbara. *Die Mystifikationen der Sophie Silber*, 1976.

(It) Ginzburg, Natalia, b. 1916. *A Light for Fools*, tr. A. Davison, 1957. *Stories of Modern Italy* (ed. B. Johnson), 1957: "Valentino."

(FC) Hébert, Anne, b. 1916. *Kamouraska*, tr., 1973. *The Torrent*, 1963: "The Death of Stella."

(Ge) Huch, Ricarda O., 1864–1947. *Eros Invincible (Erinnerungen von Ludolf Ursleu dem Jüngeren*, 1892), tr. W. A. Drake, 1931.

(In) Jhabvala, Ruth Prawer, b. 1927. *How I Became a Holy Mother and Other Stories*, 1976: "In the Mountains."

(F) LaFayette, Marie-Madeleine Pioche de la Vergne, 1634–1693. *The Princess of Cleves*, 1678.

(Sw) Lagerlöf, Selma, 1858–1940. *Charlotte Lowensbold*, 1928; *Anna Svard*, 1931.

(FA) Lamsine, Aïcha. *La Chryside: chroniques algériennes*, 1976.

(P) Lispector, Clarice, b. 1925. *Family Ties*, 1960.

(It) Lussu, Joyce Salvadori, b. 1912. *New Italian Writers, collected from Bottegbe Oscure*, 1950: *The Bambina," "The Matriarch," tr. W. Packer.

(F) Mallet-Joris, Françoise, b. 1930. *Cordelia and Other Stories:* *"Marie" (*Cordélia: récits*, 1956), tr. P. Green, 1965.

(It) Maraini, Dacia, b. 1936. *The Age of Malaise* (*L'Età del Malessere*, 1962), tr. F. Frenaye, 1963.

(In) Markandaya, Kamalá, b. 1924. *Nectar in a Sieve*, 1954.

(SpA) Matute, Ana Maria, b. 1920. *Primera memoria*, 1960.

(Sw) Morris, Edita. *Dear Me, and Other Tales from My Native Sweden*, 1967: "After the Ball," "A Little Egg."

(Gr) Nakos, Lilika, b. 1899. *The Lost*, 1935. *Toward a New Life*, 1960.

(It) Ortese, Anna Maria, b. 1914. *Stories of Modern Italy:* "A Pair of Glasses," tr. F. Frenaye.

(FB) Philipe, Anne, b. 1917. *Les Rendez-vous de la colline*.

(Ne) Prou, Suzanne. *The Terrace of the Bernardini* (*La Terrasse des Bernardini*, 1973), tr. A. Foulke, 1976.

(Ne) Rochefort, Christiane, b. 1917. *Les Petits Enfants du Siècle*, 1961.

(FC) Roy, Gabriella Carbotte, b. 1909. *Rue Deschambault*, 1955. *The Tin Flute* (*Bonheur d'occasion*, 1947), tr. H. Josephson, 1947.

(F) Sand, George/Amandine Aurore Dupin Dudevant, 1804–1876. *La Confession d'une jeune fille*, 1862. *Rose et Blanche*, 1831. *Voyages en Auvergne*, 1829.

(F) Sarrante, Nathalie, b. 1900. *Martereau*, tr. Jolas, 1953. *Le Planétarium*, 1959. *Tropismes*, 1957.

(Ne) Sarrazin, Albertine, 1937–1967. *L'Astragal*, 1965. *The Runaway* (*La Cavale*, 1965), tr. C. Markmann, 1967.

(It) Serao, Mathilde, 1856–1927. *All'erta, sentinella*, 1889: "Terno secco."

(PA) Silveira de Queiroz, Dinah, b. 1911. *Modern Brazilian Short Stories* (ed. W. Brossman), 1967: *"Guidance" ("A Moralista").

(Ge) Struck, Karin, b. 1947. *Die Mutter*, 1975.

(Ne) Thomas, Édith, 1909–1970. *Bedside Book of French Stories* (ed. B. Becker and R. N. Linscott), 1945: "The Professor and the Mussels," tr. M. Jolas.

(SpA) Turner, Clorinda Matto de, 1854–1909. *Aves sin nido*, 1889.

(No) Undset, Sigrid, 1882–1949. *The Faithful Wife*, 1937. *Kristin Lavransdatter*, 1920–22.

(F) Wittig, Monique, *The Opoponax* (*L' Opoponax*, 1964), tr. H. Weaver, 1966.

(FB) Yourcenar, Marguerite/Marguerite de Crayencour, b. 1903. *Souvenirs pieux*, 1974.

IV. POETRY

A. Twentieth-Century Poetry in English

Atwood, Margaret, b. 1939. *Procedures for Underground*, 1970: "Woman Skating."

Brooks, Gwendolyn, b. 1917. *The World of Gwendolyn Brooks*, 1960: "Jessie Mitchell's Mother."

Giovanni, Nikki, b. 1943. *Black Judgment*, 1968: "Nikki-Rosa." *My House*, 1972: "Legacies," "Mothers," "Scrapbooks." *The Women and the Men*, 1975: "Once a Lady Told Me," "Mother's Habits."

Griffin, Susan, b. 1943. *Like the Iris of an Eye*, 1976: "Archeology of a Lost Woman: Fragments," "Chance Meeting," "Daughter," "The Great Mother," "Grenadine," "White Bear."

I Hear My Sisters Saying: Poems by Twentieth Century Women (ed. C. Konek and D. Walters), 1976.

Jong, Erica, b. 1942. *Half-Lives*, 1973: "Mother." *Loveroot*, 1976: "Dear Marys, Dear Mother, Dear Daughter."

Kaufman, Shirley, b. 1923. *The Floor Keeps Turning*, 1970: "Mothers, Daughters."

Kumin, Maxine, b. 1925. *The Retrieval System*, 1978: "Birthday Poem," "The Longing to Be Saved," "Parting," "Sunbathing on a Rooftop in Berkeley."

Lorde, Audre, b. 1934. *From a Land Where Other People Live*, 1973: "Black Mother Woman," "Dear Toni Instead of a Letter of Congratulation Upon Your Book and Your Daughter Whom You Say You Are Raising to Be a Correct Little Sister," "Generation II," "Progress Report."

Millay, Edna St. Vincent, 1892–1950. *Wine from These Grapes*, 1934: "III Childhood Is the Kingdom Where Nobody Dies," "II In the Grave No Flower," "IV The Solid Sprite Who Stands Alone," "VI Sonnet," "V Spring in the Garden," "I Valentine."

Morgan, Robin, b. 1941. *Monster*, 1972: "Matrilineal Descent." *Lady of the Beasts*, 1976: "Network of the Imaginary Mother."

Pastan, Linda, b. 1932. *Aspects of Eve*, 1975: "Rachel," "To a Daughter."

Pitter, Ruth, b. 1897. *Poems, 1926–1966:* "May, 1947," "The Solitary," "The Weed."

Plath, Sylvia, 1932–1963. *Ariel*, 1965: "Balloons," "Kindness," "Lesbos," "The Moon and the Yew Tree," "Morning Song." *Crossing the Water*, 1971: "Maenad," "Magi," "Two Sisters of Persephone." *The Colossus*, 1960: "All the Dead Dears," "The Disquieting Muses," "Poem for a Birthday," "Point Shirley."

Rich, Adrienne, b. 1929. *The Dream of a Common Language: Poems 1974–1977*, 1978: "Sibling Rivalries." *Poems: Selected and New, 1950–1974*, 1975: "The Mirror in Which Two Are Seen As One," "Mourning Picture," "Night-Pieces: For a Child." *Snapshots of a Daughter-in-Law: Poems 1954–1962*, 1967: title poem, "A Woman Mourned by Daughters."

Rukeyser, Muriel, b. 1913. *The Gates*, 1976: "Double Ode," "Ms. Lot," "Trinity Churchyard."

Sexton, Anne, 1928–1974. *All My Pretty Ones*, 1961: "Housewife." *The Awful Rowing Toward God*, 1975: "Mothers." *The Book of Folly*, 1972: "Dancing the Jig," "Dreaming the Breasts," "Mother and Daughter," "The Red Shoes." *45 Mercy Street*, 1976: "The Consecrating Mother," "Talking to Sheep." *Live or Die*, 1966: "Christmas Eve," "Little Girl, My String Bean, My Lovely Woman," "A Little Uncomplicated Hymn," "Pain for a Daughter." *To Bedlam and Part Way Back*, 1960: "The Division of Parts," "The Double Image."

Sitwell, Edith, 1887–1964. *Collected Poems*, 1954: "Anne Boleyn's Song," "Colonel Fantock." *The Sleeping Beauty*, 1924.

Tangled Vines: A Collection of Mother and Daughter Poems (ed. L. Lifshin), 1978.

Walker, Margaret, b. 1915. *For My People*, 1942: "Lineage."

B. Poetry in Other Languages

(Sp) Frenk Alatorre, Margit. *Lírica hispánica de tipo popular: edad media y renacimiento*, 1966: anonymous Cancioneros, apparently feminine origin, 1450–1650.

(F) Houville, Gérard, 1875–1963. *Les Poésies*, 1931: *"La Robe bleue."

(Sp) Ibarbourou, Juana, b. 1895. *Joyas poéticas:* "Lullabies," tr. P. T. Manchester, 1951.

(Ge) Langgässer, Elisabeth, 1899–1950. *"Frühling," 1946.

(PA) Meireles, Cecília. *An Anthology of Twentieth Century Brazilian Poetry* (ed. E. Bishop and E. Brasil), 1972: "Ballad of the Ten Casino Dancers" ("Balada das dez Bailarinas"

(Ge) Miegel, Agnes, 1879–1964. *Gesammelte Werke*, Band 2, 1953: "Schöne Agnete."

(SpA) Mistral, Gabriela/Lucila Godoy y Alcayaga, 1889–1957. *Luggar (Wine Press)*, 1954: "Canción del maizal," *"Herramientes." *Selected Poems of Gabriela Mistral*, tr. L. Hughes, 1957: *"Cascade in Sequedal," *"Fear," "Midnight," *"Mother," "The Parrot," "Poem of the Son," *"Tell Me, Mother," "Thrown Out," "What Will it be Like?" *Tala (Felling)*, 1938: *"Beber," *"Muerte de mi madre," "Pan."

(F) Navarre, Marguerite de, 1492–1549. *Dernières Poésies*, 1895: *"Épitre de la royne à madame la princesse."

(It) Negri, Ada, 1870–1945. "I canti dell'isola," 1925: *"Nel paese di mia madre."

(SpA) Storni, Alfonsina, 1892–1938. *Irremediablemente*, 1919: *"Bien pudiera ser . . ."

V. INTERDISCIPLINARY BACKGROUND

Adami, Marie. *Fanny Keats*. New Haven, CT: Yale University Press, 1938.

Aguilar, Grace. *Home Influences: A Tale for Mothers and Daughters*. New York: Harper and Bros., 1848. *Mother's Recompense: A Sequel to Home Influences*. New York: D. Appleton & Co., 1851.

Auerbach, Nina. *Communities of Women: An Idea in Fiction*. Cambridge, MA: Harvard U. Press, 1978.

Barber, Virginia and Merrill Skaggs, *The Mother Person*. Indianapolis: Bobbs-Merrill, 1977.

Bardwick, Judith M. *Psychology of Women*. New York: Harper & Row, 1971.

Beauvoir, Simone de. *The Second Sex*, 1949. Tr. & ed., H. M. Parshley. New York: Knopf, 1952.

Bem, S. L. and D. J. Bem. "Case Study of a Nonconscious Ideology: Training the Woman to Know Her Place." In *Beliefs, Attitudes and Human Affairs*. Ed. D. J. Bem. Belmont, CA: Brooks/Cole, 1970, pp. 89–99.

Bernard, Jessie. *The Future of Motherhood*. New York: Penguin, 1974.

———.*Women, Wives, Mothers: Values and Options*. Chicago: Aldine, 1975.

Blumenfield, Samuel L. *The Retreat from Motherhood*. New Rochelle, NY: Arlington House, 1975.

Brée, Germaine. "George Sand: The Fictions of Autobiography." *Nineteenth-Century French Studies*, 4 (1976), 438–449.

Chesler, Phyllis. *Women and Madness*. New York: Doubleday, 1972.

Chess, Stella and Jane Whitbread. *Daughters: From Infancy to Independence*. New York: Doubleday, 1978.

Child, Lydia Maria. *The Mother's Book*. Boston: Carter, Hendee and Babcock, 1831.

Chodorow, Nancy. *The Reproduction of Mothering: Psychoanalysis and the Sociology of Gender*. Berkeley, CA: U. of California Press, 1978.

Cott, Nancy F. *The Bonds of Womanhood: 'Woman's Sphere' in New England, 1780–1835*. New Haven, CT: Yale U. Press, 1977.

Daly, Mary. *Beyond God the Father*. Boston: Beacon, 1973.

Deutsch, Helene. *The Psychology of Women*. Vols. I–II. New York: Bantam, 1973.

Dinnerstein, Dorothy. *The Mermaid and the Minotaur: Sexual Arrangements and Human Malaise*. New York: Harper & Row, 1976.

Dworkin, Andrea. *Our Blood*. New York: Harper & Row, 1976.

Erikson, Erik H. "Reflections on Womanhood." In *The Woman in America*. Ed. R. J. Lifton. Boston: Beacon, 1964, pp. 1–26.

Feminist Studies, 4 (2) June 1978: "Toward a Feminist Theory of Motherhood." [Special Edition]

Fox, Greer Litton. "'Nice Girl': Social Control of Women Through a Value Construct." *Signs*, 2 (1977), 805–817.

Fraser, Antonia. *Mary, Queen of Scots.* New York: Delacorte, 1969.

Friday, Nancy. *My Mother My Self: The Daughter's Search for Identity.* New York: Delacorte, 1977.

Frontiers: A Journal of Women Studies, 3 (2) 1978: "Mothers and Daughters." [Special Edition]

Gallagher, Dorothy. *Hannah's Daughters.* New York: Crowell, 1976.

Gardiner, Judith Kegan. "The New Motherhood." *North American Review,* Fall 1978.

Gros-Louis, Delores. "Pens and Needles: Daughters and Mothers in Recent Canadian Literature." *Kate Chopin Newsletter,* 3 (1976–77), 8–13.

Gutwirth, Madelyn. *Madame de Staël, Novelist/The Emergence of the Artist as Woman.* Urbana, IL: U. of Illinois Press, 1978.

Hall, Nor. *Mothers and Daughters: Reflections on the Archetypal Feminine.* Minneapolis, MN: Rusoff Books, 1976.

Hammer, Signe. *Daughters and Mothers, Mothers and Daughters.* New York: Quadrangle/New York Times, 1975.

Hogrefe, Pearl, *Women of Action in Tudor England.* Ames, IA: Iowa State University Press, 1977.

Horney, Karen. *Feminine Psychology.* New York: Norton, 1967.

Howard, Jane, *Families.* New York: Simon and Schuster, 1978.

Jacobson, Edith. *The Self and the Object World.* New York: International Universities Press, 1964.

Kerényi, C. *Eleusis: Archetypal Image of Mother and Daughter.* Bollingen Series LXV. 4. New York: Pantheon, 1967.

Kessler, Carol Farley. "The Elizabeth Stuart Phelpses: Mother-Daughter Regionalists." *Proceedings of the National Popular Culture Ass'n. Convention* (microfilm). Bowling Green, OH: Bowling Green State University Press, 1977.

Latimer, Caroline Wormeley. *Girl and Woman: A Book for Mothers and Daughters.* New York and London: D. Appleton, 1910.

Lerner, Gerda, ed. *The Female Experience: An American Documentary.* Indianapolis: Bobbs-Merrill, 1977.

Maccoby, E. E. *The Development of Sex Differences.* Stanford, CA: Stanford University Press, 1966.

Maccoby, E. E. and Jacklin, C. *The Psychology of Sex Differences.* Stanford, CA: Stanford University Press, 1974.

Mander, Anica Vesel. *Blood Ties: A Woman's History.* Westminster, MD: Moon Books/Random House, 1976.

Michel, Sonya. "Mothers and Daughters in American Jewish Literature: The Rotted Cord." In *The Jewish Woman: New Perspectives.* Ed. Elizabeth Koltun. New York: Schocken Books, 1976, pp. 272–282.

Moers, Ellen. *Literary Women.* Garden City, NY: Doubleday/Anchor Books, 1977.

Neisser, Edith G. *Mothers and Daughters.* New York: Harper & Row, 1973.

Neumann, Erich G. *The Great Mother.* Tr. Ralph Manheim, Bollingen Series, 47. Princeton, NJ: Princeton University Presss, 1955.

Niethammer, Carolyn. *Daughters of the Earth.* New York: Macmillan, 1977.

Nye, F. I. and L. W. Hoffman. *The Employed Mother in America.* Chicago: Rand McNally, 1963.

Pildes, Judith. *Our Mothers' Daughters.* Berkeley, CA: Shameless Hussy Press, 1979.

Psychoanalysis and Women. Ed. Jean Baker Miller. New York: Penguin, 1973.

Rich, Adrienne. *Of Woman Born: Motherhood as Institution and Experience.* New York: Norton, 1976.

Rigney, Barbara Hill. *Madness and Sexual Politics in the Feminist Novel.* Madison, WI: University of Wisconsin Press, 1978.

Ryan, Mary P. *Womanhood in America: From Colonial Time to the Present.* New York: New Viewpoints, 1975.

Silverman, Elaine. "In Their Own Words: Mothers and Daughters on the Alberta Frontier, 1890–1929." *Frontiers: A Journal of Women Studies,* 2 (1977), 37–44.

Smith, Liz, ed. *The Mother Book.* New York: Doubleday, 1978.

Smith-Rosenberg, Carroll. "The Female World of Love and Ritual: Relations between Women in Nineteenth-Century America." *Signs,* 1 (1975), 1–29.

———. "The Hysterical Woman: Sex Roles and Role Conflict in 19th-Century America." *Social Research,* 39 (1972), 652–678.

———. "Puberty to Menopause: The Cycle of Femininity in Nineteenth-Century America." In *Clio's Consciousness Raised.* Ed. Mary Hartman and Lois W. Banner. New York: Harper & Row, 1974, pp. 23–37.

Spacks, Patricia Meyer. *The Female Imagination.* New York: Knopf, 1972.

Stack, Carol. *All Our Kin: Strategies for Survival in a Black Community.* New York: Harper & Row, 1974.

Thompson, Clara. *On Women.* New York: New American Library, 1964.

Todd, Janet M. "Frankenstein's Daughter: Mary Shelley and Mary Wollstonecraft." *Women & Literature,* 4 (Fall 1976), 18–27.

Wolff, Cynthia Griffin. *A Feast of Words: The Triumph of Edith Wharton.* New York: Oxford University Press, 1977.

Wollstonecraft, Mary. *Thoughts on the Education of Daughters: With Reflection on Female Conduct, in the More Important Duties of Life.* London: J. Johnson, 1787.

Woman, Body and Culture (Ed. Signe Hammer. New York: Perennial Library, 1975): Grete Bibring, "Some Specific Psychological Tasks in Pregnancy and Motherhood" (1965). Lois Wladis Hoffman, "Early Childhood Experiences and Women's Achievement Motives" (1972). Evelyn Goodenough Pitcher, "Fathers, Mothers, and Sex Typing" (1957).

Woman, Culture and Society (Ed. Michelle Zimbalist Rosaldo and Louise Lamphere. Stanford, CA: Stanford University Press, 1974): Sherry B. Ortner, "Is Female to Male as Native Is to Culture?" Michelle Zimbalist Rosaldo, "Woman, Culture, and Society: A Theoretical Overview."

Women and Analysis: Dialogues on Psychoanalytic Views of Femininity (Ed. Jean Strouse. New York: Grossman, 1974): Sigmund Freud, "Female Sexuality" (1931); "Some Psychical Consequences of the Anatomical Distinction Between the Sexes" (1925). Robert J. Stoller, "Facts and Fancies: An Examination of Freud's Concept of Bisexuality" (1973).

Women and Men: The Consequences of Power (Ed. Dana V. Hiller and Robin Ann Sheets. Cincinnati: Office of Women's Studies, University of Cincinnati, 1977): Nina Auerbach, "The Mater familias: Power and Presumption." Judith Gardiner, "The Heroine as Her Author's Daughter." Susan Gubar, "Mother, Maiden, and the Marriage of Death: Women Writers and an Ancient Myth."

Women's Studies, 6 (2), 1979, ed. E. M. Broner and Cathy N. Davidson: "Mothers and Daughters in Literature": Helen M. Bannan, "Warrior Women: Immigrant Mothers in the Works of their Daughters." Jacqueline Berke, "Mother I Can Do It Myself: The Self-Sufficient Heroine in Popular Girls' Fiction." Susan Friedman, "Psyche Reborn: Tradition, Re-Vision, and the Goddess as Mother-Symbol in H.D.'s Epic Poetry." Deborah Tannen, "Mothers and Daughters in the Modern Greek Novels of Lilika Nakos." Grace B. Stewart, "Mother, Daughter, and the Birth of the Female Artist."

Notes on Contributors

The Editors

E. M. Broner is Associate Professor of English at Wayne State University. Her novels include: *Journal/Nocturnal* (Harcourt, Brace and World), *Her Mothers* and *A Weave of Women* (both from Holt, Rinehart, & Winston). She has had plays produced and has published articles and stories in numerous periodicals including *Ms.*, *Commentary*, etc. She is currently under contract for a new novel. Esther is descended from Bronya of Russia. Her grandmothers were sisters, the tall one, Nechama (Consolation), the small one, Tsivia (Doe). Her own daughters are named for them: Sari, for Tsivia, and Nahama. Her twin sons, Adam and Jeremy, are named for their grandfathers.

Cathy N. Davidson, Assistant Professor of English at Michigan State University, has published some twenty-five articles on American literature, Canadian literature, and women's studies. She is currently coediting a collection of essays on Margaret Atwood (Toronto: House of Anansi, 1979), editing a collection of essays on Canadian women writers and is finishing a book on early American fiction.

The Contributors

Helen M. Bannan is Assistant Professor of American Studies at the University of New Mexico. A year of teaching on the Fort Belknap Reservation in Montana sparked her interest in Native American cultures, an interest she has pursued on a fellowship at the Newberry Library's Center for the History of the American Indian, and at a MLA Summer Seminar on Native American Literature. She is grateful to her German-American mother who remained close to her daughter, despite an educational system that emphasizes differences, rather than similarities, between cultures and generations.

Jacqueline Berke, Professor of English at Drew University, graduated from

Columbia School of Journalism. After working as a free-lance journalist for many years, she returned to earn a degree in English literature from Rutgers Graduate School. Coordinator of the writing program at Drew, she is author of *Twenty Questions for the Writer* (Harcourt, Brace, Jovanovich). She has also presented numerous papers on popular culture and women's literature, including "Jane Austen, a Feminist for All Seasons" (at the Jane Austen Bicentenary).

Laura Berke, born in New York City in 1945, is a Ph.D. candidate in English at New York University. A one-time high school teacher and editor of college texts, she now lives in Greenwich Village with her husband and young daughter, Catherine, known as Katie.

Lynn Z. Bloom is an Associate Professor of English at the College of William and Mary. Her publications on biography and autobiography include *Doctor Spock: Biography of a Conservative Radical* (Bobbs-Merrill, 1972); an edition of *Natalie Crouter: A Diary of Captivity*, American Women's Diary Series (Burt Franklin, 1979); and articles on Anaïs Nin, Gertrude Stein, Dorothy Parker, John Nichols, women autobiographers, and various aspects of biographical theory and practice.

Mary Lynn Broe presented an earlier version of her paper at the MMLA Women's Caucus Workshop on Mothers and Daughters in Literature, which she attended with her mother. She is Assistant Professor of English at SUNY/Binghamton. Dr. Broe has completed a book-length study about Sylvia Plath.

Irene G. Dash teaches English and Women's Studies at Hunter College, CUNY. Her career has ranged broadly, including work in art and business, as well as English. She holds a Ph.D. in English from Columbia University, has presented numerous papers on women's studies and Shakespeare, and is currently writing a book, "The Mind of Shakespeare's Women" (Frederick Ungar Publishing).

Erika Duncan's first novel, *A Wreath of Pale White Roses*, was published in 1977, and she is currently working on her second. Her critical articles have appeared in *New Boston Review*, *Changes*, *Human Behavior Magazine*, and *Book Forum* where she is a contributing editor. She lives in New York City with her three young daughters, Rachel, Gwynn and Jane, and where monthly The Women's Salon meets in her house, bringing together hundreds of women writers from all parts of the country.

Karen Elias-Button, Assistant Professor of English at SUNY/Oswego, is presently revising for publication her dissertation, "Medusa's Daughters: A Study of Women's Consciousness in Myth and Poetry." Her articles and poems have appeared in *Discourse*, *Anima*, *Thirteenth Moon*, *Second Wave*, *Women/Poems* and *Feminist Studies*.

Katherine Fishburn teaches contemporary literature at Michigan State University where she holds the 1978–79 Academic Administrative Internship for women. She is the author of *Richard Wright's Hero* as well as other scholarly articles. Her bibliographical essay, "Women in Popular Culture," will appear in *A Handbook of American Popular Culture*, Vol. II, and she is currently working on a book about Doris Lessing.

Lorna Irvine, Assistant Professor of English at George Mason University, is working on a book on the feminist perspective in Canadian literature. She is a Canadian and the mother of a daughter.

Carol Farley Kessler teaches women's studies at the University of Pennsylvania and is writing the Twayne United States Author's monograph on Elizabeth Stuart Phelps (1844–1911). She is the mother of a daughter.

Deena Dash Kushner is completing her doctoral dissertation in business at the University of Georgia. She received her B.A. in English from Brandeis University but then went on to a successful career in the business world. She is coauthor of a book *Making the Most of Energy in Real Estate*, and is a mother of a young son and a two-year-old daughter.

Jane Lilienfeld, Assistant Professor of English and Women's Studies, Assumption College, Worcester, Massachusetts, has published articles on Margaret Atwood and Virginia Woolf. She is currently writing *The Possibility of Sisterhood: Literary Women and Their Mothers from Mary Wollstonecraft to Adrienne Rich*.

Susan Peck MacDonald is Associate Professor of English at Eastern Connecticut State College. She is just completing a study of male Victorian novelists' views of women (written with two other Victorian scholars) and was an American Council of Learned Societies Study Fellow for 1978–79, studying the history of nineteenth-century science.

Nan Bauer Maglin, who received her doctorate from Union Graduate School, has taught English and Women's Studies at Manhattan Community College-CUNY since 1970. Her work on matrilineage grew out of her participation in the 1977–78 Modern Language Association project, "Teaching Women's Literature from a Regional Perspective." She has published widely in academic and women's studies journals. She is the mother of an adopted daughter.

Ann M. Moore is completing her dissertation on Mme. Marie-Madeleine de Lafayette (1634–1693) at the University of Oregon. She, like the other bibliographers, has a daughter.

Deborah Dash Moore teaches Jewish Studies at Vassar College and American Jewish History at the Max Weinriech Center for Advanced Jewish Studies, YIVO. Her research interests (including work on two books) focus on second generation Jews in New York City. A mother of two sons, she is glad to have shared her experience as a daughter with a sister.

Barbara Ann Clarke Mossberg, daughter of a matriad of lost names (Rumore, Slovik, Todaro), is Assistant Professor of English at the University of Oregon.

She has recently completed a full-length study of Emily Dickinson as daughter, *When a Writer Is a Daughter*, and is in the process of writing its sequel, *Kangaroos among the Beauty: Writer-Daughters in America*. Some of her own published poetry concerns the mother-daughter relationship.

Mitzi Myers has her Ph.D. from Rice University and is currently teaching at California State Polytechnic University, Pomona, California. She has written essays on William Godwin, Elizabeth Inchbald, Mary McCarthy, and Mary Wollstonecraft. Her principal area of interest is women writers from 1750–1870. She is working on a study of eighteenth-century feminine ideology.

Judith Ochshorn, Director of the Women's Studies Program at the University of South Florida, has completed a book on sexual identity in polytheistic and monotheistic religions of the ancient Near East. Her interest in the history and socialization of women stems partly from the strength and insight she gained from her mother's life which she shared, in love, with her own daughter.

Natalie M. Rosinsky is a Ph.D. student in English at the University of Wisconsin-Madison. She is the granddaughter of a Jewish woman who immigrated to America by herself at the age of nine.

Gail M. Rudenstein, Assistant Coordinator of the Women's Studies Program at the University of Pennsylvania, is writing a dissertation on the mother-daughter relationship in American novels and magazine fiction, 1918–1930. She is the mother of two daughters.

Myra Glazer Schotz teaches at Ben Gurion University of the Negev. She has written on William Blake, D. H. Lawrence, and, most recently, on Israeli women poets.

Nikki Stiller, a poet and medievalist, took her Ph.D. at The City University of New York. Her work has appeared in many journals, including *College English*, *Primavera* and *Midstream*. She is currently teaching English at the University of New Orleans. Her mother, working since her arrival in this country at age 14, has been of continuous support in her daughter's struggle.

Adeline R. Tintner is an independent scholar who has published widely in the humanities. She began her career in the 1930s and 1940s with numerous essays on art and architecture. More recently, she has published widely on Edith Wharton and Henry James in journals such as *PMLA*, *NCF*, and *MFS*. She is a daughter and a mother of two daughters, one a dancer and one an Oxford trained scholar.

Carol E. W. Tobol graduated from Wellesley College and received her masters degree in classics from Johns Hopkins University. Before the present collaboration she coauthored two articles with her mother, Ida H. Washington. She is now on leave from the academic world and living in California.

Betty S. Travitsky, Assistant Professor of English at Touro College, completed her Ph.D. in 1976 at St. John's University. She has recently compiled an anthology of writings by Renaissance Englishwomen. Her checklist of writings by Renaissance women is scheduled to appear in the spring of 1979 in *Bulletin of Research in the Humanities*. She lives in Brooklyn with her family, which includes two daughters.

Linda W. Wagner has published fifteen books on modern American literature. Professor of English at Michigan State University, she is currently editing collections of essays on Denise Levertov and Joyce Carol Oates, and plans to write a full-length study of Ellen Glasgow in the near future. She had an exemplary mother (who lived her own life, against odds) and is blessed with an equally self-directed daughter.

Ida H. Washington graduated from Wellesley College, received a master's degree from Middlebury College and a Ph.D. from Columbia University, both in German, and is presently Professor of Modern Languages at Southeastern Massachusetts University. She has published numerous articles in scholarly journals, two of them in collaboration with her daughter, Carol E. W. Tobol.

Bonnie Zimmerman is Lecturer in Women's Studies at San Diego State University. She has published in *Criticism, Feminist Studies,* and *Sinister Wisdom*. She has successfully struggled to create a mature and nonneurotic relationship with her mother.

In the production of *The lost Tradition*, book design and cover design are by Jacqueline Schuman, who is also mother of a daughter. The cover photograph was taken originally in 1899 by Gertrude Käsebier.